SURVIVAL
in the
NEW MILLENNIUM

SURVIVAL
in the
NEW MILLENNIUM

TOWARD A CIVILIZED WORLD

Don R. Dooley

COSMOPOLITAN PUBLISHING
Green Valley, Arizona

Copyright © 1998 by Don R. Dooley

All rights reserved. No part of this book may be reproduced or transmitted in any form or by any means, electronic or mechanical, including photocopying, recording, or by any information storage and retrieval system, without permission in writing from the author.

Although the author and publisher have made every effort to ensure the accuracy and completeness of information contained in this book, we assume no responsibility for errors, inaccuracies, omissions, or any inconsistency herein. Any slights of people, places or organizations are unintentional.

This special edition was prepared for printing by
Ghost River Images
5350 East Fourth Street
Tucson, Arizona 85711

Cover illustration by: Don R. Dooley

ISBN 0-9659938-0-9

Library of Congress Catalog Card Number: 97-92431

Printed in the United States of America

First Printing: 1998

10 9 8 7 6 5 4 3 2 1

Centuries from now, the Earth's inhabitants will look back with disdain and unbelief on the prejudiced, illiterate an uncivilized world of today. This book is dedicated to those future generations who must turn their backs on those prejudices and failed philosophies.

ACKNOWLEDGMENTS

I am particularly grateful for considerable data gleaned over the years from the Wall Street Journal. Most Journalists consider it to be one of the finest daily newspapers in the world and a source of abundant information. It is a textbook of society - for society. I am also indebted to the staff of Publisher's ExpressPress for their knowledgeable advice on book production and especially to Michael White of Ghost River Images for his design, layout and very helpful suggestions, in the final compilation. And finally and most importantly I wish to thank my wife, Dorothy, without whom the book would never have been completed. She has been my inspiration and collaborator in every phase of its development including the computerization and tedious editing of many drafts. The responsibility of what is in the book is mine, but without her help it would not exist.

Contents

INTRODUCTION

PART I

PROLOGUE: A DYSFUNCTIONAL WORLD 1

Chapter 1 GLOBAL CRISIS 3
Chapter 2 THE RISE AND FALL OF SOCIALISM 19
Chapter 3 ETHNIC RETARDATION 53
Chapter 4 DECLINE OF DISCIPLINED SOCIETY 73

PART II

TOWARD A NEW WORLD ORDER 91

Chapter 5 DAWN OF A NEW CIVILIZATION 93
Chapter 6 NEW BEHAVIORAL PATTERNS 103
Chapter 7 CONTROL OF CHEMICAL-INDUCED BEHAVIOR .. 153
Chapter 8 SECURITY 175
Chapter 9 A RESTORED ENVIRONMENT 203
Chapter 10 A DYNAMIC NEW ECONOMY 231
Chapter 11 FREEDOM AND RIGHTS OF THE INDIVIDUAL 275
Chapter 12 A NEW GOVERNMENT THAT WORKS 319
Chapter 13 A NEW WORLD ORDER (Summary) 367
Chapter 14 FINAL CHALLENGES OF MANKIND 371

NOTES 387
INDEX 401

INTRODUCTION

"No lasting civilization will ever be founded upon philosophical and social ideologies. The democratic ideology itself, unless reconstructed upon a scientific basis has no more chance of surviving than the fascist or Marxist ideologies." Alexis Carrel, from "Man the Unknown" (June 15, 1939)

In August of 1995 a non-partisan survey by Democratic pollster, Stan Greenberg and Republican pollster, Fred Steeper, indicated seventy percent of those polled couldn't trust the government to do the right thing. This belief was the same among conservatives and liberals, the affluent and the poor, and people of both sexes. The function of democracies, the world's greatest hope for fair government, appears to be seriously flawed.

Rapidly growing centralized governments in the world are also gradually usurping the power of their citizens. In many countries, most liberties are non-existent. Bureaucratic waste and corruption eat up resources from increased taxation. Hyperinflation is rampant in many nations. Crime is out of control. The world is enmeshed in ethnic and cultural prejudice creating distrust, protests and finally terrorist attacks. Nationalistic, ethnic, and religious conflicts are everywhere. Nuclear weapons are still intact ready to destroy huge metropolises. Vast amounts of chemical and biological weapons capable of destroying most of the world's population are stored by some nations and even by terrorists. The earth's ecosystem is being destroyed by exploding hordes of humanity. People are clamoring for change, for an end to this madness.

The bipartisan National Commission on America's Urban Families reported in 1993, "The family trend of our time is the deinstitutionalization of marriage and the steady disintegration of the mother-father child raising unit."

These are very serious indictments of our present society. It is evident that change is necessary, perhaps, imperative for survival of the human race.

Survival in the New Millennium, is a result of voracious research into economic and socio-economic policies and contains data collected over twenty five years and begun during the vast social transformation of the late sixties. Each chapter explores different aspects of a socio-economic malfunction and its cause reaching back through history. Each suggests how specific, non-political solutions for resolving these problems may occur through dramatic changes in the world's social structure in the new millennium.

It is my opinion that we, humans, are still living in a primitive society, one that is not civilized in the truest sense. This is dramatically described in Part I : *A Dysfunctional World* where the stage is set for future crisis and finally change.

To some readers the second chapter in Part I, *The Rise and Fall of Socialism*, may seem incongruous with the rest of Part I. But, after a closer study of the problems arising from socialist economies, it becomes apparent the great socialist experiment of the 20th century has ended in economic devastation and seriously delayed civilized growth in a large part of the world. Still, the problems persist and are hindering the world's economic progress. (i.e. proponents of government-run economies still cannot understand that socialist economic systems are malfunctional.)

This chapter was first written in the early 1980s in which I predicted the collapse of the Soviet Union. The prediction was based primarily on the inevitable failure of government-run industries in a centrally-controlled economy. Because the prediction became a reality before the book was finished, it became necessary to modify the chapter's ending.

Ethnic Retardation (chapter 3), suggests that the inability of certain ethnic groups to progress is due to lack of discipline and motivation by parents passed down from generation to generation in those cultures. This results in uneducated and undisciplined offspring who are unemployable and, therefore, are poverty-stricken or prone to hustling drugs or other criminal activities to survive. The vicious cycle, then, continues as young illiterate men beget more of these children but are unable to either support or motivate them to higher standards of education and morality. Some successful solutions to this problem are sure to be adopted in the future and are outlined under *New Behavioral Patterns* (chapter 6).

In a Newsweek poll in 1994, three-fourths believed the United States was in a deep moral decline. An NBC/Wall Street Journal poll taken in December of 1996 reported, "By a healthy margin (51% vs 37%), Americans believe the roots of crime and other social ills stem from a fundamental decline in moral values rather than economic pressures on families." *Decline of Disciplined Society* (chapter 4), describes how far social behavior has actually fallen. It encompasses every conceivable attack on civilized conduct since the 1960s and concludes Part I. It is interesting that contemporary youth, observing such behavior, assume it has always existed and is normal conduct. Only more mature adults, who have lived through the decades preceding the general moral collapse, can assess the degree of decline.

Although Part I illustrates the overwhelming seriousness of the contemporary state of global life, Part II, *Toward a New World Order*, is upbeat and predicts an optimistic outcome through critical changes in our socio-economic structure. I attempt to uncover the reasons for uncivilized behavior and propose how they may be dealt with by future generations.

Dawn of a New Civilization (chapter 5) is my attempt to arrive at some type of event that would start mankind on the road to a civilized world. In all probability, the actual event or events may be considerably different. Nevertheless, the overall solution will recognize the interrelationship of all dysfunctions. Social responsibility by the individual will also be an important requisite.

In chapter 6, I indicate one of the keys to solving society's problems is early behavioral education. It is needed to overcome survival-selfishness which evolved through centuries of natural selection in order for the human race to endure. It must be based on a scientific analysis of the intricate processes that motivate the mind to function as it does.

Logic insists solutions to global malfunctions are obvious. So why then do we ignore them? For centuries religious and ethnic prejudice have combined with illiteracy and selfishness to obscure our path to social righteousness. If these three culprits of uncivilized behavior - illiteracy, prejudice, and selfishness - could be substantially reduced, then most of the world's problems would be much easier to resolve. The quality of life would then soar.

Such an assumption is considered naive by many who believe we are helpless to change our continuing barbaric behavior. However, it is difficult to believe that human intelligence, which has astounded even the optimists among us by advancing science and technology to incredible levels, cannot discover the means to understand ourselves and then mold our behavior in such a manner that the human race will eventually evolve into a truly civilized society.

Predictions of future society continue in subsequent chapters as solutions to overwhelming global dysfunctions are anticipated. How the great debate over de-criminalization of addictive drugs and the end to uncontrollable drug crime will be resolved is foreseen. The criminal-justice system will be radically changed. Juries and prisons will be abolished, but permissiveness in tolerating criminals will have evaporated as will most crime itself. A global disarmament conference will finally end the enormous cost and threat of war.

The incredible harm to the earth's environment by the population explosion will end with mandated family limitations. The world's natural resources, including land, will be closely supervised and protected from environmental calamities. Economic innovations will eliminate income taxes, improve free trade, and give the individual basic economic opportunity and security without the loss of incentive. The scourge of inflation will be gone.

Workplace, lifestyle, and transportation in the new millennium are described in *Freedom and Rights of the Individual* (chapter 11). In *A New Government That Works* (chapter 12), democracy is shown to be seriously defective and will be replaced by an improved form of governance - one devoid of politics. It also appears that a single world government will evolve if mankind is ever expected to be at peace with itself.

The exponential advance in knowledge within the last century, projected into the future, portends extraordinary scientific achievements ahead. The possibilities are beyond present comprehension. These achievements must be used to insure our survival through colonization in a hostile universe. Later as outlined in the last chapter, *Final Challenges of Mankind*, these advances will be used to unlock the many secrets of the universe. This may be the future evolution and destiny of human intelligence.

Each chapter, in Part II through chapter 12, consists of passages depicting the *Historical Background* followed by The *New Society*, descriptions of how world problems may be overcome generations and perhaps centuries from now. It is a description of what the future socio-economic structure of the world may be or an unusual blueprint for radical changes in a new highly-civilized global society.

Passages of *The New Society* are depicted in the present tense as if being told by a member of that future society. In today's world some of these portrayals of the future may appear unreal or impossible, but how would today's world have appeared to medieval people?

It is my hope that some of the ideas expressed to improve world society may instill a resolve by others in future generations to radically move forward in those directions. At first glance, some readers may adamantly oppose some of the presentations in *Survival in the New Millennium*. I ask only that the reader keep an open mind while analyzing the pros and cons of each.

Utopia will never exist, but the attempt to bring it into being can only end in a truly civilized world and perhaps its very survival. If we are determined to utilize the vast potential of the human mind and have overwhelming faith in our ability to create an ideal environment for future generations, then it will surely come to pass.

***

The reader will notice that in referring to both sexes, I have used the traditional masculine pronoun or noun (such as mankind). This is not meant to deride the feminine sex but only to expedite clarification. I completely support equal rights for women throughout the world. The inequality that exists, especially in some third world countries, is another example of our uncivilized society.

PART I

PROLOGUE: A DYSFUNCTIONAL WORLD

AN IMPORTANT NOTE TO THE READER:

To fully appreciate how to read this book, it is suggested that the Introduction be read first. This will enable the reader to understand the method the author has elected to portray the future.

Chapter 1

GLOBAL CRISIS

Flames leaped high in the skies above great metropolises as burning and looting heralded the approach of Apocalypse. The time was decades from now. Bandit-gangs roamed the streets at will, robbing, raping, and killing. Isolated pockets of remaining soldiers stood by helpless to prevent the carnage - held down by urban guerilla snipers. The police had, long ago, deserted.

***

It wasn't long before, that developed countries were smug in the belief society had made extraordinary gains and became civilized by the end of the twentieth century. The average life-span had reached the mid-70s at the beginning of the new millenium, whereas, historical records revealed as late as 1775 life expectancy was less than thirty years. Most inhabitants in the 18th century lived in cramped, dirty hovels, and produced what they consumed by arduous outdoor work. Even in the more civilized European countries it was a desperate struggle. The masses lived hand to mouth, never knowing when their next meal was coming .

As late as 1900, with the exception of a few wealthy people, the quality of life had little meaning. For most, the struggle for food and shelter was all encompassing. Nearly everyone lived in poverty compared to the more affluent life-style of the developed nations in the late twentieth century.

As technology grew, some in society became aware they were not as civilized as previously thought. In fact, future generations looked back in disdain on this period and considered it primitive.

They were appalled at what occurred. Crime could no longer be controlled in many parts of the world especially in Brazil, Russia, and the United States. Its subjugation was beyond the ability or resolve of governments. This was ironic because the main purpose, for humans to band together since pre-historic times, was for mutual protection. Yet, politicians devoted the largest resources to everything but the security of their citizens, and much of that was being squandered in bureaucratic mismanagement and corruption. One reason was the lack of an organized citizen lobby to fight crime as existed in other social programs. A special interest did not exist until the individual was a victim. Then it was too late, and other citizens had little interest in some other person's unfortunate experience. Large sums were spent by all nations in preparation for war, but in comparison, little was spent in the protection of citizens from criminals.

Because the governing bodies in the United States were unable or unwilling to discharge their most fundamental obligation to protect their citizens from violent crime, it became commonplace for citizens to develop their own methods to protect property and life. Homes were enmeshed with intricate alarm systems, special locks, iron-barred windows, and flood lights. Watch dogs were placed on guard, and owners armed themselves to the teeth with guns. Many women carried mace or hot-pepper sprays to immobilize attackers. Walls were erected around some neighborhoods with gates guarded by private security men. Gates were placed across some streets to prevent drive-through shootings, and curfews were imposed on teenagers.

In urban Rio de Janeiro, residents placed special devices on their automobiles that cut off the fuel supply when a thief drove only a few blocks. Official annual homicides in the city rose from three thousand in 1983 to eight thousand in 1989; most killings didn't get into the records. One police official said the true figure was nearer twenty-thousand murders a year in metropolitan Rio.

Sales of firearms mushroomed as people trusted only their guns for protection.

Todd Lewan, a reporter for the Associated Press in Rio in 1990 stated, "Bodies are dumped in the streets every day, sometimes outside police stations. One Sunday in January, ten were found in a group, shot through the head. A month later, a record fifty-seven corpses turned up in a single weekend.

"City police, poorly equipped, trained and paid, are no match for the well-armed criminals. There is temptation for officers to break the law, and little incentive for them to enforce it. Death squads, generally off-duty policemen fed-up with inefficient courts and turn-style justice, make another kind of law. They simply kill known criminals or suspects often for pay from merchants."[1]

***

The sale of addictive drugs for profit engulfed the world. Prohibition bestowed awesome overnight wealth on drug lords and their dealers. The profit was so great it overwhelmed the morality of everyone it touched: attorneys who defended the drug mafia, bankers who laundered the money, law-enforcement officers, judges, and even some in the government to say nothing of the ordinary person eeking out a living. A few C.I.A. agents, doing counter-espionage work, were even suspected of receiving vast sums of money at the behest of drug lords.

Greed for even greater wealth resulted in constant gun battles between rival drug gangs. Murders, including those of innocent bystanders, were common. The greatest tragedy was the deliberate promotion of addiction on all walks of life, including school children, in order to increase the demand for their product. Addiction resulted in a rapid increase in burglaries, purse-snatching, robberies, and assaults in order to maintain the habit.

Hospitals were on the front-line of a losing battle treating overdoses of "crack" or heroin nearly every day. Women sold themselves to anyone to buy drugs, and many, therefore, were infected with syphilis or AIDS. Pregnant women would "free-base" until delivery day. Their babies were born addicts sentenced to live months or even years as "boarder babies" in hospital wards costing as much as two-hundred thousand dollars each annually. Some crack babies suffered strokes while in the uterus. Others were abandoned by the mother at society's expense. Still, others were born with AIDS.

There were long waiting lists of addicts for treatment at rehabilitation programs; even the lucky few who entered, had difficulty recovering completely and most eventually returned to drugs. Prison programs were also swamped as were the prisons themselves. Courts were inundated with drug-related cases. Many were postponed for months. This resulted in a continued crime-wave by the accused in order to maintain the habit.

The total cost to the world's citizenry was enormous, to say nothing of the cost to governments trying to interdict the flow of drugs. All was for the benefit of a few who profited obscenely at the world's expense.

The AIDS pandemic, once established, spread rapidly from the use of infected drug needles and addicted prostitutes as well as from homosexuality. Those who were infected, then spread it to spouses, sexual partners, and offspring. By 1991, AIDS had already become the number one killer of young black women in parts of the United States as well as Africa. The cost for treatment was enormous, and in most cases, had to be born by the rest of society. In Africa, because of the cost, treatment was prohibitive, and death was everywhere in communities hard hit by the malady. It was the major killer of third-world children by the end of the century.

***

Each time bacteria was exposed to antibiotics, there was a good chance that a genetic mutant would survive and become resistant to medication. As mutant bacteria multiplied and spread, previous commonly-controlled diseases such as tuberculosis, pneumonia, meningitis, gonorrhea, and many others became pandemic throughout the world. This was especially true in third-world areas with inadequate sanitation; hundreds of thousands died.

Worse yet, new mysterious diseases rose from remote virgin jungle areas that were being stripped by logging, mining, or otherwise disturbed by humans. Many, like AIDS, were incurable at the time; some were extremely deadly. Increase in population appeared to go hand in hand with the explosion of new viruses. Thousands of unidentified viruses had yet to be discovered. Most individuals were not aware that the very existence of humanity was vulnerable to some of them.

There were some who thought AIDS, new antibiotic-resistant bacteria, and other newly-evolved mystery diseases were only "nature's" way of controlling the world's exploding population.

***

In many developing parts of the world, women were still considered inferior citizens or suffered discrimination. In India, "dowry deaths" were common. If a bride didn't bring enough money into the marriage, she would be murdered. The husbands were then free to remarry and claim another dowry. Authorities looked the other way. Girls were considered burdens by their parents because women's status was considered low and devalued. Many were killed at birth. In most of Asia, boys were still preferred so if the sex was detected before birth, mothers would abort females. In China, India, and Bangladesh, female children were given less nourishing meals than boys; many suffered from chronic malnutrition. The primitive ritual of female circumcision, the mutilation of external genital organs using unsterilized razor blades without anesthesia, was practiced by many faiths in two dozen black African countries as well as in the Sudan and Egypt.[2] The World Health Organization estimated 120 million women and girls were living in 1996 in three dozen countries who had been circumcised.

Most Islamic countries continued to relegate women to second class citizenship prohibiting them from many everyday activities including driving an automobile. They were not allowed in mosques and were required to stay in a separate parlor from the men while in their homes. Most of the world considered women inferior to men. Even in some of the more developed countries, discrimination was accomplished in more subtle ways such as limiting salaries and promotions. It was almost as if there existed a caste system.

***

Another serious and uncontrolled problem was the incessant proliferation of weapons of war throughout the world. During the Cold War, the Soviet Union furnished weapons to any Marxist group trying to take or maintain power. The United States countered by supporting the opposition with armaments. This was in addition to the huge build-up in nuclear and conventional weapons by the two super-powers. After the Cold War ended and the two began to scale-down their defenses, excess armament capacity was used to improve trade and prevent their economies from suffering. Many of these weapons were then sold to Third-World countries. As arms spread, conflicts errupted everywhere. Most were ethnic or religious in nature.

After the Soviet Union was dismantled, there were thousands of military and nuclear scientists and technicians without jobs or income. The Chinese media reported that at least three-thousand of these military experts were recruited to help expand China's war machine and intercontinental nuclear missile capabilities. China began to build a military machine that would match that of the old Soviet Union. In addition, thousands of nuclear missiles in both Russia and the United States remained poised ready to blow up the world. The threat of intercontinental nuclear war had not been eliminated.

China's adoption of the free-market system propelled the economy into a dynamic phase. Coupled with its vast human resources and totalitarian discipline, another super-power and threat to the Western world was created.

Nationalism was rampant especially within a country's borders where stateless nationalities fought for recognition or sovereignty. In Yugoslavia, Slovenia broke away to become independent. Serbs fought the Croats and the Bosnian Muslims, and Muslims fought both in a vicious civil war. The Kurds fought for a homeland within the borders of Iraq, Turkey, Syria, and Iran. The dismemberment of the Soviet empire created additional nationalistic conflicts as the individual components turned on one another. The horrible destruction in Chechnya was an example. Pent-up ethnic prejudices were the primary cause. Throughout the world, nationalistic conflicts with neighboring countries or civil wars within added to human misery. Genocide and ethnic cleansing became common as prejudiced, militant groups fought one another bringing enormous grief and suffering to humanity.

Religious conflicts also continued throughout the world. The Catholic-Protestant terror in Northern Ireland was typical, but the greatest threat were Muslim fundamentalists terrorizing not only the West but other Arabic countries as well. Some had built nuclear arsenals for this purpose. Most condemned the culture and institutions of the West believing they had to be eradicated. This threat, along with the hordes of Muslim immigrants, dominated Western European thinking as the most divisive social issue in the 1990s.

Throughout Western Europe the need for additional laborers created an explosion of African and Arab immigrants. The differing cultures collided until it became one of the greatest problems facing the European community. Swedish youths firebombed refugee camps, masked Italians rampaged through the streets of Florence clubbing and knifing North Africans, and German Neo-Nazis assaulted Turks and Africans, setting fire to their homes.

In the United States, the steady stream of Asian immigrants and the swarms of illegal Mexicans and other Hispanics overwhelmed the Los Angeles metropolitan area. Whites, drawn to Southern California for decades, left in droves during the 1990s. Nevertheless, the area's population rose sharply because of immigration and high birth rates among Hispanics and Afro-Americans. Into the early 21st century the city's white population dropped below one-half. Hispanics were in the majority with Asians and black Americans making up the balance. However, these ethnic groups did not blend into a homogeneous society. The population, instead, became a diverse mixture of cultures and economies each with strong ties to their home country. They were unable to live side by side without prejudice, ethnic conflict, and periodic racial riots.

The inner-cities of many large metropolitan areas, both in the United States and England as well as Western Europe, finally degenerated into Third-World enclaves as their minority populations exploded and their literacy declined.

***

Special interest groups in most nations helped to curtail free trade. Tariffs were imposed when the cost of imported goods was less than those produced domestically, or if the quality was superior. Consumers were then forced to buy domestically produced goods and pay higher prices for inferior quality in order to subsidize farmers as in Japan and France and labor unions as in the United States.

Free trade improved in the 1980s and early 1990s, but then declined again as politicians opted to please inefficient industries, labor unions, and farmers for votes at the expense of the unorganized consumer.

When other nations responded by adding tariffs to their imports, trade wars errupted, international trade declined, consumer prices rose, and quality deteriorated. No longer did an efficient world market exist. Nationalistic ferver rose in many areas, antagonism, and conflicts replaced economic cooperation between nations.

In many third-world countries, nationalism and the lingering hatred of colonialism prevented foreign investment and impeded economic development causing their people to suffer.

After the collapse of the socialistic economic system in the Soviet Union, it became abundantly clear to most nations that the market-economy was the future. This was demonstrated in Western Europe, Japan, the United States, and the Asian "tigers" of Taiwan, South Korea, Hong Kong and Singapore. So most countries in Latin America, Africa, Eastern Europe, and the new nations of the former Soviet Union began to dismantle their government-owned businesses in favor of the more efficient private enterprise system.

But the fight against change continued to hold back development and growth. This resulted in continued deterioration in the standard of living in many countries.

Even in the United States continual government interference in the market-economy existed to the detriment of its people. Some examples were: farm and business subsidies; a proliferation of costly, unneeded, and obsolete regulations and restrictions; periodic price controls in some sectors; punishment of savings and reward for spending through the tax code; inefficient government-run postal and educational systems.

In many countries the cost of continuing to subsidize inefficient government-owned businesses, instead of privatizing them, was enormous. Unable to compete in world markets against more efficient free enterprises, they posted huge losses for their respective governments. Nevertheless, the unions, bureaucrats, and politicians, supported them and vigorously fought privatization.

To pay for these mounting losses, government subsidies were increased resulting in soaring national debts and increased taxes. More bureaucracy and regulations were imposed on small business. To cover increasing national deficits, treasuries printed worthless money resulting in runaway-inflation. As a result, the general citizenry suffered. Many resorted to a black market to survive the inflation, rising taxes, and entrenched bureaucracies.

"The only way to earn enough to feed your family is to be self-employed and ignore the government, its red tape and its taxes," said Claudio Tavares, a street peddler on a busy street corner in downtown Sao Paulo, Brazil. To make a simple business decision, involved dealing with thirty-eight government entities, inspectors (and bribes), and massive amounts of paperwork. Economist Nelson Barrizzelli of the University of Sao Paulo said, "The government, with its interventionist and highly centralized economic policies, is a virus that attacks the country's economic organism."[3]

In addition to the above, armaments and a proliferation of welfare programs took vast sums of money that added to national debts. In the United States the federal debt became staggering, but Congress continued to appropriate more funds for various programs than was available from taxes. The desire to be reelected, took priority over fiscal prudence which resulted in unabated funding for special interests until the interest on the debt became the costliest part of the annual budget.

Government waste was overwhelming. The United States Comptroller General of the General Accounting Office estimated in 1990 that money being lost to corruption, waste, and mismanagement totaled one-hundred and fifty billion dollars annually. This was enough to reduce the deficit substantially without even eliminating any government programs or agencies.

In addition, many insured programs amounting to hundreds of billions of dollars were outside the functioning government that posed future financial risk to the taxpayers. Some of these included the notorious Saving and Loan Deposit Insurance system, and the Pension Benefit Guaranty Corporation which insured private pension plans. The later resulted in an obligation to pay over four billion dollars in defunct plans as early as March 1990. Another insured program was the Federal Housing Administration mortgage insurance which had guaranteed billions of dollars in real estate mortgages and was vulnerable to large losses. Billions of dollars in unpaid student loans were guaranteed by the government, and the Farmers Home Administration, which loaned to farmers, was delinquent by an estimated eight billion by 1990. It was estimated $7.7 trillion in direct loans, loan guarantees and insurance had accumulated that was in addition to the national debt.To make matters worse, the Internal Revenue Service estimated uncollected taxes totaled sixty-four billion dollars. These were not tax evasions or disputes, but taxes that the I.R.S. failed to collect.[4]

The greatest threat to American governmental financial solvency was the unfunded pension plans of local, state, federal civilian, and military employees. The gap between what had been set aside and what would be required was an unbelievable $1.24 trillion dollars! Sooner or later it had to be made up through increased taxes or by reducing the pensions. Most taxpayers were unaware of this threat; politicians preferred to forget it.

Everytime Congress addressed the overwhelming deficit created by themselves, its first and sometimes only answer was to find new ways to raise taxes. Then it would spend the new revenues on new programs without applying them to the deficit. By raising taxes, a little more income was whittled away from consumers resulting in a little more reduction in their standard of living. Most were not aware this was one of the reasons living standards were gradually being eroded. In 1994 the average American family paid more in all the various taxes than it spent on food, clothing, and shelter combined. Nearly one-half of the country's income was spent, not by the workers and producers who earned it, but by the local, state and federal politicians and bureaucrats that taxed it from them.

The national debt continued to grow, not only in the United States, but in all countries where deficit spending was out of control. As early as the 1990s, South Americans and youths in particular, were angry at the widespread patronage and corruption in government bureaucracies and blamed government officials for the nation's problems. There was no solution in sight for the indebtedness, inflation, joblessness, and economic stagnation. Disinchanted military officers, drug lords, and guerrillas were constantly challenging their respective Latin-American governments. Drug and alcohol abuse was rampant, much of it the result of educational shortcomings and idleness due to unemployment.

Desperation turned to violence during that time. Helio Jaguaribe, a leading Brazilian sociologist said, "Many of the poor have reached the point where they feel violence is an act of social justice. Driving through poor areas of Rio, the affluent are routinely stopped and robbed or killed as if they were colonial exploiters who had stumbled on a primitive tribe."[5]

At the same time in Venezuela, Carlos Ball, a former editor in chief of a Caracas newspaper noted, "The people are fed up with government corruption; an obscene concentration of wealth of those close to the presidential palace; rising inflation; and huge investments in money-losing state corporations, while public hospitals have no medicines or modern equipment. The air force flies F-16s and Broncos, but there are no policemen after dark to protect citizens and their property from criminals. Water is insufficient and unclean in most cities, including the capital.[6] Most of these problems were prevalent in nearly all Third World countries and in some developed countries as well.

In remote Pakistan, cities were overcrowded and most services were lacking while politicians doled out government assets with abandon to gain votes. "The public has realized that our leadership is as bad as the next, that the politicians are always the same," said Moazzam Malik, an investment banker in Karachi.[7]

In Africa, power-hungry Marxist dictators borrowed large sums of money from the developed world in order to promote their economies. Most of it was wasted through mismanagement or corruption. The balance was used to develop government-run business that eventually failed from lack of efficiency and the inability to compete in world markets. The result was a vast foreign debt whose servicing took two-thirds of the region's gross domestic product. Following the economic collapse of the Soviet Union, African socialists became aware, like everyone else, that the answer to some of their problems was a market-oriented economy. By then, saddled with an enormous foreign debt, entrenched corrupt bureaucracies, and an exploding population, it was extremely difficult to rectify.

It became abundantly clear that all governments worldwide were failing miserably to function for the needs of their citizens because of bureaucratic gridlock in their various institutions, waste, corruption and the greed for political power by the officials in charge. Burdensome national debts resulted in higher taxes, and more paper money printed to help pay for the mismanagement. The result was inevitable inflation and the decline of global living standards.

***

Long-term interest rates gradually rose during this period in order to entice lenders to continue loaning the vast sums needed to keep the burgeoning national debts afloat. Borrowing became too exorbitant to develop new businesses and jobs, and growth of older firms stagnated. Governments then borrowed even more to desperately try various new programs to get their economies moving again. The result was even greater debt and higher rates of interest. But most nations merely printed more paper money to pay for their subsidies and programs.

More money chasing the same amount of merchandise led to rapidly rising inflation that occured so many times in the past. Early on, inflation turned to hyperinflation in South America and later in Russia. In 1989 inflation exceeded one-thousand percent annually in Brazil! By 1992 it was out of control in Russia. Some of this was later alleviated by the abolishment of many inefficient government-run businesses.

As hyperinflation spread to other countries in the 21st century, loans had to be repaid in a week at double the amount borrowed. Wages were raised almost daily, and upon receiving payment, everyone scurried to get rid of the worthless paper money by buying food and other tangibles. Almost overnight, retirees on fixed income became destitute. It was impossible for businesses to make plans. Money instead had to be invested immediately before it lost its value; therefore, a speculative bubble was created. Generally there was little money for productive purposes. Consequently, industry slowed and became stagnant. In some parts of the world, this created shortages in food and other essentials. Crowds roamed the streets protesting, culminating in riots and looting.

Those, who had inherited or accumulated wealth, were able to survive because the value of their assets grew with inflation. Whereas, most young people, with little or no tangible assets to appreciate, had difficulty buying necessities. The gulf between the two distinct economic classes grew wider. The elderly, living on a small pension, were doomed.

***

But one of the world's greatest catastrophes was the destruction of its environment by the exploding masses of people. By the 1980s the world's population was doubling every forty years. It required more farmland, more production and mining facilities, more highways, larger cities, and more natural resources with which to build and support them.

Editors of The Environmental Fund noted early on, " ... exponential population growth is basic to most of our social problems. It is one of the causes of inflation, unemployment, food and energy shortages, resource scarcities, pollution and social disorder. The quality of life of the world's peoples can only deteriorate, if population growth continues."[8]

The 21st century became an environmental nightmare. Remaining rain- forests were ravaged as Third-World inhabitants burned and butchered the vegetation in desperate attempts to obtain firewood and to carve out needed farmland to support their growing families. But it wasn't enough, and thousands perished from starvation and disease. Large sections of topsoil eroded away. Marine fisheries were no longer able to keep up with the voracious demands of population growth. As they dwindled, many were depleted beyond recovery. Precious remaining minerals and fossil fuel resources appeared to be nearly gone, but research for alternatives continued to lag. Energy throughout the world was rationed.

Swarms of humanity were also polluting the air, water, and soil with toxic waste. Where water wasn't poisoned, it was contaminated by lack of basic sanitation. Sufficient funds were not available to help; instead, they went for the basic necessities of food and shelter. Many scientists believed the ozone layer was being destroyed by man-made chemicals, and the atmosphere was being carbonized by pollutants. NASA satellites detected hydrogen fluoride in the stratosphere, which mostly originated from manmade sources although some came from volcanic activity. The human animal was literally overrunning the earth's surface!

As shortages escalated and the standard of living dropped, constant tension developed between most countries which had significant economic differences. Cultural, linguistic, and general nationalistic differences added to the tension. Regional wars became more frequent than in the past.

The chasm between the haves and have-nots grew wider as literacy declined even further. Those unable to obtain a good education, were forced to accept lower-paying jobs, and consequently, lower living standards. The few with higher education were in great demand and received much higher salaries because of rapidly advancing technology. If the education system was poor, as in many Third-World countries, the inhabitants had little opportunity to compete with other educated workers in world trade and were destined to a life of poverty. The same was true for school-dropouts in the more developed countries. As the chasm in income and wealth grew wider, many could not comprehend that the real culprit was the gap in literacy in the new computerized Information Age. They preferred to suspect something more sinister.

As education systems disintegrated, illiteracy became widespread, and poverty eventually enveloped much of the world.

This was accompanied by increased regimentation in everything but standards of conduct, resulting in dwindling choice and initiative and mass conformity. Most inhabitants became dependent on giant politically motivated government-machines, stripped of ambition and their pride of achievement. Life had no purpose except to exist, and even that became a desperate fight.

Morality continued to degenerate. The corruption of youth was allowed to continue by permissive adults. Civilized decency was overwhelmed with indifference, callousness, rudeness, and vulgarity. Drug and alcohol addiction soared. Much earlier, a noted Russian philosopher, Alexander Solzhenitsyn, who observed American society, called it "decadent".

Criminal law completely broke down. Looting, burning, rape and killing were common. Everyone was armed. Courts were gridlocked. There weren't enough prisons to hold the criminals so they were placed in huge outdoor stockades like wild animals. Police were so overwhelmed in large metropolitan cities, the military had to be brought in to maintain order.

As early as 1994, heavily armed Brazilian soldiers, tanks, and helicopters rolled into large areas of Rio De Janeiro. They erected barriers to cut off weekend drug trafficking that had spiraled out of control. They parolled the streets to inhibit the shooting and violence which could not be controlled by the police.

Well into the 21st century, robber-gangs roamed the third-world countryside amid starving and disease-ridden inhabitants. Hordes of immigrants, fleeing starvation and environmental ravage, tried to storm across borders of more-developed nations. Some were driven back at gunpoint by the military patrolling borders. Deadly pestilence sprang up from unknown sources. Horrendous ethnic and religious wars were commonplace. Terrorists used poisonous gases killing thousands in confined areas, such as subways in large metropolitan cities, to achieve their demands.

Much later the religious revolt of the Islamic Fundamentalists spread across north Africa and finally to Saudi Arabia. A holy war was launched against the Christian West when the radical Moslims cut off all oil from the Mideast. Devastating terrorist attacks errupted in all large cities of the West. Hordes of civilians were mangled and butchered. It became a bloody holocaust, a fanatic and total disregard of humanitarian law.

***

How did this madness develop? What were the causes of this uncivilized behavior? Most of the world's inhabitants were aware of the problems that affected them, but few had any idea of the causes. Even fewer had any idea how to solve these enormous global dysfunctions.

The next three chapters illustrate the basic causes of economic malfunction, ethnic malbehavior, and the general decline of disciplined society. *The Rise and Fall of Socialism,* the first of these chapters demonstrates how centralized government-run economies resulted in bureaucratic waste and corruption that ate up resources from increased taxation and increased government debt which eventually ended in hyperinflation for the populace.

Chapter 2

THE RISE AND FALL OF SOCIALISM

The faint glow of daybreak revealed the largest massed army in the history of the world, three million troops, silently moving eastward across the vast plains of the socialist empire. It was the longest military front ever, extending from the shores of the Baltic 2000 miles south to the sands of the Black Sea.

In the pre-dawn hours of June 22, 1941 Operation Barbarosa had begun. A massive German juggernaut opened the door to the most appalling battles of death and destruction in the annals of warfare - a struggle intent on decisively changing the history of the world.

Several popular reasons have been given for this savage invasion - to preempt further expansion by the Union of Soviet Socialist Republics, [1] to erase the threat on Hitler's eastern flank and thus eliminate the possibility of a two-front war, and to destroy the bastion of Communism while completing the German domination of continental Europe.

Hitler was a geopolitician and early recognized that control of the Eurasion heartland could eventually result in control of the world. Hegemony could extend into Africa and probably Australia, as well as Europe and Asia. Furthermore, it was thought the dominant power in the Eurasian land mass would be self-sufficient in all natural resources unlike the American colossus in the smaller western hemisphere. The United States would then be isolated and more easily influenced by the new world power.

The onslaught was awesome. Within ten days 1200 tanks and 150,000 Russians were captured. Thousands more were killed and wounded. A major part of the Soviet air force was destroyed on the ground, and shortly after the Luftwaffe completed air supremacy over Russia. In eighteen days the large industrial city of Smolensk, only 200 miles from Moscow, was surrounded. Hitler declared, "Russia is broken. She will never rise again."

Near the end of summer Leningrad, the second largest city, had been completely encircled. The Ukraine and 50,000 square miles were over run. Hundreds of thousands of Ukranians, alienated by Stalin's ruthless supression, welcomed the Germans as liberators. In the south the Blitzkrieg rolled across the Crimea, captured the large seaport city of Rostov at the mouth of the Don, and were in striking distance of the Caucasian oil fields. The future of socialism appeared doomed.

As Moscow tottered, the German general staff recommended concentrating all available forces on the city's immediate capture. But Hitler's strategy, the wrong one, prevailed. It was to create gigantic pincer movements with separate armies attacking Leningrad and the southern Ukraine leaving only General Von Bock's forces to converge on Moscow.

Without help, Von Bock's army could not deal a quick and final blow to the Russians who had by then concentrated their main reserves to protect Moscow. By November it began to snow, but once again, Hitler ignored his generals' pleas to bring up winter supplies and reserves and solidify positions for a final spring drive. Instead, he called for another offensive to encircle Moscow from the rear.

During the attack General Guderian, the brilliant tank strategist, actually entered the suburbs of Moscow. The Kremlin towers could be seen in the distance through the falling snow. Moscow seemed about to fall, and the Soviet Government fled to Kuibyshev over 500 miles to the east.

Then the full fury of the Russian winter settled in on the lightly clad Germans. Temperatures dropped below zero. Supply lines bogged down. Food and gasoline became scarce. Engines froze.

The Russians, equipped for winter, counterattacked. An imminent German victory turned into a nightmare, a fight to survive the winter.

The Germans were able to muster a 1942 offensive but the tide of war had changed in the fall of 1941. Hitler's two momentous tactical errors changed world history forever.

After Germany's defeat the USSR rose from the ashes of war, sought revenge, and determined never to allow the motherland to be ravaged again. So during the Potsdam Conference in 1945, they insisted on creating an extensive buffer zone between the pre-1939 Soviet boundary and western Germany and to enlarge their territorial empire.

The Russians were intransigent throughout the conference insisting on innumerable concessions from their former allies, the United States and Great Britain. In the words of historian Louis Snyder, "They were cold, hard, unyielding, unrelenting, demanding ever more and more, using every weapon from sarcasm to vituperation to threats. To the monolithic minds of the Kremlin, negotiation meant one-hundred percent their way..." They even went so far as to demand trusteeship over the former Italian colony of Libya which was not even in their theatre of war! This attitude may have contributed to the Cold War that soon followed.[2]

The USSR was allotted the northern part of East Prussia (Germany). The Soviets had already annexed half of pre-war Poland following its bilateral invasion with Hitler in 1939; so the eastern half of pre-war Germany was added to Poland to compensate for what the Russians had taken. The rest of Germany was divided into two parts and occupied by the victors. It was militarily dismantled; most heavy machinery and industry was moved to the USSR as reparations. Other reparations were also demanded from all east European countries including Austria and ran into the billion of dollars.

Chunks of eastern Finland were also added to the Soviet Union under the agreement. A prolonged occupation, by Russian troops of Eastern Europe, resulted in the annexation to the USSR of a large southeastern section of Romania, the eastern part of Czechoslovakia, and the permanent establishment of a communist state in divided East Germany. The socialist empire had greatly expanded.

The occupying troops also enabled the Soviets to establish puppet Communist governments in Poland, Czechoslavakia, Hungary, Romania and Bulgaria. Once established, these totalitarian governments continued in absolute political control for decades.

The underground Communist parties had fought the Axis occupation in the Balkans, so they took easy control of the governments in Yugoslavia and Albania once the Germans surrendered. In Greece, however, a civil war broke out between the Communists and the elected government. The Communists were supported by the USSR through supply lines in Yugoslavia until that country broke with the Soviets. The Truman Doctrine of 1947 gave American assistance to the Greek government, and the threat of a Communist take-over ended.

The conference to finalize a peace treaty for Germany became even more acrimonious. The Soviets suddenly demanded additional financial reparations from West Germany which the U.S. was rehabiliting with financial assistance (i.e. The U.S. would be paying the reparations). Finally after several meetings in various capitals, any chance for agreement vanished; Germany remained divided.

It had been agreed that Berlin, the largest city, would be divided into military zones, each to be occupied by one of the victorious powers. All provisions for the Western zones had to be brought in from the west across 100 miles of Soviet occupied East Germany.

In 1948 the Russians blockaded Berlin. They cut off all transportation and communications from the west hoping to compel the Western powers to abandon the city. However, the incredible American and British airlift of supplies, even including coal, into Berlin was successful; the Soviets lifted the blockade.

This was followed by the reconstruction of West Berlin into a showcase of Western development in contrast to the bleak conditions in East Berlin. The Communist government of East Germany responded by building the Berlin Wall. It separated the east and west sections and prohibited free movement of people into West Berlin.

In the later days of the war with Japan, the Soviet Union occupied the Kurile Islands and southern Sakhalin and drove the Japanese out of the northeastern Chinese province of Manchuria. The Russians then proceeded to strip this heavy industrial section of all its machinery and plants before returning it to China. Following the Japanese Peace Treaty in 1952, the Russians refused to return the southern half of Sakhalin and the Kurile Islands to Japan.

Korea, the former Japanese colony, was occupied by the Americans in the south and the Russians in the north. The United Nations resolved that the Korean people should elect a government for the entire country, but the Soviet authorities refused to allow the people in the north to participate. After a democratic election in the south, the North was proclaimed a Communist state in 1948. Then in June 1950, North Korean troops invaded South Korea. The United Nations, with major help from the United States, eventually pushed the invaders back and hostilities ended with an armistice in 1953.

The early socialist expansion actually began years earlier in Asia in 1924. In Outer Mongolia a Communist revolution, fostered by Soviet agents, created the Mongol People's Republic. In reality, it became a Soviet satellite carved out of China.

In China the Communist party formed a coalition with the Nationalist party in the new Kuomintang government. During the military expeditions to drive out foreign interests and subdue the old military factions, some elements of the Communist wing created considerable civil strife among the citizenry. Finally in 1927 after the Nationalists purged some of the more radical Communists, an irreconcilable break occurred .

By 1930 a sizeable Red army occupied several large areas in southern China. After five campaigns it was defeated in 1934 by the Nationalists, forced to retreat to the west, and thence ended in the long devastating march to the north.

In the late 1930s it was in the interest of both the Nationalist government and the Communists to once again form a coalition in a united front against the Japanese. The scattered areas controlled by the Communists grew during the war until they covered large portions of north and east China. When the Japanese surrendered in 1945, Red army troops began moving out of their guerilla bases to occupy all of north China.

As the Nationalist armies moved north to meet the threat, a full-scale civil war broke out. By 1948 the Nationalist armies were defeated in the north and began a retreat southward. Eventually they were driven from the mainland and forced to move their capitol to Taipei in Taiwan, formerly Formosa under the Japanese.

A Communist government, the Peoples Republic of China, was finally established in 1949. Taking complete control of the Chinese mainland, it brought a massive part of the world's population under the direct control of socialism. The Red army then invaded Tibet in 1950 and forced its amalgamation into China completing the socialist domination of the Euro-Asian heartland.

Victims of inhuman poverty, inhabitants of former colonies, and those living under military oppression were particularly susceptable to the call of revolutionary socialism. But many educated people in advanced industrial nations also saw Communism as new, exciting, and logical.

Idealists and revolutionaries throughout the capitalist world were indoctrinated and trained not only in Moscow, Peking, and other Communist cities but in "cells" worldwide. In the United States subtle forms of subversion were also at work. The educational system and media groups were targeted. The objective was to control the mind through innuendo. Labor movements and government bureaucracies were also fertile ground. Later some world church organizations responded to the call for social justice and supported Communist revolutions. A trojan horse was being erected in every non-socialist country just as the Nazis "fifth column" had infiltrated its victim countries.

Earl Browder, former leader of the Communist party in America, stated in 1950, "...In the decade 1939-49 ... State Capitalism has progressed farther in America than in Great Britain under the Labor government, despite its nationalization of certain industries, which is a formal stage not yet reached in America; the concentration of the guiding reins of the national economy in government hands is probably on a higher level in the U.S.A." He appraised twenty-two specific governmental economic controls and said, " this growth of economic power, ... represents the maturing of the prerequisite for socialism, ... which makes socialism inevitable."

Commenting on the Communist seizure of power, a statement by Oldrich John, the Communist speaker of the Czechoslovakia parliament in Prague, was typical of the philosophy that demanded a socialist world. He proclaimed, " February 1948 was not a decision concerning only our country, but the whole world. Our February ... belongs to the working class of the whole world which is expecting its February. It will have it."[3]

Communism spread world-wide by the 1970s. Every country had either a Communist party, or if prohibited, a core of party intellectuals determined to bring revolutionary socialism to their nation.

In Europe even nations aligned with the west and North Atlantic Treaty Organization had large Communist parties. They were particularly dominant in France, Italy, Greece, Spain, and Portugal and at times very influential in national policies. They even held power for a time in Portugal when it was a member of NATO. In France, another NATO member, a Communist was appointed to the cabinet. In Spain the civil war of the 30s was a direct confrontation of the Communist-Socialist Popular Front backed by the USSR and a military-led faction under General Franco. Following Franco's death, Spain's Communist party once again became an important voice in the conduct of national policy.

Nearly all of the new independent nations of Africa anxiously adopted socialism. Most were ruled by militant dictators many of whom had been indoctrinated in Marxism either in the Soviet Union or while attending a Western university. Existing governments were overthrown in Ethiopia and Rhodesia and replaced with Communist ones. In Angola and Mozambique Communist governments fought bitter counter-revolutionary wars to retain power.

Communism was spreading throughout Asia and the Middleast. Following WWII Communist guerillas in Malaysia tried to gain control but were finally overcome by the British. Indonesia's large pro-Peking Communist party attempted to seize the government in 1965 but failed, and thousands were executed. Even the overwhelming religious fervency of Iran and India could not deter a large Communist party from developing in both countries.

In Vietnam one of the bloodiest wars unfolded in the 1960s as the Communists from the north infiltrated and later invaded the non-Communist south. Overrunning South Vietnam, Laos, and Cambodia they created a solid socialist block in Indo-China. Afghanistan adopted a puppet Communist government with the aid of the USSR, and a terrible civil war ensued. In the Philippines Communist insurgents gained control of large portions of the archipelago. Even in capitalist Japan the Communist party became extremely vocal, and the Red Brigade terrorized the populace with its demonstrations.

With an exploding population living in poverty, Latin America was even more vulnerable to socialism. In 1959 Cuban revolutionaries overthrew the corrupt regime of Batista. The Communist element quickly forced the newly appointed president to resign, and Fidel Castro became head of the government.

The Marxist Allende was elected president in Chile by a small margin in 1970 professing not to socialize the country. Nevertheless, by 1972 all major industries and large farms had been brought under government control causing the economy to plummet. The result was middle-class riots and street demonstrations protesting food shortages. This led to a military coup which overthrew the government. For years after, the left protested, fought the return to capitalism, and bitterly divided the country.

In the rest of South America, Marxist guerillas appeared everywhere especially in Columbia, Venzuela, Bolivia, and in Peru where the Shining Path was creating havoc destroying government installations. In Central America the despotic Samoza regime in Nicaragua had been overthrown by the Sandinistas. A Communist government was installed with the support of the USSR and Cuba. Sandanista-supported guerillas dominated much of the rural area of El Salvador. To the north in Mexico the socialist front led by Cardenas, a Marxist, nearly captured the presidential election in 1988.

By the late 20th century the entire world was divided into two bitterly fighting armed camps. Marxist wars of "liberation" were going on everywhere to overthrow existing governments or to prevent a counter-revolutionary movement. Terrorists trained in Moscow, or by one of its surrogates, also spread the fight. The Red Brigades of Italy and Germany and the radical Marxist wings of Libya and the Palestinian Liberation Organization were typical. A

Marxist element even infiltrated the Basque movement for independence in northern Spain and the Irish Republican Army in Northern Ireland. In remote southeastern Turkey the revolutionary Kurdish Labor Party sought to establish a Marxist state.

At times it became open warfare; at others it took the form of indoctrination, subversion, or terrorist acts. Hardly a country in the world was left untouched. Even in the capitalist democracies, the political struggle went on between the status quo and the growing class of Marxists and socialist intellectuals.

Leonid Brezhnev, premier of the USSR, declared in December 1972, "The Communist party of the Soviet Union has proceeded and still proceeds on the basis of the continuing class struggle between the two systems - capitalist and socialist - in the spheres of economics, politics and, of course, idealogy. ... the world outlook and class aims of socialism and capitalism are opposed and irreconcilable."[4]

Later in 1977 the Brezhnev constitution stated it was a duty to spread Communism to all countries of the world including supporting " wars of national liberation" and guiding local revolutionary forces to Marxist-Leninism. Once established, it declared the Soviet Union would use military means to prevent its overthrow.

The truth was the Communist and capitalist worlds had been in a deadly struggle since the end of World War II. Concerned about possible nuclear hostilities in the future, most failed to recognize the world was already at war!

* * *

What motivated people to this great doctrine called socialism that was sweeping the world?

In a very broad sense, socialism was a movement for the promotion of the greatest well-being and happiness for the greatest number of individuals. It embraced a classless society, the abolition of physical want, and world-wide brotherhood. Despots aside, most agreed these were very worthwhile goals.

Since Plato, intellectuals have envisioned an ideal society based on certain aspects of socialistic behavior. Sir Thomas Moore coined the word " Utopia" in 1516, and Sir Francis Bacon reflected on a utopian world built upon science and human achievement in 1627.

It wasn't until the 19th century that the germ of socialism began to spread. In 1825 the word socialism was adopted to mean a complete transformation of society by substituting social for individual control in the organization of life and work.

Various socialists during that period contributed to the theory. Robert Owen, the founder of British socialism, denounced capitalism as the exploiter of labor. William Thompson developed the doctrine that labor was the sole true source of value and should receive all of the benefits. Louis Blanc originated the formula, "From each according to his abilities; to each according to his needs." Edward Bellamy and William Morris wrote respectively of a regimented transitional society and revolution as a prelude to socialism.

Albert Einstein, like most of the other great thinkers of the early 20th century was an exponent of socialism and a deep believer in social justice and world government. Even the great science-fiction writers, H.G. Wells and George Orwell, both socialists, wrote of future socialist worlds.

The first clear proclamation of revolutionary socialism was documented in 1848 when Karl Marx and Friedrich Engels wrote the *Communist Manifesto*. It later became the bible of the Communist world. To the authors, the word Communism was synonymous with socialism and meant a system based upon common property and an equal distribution of income and wealth.

Marx believed all institutions of society were a direct result of economic circumstances. He deduced that profit and interest were merely payments for the use of capital which, in turn, was created by labor. He developed the theory of surplus value - profit, interest, and rent (land was a passive agent) were distributed undeservedly to the capitalist which created a society of unequal classes. [5] As a result, Marx was convinced of the inevitability of class warfare or revolution.

It is important to note that most of these theories appeared during the early industrial revolution when the economy was suddenly changed from agrarian to one based on industrial mining and manufacturing. The change was so swift that factories and sweat shops quickly sprouted without plans, regulations, or even thought for the welfare of the workers. The emancipation of labor was, therefore, dominant in the minds of early socialists.

Although Marxism spread throughout Europe during the last quarter of the 19th century, most followers opted for an evolutionary approach. The plan was to attain socialism through education and the machinery of existing states without revolutionary confrontation. The evolutionary form generally encompassed government control and subsidies of large industrial enterprises, some price controls, resource allocation, and especially social welfare. England, France, Sweden, Mexico, and India were typical examples in the post WWII era.

Probably the most important political party created for this purpose was the Social Democratic party. For decades, it became a dominant political force in Europe. In England the British Labor party in 1918 committed itself to support only programs which would lead to a socialist society. Even in the capitalist United States the programs of the New Deal and the Great Society not only attracted many socialists but were also influenced by them. These individuals made great strides in influencing the growth of trade unions, social insurance, and welfare; and the comprehensive regulation of agriculture, finance, business, and industry. Through increased taxation on higher incomes and the redistribution of those funds for welfare and other social programs, they attempted to transfer income from one group to another in order to try to create a classless society.

Although the principles and objectives of socialism remained unchanged, the movement broke into two distinct groups to achieve those aims after the disposition of the Czar. In November 1917 the evolutionary socialist government of Kerensky was overthrown in Moscow by the revolutionary socialists under Lenin. Lenin's interpretation of Marxism was the complete destruction of the old government and replacment with a dictatorship of the proletariat. It was this interpretation that prevailed in all economic revolutions throughout the 20th century.

More important, Trotsky, Lenin's close collaborator, and others believed the Russian Revolution would fail unless it was followed by Communist revolutions in advanced capitalist countries.

This Trotsky doctrine subsequently was modified in later years in a more sophisticated manner to embrace gradual world-wide indoctrination and revolution. With this approach the advanced capitalist countries would be last to fall after being isolated and infiltrated. It would mean the complete and final socialization of the world.

All socialists, nevertheless, had a common objective, the ultimate control of the economic and social system by a central government. The revolutionaries, however, believed that any means whatever justified this end. But morality lay in means as well as in the end. It was shown many times that absolute socialism wherever practiced, not only led to inequity, but cruelty wherever practised.

Extreme examples were the liquidation of millions in the Ukraine in the 1930s, and in the killing fields of Cambodia after the vietnam war. It was genocide that even dwarfed the Jewish holocaust of WWII. Yuri Afanasyev, historian and archivist, published evidence from KGB and Communist party documents showing seven million executions in Soviet prisons alone between 1935 and 1941.

"It was a well known fact there was a quota for how many people were to be liquidated. The most dangerous people for any totalitarian regime were people who could think," said Edwaed Keonjian, a Russian scientist living in an apartment building in Leningrad at the time of the exterminations. "The quota was very high for that building, it was full of scientists."[6] As late as 1989 thousands were ruthlessly massacred by the Chinese army in Beijing to eradicate protesters for political reform.

In the later half of the 20th century most non-socialists in the capitalist West were unable to comprehend either the philosophy or the fervency of these Marxists. Smug in their own democracies, free from dictatorial rule, and living an affluent lifestyle, they went about their daily lives giving little thought to the world about them. Meanwhile, many of their offspring were being indoctrinated with anti-business and anti-capitalistic subtleties in the classroom, the movies, and on television by an increasing number of people dedicated to expanding socialist thought.

By 1982 some academics bragged that hundreds perhaps thousands of socialist-leaning professors were spreading Marxist doctrine in colleges and universities. One of the leading Marxist professors, Bertell Ollman of New York University wrote, "A Marxist cultural revolution is taking place in American universities. It is a peaceful and democratic revolution, fought chiefly with books and lectures." His textbook, *Alienation : Marxist Conception of Man in Capitalist Society.* was being used in more than a 100 universities.[7]

Jan Van Houten,a Dutch journalist, correctly perceived what was occuring in Europe and especially in Germany, "The left has discovered that today power means first and foremost control of the means of communication and socialization - schools, universities, churches and above all, the mass media. It's in these institutions that public opinion is shaped ..." Even Alexander Solzhenitsyn, the exiled Russian author, noted in 1976 that Western society had failings and weaknesses which caused a fatal drift toward socialism.[8]

The ultimate factor in those years which helped to erode the capitalistic system was the fanaticism of those beliefs. To socialists it was a religious call to the great struggle for fairness and decency in their everyday life and workplace. In theory it was mankind's final answer to the economic and social shortfalls in the world. Their belief was deep and irrevokable. All other political philosophies and religions were heresy. They preached wherever they could. They indoctrinated and infiltrated. As a result it spread like a religion.

Unable to comprehend this fanatacism, negotiating statesmen from the West were always at a disadvantage. They could not understand that Soviet supported Marxist wars and supression of individual freedoms were non-negotiable (i.e. rights of the state were more important) whereas nuclear arms treaties were negotiable. The Soviets continually and successfully resisted any linkage between progress on arms control and progress in areas of Soviet behavior which posed the real strategic threat to the interests of the West. The Soviets took a long-term view of achieving a socialist world whereby the particular means to achieve their objective could only be compromised temporarily before being renewed.

On the other hand, mutual arms reductions involved no political concessions. Andrei Gromyko, the long-time foreign minister and architect of Soviet diplomacy, confided to his aide, a senior United Nations official who later defected, that American statesmen "don't comprehend our final goals and they mistake tactics for strategy."

Not only had the political philosophy of socialism risen to dominancy, but the Soviet Union also rose from the devastation of World War II to become a world super power that threatened Western democracies.

The catastrophic invasion by the Germans during WWII fostered a psychosis within the Kremlin that created distrust and hostility everywhere they looked. Any foreign development or incident immediately became a threat. Even during WWII, these fears helped create a vast network of spies throughout Russia's allies: England, Canada, and the United States. Afterwards, it resulted in a series of spectacular espionage trials. The Soviets were unyielding and unrelenting in their negotiations with their "enemies", the capitalistic West.

The possession of the atomic bomb by the United States was an intolerable situation until they were able to obtain its secrets principally through espionage.[9]

The most humiliating incident occured when the Soviets were forced by American naval elements to turn back their ships bearing nuclear missiles to Cuba in 1962. To succumb to the overwhelming naval and nuclear power of the capitalist United States, in the eyes of the world, was indicative that the USSR was only a second-rate military power when compared to the United States.

From that day forward, the Soviets went on a war-economy and embarked upon the greatest military build-up in history. By 1980 they had numerical superiority in nearly every weapons categrory. Suddenly the United States reversed its decline of preparedness and began a massive military expansion in order to quickly reach par with the Soviet Union.

As the arms race heated up during the 1980s, it became evident to the Kremlin that it would be difficult for the Soviets to keep up the pace. Their domestic economy had already been sacrificed during the many years attempting to become a military superpower and had declined to the level of a third world country.

Productivity, in the consumer economy under state controls, dropped to its lowest historical level. The economy was stagnant, a disaster. It called for immediate action.

Under Premier Gorbachev the Soviets developed a new strategy. They relaxed some of the dogmatic and dictatorial controls on the populace and temporarily suspended support of Marxist wars. Then they negotiated a cessation in the arms race so national efforts and monies could be diverted to modernizing the economy. Under this apparent peaceful change, they solicited billions in credit, technology, and management expertice from the capitalist countries.

The intermediate objectives appeared to be the consolidation of Soviet gains, the temporary end to further world revolution, and to catch up with the collossal capitalistic economic machine. It was very important, however, that this be achieved with only superficial modifications to Marxist principles. The Communist party also had to remain in full control of the economy and the political system.

***

The control of the economic system by a central government was probably the most important goal of the early socialists. They theorized this would equalize income and wealth and result in a classless society. All instruments of production and distribution were, therefore, in the hands of the state. All private ownership and the free-market system had been abolished. In an attempt to assure full employment and set salaries and wages, the state controlled labor.

A centralized bureaucracy planned production quotas, standards of quality, allocation of resources and credit, means of distribution and set all prices. These were usually formulated in the capitol far removed from the realities of consumer markets or the manufacturing plants and collective farms. The consumer could not vote by purchase in the market place on what or how much he needed, but had to accept whatever was offered by bureaucratic proclamation. Nor could he shop for the best price or quality because there was only one quality at one price.

The key problem with the planned economy was the elimination of competition. Instead, a non-competitive supplier for a particular product or service would be created, owned, and run by the government's planning agency without a practical means to determine consumer demand for the product. Unless the consumer had a choice of products, bureaucrats had no way to tell what he preferred. Without this information, the central planners set a quantity of "widgets" to be made based on a guesstimate, quality standards at a bare minimum, and a price they hoped would cover production costs.

The result, of course, was an oversupply of items that were in small demand and a shortage of items in great demand. Rationing and long lines to obtain scarcities became commonplace. Black markets and bribery arose. On the other hand, overproduction of some items resulted in gross waste in both resources and labor that were badly needed elsewhere.

Incentives were lacking for government-run businesses to develop new and better products or services since they had a monopoly, and consumers did not have the freedom to turn to a competitive source. In fact, there was no way that government-managers could tell whether their merchandise was good or bad unless it was totally shunned; so many products continued to be produced for years in their original obsolete form. Consequently, technological innovations to improve the standard of living fell far behind those of the capitalistic countries.

Lack of incentive for labor and management in the civilian economy was no different in the military economy. Yet the military was able to develop an advanced war machine second to none. This was due to several factors. First, unable to develop and utilize technological advances in the civilian economy, the Soviets bought as much technology as possible from the West; secondly, their vast espionage network was able to penetrate most military secrets of the West; finally, a massive amount of the gross national product was diverted from the civilian to the military sector of the economy. Most important, both the Soviet and American military programs were still profoundly wasteful and inefficient because they both operated as government-controlled monopolies in a non-competitive environment. In other words, the development of military hardware in the United States did not have a capitalistic advantage over the USSR except for the technological advancements from its civilian marketplace.

Soviet salaries and wages were arbitrarily set by bureaucrats rather than what the free market in a particular labor category would support. Since most salaries did not reflect supply and demand, they varied little. As an example, doctors' salaries were set only slightly higher than routine jobs. Most monetary incentives were forbidden, but a worker could never be fired except for gross misconduct.

All of these things resulted in little incentive by the worker to seek better employment or to work harder to better his position. New workers, that started out producing efficiently, soon gave up after observing their fellow-workers "goofing off." The result was inertia by all workers. Laziness, bureaucratic indifference and corruption, and declining productivity abounded. Many times a shortage occurred in one labor category and an oversupply in another. At other times insufficient training developed in some and overqualification in others. When productivity dropped, everyone eventually suffered a decline in their standard-of-living

There were attempts later to add incentives for workers in the form of bonuses for increased quantity quotas and better quality. However, in a non-competitive market there was no practical way to measure improved quality. Besides, improving quality meant the slowing of quantity output. In turn, this affected the manager's volume quotas handed down from centralized planning.

Of course, labor negotiations and strikes were barred to facilitate the control of labor by central planning bodies. Turning down a job was also subject to prosecution for "parasitism".

Factories, operated by central planning bureaus, had profits and losses like any business in the capitalist countries, but unlike their counterparts, the bottom-line results were not critical to the workers or managers. If costs rose and losses piled up, the government's planning bureau merely subsidized the plant or business with more government funds. This was true not only in the Communist economies but in India, Mexico, Brazil, and other semi-socialist economies where the government owned and operated many large businesses. Even in capitalist America, Amtrack and the Postal Department were examples of highly subsidized and badly-run government monopolies.

Consequently, there was no incentive to increase sales through an improved and less-expensive product, to reduce excessive costs and waste, or to increase the productivity of workers. Instead, inefficiency continued, and consumers paid for it in lower quality and in higher prices as well as increased taxes and deficits to finance the subsidies. It was evident, therefore, that the discipline from profit and loss was absent in a planned economy. It resulted in a deterioration of efficiency in industry and stagnation in the living standard for all.

In order to distribute the fruits of labor more equitably, the main objective of socialism was a better economic system than under capitalism. "The economy," said Lenin," is the main field of battle for Communism." This was ironic since the biggest problem confronting socialists was the economy. It was the problem that beleaguered all socialist governments since the Bolshevik Revolution.

Lacking incentive of any kind, the inefficient production and distribution system continued to result in chronic shortages, rationing, and price controls.

Although the economic system had been in a state of gradual decay in nearly all socialist countries by the late twentieth century, most of their leaders were dogmatic in their belief that the general principles were correct; so, they pursued them with little modification to the great disbelief of the West. At times they appeared to be changing to capitalism when they sought Western methods of management, production, technology, and credit. Some even allowed profit in very small businesses. Still, anyone, who understood socialism, knew significant change was impossible; the ultimate goals: a state-planned economy, abolition of private property, and distribution of wealth and income always remained.

The vision of most frustrated socialists was obscured by the need to create equality in income and wealth. To achieve equality, force was necessary. People were required to part with their labor and earned wealth in order to satisfy an arbitrary concept of equity.

Socialists held to a deep prejudice which rejected anything derived from the "evil" capitalistic system regardless of the outcome. Thus they were slow in uncovering the real reason that planned economies failed.

Moreover, planned economies began with the ultimate solution to economic problems and ignored the effect that the means had on the outcome. In other words, the planners had a pre-conceived assumption of perfection in its workers and managers. There was no regard to the motives which caused workers to individually take actions for themselves or to react differently when incentives were absent. As a result, the economic outcome was different than originally planned.

***

Following the feudalistic days of the Czar, a huge productive vacuum existed in Russia. Consequently, under a totalitarian planned economy and with revolutionary determination, it was obvious considerable progress would be made in closing the gap initially between it and the industrialized nations of the West.

After fifty years of waste, mismanagement, inefficiency, and planning gone berserk, it was generally recognized by everyone, including the more dogmatic Marxists, something was fundamentally wrong with the socialist economic system. The standard-of-living remained far below that which existed in the West and economic problems of all types were widespread. This was recognized as early as the 1960s.

Although Yugoslavia was one of the first Communist countries to begin adopting some capitalistic methods, it wasn't until under the term of Premier Krushchev, that a serious effort was made in the Soviet Union. He complained in 1962 that the inferior production of plant equipment resulted in massive amounts of capital and labor to keep the equipment in repair. It was estimated it took an additional two million workers and 800,000 machine tools to accomplish this. Soviet manufactured aircraft engines had a service life of only five hundred hours compared to twenty-five hundred for British engines. Petrochemical plants complained of certain units with forty percent of the parts defective.

Krushchev was especially influenced by Evsei Liberman, a Kharkov professor of economics, who urged a switch from rigid centralized planning to profit guidelines in 1963.[10]

Several factories were placed on a trial competitive basis. Profits on invested capital, flexible prices which responded to supply and demand in the market, and interest charged on the use of government money by industry were instigated. The system was altered six times in ten years in a vain effort to recentralize and find the magic mix for a better economy. The massive and entrenched planning-bureaucracy was too great an obstacle, and each time it failed.

A Supreme Soviet Deputy at the time cited a typical example of a factory that received seventy different official instructions from nine state committees, four economic councils, and two state planning committees all authorizing production orders. Factory output goals were measured in quantity by the planners so a factory manufacturing knitted caps and sweaters produced only caps and in only one color because they were easier and quicker to manufacture. In the Russian Republic, deliveries from 257 factories had to be suspended because their goods simply would not sell.[11]

Later Premier Kosygin, an economist in his own right, continued Krushchev's attempts to reform the economic system in his budget of 1965. Central economic councils were abolished in favor of ministries for separate industries, but it was too little and too late to make significant advances. Party members and bureaucrats, seeing a curtailment of their control, insisted on retrenchment and a scrapping of the experiments.

Then in the mid-1980s other Soviet economists began expressing considerable doubt about the economics of socialism. Leonid Ivanovich Abalkin at a 1986 Communist rally in Yugoslavia, conceded that capitalism outpaced socialism in many scientific and technological fields. More important, he said, "We have now reached an era in which many illusions about socialism's 'automatic' advantage over capitalism must be reassessed."[12]

Nikolay Shmelyov, a Moscow economist, castigated the system in a 1987 issue of *Novy mir*, the Soviet's leading political and literary journal. He remarked, "Persistent long-term efforts to overthrow the laws of economic life and crush natural incentives to work brought on results opposite to those anticipated. We now have an economy out of whack and plagued with shortages. Industry rejects eighty percent of new technical inventions and decisions. Our level of efficiency is among the lowest in the industrialized countries."[13]

He elaborated further, "We need to realize there is such a thing as natural unemployment among people looking for work or changing their place of employment. Only profit can ... permit us to relate production costs to results effectively. It simply tells whether you are working well or not. Consumers need to have the opportunities to take what is offered or turn it down. That means they have to have a real choice. And the producer must be faced with the real possibility of loss and even bankruptcy if the goods he produces cannot be sold."[14]

In the same year Igor Birman, a Russian economist who helped design the failed economic reforms under Premier Kosygin, said simply, "The only cure for socialism is capitalism."[15]

On a visit to the USSR in 1984, *Washington Post*'s Robert Kaiser commented, "There is evidence of social disintegration - dramatically declining life expectancy for men; rising infant mortality; increasing alcoholism, affecting ever-younger age groups; increasing crime, corruption and cynicisim." He was amazed to be told by a knowledgeable Muscovite, "Most of the clinics where babies are born in this capital city are contaminated with staph infections which a large percentage of newborns catch and which Soviet drugs often fail to cure. Many Moscow hospitals now have virtually no nursing staff, so patients must depend on friends and family for nursing care. A third of patients being treated for alcoholism began drinking before they were ten years old."[16]

Dr. AbelAganbegyan, another leading Soviet economist said, "There has been no breakthrough in production efficiency ... the return on capital and the efficiency of capital investments have not improved ... "[17]

By 1988 food was rationed in 8 of the 15 Soviet republics. The agricultural production system was in complete disarray. Cows and pigs were held up for days at slaughterhouses because there wasn't enough cold storage facilities. At the other end consumers lined up for hours outside of stores because there wasn't enough meat to go around. More than $22 billion of farm equipment was lying unused in farm fields and storage areas because it was either the wrong kind, improperly made, or not needed for that particular farm operation. Thousands of tractors were left outside to rust in the winter weather simply because there were no sheds to house them. A chronic shortage of veterinary care reduced livesock herds by one-third. Millions of tons of food went to waste because of inadequate storage and transportation facilities.[18]

Most socialists world-wide could not bring themselves to admit that after seventy years of trying, a government-planned and run economy was completely inferior to a free one. They continued to try reforms without abandoning the basic system. Unfortunately, the status quo served the bureaucratic class in charge. A factory manager had no personal interest in reform because it would upset the accustomed routine and would only make new demands leading to trouble. Officials at the ministries would lose some of their power so they were not in favor of reform. Workers, used to loafing were afraid of having to work harder under new reforms. So they too did all they could to frustrate whatever changes were planned.

When Gorbachev was only a second secretary of the Communist party he recognized this problem. He observed the administrative bureaucracy, that stubbornly blocked reforms in the past, could ever be persuaded to go along with significant changes. Yet, he persisted by telling a televised news conference in 1990 that the creation of a market economy in the Soviet Union was "essential." He declared, "The market is not an invention of capitalism. It has existed for centuries. It is an invention of civilization."

In September of the same year, Boris Yeltsin, the newly elected president of the Russian Republic, said, "A transition is needed from an idealogy-ridden economy to an efficiency-driven economy. We know that poverty, even misery, are widespread and that the standard-of-living continues to fall."

Communist China already began significant efforts to develop some free markets and enterprises in the late 1970s. Profits and other incentives were adopted, and the de-centralizing of vast industrial bureaucracies was started. The changes began to make gradual improvements in the standard-of-living for the average Chinese.

By 1989 the rapid growth in economic freedom brought demands for more political freedom. The ruling elite of the Chinese Communist party saw signs of the eventual loss of their status in both power and affluence, so the protests culminated in the infamous massacre at Tienamon Square in Beijing. It was immediately followed by a retrenchment in economic reforms as well as political. But, the Chinese leaders, unlike the Soviets, soon saw their mistake and returned to the promotion of even faster economic growth by further expanding the market-economy.

Yugoslavia, under Tito, was one of the first Communist nations to gradually fashion a market-oriented economy. However, it never completely licked the problem of allowing bureaucrats, with little understanding of the free market, to make big decisions allocating resources on projects without fully subjecting them to the rigors of the market-place. Typical was the $300 million of borrowed Western capital invested in the spectacular Feni smelter. Having never broken even, operations were suspended after a brief twenty-six months.[19]

"The lesson of Yugoslavia is that there is no compromise between a market economy and a centrally planned economy," said Ivan Ribnikar, an economist at Yugoslavia's University of Ljublzana. "One must have a true market economy."[20]

In Communist Vietnam, the principal result of the invasion and socialization of the South was to make it nearly as poor as the North. After nearly fifteen years of disastrous economic control and with the help of more pragmatic leaders, the Communist party in 1986 admitted the need for real reform and the adoption of a market-economy. It finally had to embrace the American-promoted capitalist system it once fought with fanatical fervor.

They granted autonomy to state-controlled enterprises and lifted most restrictions on private business. By 1990 the central-planning apparatus nearly disappeared. The government claimed the new economic policy was irreversible. Yet, socialism remained the official ideology and long-term objective.

Socialist countries all over the world laboured mightily to try to find some way to reinvent the market system; they tried to make use of the discipline and incentive of profit and loss to achieve greater economic rewards without giving up control of the economy. Most economists agreed that such a combination could not work successfully. It had been tried in the semi-socialist countries of Mexico, India, Brazil, and many other third-world countries with little or no success.

***

Examples of the gross errors and unmitigated disasters of a planned economy and government-run industries were numerous. None were as obvious as in the Soviet Union. Typical was a giant hydroelectric plant that was built on the Angara River in Siberia. When it became operative in 1974 there were no nearby industrial facilities or none in the planning stage to use the power.

An article in *Pravda* described another example of waste in bureaucratic control. When a Soviet citizen named Yurier saw four ferryboats crossing the Neva River in Leningrad with no passengers aboard, he called the Leningrad passenger agency and asked why the boats were running empty.

"What do you mean, why?" an official asked. "They're carrying passengers."

"But there are no passengers," Yurier said.

"That's true. The passengers don't need this ferry line. It's faster and cheaper to go by train," the official said.

"Why not cut out the line or have fewer boats?"

"These are orders from higher up."

But the official referred Yurier to a higher official named Veselov who told him, "I gave the order the line be eliminated."

Yurier said the four ferries were still running. Veselov said if so, they would stop. But three and a half weeks later *Pravda* verified, "The four ferries were still running despite the orders, common sense, and interest of the state."

The planning from above, rather than in response to consumer demand below, resulted in a chronic struggle by the average Russian to obtain desired merchandise. Scarce items could not be found. They were not permanently out of stock, but their presence was unpredictable. Hedrick Smith, an American Journalist, noted in his book, *The Russians,* in the early 1970s that many common consumerables were difficult to procur such as toothpaste, towels, dishes, and cooking utensils. A consumer had to wait four to six years for an automobile, and such things as clothes dryers, dish washers, and freezers weren't even manufactured or sold.[21]

A Russian city may have had a glut of radios, but for months, be without dishwashing soap. Part of the problem was an inefficient distribution system even if a product was available in abundance somewhere else.

Desired items were sold out in a hurry. Consumers prowled the stores in search of something nice that may be available. Advertising to assist the consumer was non-existent, and helpful "Yellow Pages" did not exist. To alert the consumer to new, hard-to-get, or specially-priced items and discounts was unheard of. Everyone always carried a bag wherever they went in the odd chance they might unexpectedly run into something. Normally three lines formed for the purchase of each product: the first to select and price the product, the second to pay the cashier, and the third to pick up the item with the receipt. Therefore, if one went into a store to buy butter, cheese, and sausage, he would end up getting in nine different lines! Workers organized shopping pools to rotate the daily chore of shopping for food. It was estimated the average Soviet woman spent two hours in line each day, seven days a week![22]

The Soviet magazine *Ogonek* reported that between 1980 and 1986 exploding television sets caused 18,000 fires and nearly a thousand deaths. Yet these television sets were in great demand by all Russians even though it cost seven-hundred hours of labor to purchase.[23]

In the hinterland outside of Moscow, economic conditions were far worse. An example was Magnitogorsk, a large steel manufacturing city in the Urals. Chronic pollution, food rationing, and lax safety standards resulted in an average life expectancy of just fifty-three years. About a dozen workers died every year from mishaps at the gigantic Lenin steel mill. Inadequate housing necessitated thousands living in dormitories .[24]

Salesclerks normally stashed away a portion of attractive or hard-to-find items and sold them for bribes to steady customers. A system of mutual favors arose that permitted a customer to gain access to a scarce product or service in return for a similar favor.[25]

Economic cheating and stealing from the state by Russian citizens ran into billions of dollars each year. Government ownership and management made the practice easily acceptable or tolerated. This was also common in all countries, including capitalistic ones, where the product or service originated in or was sold to government bureaucracies. Cheating and misuse of funds in government agencies, in defense contracts, for farm subsidies and crop insurance, in government insured loans, in government-run Navy yards, postal service, and even public school systems were examples in the United States.

Most government workers assumed that stealing from the vast resources of a large anonymous structure would never be missed so everyone did it. Most important, no one seemed to care. Unlike a privately-owned business working on a profit or loss basis, the need to closely watch waste and pilferage was absent because all losses were made up (subsidized) by the government. Consequently, little effort was made to seriously curtail the activity.

In the USSR consumer goods were lifted from production lines or warehouses. Farmers on collective farms stole grain to feed their own animals. State gas station operators failed to ring up most sales and pocketed the money. Large rings of employees would swindle the government by padding the sales of merchandise and farm produce. Huge amounts of goods were diverted and bootlegged to black markets in a different province. Embezzlement of government funds proliferated. Typical was a ring of sixty-four farm and canning employees in Azerbaijan that cheated the government out of $12 million dollars by selling it nonexistant vegetables.[26]

The black market (free market) had long played an important role in Soviet society enabling citizens to overcome the inadequacies of the state-run economy. Well organized groups of black marketeers worked closely with corrupt managers of state stores, diverted truckloads of goods, and sold them in huge underground department stores.

***

It was unbelievable that any society could impose upon itself such a masochistic economic system, but as late as the 1980s most developing countries in the world were quick to adopt the socialistic economic system. The Soviet Union did not have a monopoly on market maladjustments. Any capitalistic or semi-socialist government, that interferred with the free market, inevitably had increased dislocations in its economy.

Worker indifference resulted in massive waste and inefficiency in China in the 1970s. A British exchange student who was required to put in a stint at a Shanghai factory remarked, "Shifts seldom started on time, and the whole day was punctuated by unofficial breaks." An American resident in Peking said, "All the elevators work automatically, but you still find that each has an operator, or sometimes two or three, who do nothing except ride up and down all day." Hong Kong residents, traveling in China, observed snarled train schedules while rail workers were playing cards instead of tending to their duties. One exasperated foreign executive complained, "If you want to move a machine from one room to the next, the workers have a meeting."[27]

In a government-run sugar mill in Mexico that hadn't turned a profit in a decade, Marta Sanchez, a chemist there in 1988, left work at two sharp in the afternoon for her aerobics class. "That was working late by our standards," said Mrs. Sanchez. Later the new superintendent, Sergio Villa Godoy, said, "Efficiency and honesty from workers never mattered because the mill could always count on the state to cover for its errors."

In India government-run industries produced only one-fifth of the gross national product, yet controlled three-quarters of India's productive capacity. In a one-day strike to protest free-market reforms proposed by the government, millions of India's workers walked away from their jobs. Their unions feared reforms would lead to layoffs at inefficient government-owned businesses (1992).

Following the election of Marxist president, Salvador Allende, a coalition of Communist, socialist, and other left-wing parties took control of Chile. Attempts to build a type of government-run farm system resulted in a drastic drop in agrculural production. After taking control of more than five-hundred private businesses, the firms were loaded with incompetent patronage employees, and worker discipline collapsed. Following two years of a centrally-planned economy, inflation soared more than one-thousand percent; the national treasury was nearly empty; production fell until virtually none existed in the final months before the military intervened.

In Communist Poland appalling filth and safety conditions were prevalent in factories everywhere; substandard health care prevailed; food shortages were widespread despite rationing; it took as long as fifteen years to wait for an apartment.

" ... the personal humiliation inflicted by the permanent lack of the most elementary consumer goods: the humiliation of silent and hostile lines; the humiliation inflicted on you by sales people who seem angry to see you standing there; the humiliation of always having to buy what there is, not what you need. The systematic penury of material goods strikes a blow at the moral dignity of the individual," wrote Tzvetan Todorov, a Bulgarian author, about life in Bulgaria in the June 25th 1990 issue of the *New Republic*.

As East Germany merged with the West, Juergen Kamjunk said, "We are accustomed to this misguided planned economy where no one works very hard and nothing works very well. I know we can't expect to achieve West German living standards with our current work habits."[28] Marlies Breite explained after arriving in West Germany from the East, "It is the yearning for the little luxuries that are daily conveniences here (West Germany). The daily irritations keep building up in you - no bananas, bread only in the morning, standing in line. It's like a fairy tale (here)." Her husband, Olaf, remarked, "The materials, equipment and technology are as different as night and day."[29]

By 1982 after twenty-four years of Marxist-style totalitarian government, the African Peoples Republic of Guinea was in economic shambles. A bauxite-mining operation finally had permission to be run by a consortium of Western companies. It consistently outproduced another run by the Soviets and yielded far more profits for the Guinean government.

Even in the United States in the last half of the twentieth century, farm production was controlled and subsidized by a central agency, the Agriculture Department, rather than left to a free market. Large subsidies paid by the taxpayers supported corn, wheat, rice, and cotton. In the late 1980s for various reasons, subsidies hadn't been placed on oats or soy beans. Farmers, therefore, elected to grow subsidized crops instead. This created large surpluses while the oats and soy beans acreage declined. Latin America and other world- farm areas picked up the slack and began to dominate those two markets. All of this occurred when American farmers badly needed to increase their exports. Finally in 1988, an acute shortage of oats and soybeans in the United States necessitated American processors to begin importing large amounts. It was but one example of the tragic dislocation of free markets in the American farm program which were artificially manipulated by a government agency.

In most socialist countries the goal of a classless society deteriorated into one of a party elite. It dispensed thousands of patronage jobs, controlled the press, and virtually ran the administrative bureaucracy free of any interference by the average citizen. Communist officials and those holding important bureaucratic offices enjoyed special housing, private cars, scarce food items, and other privileges beyond the reach of the average Russian. A study by *Pravda* revealed that these officials and their families consumed the best of the free health care, used the best subsidized recreational facilities, and educated their children in the best of the free schools and colleges. Special stores, stocked with imported goods and hard-to-get gourmet foodstuffs and other desirable merchandise, were available only to the elite.

***

By 1989 there was economic chaos throughout the Soviet Union. The situation became extremely volatile verging on anarchy. Aleksando Zaychenko, an economist, cited figures showing Russians ate worse than those under the Czar in 1913. According to official figures, eighty-three percent of everyday consumer items were in short supply. "The entire economy operates on the edge of crisis," said Anatoly Anshitz, a Soviet journalist, "It is geared to producing as little as necessary." An opinion poll commissioned by government economists found ninety-four percent of Soviet citizens believed the economy was in a "critical" or "unfavorable" condition.[30]

The summer of 1990 promised to be the biggest Soviet grain harvest ever. While millions of tons of wheat ripened in the fields, bread was rationed and completely disappeared from Moscow's bakery shelves. Harvesters gathered millions of tons of vegetables, but shoppers could find little more than cabbages.

An American journalist, Elisabeth Rubinfien, unable to comprehend such irony, took a tour from farm to store and discovered everything going wrong. There were labor shortages in many farm areas where farmers threatened to withold food for cities unless factory workers helped. There wasn't enough farm machinery on one state farm near Moscow so they relied heavily on horses. Individual initiative to get things going was stifled by bureaucratic lethargy and indifference.[31]

When she visited the produce distribution center, tomatoes remained unsorted while workers were told to wait. Finally, they were assigned to peel garlic but had no knives. Soldiers unloaded a train-car of watermelons because no one else would. Still, no trucks arrived to deliver them. The cold storage director complained of apples sent to him by a government-run farm. In order to fill its quota, the farm sent many rotten ones. When produce was finally delivered to stores, many times they refused it because that type of product was not needed.[32]

At one of the stores Ms. Rubinfien visited the store director, Lydudmeva Shevlugina, who cried as she described the latest catastrophe. A week earlier the distribution center sent her three tons of potatoes in paper sacks. She tore open the sacks and pointed to the oozing mold. "I told them the potatoes are no good, but they say it isn't their problem," she said, "And now, I'm supposed to sell three tons of potatoes, but they're all rotten. How is a person supposed to work when it's like this?"[33]

By 1991 there should have been no doubt in the minds of everyone that socialism did not deliver what it promised. Most people looked back in shock at the monumental folly that caused many intellectuals to buy what Hayek, the great Austrian economist, called the "fatal conceit." The old French saying was never truer, "If you are not a socialist at twenty, you have no heart. If you are still a socialist at forty, you have no head." It was universally acknowledged the free-market worked, and the government economic-decision-making apparatus did not.

***

It was amidst this chaos that the Soviet empire began to crumble and break up into independent states.[34] Communism was renounced; economic reforms, based on a free competitive market, were attempted. The great struggle, the Cold War, between the diverse economic systems of capitalism and socialism finally ended in victory for the market-driven economy.

The disintegration of planned economies in powerful socialist nations, especially the Soviet Union, was recognized by socialist countries in Africa and other developing areas. So, they began gradual moves to free their economies from the strict rigidity of bureaucratic planning and to attempt changes. This also occurred, as well, in the semi-socialist ones with state-run industries such as India, Mexico, Brazil, and Argentina.

***

Incredibly, some socialists still attempted to limit the degree of acceptance of the free market and the profit and loss system, to somehow amalgamate the free market within a government-controlled economy. They could not decide whether incentives be allowed or income remain equal. If incentives, to what degree could standard-of-living be allowed to differ? How far could inefficiency, low productivity, and a resulting lower standard of living be tolerated in order to maintain equality without incentives?

Apathy, class-hatred, the prejudices of the have-nots, and age-old suspicions prevailed; so many government-economies continued to struggle especially in the former Soviet Union, Eastern Europe, Africa, Latin America, and other undeveloped areas. Even in the developed capitalist countries, additional government-controlled markets arose periodically when things went awry in the economy. It didn't matter that the original cause of the problem lay in excessive government interference.

The newly formed Russia, Ukraine, Belarus, and other independent republics continued to subsidize many government-run enterprises with funds obtained by merely printing paper money. This resulted in runaway inflation, worsening productivity, and a continued decline in the standard of living.

Although in just a few years, many enterprises were privatized, a more serious attack began on privatization in 1996. Part of the problem was bribery, cronyism, and general corruption in the way privatization was handled and businesses sold off to employees, citizens, and private investors. Government-created inflation worsened and added to the woes of the average citizen especially the elderly. Many had never lived in a free economic society and were unable to carry on every-day duties without orders from government bureaucrats.

The Russian population was in a desperate mood ready to grasp at any straw for help. The result was constant political turmoil in parliament and the administration. Demagogues arose in search of power.

Even China, where its rapid move to a market economy allowed the large urban and coastal areas to prosper, experienced relative backwardness in its predominately agrarian interior because huge government-run companies and farms still employed three-quarters of the country's workers there.

Three factors hindered the movement to true market economies in all nations: entrenched bureaucracies, party bosses unable to relinquish power, and genuine socialists who incredibly still believed in the socialistic system in spite of the obvious superiority of a free-market economy.

For example. Nikolai Ryabov, the deputy to the Russian parliamentary chairman said in 1993, "Nobody has proved that the economic course the government is pursuing is right for this country. In fact, I think that an effective market-economy is nonsense." Chris Hani, a white member of the African National Congress, said "The advance to socialism in South Africa is unstoppable." and urged the world-wide Communist movement to regroup and reassert itself.

As late as 1994 general Party Secretary, Jiang Zemin, came out strongly in defense of public ownership in China despite the bad performance of state industries in previous years. He said it remained the core of the economy notwithstanding rapid growth in the private sector.

In the developing country of Brazil increased foreign investment, moving in and out to enforce budgetary discipline and the reduction of government expenditures and debt, reduced inflation considerably by 1996. Nonetheless, President Fernando Cardoso, was still slow to address the underlying cause of inflation: government spending to support unprofitable government-run business. A left-wing sociologist, Mr. Cardoso had earlier written and edited twenty books supporting socialism.

In France, an attempt to cut government spending for huge subsidies of government-owned industries such as railways, airlines, telephone companies, postal service, electrical and gas utilities ended in a crippling twenty-four day strike in 1996. All of these businesses were losing massive amounts of money adding to France's big budget deficit. Air France, like other government-run airlines in Europe, lost $254 million in 1994 while privatized airlines, such as British Airways, made a profit of $514 million. Government workers in France were guaranteed jobs for life, retired at age fifty-five, and had six weeks of annual vacation; they were adamant about ever having their jobs privatized. The French people, afraid of further privatizing by the party in power, returned the Socialist party to power in 1997 after many years of absence. During the same year Deutsche Bank chief economist, Norbert Walter, said, "With government spending at 51 percent of GDP, Germany is still nearer to socialism than to a market economy." Both countries were steadily losing business in the competitive world market creating rising unemployment and larger government deficits.

And in Britain, the Labor Party was elected to govern in 1997 also after many years in absence and in spite of one of the strongest free market economies in Europe fostered by the previous Tory party. The Socialist Worker's Party recruited more new members than at any time in the previous twenty years, and class-warfare rhetoric was uttered daily in the political arenas. There were still those who sought to gain power by pitting class against class and expounding the equal distribution of income to all. And there were always have-nots ready to believe it was the answer to their problem.

The endowed socialists, like religious zealots, could never be budged from their beliefs. *It was always going to be different next time.* Typical was Gorbachov who said in his memoirs after the disintegration of the Soviet Union, "I am (still) a confirmed supporter of the idea of socialism."

The great battle between Hitler's fascism and Stalin's proletarian dictatorship ended in continued oppression by the socialists. As Alvin and Heidi Toffler so appropriately remarked, " ... socialism led not to affluence, equality and freedom, but to a one-party political system, a massive bureaucracy, heavy-handed secret police, government control of the media, secrecy and the repression of intellectual and artistic freedom." One might add, "And to complete economic disintegration!"

Regardless of the above, the call for a truly competitive market, without dysfunctional interference of governments, continued and went unheeded by many. The pleading to stop the disintegration of civilized conduct and eliminate dysfunctional family-life also went unheeded as we shall see in the next two chapters..

Chapter 3

ETHNIC RETARDATION

Beginning in the nineteenth century and continuing through the twentieth, an exasperating problem existed in merging underdeveloped ethnic groups into the social and economic mainstream. These included such diverse groups as the Indians of North and South America, Eskimos, native Hawaiians, Australian aborigines, and black Africans who had migrated world-wide. True, a few were able to educate themselves and move up in society, but the majority were hopelessly mired in poverty and squalor.

On the other hand, Europeans, Orientals, and Jews had no problem developing social and economic skills. In his book, *Economics and Politics of Race,* Thomas Sowell pointed out that even among the Europeans, some were able to adapt better than others. Generations of Scottish-Irish and German immigrants settled in the same areas in the United States. Both groups were predominantly family-farmers; the Scottish-Irish usually had the first choice of land. Mr.Sowell wrote, "The Germans prospered and the Scottish-Irish produced some of the most enduring pockets of poverty to be found among European-Americans."

In Central America, twentieth century Belize was populated with Latin-American Indians, Blacks, East Indians, and a few Europeans. Although there was an adequate educational system, poverty and sanitation was frightening.

Bonita Mueller immigrated from Germany when she was 73. The Belize government granted her one hundred acres of jungle which was free and available as a homestead to all inhabitants. In seven years she had cleared most of the land with the help of her sons. They built fences, thatched-roof outbuildings and a farm house, raised twenty-two head of cattle, numerous sheep and other livestock. Her farm was primitive, but Bonita was wealthy by local standards. She was asked how she could carve out a better life than the non-Europeans when the land was also available to them.

"Very hard work," she said. "You cannot believe how much work it was."

And why didn't the others do the same? She answered, the difference was in the culture transmitted from one generation to another. The native people didn't have the ambition, the will to work, the intolerance of squalor, and the Teutonic concern with order and detail which came naturally from the German heritage.[1]

Jews were classic examples of destitute immigrants from the ghettos of Europe who eventually became the most economically successful of any ethnic group. In another of his books, *Ethnic America*, Thomas Sowell wrote, "The Jews seized upon free schools, libraries, and settlement houses in America with a tenacity and determination unexcelled and seldom approached by others." Jews were driven toward upward mobility by the values of the Jewish family.[2]

Early in the 20th century thousands of Japanese were imported into the Hawaiian Islands to work as cheap labor in the cane fields as well as laborers on the mainland. Pay discrimination and efforts to prevent their rise into skilled occupations prevailed. They were prevented by laws from becoming citizens or to own land. Other ethnic groups turned against the Japanese because, unlike many of them, they were very thrifty and saved small amounts from their meager wages. Their diligence and ambition to work harder doing piece-work in the fields than whites and other groups, was resented.[3]

Yet, by the middle of the century the Japanese had risen to control the Island's wealth and dominate its political offices. On the other hand, native Hawaiians continued to languish in substandard living conditions and menial jobs while their political influence diminished.

In 1908 several hundred Japanese immigrants landed in Brazil as cheap labor to replace black slaves on coffee plantations. There was great emphasis on the Japanese values of honesty, education, and dedication. By the late twentieth century, they became a dominant force in the Brazilian economy.

Thomas Sowell, again, points out possible reasons for the distinction between their disciplined drive and those that were less-motivated. He noted that Japanese families had few divorces, and therefore, were stable influences on their children. Although strictly disciplined, the children were of paramount importance to the parents. Upholding family and Japanese honour were taught as they had been for generations. The results were children who were notable in school for being obedient, polite, and hard-working. Unbridled individualism or permissiveness was not part of the Japanese culture. Japanese communities lacked crime, juvenile delinquency, and other forms of social pathology.[4]

In the late nineteenth century Chinese coolies were imported as laborers to help build the transcontinental railroads in the United States and Canada. They worked in appalling conditions and were constantly abused by the European-Americans. In 1903 a Canadian government commission determined that Chinese and Japanese immigrants were "unfit for full citizenship." Chinese-Canadians were only granted the right to vote in 1947. Nevertheless, the Chinese rose in both countries from extreme poverty to become prosperous and influential in their communities.

In Malaysia and Southeast Asia the Chinese were once banned from better jobs, singled out for special taxes, restricted to ghetto-type areas and even subjected to physical violence. Despite this discrimination, the Chinese gradually achieved a considerable degree of prosperity surrounded by poverty-stricken natives who were persecuting them. Most remarkable, was the Chinese Prime Minister of Singapore, Lee Kuan Yew, who by 1989 had led his city-nation to become one of the most progressive in the entire world. It became an economic engine of prosperity, clean, and free of crime, polution, and debt. This was in sharp contrast to the large cities in the United States. Many of which were ridden with crime, drugs, squalor, and poverty. Most were heavily populated with blacks and run by black mayors.

Natives of India came to the Fiji Islands in 1879 as indentured laborers to work in the sugarcane fields. By 1997 they dominated the business and professional life of the country. The original Fiji natives could not keep pace.

In the 1980s Korean immigrants worked intensively often twelve to fourteen hours a day for seven days a week. They worked as family units; raised capital for their small businesses from hard-won savings and from relatives' loans; succeeded in the United States where opportunities were offered that eluded them in Korea. Many became successful entrepreneurs of grocery stores, flower shops, and other small businesses. According to a Census Bureau survey in 1987, Koreans had the highest business-ownership rate of any ethnic group including whites. One in ten was a business owner as contrasted to one in sixty-seven for blacks.

Early Jews from the Eastern-European ghettos and Vietnamese refugees did the same. Most arrived with only the clothes on their back, had limited education or occupational skills, could not speak English, and suffered cultural shock. They adapted with little complaint.

In a few years the Vietnamese had climbed out of poverty. By their fortieth month their earnings averaged twice the poverty level of families in the United States. In the meantime, Vietnamese children made remarkable academic progress. Nathan Caplan, professor of psychology at the University of Michigan and co-author of *The Boat People and Achievement in America,* noted that in Garden Grove, California in 1985, "The Indochinese refugee community made up less than twenty percent of the school population, yet twelve of the fourteen high school valedictorians were of Indochinese refugee background."

On the other hand, by the late twentieth century many Indians and Afro-Americans in the United States remained uneducated and impoverished continuing to live in misery and filth. Moreover, they blamed their predicament on everyone but themselves.

Mr. Sowell, an Afro-American himself, concluded, "Groups that arrived in America financially destitute have rapidly risen to affluence, when their cultures stressed the values and behavior required in an industrial and commercial economy. Even when color and racial prejudice confronted them - as in the case of the Chinese and Japanese - this only proved to be an impediment but was ultimately unable to stop them."

Most Indian reservations in Canada and the United States were scenes of public drunkeness and family violence. A Senate panel was told in 1990 by tribal social workers that one of every five Indian children in Michigan suffered abuse. Residences generally consisted of ramshackle houses with yards strewn with junk and even abandoned automobiles. According to Tom Velk, a professor of economics at McGill University in Montreal, most Indians died younger than whites, had more disease, less education, and poorer nutrition. Still, he noted the average Canadian Indian family in 1990 received more than $60,000 in cash and in-kind benefits from the government, a sum considerably in excess of the average citizen's income.

Following the evacuation of colonial rulers in the 1940s, independent black nations rose across Africa hopeful of extending the benefits and ammenities brought to their lands by the Europeans. Unfortunately by 1985, black Africa was grossly overpopulated in many areas, lacked enough food, and was destroying their land and forest resources; it mismanaged nearly everything else. Educational standards declined significantly and it was estimated that health care had regressed about one-hundred and fifty years behind Europe and was continuing to decline. President Nyerere of Tanzania, after eighteen years of government confiscation and mismanagement of former British plantations, said, "If I called the British today to look at their former estates, I am sure they would laugh at us because we have ruined them."[5]

George Ayittey, a Ghanaiian economist and author of *Africa Betrayed,* stated, "They ruined one African economy after another with brutal efficiency and looted African treasuries with military discipline. Out of forty-five black African nations, just four ... allow their people to vote, choose their leaders, and express themselves freely. Twenty-three are military dictatorships where no political parties are permitted. The rest are one-party states ruled by dictators-for-life. Worse, it has degenerated into savage barbarism in ... many of the countries.

"The ruling elites also smuggle, embezzle funds, plunder state treasuries, and illegally transfer their booty abroad. ...many leaders have declared their countries one-party states and liquidated the opposition. To many, independence has meant oppression and economic deprivation.

"In Zaire, officials each earn between $5000 and $9000 a month while a peasant is lucky to make fifty dollars a month. Cameroon, with a per-capita income of less than $1000 a year, is the world's ninth largest importer of champagne,"[6]

Corruption, coups, tribal warfare, massacres, and butchery became common. There were even reports of symbolic cannibalizing of enemies by some tyrants.

In Out of Africa: A Black Man Confronts Africa, Keith Richbuy astounded many black Americans when he reflected on his enslaved African ancestors by saying, "Thank God my ancestors got out, because, now, I am not one of them (Africans) ... In short, thank God I am an American." Traveling to Africa in search of his heritage, he encountered unbelievable poverty, political corruption, brutal dictators, devastating illness and sadistic violence among its inhabitants.

For years there was a net black migration into South Africa from bordering countries despite segregation under Apart-heid. They came from countries whose economic conditions were intolerable under black independence. Amazingly, they sought a job and a better way of life in a country controlled by whites through blatant discrimination.

The leader of Zambia was one of the most vociferous critics of oppression in South Africa. Yet since its independence in 1964, Zambia remained a one-party state where freedom of expression or assembly was forbidden. The remaining countries bordering South Africa were also ruled by one-party with lifetime-presidents and vicious violation of human rights.[7] The white residents of South Africa, observing the massive economic and governmental disintegration and chaos in the black nations to the north of them, were reluctant to turn over control of their country to the black majority. Apartied was finally relaxed and gradually eliminated. Most whites were apprehensive as blacks began to share in the governing process.

***

Many Afro-Americans had worked hard, educated themselves, and became responsible, well-respected, and successful citizens in their communities and on the national scene. Yet by the 1980s the situation for most blacks reached a deplorable state in the United States. Social irresponsibility in every facet of life soared: parental indifference, school dropouts, illiteracy, indifference to job-training or job responsibility, youth gangs, teen-age pregnancy, fatherless homes, drug use, and exploding crime. Studies overwhelmingly indicated that Afro-Americans accounted for a disproportionate number of unemployed, on welfare, infant mortality victims and involved in crime. Yet, they represented a small portion of the total population, about twelve per cent. The results were being recorded decades after the civil rights bill passed, and the Great Society social programs begun in the 1960s, both primarily benefiting Afro-Americans.

Evidence in various statistics and studies was overwhelming. For example, a study of Los Angeles high schools in 1987 found Afro-Americans and Hispanic students lagging further behind whites in reading, writing, and mathematics.[8] The National Assessment of Educational Progress found one-half of seventeen year old blacks were grossly illiterate compared to only thirteen per cent of whites. A study by the National Academy of Sciences also found a disportionate number of minority students in special education classes.[9]

There was tremendous peer pressure on young Afro-Americans to avoid higher academic pursuits. High grades by Afro-Americans were ridiculed by other black students as symbols of whites. Much of this originated in the late 1960s by the Black Panthers. They decided blacks should stop excelling in "the white man's school;" that the poorest and least-skilled blacks were the noblest of their race; that blacks should develop their own speech patterns.

In some large inner-city schools the attendance rate had dropped below fifty per cent. A study, by Dr. James Banks of the University of Washington's College of Education, indicated lack of parental involvement may have been the determining factor in whether a black child failed academically.[10]

Teenage pregnancy was twice what it was for whites. Ninety per cent of all babies born to blacks in that age group were born out of wedlock. The Urban League reported in 1983 that roughly one-half of all black families was headed by just one parent; by 1997 it was sixty percent. One-half of all black teen-agers were also unemployed.

Asa Hilliard, a professor at Georgia State University said, "The main reason black families are falling apart is that men can't get jobs, so they leave home." Some thought such reasoning was a simple explanation to a very complex problem. Indeed, Richard Freeman, a Harvard economist using 1984-87 data from the Census Bureau, found during the growing economy of the 1980s, unemployment dropped from over forty percent to seven among young black males with little education and living in large urban areas. This was about the same decline as for white males with the same background. He also found earnings of blacks had increased substantially at the same time. It indicated, in a strong economy, blacks benefited as well as whites.

Even under these conditions, there was a large percentage of all young black males that were still not working. Many thought it was because they had become so discouraged looking for a job, they finally gave up. In 1989 following the economic boom, labor-force absence among all young black males remained at thirty seven per cent, the same level it had been a decade earlier. Labor-force absentees are not counted in the government unemployment data because they have not indicated they are looking for work.

Charles Murray, author of *In Pursuit: Of Happiness and Good Government,* addressed the problem by asking, "What are they doing? Judging from the narrative accounts of such young men, the answers are varied. Sometimes they have worked in the past, moving briefly into the labor force, then lost the job because they quit or were fired for cause. While out of the labor force, they survived off relatives, girl friends, hustles, maybe drugs or crime. What they aren't doing is saving for the future, marrying the woman they get pregnant, supporting the children they father. Neither are they acquiring the job skills and getting the job networks that would give them a secure niche as they age ... "

Mr. Murray points out that an environmental survey of Boston youth indicated "Labor-force absence came from several sources: from a single parent home; from a teen-age mother; living in public housing; low parental income and education; and living in a neighborhood with many other unemployed youths."[11]

It was obvious to many that the main reason for their high unemployment was illiteracy; many were unable to read and communicate in some of the most basic functions as an employee: filling out a job application, reading labels, making change, accepting checks and charges, and reading and understanding simple instructions. They were illiterate because of many reasons: most inner-city schools maintained little discipline and were permissive of disruptive students, teachers were intimidated or abused by some students and became indifferent, drugs eliminated motivation of some students, and a large portion merely dropped out of school.

These were but symptoms of the real cause, the lack of discipline and motivation from parents. This was usually because many parents were uneducated, on welfare, on drugs, living in squalor, and unable to comprehend a life that could be different for themselves or their children. So it became a vicious cycle in black families. Each succeeding generation was offered little hope or encouragement to improve. Total desperation and indifference permeated most young Afro-Americans as they perceived a future devoid of the successes and rewards available to most in the white community.

In *Mothers, Leadership and Success,* Guy Odom expresses it succinctly, " ... differences in cultures affect the nature of what is seen as success or failure ... The non-dominant mother rears her children by the only way she knows, the way she was brought up. The result shows up during school years in poor attendance, low grades and early dropping out and later in lack of marketable skills. This group of non-dominant individuals comprises a large and rapidly growing percentage of our population. It has caused the average standard of living to decline and the gap in income and wealth to widen."[12]

Black men accounted for six per cent of the population but made up half of the prison population. Murder was the leading cause of death among young black men and was seven times higher than for white men the same age. Most were killed during arguments by people they knew. A hand-gun was the most-often used weapon. The National Center for Health Statistics in 1986 reported that for the first time in the twentieth century the life expectancy of Afro-Americans fell in two successive years while that of whites continued to increase.

Black women were three times more likely to be murdered than white. Judy Belk, a black female victim, was driving along a street in Oakland, California minding her own business. She said, "Suddenly a car crowded with young black men came charging toward us, weaving dangerously on two flat tires. I struggled to get out of its way. As the car sped past us, a gun was fired. There was an explosion of glass and my window shattered around us. I couldn't move."

Luckily Judy was only wounded, but later her sister Vickie was abducted on her way home from a government job in Washington, D.C. and killed with a bullet through the head. Investigators strongly suspected she was one of several victims randomly killed by two black men on a rampage while high on drugs. Still later, Judy's cousin, Darryl, was murdered in a spray of bullets by black assailants packing machine guns as a result of an earlier quarrel.

Judy continued, "Mostly, I'm afraid for the black community. I know what ails us, but I'm groping for the answers and the role I can play. The solutions must involve a re-emphasis of the values that have helped many blacks succeed: respect for the family, for the community, for one's self."[13]

In 1989 a twenty-eight year old investment banker was attacked, while jogging in Central Park, New York, by a gang of black teens aged fourteen to sixteen. Police said the boys hunted her down in a wolf-pack sequence, savagely beat and raped her, and left her for dead. Upon arrest the boys joked, rapped, and sang. Asked why he beat her head with a lead pipe, one was quoted by investigators as saying, "It was fun." These were not crimes due to drugs, race, or robbery.

"What distinguishes these boys is ... their lack of moral faculty. Acts of rage are usually followed by reflection and shame. In this case, these characteristics appear to be entirely missing. They were 'wilding.' Wilding is not rage, it is anarchy. Anarchy is an excess of freedom. Anarchy is the absence of rules, of ethical limits, of any moral sense. These boys ... have lost, perhaps never developed, that psychic appendage we call conscience," said Charles Krauthammer, a columnist for *Time*.

To illustrate the utter lawlessness and disintegration that prevailed in black neighborhoods, take the typical early childhood of Lafayette Walton in Chicago. Lafayette was twelve and lived in a neighborhood where gunshots were common. He watched men being brutally beaten and saw friends shot. Two years before at age ten, he stood over a dying teen-ager who had been gunned down outside the Walton's apartment. His mother permanently lost the use of two fingers when she was attacked by knife-wielding muggers. During the summer at Lafayette's apartment complex, according to police reports, an average of one person was beaten, shot, or stabbed every three days.

His father, a bus driver for the city, stayed with the family sporadically. Lafayette only shrugged when asked what he wanted to be when he grew up. He rarely laughed.

Lafayette and Pharoah, his younger brother, got headaches when they heard the gunfire. Pharoah sometimes shook uncontrollably when surprised by a loud noise. One evening Pharoah fainted after pleading with his mother to stop the shooting outside.

"These children are surrounded by a very real and immediate world of violence, gunfire and death," said Theodore Cram, the assistant to the United States surgeon general.

Psychologists and social workers found that many black youngsters routinely exposed to violence, exhibited the same post-traumatic stress symptoms that plagued Vietnam combat veterans. Many frequently suffered nightmares, depression, and personality disorders. Some withdrew and gave up hope; others became more aggressive.[14]

Drugs proliferated the inner-cities of Afro-Americans. It had grown to uncontrollable proportions in Washington, D.C. where blacks predominated. Even the black mayor was convicted for cocaine and other drug abuse. Many pregnant black women were taking crack-cocaine up to the time of delivery. Most crack babies, born addictive and without pre-natal care, were kept in intensive care and then "boarded" by hospitals after being abandoned by their mothers.

In one case a mother, at the age of twenty-eight, delivered a crack baby every year for eight years. Most were abandoned in the hospital. Some were so severely damaged, they lived their entire lives in nursing care.

The financial as well as social cost to society was enormous. All the while, politicians were inventing proposals to contain runaway health costs but ignored some of the most blatant causes.

As violence, crime, and squalor grew worse in black neighborhoods, whites reacted with fear upon any encroachment by blacks into their communities. Whites were terrified that blacks would bring the same problems with them. They were especially concerned how their children would adapt to the negative behavior of undisciplined black chidren around them. Whites were also afraid of blacks bringing physical decline to their neighborhoods resulting in a drop in property values. In most cases these fears were realized.

An occasional black family worked hard, saved their money, gave excellent guidance to their children, and wanted to free themselves of the inner-city ghetto. They deserved a better environment. Unfortunately, whites could not distinguish them from other blacks. So, the majority of whites arbitrarily adopted segregation in the face of civil-right laws and tried to keep all blacks out of their neighborhoods. They also pulled their children out of integrated inner-city schools and enrolled them in private ones or moved to the suburbs and enrolled their children there. Many branded such behavior as racist and accused it of being the cause of the black's plight.

Most believed decades of slavery, repression, and second-class citizenship was at the root of all of the black's problems; that racism and discrimination by whites was the main reason blacks were not progressing. It was believed by many that blacks were helpless to progress and could not be responsible for their behavior until their treatment by whites was changed. This was despite numerous civil-right laws and special economic benefits and programs that were passed primarily for the benefit of urban minorities. Compassion for the black's plight gave way to apathy following decades of failed social policies and a never-ending demand for more tax money to finance them.

Nevertheless, leaders of the black minority continued to press for greater "economic rights" and demanded increasing amounts of financial support in the form of welfare programs. They vocally blamed whites for all their problems. This constant harranguing encouraged black followers to eventually become vehemently anti-white. So much so, even a small incident would create mob-violence, of such magnitude, that many times it ended in burning, looting, and the maiming and killing of whites or other minorities such as the Koreans in Los Angeles. Ironically anti-white racism gradually replaced racism against blacks, making matters even worse.

Nevertheless, there were still isolated incidents of vicious anti-black racism usually committed by illiterate and prejudiced individuals. Society did not condone these acts and blamed them for keeping the turmoil simmering.

In his book, *Paved With Good Intentions: The Failure of Race Relations in Contemporary America,* Jared Taylor wrote of perverse consequences when attributing all the problems of Afro-Americans to racism. He described some of these as the outright discrimination against some whites through the use of affirmative action while poor job skills, of some Blacks selected over whites, was ignored; double standards for whites and blacks in the news media such as emphasizing white-on-black crimes and ignoring black-on-black crimes, (Many in the media also refused to use the term "black male" to identify a police apprehension for fear of being accused of racism but had no problem when white males were involved); the permission of all-black clubs and organizations, but lodges and clubs for whites were illegal. Mr. Taylor also complained that to even discuss race meant the fear of retribution. He claimed his book was turned down by two publishers because he was white. Other authors faced similar reactions.

"To seek and analyze the factors that advance and retard the progress of ethnic groups is in no way to morally or otherwise grade these groups," said the brilliant black sociologist, Thomas Sowell, in his book *Ethnic America.*

Some sociologists insisted that such analysis must be made if society was to attack the problems of ethnic backwardness even though it may be sensitive to the group involved. They believed the ridiculous charge that racism was intended was merely racism itself.

Shelby Steele, another Afro-American and San Jose State professor and author of *The Content of Our Character : A New Vision of Race in America,* believed it was time for blacks to rely on themselves, take advantage of the opportunities that new immigrants found available, and to quit blaming racism for their lack of success. Mr. Steele remarked, "I challenge blacks. To me the goal of society is absolute social equality. That's what the civil rights movement was after, and we took a left turn into racial preferences that has allowed everybody to get off the hook."[15]

In analyzing the plight of Afro-Americans, Indians, and other undeveloped ethnic groups, most people overlooked other racial minorities in America: early Jewish, Irish, Chinese and Japanese immigrants; later the Vietnamese and Koreans. All were able to raise themselves from abject poverty and intense racism to an important status in society despite rampant discrimination and repression that prevailed at the time.

Still others thought that American society had failed to give enough help to all minorities, including the very early immigrants. This thinking resulted in bestowing welfare, health care, and education on illegal immigrants in the 1990s at a tremendous cost to the inhabitants of many states.

Some felt society was responsible for poverty, and poverty responsible for all the problems of minorities. They pushed for increased minority benefits through the redistribution of income and wealth via taxes and social welfare. Still others said poverty was due to exploitation. They assumed people were basically alike in their motivation, ambitions, and education. Therefore, if some were rich and others poor, it indicated wealth and higher incomes of the rich must have risen through devious means at the expense of the poor.

Others responded, "This was only an excuse for all poverty." Furthermore, they replied, "Why was it some minority groups remained in poverty while other groups became successful and affluent?"

***

Most slaves of the American South began lives after the Emancipation Proclamation as free men but with distinct handicaps. Mr. Sowell points out they were "destitute, illiterate, and unfamiliar with even the basics of hygiene, social behavior, or responsibility." Earlier it was a crime in the South to teach slaves basic literacy - most could not read or write. They were deliberately and completely dependent on the slave owners for food, clothing, and shelter to prevent them from learning how to take care of themselves. Formal families were discouraged by the slave owners as an interferance to the structure of slavery. Even surnames were forbidden. Teenagers were sold out of their families. It was only natural for slaves to develop work-evading patterns and to have incentive to work only enough to escape punishment. Duplicity and stealing also pervaded their lives. Long after slavery disappeared, these handicaps became a cultural legacy that remained for decades.[16]

An interesting comparison with West Indian slaves, both white as well as black, is pointed out by Mr. Sowell. He noted that West Indian slaves were given plots of land to raise food for themselves and to sell any surplus in the local markets. As a result they developed incentives and experience in the market-economy and became frugal, hard-working, and entrepreneurial. Unlike slaves in the South, they had centuries of experience being self-reliant.

When West Indian blacks migrated to the United States, they entered more professions and represented less unemployment than the national average. American blacks called them "black Jews," were hostile toward them, and remained separated from most. " ... the West Indian experience itself seriously undermines the proposition that color is a fatal handicap in the American economy," wrote Mr. Sowell.[17]

After the mid-60s there appeared to be a strong effort in the United States to erase the guilt of black slavery, persecution, and discrimination. The effect was to raise blacks, in many areas, faster than whites. Income of black families rose fifty-five per cent between 1961 and 1971 while the income of whites rose only thirty per cent. Blacks that enrolled in college nearly doubled between 1965 and 1972 while whites remained the same. Blacks in professional occupations nearly doubled while whites increased only twenty per cent. Blacks in Congress as well as state legislatures also doubled.[18]

This overall effort was so encompassing that many social standards were altered for the sake of Afro-Americans - black studies were invented and added to educators' curriculum; grade standards were lowered; employment qualifications were lowered to meet minority employment quotas; social behavior was allowed to become more permissive. As new standards became permanently adopted by society, it was only natural, they became the lower standards for white youths as well. Finally, it seemed to some the progress and discipline of main-stream society was deliberately inhibited in order that a backward ethnic group, representing only twelve per cent of the population, could "catch up." Yet, unemployment and welfare continued to rise in black communities during this period.

***

Reflecting on all of the above decades later, some astute sociologists asked themselves, "What on earth went awry to cause so many problems in the black community?"

After considerable study it was obvious to them that generally the difference in income, wealth, and behavior between ethnic groups was due, in large measure, to motivation, attitudes, and general culture within the society of each particular minority and not the behavior and attitudes of the larger society.

They compared such things as family and community moral standards, work ethics, the tolerance for disorder and squalor, and acceptable living standards. It appeared the lower the acceptable standards of an ethnic group in all categories, the greater the resulting misery of that particular group. This was logical, but they wondered why motivation and attitudes varied so greatly between ethnic groups.

Comparing the underdeveloped with the more developed groups, they discerned a startling difference in the degree of civilized order that was passed on from previous generations.

The more advanced ethnic groups such as the Japanese, Chinese and Europeans derived from very old, highly developed family and community structures with rigorous disciplined standards of conduct. Whereas, the less developed groups, such as American Indians, native Hawaiians, and Afro-Americans, derived from primitive family and tribal cultures. Their cultures required less discipline for standards of conduct, and they had considerable tolerance for the most rudimentary living conditions. Their amalgamation into a much more advanced society in the later part of the nineteenth century led to traumatic, cultural shock.

"Culture, as related to child rearing, is the total of living patterns built up by a group of human beings and transmitted from one generation to another. A baby is born without culture; culture comes into play at birth, when the mother transmits culture as she perceives it to her child. The mother's enculturation, in turn, came from her mother's perception of culture. Cultural transmission began in mankind's past. In each society, children learn the sum of cultural experiences through maternal agency, generation after generation," wrote Guy Odom in *Mothers, Leadership and Success*.

For years Indians and Afro-Americans had been repressed, persecuted, and isolated from the rest of American society. It was extremely difficult, therefore, for their children to finally be indoctrinated with cultural standards completely foreign to both themselves and their elders, when the European-Americans finally decided to mesh them into their society. Centuries of primitive life, as well as decades of slavery and legalized discrimination, made the transition next to impossible.

Indeed, many skeptics thought the more primitive cultural groups could never be taught to advance to the degree that more developed groups had. There was abundant evidence, however, in all underdeveloped groups that some individuals had become educated, accepted a more progressive culture, and went on to extraordinary success in their respective fields of endeavor.

It was true that in the early 1940s the average I.Q. of Indian children ranged between seventy and eighty, and that of Afro-Americans between seventy-five and eighty-five. Yet, one of the few individuals with an I.Q. of two-hundred was a young black girl. By contrast, this child had an excellent home environment and attended a good school. Her father was an electrical engineer, and her mother a college graduate and former school teacher.[19]

It was also found that black orphans raised by white families had I.Q.s at or above the national average. This was from a study by Sandra Sear and Richard Weinberg published in the American Psychologist.[20]

"Child-rearing practices, not heredity, define the degree of intelligence one has," explains Mr. Odom. Mr. Sowell concurred, "The cultural inheritance can be more important than biological inheritance ..."

However, there were many who did not agree. Probably the most prominent were Richard J. Hernstein, a distinguished psychology professor from Harvard, and Charles Murray of the American Enterprise Institute. In their controversial book, *The Bell Curve*, they claimed studies resulted in irrefutable evidence that approximately sixty percent of an individual's intelligence, measured by I.Q. tests was derived from heredity.[21] Many of these studies, in contrast to the results by Sear and Weinberg, were also of blood relatives including identical twins reared apart in separate environments.

Portions of their arguments in support of heredity were interspersed with ambiguity. For instance, they said, "The debate about whether and how much genes and environment have to do with ethnic differences remains unresolved." Later in their book they noted,"..black progress in narrowing the test score discrepancy with whites has been substantial..." They also mentioned that the average I.Q. of native black Africans was seventy-five compared to black Americans' eighty-five. This could indicate that environment may have made the difference.[22]

Christopher Jencks, Northwestern University sociologist, argued that many studies indicated education could improve cognitive functioning, contrary to what *The Bell Curve* indicated.

Dr. Jencks added that many heritable things, such as some mental illneses, could be successfully treated.

Professor of psychology at Hofstra University, Ira Kaplan, suggested *The Bell Curve* showed intelligence of most people concentrated in the middle of the curve between extremes indicating only a small percentage were not close to average. Therefore, he contested the book's premise, that there would be an increasing problem by a large and growing gap between the below-average I.Q.s and those in the above-average bracket, did not appear warranted.

***

The apparently insurmountable problem, that came to the fore in the 1990s, was how to end the vicious cycle: lack of discipline and motivation by parents, which resulted in uneducated and undisciplined children, which resulted again in the inability to qualify for even the lowest job opening, and finally permanent unemployment. This was followed by receiving welfare of various types, hustling drugs, or even resorting to crime in order to survive. These illiterate young black men, unable to support themselves, did not marry the mother of their children so the mother usually went on welfare. More children were born to these unmarried illiterates and grew up without guidance or motivation, so the cycle continued with no end in sight.

It became obvious that early behavioral teaching and other mandatory education was essential to wipe out illiteracy and unemployment. This would break the cycle and eventually end the misery of Afro-Americans and other backward ethnic groups throughout the world. Still, the world continued to ignore this premise and instead continued to attack the symptoms with all types of social aid programs and new laws to benefit these retarded cultures. The methods continued to fail miserably and the plight of these people got worse.

Chapter 4

DECLINE OF DISCIPLINED SOCIETY

Signs of uncivilized and undisciplined behavior were evident throughout the global society by the late 20th century. It accelerated in the 1960s when excesses approached outright anarchy, the counter-culture Youth Revolution. Some of this was attributed to the earlier "baby-boom" explosion that saw youth nearly outnumber mature adults. Young males were at the forefront, but studies indicated that young men in all societies, at all points in history, have committed the most aggressive actions and violence.[1]

Individuals stressed their own codes of conduct over those of society because it was thought society had no purpose. The here and now, the existential moment was thought to be life's only reality. Clare Booth Luce remarked, that for youth at the time, "Moral values were mere fantasies of the brain. Suicide and violence against the establishment became the order of the day."

Arson, vandalism, and even armed robberies of symbolic hated institutions became commonplace. Mrs. Luce said, "Drug and alcohol consumption rose rapidly among the young, and drug peddling was welcomed. Free uncontrolled sex replaced Victorian sexual hypocrisy. Jerry Rubin proclaimed the uniform of the day: long-hair and unkempt beards, dirty appearance, and scruffy clothing. All of this degenerated into common theft, muggings, rape, and murder. They proclaimed 'God is dead.'

An example, of how far the movement degenerated, was the Manson murders. Sadistic acts became liberating if they "felt good". One of the girls from the Manson gang, who repeatedly stabbed and murdered the pregnant Sharon Tate and her unborn child, dipped her fingers in her victim's blood, licked them and voiced the sensation, "Wow! Delicious!"[2]

Later, on the steps of a church in Hartford, Connecticut in 1976, a sixteen year old girl, high on LSD, slashed her wrists and arms; dripping with blood she then poked a razor to her throat while a crowd of three-hundreds bystanders cheered. Witnesses said the crowd shouted and screamed, "Do your thing. Right on!" Bottles were thrown. A whiskey bottle hit the girl and another hit the church. An officer trying to get control of the situation remarked, "I can't believe this. What has society come to?" Later police detective William Tremont reported, "The officers at the scene told me the bystanders were just like animals." [3]

Human behavior continued to deteriorate into the 1990s. Gross toys were sold in toy stores to small children that reduced civility and good taste to their lowest levels. One toy, the Grossinator, emitted raunchy sounds at the touch of a button like a revolting, putrid burp. Doctor Dreadful kits made edible ice cream that looked like gray-green vomit. "Brains" could be eaten out of a skull. Gooey Louie toys had big noses full of long, green, rubbery things. If the wrong one was pulled, his brain popped out.

In Britain and other parts of Europe, commercials on television aimed at the cynical and rebellious consumer groups, hit new lows in civilized behavior. They were filled with violent images and interspersed with four-letter expletives that condoned aggression, violence, and antisocial behavior. Typical was a jewelry ad which featured an axe-wielding undertaker chasing a scampering, severed hand sporting jewelry. The ad ends with "if you don't like it. then f____ off."

A new spectator sport called Ultimate Fighting developed in 1995 wherein two bare-knuckled fighters punched, kicked, and gouged each other until one was ripped apart and his face crushed to a bloody mess. Men expressed their innermost brutal and violent behavior and drew large crowds that paid to see the most barbaric scenes possible. It was reminiscent of the frenzied days of gladiators near the end of the Roman Empire.

Children played video games to win points for killing the most people. They watched violence-packed cartoons and listened to songs titled "Be my Slave" and "Skumkill". Or they watched movies like "Splatter University" and "I Spit on Your Grave." Sociologist, Gail Dines-Levy of Wheelock College said, "What we are doing is training a whole generation of male kids to see sex and violence as inextricably linked." [4]

In the United States satanism and other cults prevailed among teen-agers. They were permeated with violence and crime, laced with drugs and savage rock music, symbols and rituals. Carl Rashcke, director of Institute of Humanities at the University of Denver remarked in 1988, "This paranoid fantasy is becoming a major national social problem." Social workers in the State of Missouri said there was a dramatic increase in reports of serious, highly secretive satanic cults that practised bizarre rituals to cloak animal torture, drug abuse, pedophilia and child pornography. [5] Police authorities even reported human sacrifices in some rituals. Satanisim, which reveled in evil, destruction, instant gratification, as well as rituals, guaranteed to shock parents and displayed the ultimate rebellion by youth.

Many heavy-metal rock lyrics concentrated on vulgar, sadistic, and violent explicit sex. The more degrading and shocking, the more youth applauded. One rock performer included such excesses as biting the head off a bat. Such savage conduct dragged culture to new depths of uncivilized behavior reminiscent of earlier tribal atrocities. Sociologists were appalled.

A comic (?), named Dice Clay, attracted huge crowds in places like Madison Square Garden in 1990. He was quoted by Richard Corliss of Time, "I know you know the old s____, but it's a new decade and I got new filth for ya." The crowd roared. Mr. Corliss reported the heavy-metal rock band, Motley Crue, presented images of satanism; the Beastie Boys mimicked masturbation on stage; Two Live Crew called for war against the police and the most hellish explicit sex. Language filth became a required ingredient of movies, finally common and acceptable. *Pulp Fiction* was nominated for seven academy awards in 1995. Its bloody violence, sleeze, glorification of drug use and the worse type of criminal element, and the deliberate degradation of anything civilized was considered hilariously funny. Filthy four-letter words dominated every line.

Mr. Corliss said, "The new music (in the 50s) took rhythm, danger and sexuality from the underground black culture, cranked the volume up, electrified it and handed it to a brand new consumer group: white teenagers. White soldiers in Vietnam picked up blacks' raw vocabulary, in which 'mother f____' is routinely used. ... this urban-black music(?) is often politically or sexually explicit. Niggers With Attitude, a rock group, received an admonishing letter from the FBI for their song F____ Tha Police, in which the singer warns ... 'Ice Cube will swarm /On any 'mother f____ in a blue uniform ... / A young nigger on the warpath. / And when I finish it's gonna be a bloodbath.' " [6]

The new obscenity of the 1990s grew from explicit sex to violent sex and then to violence against law and order. Raunchiness ruled and was worshipped by youth. One of Niggers With Attitude's gangsta rap albums went straight to number one on Billboards Top 200, shocking even the music industry and indicating how much young people approved of this filth and degradation of civilized conduct. American social culture degenerated from subtle and polite discourse to gross filthy advocacy of racism (both white and black), rape, and anarchy.

Sympathy for the criminal in many cases exceeded that for the victim because of the overwhelming desire by some to blame society for the crimes of certain ethnic groups. So crime, commited by minorities, became even more permissive. A typical case was that of Bonnie Garland. Her estranged boyfriend went up to her bedroom in the night and cracked her head open with a hammer "like a watermelon" as he was later quoted as saying. A Hispanic from the Los Angeles barrio, he was recruited to Yale because of his minority status. He was out on bail and accepted in another college within a few weeks. [7]

Examples, of the violent crime epidemic in the 1990s, indicated it was completely out of control. Two teenagers were arrested in Jacksonville, Florida for the rain of sniper-fire on freeway motorists that killed one and injured others. In about a six month period two-hundred and forty-five carjackings occurred in Washington, D.C. alone, five of which ended in murder. A New York motorist, kidnapped by carjackers, was thrown off a twenty story roof. In Virginia, a woman was dragged to death, and her baby tossed from the car by carjackers.

In Phoenix, gang-snipers shot at police who entered their neighborhoods so police had to respond to a call with six officers - four to watch for snipers while two dealt with the call. In some sections of Los Angeles and Washington, D.C., police didn't go into some neighborhoods for fear of being shot by gang members. In those communities, criminals controlled society.

Peter Fimrite of the San Francisco Chronicle reported an incident in Oakland in 1993 in which a young black woman accused of smoking crack was attacked in an apartment hallway by another young black woman. She was pursued outside across the street. She was then surrounded by fifteen to twenty teenagers and young adults who had been loitering and selling drugs on the corner. As the mob began kicking her, one hit her over the head with a bottle as they chanted, "Kill her, kill her." As she lay helpless, the other young woman stabbed her three times in the chest. The victim's last words were "Help me."

Mr. Fimrite wrote that hardened detectives investigating the crime were shocked. He reported that Troy Duster, director of the Study of Social Change at the University of California said, "What seems to be going on here is that the passive observation of brutality has been replaced by a more active egging on." It had gone one step further than the case in New York in 1964 when a young woman was repeatedly stabbed to death while she begged thirty-seven of her neighbors for help. They watched and did nothing. Mike Nisperos, director of the Oakland mayor's Office of Drugs and Crime, said the complete disregard for human life was cultivated in movies, television, and rap music. [8]

In Miami a thirteen year-old offered a man a slice of pizza, but grew angry when he took two. The boy returned a half hour later with a gun and calmly shot the man in the chest, killing him. About the same time, in 1993, another thirteen year-old was charged for his fifty-seventh crime in Fort Lauderdale, Florida. In Portland, Oregon a nine-year old boy got his father's rifle, loaded it with cartidges, and shot and killed his five-year old sister because she refused to go to her room while he was baby-sitting her. His newsphoto depicted a handsome, well-groomed, innocent-looking child. Near Orlando, Florida a thirteen year-old and a fifteen year-old were arrested for the slaying of a British tourist at a highway rest stop. "You've got a whole generation of these conscienceless young people running straight at you," said John Spencer, a Broward County, Florida forensic psychologist. "The ordinary man walking down the street has no experience to relate to this - can't even imagine the perils that he faces." [9]

The total disregard for human life was shown in Inglewood, California in 1996 when a pedestrian dropped his package on the street while he was accidentally bumped by another man. The second man picked it up and apologized. Instead of accepting the apology, the first man pulled a gun and shot him five or six times and killed him after the victim and neighbors pleaded for his life. In Flagstaff, Arizona a grand jury indicted a woman after she allegedly placed her two year-old son on the tracks of an oncoming train. There was no end to the horror stories of unconscionable acts that continued daily.

But the barbarisim of the late twentieth century was not restricted to the United States. By the 1990s the Soviet Union, later Russia, was also in the midst of a crime wave. In Rio de Janeiro, Brazil killings averaged five a day in 1988; in one year it had risen to five hundred murders in one month.

In Rio a nine year-old street fruit peddler, Patricio da Silva Hilario, was found strangled. A note pinned to his small body read, "I killed you because you did not work or produce anything." He refused to work for drug peddlers. Francisco Ferreira Santos, a maid in Rio, woke up one morning to find a neighbor's head nailed to the wall above her door. His body was missing. No one knew why he, a bus conductor, was killed.[10]

In India wives suffered atrocities comparable to the medieval dark ages. They were mutilated and beheaded for alleged infidelity and banished for witchcraft. Many were doused with kerosene and ignited by husbands wanting to remarry and obtain a better or additional dowry. It was customary for the authorities not to interfere with the husband's "rights." In the town of Kanpur, police reported a grissly incident wherein a native man kidnapped children and sold them to a restaurant where they were cooked and served! He had confessed selling fourteen for forty dollars each.

Mexico City's chief prosecutor, Jose Antonio Gonzalez, said a violent crime was committed every two minutes in the Mexican capital in 1996, and Mexicans felt more insecure and less protected by the law than ever before.

***

By the 1970s, the close-knit family life in the United States began to fall apart. This was due to several factors. Women began to enter the work force in increasing numbers leaving children without close supervision. Divorces soared while marriages declined. Textbooks in schools and colleges began to represent divorce as part of a normal family life cycle. No longer did parents put the welfare of their children before their intolerance for one another. The self-gratification of the individual parent, an inheritance of the 1960s philosophy, was more important. By 1990 demographers indicated that only one of every three adolescents lived continuously in an intact family. Social scientists predicted untold social and psychological traumas would be left in the wake of broken families.

Cohabitation out of wedlock became commonplace. In 1975 a U.S. census report indicated illegitimate births had doubled since 1955, and one-third of the children did not live with their natural parents. During the 1970s the Census Bureau reported single-parent families doubled; families headed by unwed mothers quadrupled. The report suggested almost half the children being born in 1981 would spend a significant portion of their lives in a single-parent family. By 1992 illegitimacy had increased four-hundred percent over 1960. An astonishing sixty-three per cent of black children were born out of wedlock.

As in any animal, most men impregnated as many females as the opportunity presented. Both in animals and humans, this was, no doubt, the natural behavior evolved over eons to insure the existence of their genes in future generations. Nonetheless, as late as the 1950s, men assumed the responsibility of raising their offspring whether married or not. By the 1990s not even marriage was binding in this respect for many males.

In most cases a single female parent was unable to support her child and had to resort to welfare. Welfare spending rose *sevenfold* in only thirty years. The increased financial burden in taxes on the remaining two-parent families was tremendous and an unfair penalty. Promiscuous sexual behavior was indirectly rewarded by placing the financial responsibility of having an illegitimate baby on society rather than its biological parents. Over half of all officially poor families were headed by females by 1987. They had the largest income shortfalls, the longest time-period below the poverty line, and the heaviest demand for funds from society.[11]

The number of children having children began to soar. In Hill County of West Virginia, pregnant twelve and thirteen year-old girls waited in labor rooms - carrying crayons and coloring books. The Guttmacher studies reported that the incidence of sexual intercourse among unmarried teenage girls increased by two-thirds during the 1970s. Dr. Sol Gordon, a professor of child and family studies at Syracuse University, reported 1981 teen pregnancies increased by thirty per cent in only one year. Two-hundred thousand youths contacted gonorrhea during the same year. In 1983 more than half of teen births were illegitimate as compared to less than fifteen percent in 1950. He termed the statistics as a horrendous situation and a national disaster; and concluded they could only result in psychological, emotional, and marital problems later in life.[12] By the 1990s, it became even worse.

A survey of the Mount Sinai Hospital in Chicago indicated the majority of young mothers having babies were Afro-American and Hispanic teenagers. More than half were on Medicaid contributing to the sharply rising health costs paid by taxpayers. Frequently they lived with their mother, hadn't completed high school, and had little job experience. Over forty per cent of the babies in intensive care were born to substance abuse women, and once again, it contributed to the rising cost of health care paid by others.[13]

Leon Dash, the black author of *When Children Want Children : The Urban Crisis of Teen-age Childbearing,* and whose series made him a Pulitzer finalist in 1987, did many interviews among black families. He originally thought black teenage pregnancy grew out of ignorance of birth control methods or the cynical manipulation by boys. Instead Mr. Dash wrote, "Pregnancies were not accidents. (They) knew the consequences of sexual activity, and they knew about birth control, but they wanted children for a variety of reasons - to achieve something tangible, to prove something to their peers, to be considered an adult, to get their mother's attention, and to keep up with an older brother or sister ... to meet some basic human needs - essential requirements that the adolescent children of the more affluent fulfill in other ways." The picture he drew of family life was filled with violence, anger, disaffection, and indifference. Mr. Dash felt the solution lay primarily in education.[14]

Child abuse also soared. The reported cases in 1992 were four times the number in 1976. Many of the victims were at the hands of the mother's live-in-boy-friend or a parent too immature to understand why their child was crying. Their doll-like play things suddenly developed into emotional behavioral beings too complex for young parents to comprehend.

Newly accepted promiscuous sex spread venereal disease. After having declined for many years, gonorrhea and syphylis became rampant. New and more exotic venereal diseases arose: chondria, herpes, and AIDs. Some of these were incurable at the time resulting in tortuous lives and many times death.

By 1990 the United States, an economic superpower, ranked twentieth in the world in the prevention of infant mortality. This did not make sense to most because the government sponsored over ninety-three programs costing over seven billion dollars a year to keep children alive.

Mrs. Harmeet Singh, the assistant editor of *Policy Review,* pointed out that in Washington, D.C., for example, prenatal care was free to any woman with a family income less than twenty thousand dollars. A Maternity Outreach Mobile system toured the city's poorest areas every day locating pregnant women, reminding them of appointments, and taking them to the clinics if transportation was needed. But despite all this the infant mortality rate in Washington, D.C. was three times the national rate.

Why? Mrs. Singh's answer was, " ... the most important reason for America's high infant mortality: the behavior and motivation of mothers themselves." She wrote that most pregnant women in D.C., which she had contacted, knew they could get free care but didn't consider it seriously or were unaware of their pregnancy. Nearly two-thirds of the city's newborns had unmarried mothers - three times the national average. Another two-thirds were also born to women who used drugs or alcohol while pregnant. Dr. George Graham, a professor at John Hopkins University, confirmed her observation, "I don't know how spending more on prenatal care is going to make any difference to the woman who uses crack. A 1990 study found that nearly a third of the babies born in New York were addicted to crack." Mrs. Singh concluded, "America's high rate of infant mortality is more of a social than a medical problem. Spending more won't fix it."[15] Many, who were outraged by the high rate of infant mortality, still insisted the problem was lack of sufficient funding by the government.

***

The use of marijuana, cocaine, heroin, and other drugs became epidemic and spread even into elementary grade schools. The American Medical Association reported in 1995 the use of marijuana by eighth-graders doubled in just four years. Addiction snow-balled fostering increased criminal activity to support the habit. In 1988 it was estimated Americans were spending one hundred billion dollars for illicit drugs annually. By 1989 it was estimated thirty per cent of the population was using drugs. This waste of money was in the face of an inability to increase expenditures for social programs and the need to reduce deficit spending which exceeded one-hundred and fifty billion dollars. In other words, the annual cost for drugs was nearly the amount needed to balance the budget.

Hospitals were overtaxed with proliferating crack-babies resulting in additional spiraling health-care costs to the public. Venereal disease spread as more people turned to prostitution to support their habit. Addiction spread from the inner cities into the suburbs and even into rural America. Addicts had no ambition, made no pretense to work, and pedaled the drug to maintain their habit. The demand was so great, governments of some Latin-American countries became multi-billion dollar drug rings. Government functions were paralyzed amidst this bed of official corruption.

In the Soviet Union and later in Russia, alcoholism became so rampant, it was necessary to restrict the supply of vodka in government stores. This created long lines when the supply was available. Sugar supplies became acutely short as the number of home distilleries grew. A national edict called for sobriety and reduced consumption. Drug consumption was also taking its toll as in most other countries.

In the United States dishonesty became acceptable if one could "get away with it." Shoplifting reached an estimated forty billion dollars by 1990! The FBI said shoplifting increased over a third in only four years between 1984 and 1988. It became so rampant and lucrative that even burglars shifted to less risky shoplifting. Of course, these losses were only temporarily absorbed by the retailers. They soon were passed on, as an expense of doing business, to honest consumers in the form of higher prices.

One Justice Department study estimated thievery by employees accounted for seventy per cent of retailers losses. Retail industry executives said by 1992 it was a larger loss than from shoplifting. As many as a third of all employees interviewed in studies by academics and other specialists, admitted stealing from their employers. Studies also showed three-fourths of all retail employees knew at least one colleague who was stealing.

Honest consumers ultimately paid for the dishonesty of employees and shoplifters. Most consumers, however, generally were not aware how such anti-social behaviorial could effect them.

School dropouts in American cities became a raging epidemic by the late 1980s. According to the National Dropout Prevention Network, more than four million students skipped school each day. In Newark, New Jersey most children cut classes by the fifth grade. Some of the reasons were laziness, learning problems, peer pressure, and primarily a lack of parental motivation and supervision. A third of the city was on some sort of public assistance, and half of the households were headed by a single parent. On the third day of each month, many students were expected to stay home to make sure the welfare check was not stolen from the mailbox. Since stylish clothes in ghetto schools was a status symbol, some stayed home if they couldn't steal or afford to buy them. In Phoenix, Arizona over half of welfare recipients and eighty-two per cent of prison inmates were dropouts. [16] As a result, school dropouts, especially from large inner-cities, were rapidly becoming a social disaster: a minimum-wage and welfare society at best, a criminal society at worst.

In only thirty years (1960 to 1990), violent crime in America increased five-hundred sixty per cent even though the population had increased by only forty per cent. Some sociologists thought illegitimate births, the rise in divorce, and single parenthood contributed to these criminal statistics.

Youthful vandalism occurred everywhere: wanton destruction of public signs and property, landscaping, cars, schools, unoccupied homes and even church alters. Incest, rape, pedophilia, and other violent and heinous sex crimes increased. Burglaries and armed robberies proliferated. At one time in large metropolitan areas, a bank was being robbed every other day. Burglaries became so common in large cities, hardly a household escaped. Illinois was an example of the scourge. In just one area, a six year federally-sponsored study showed a third of all juveniles committed a serious crime. Corruption and fraud also increased in the political and business world as new players took control, reflecting the new philosophy of self-gratification.

A 1976 Gallop poll and another again in 1994 showed that the greatest problem in communities of all sizes was crime and lawlessness, whereas, twenty-five years before, they were seldom mentioned as top local problems. Indeed, the survey of 1976 found two-thirds believed people did not lead as honest and moral lives as people did in the past. Of course, this thinking historically had always been prevalent, but when the same question was asked ten years earlier, the proportion was only fifty-two percent. In 1952 it was only forty-seven. [17] A Newsweek poll in 1994 indicated three-fourths believed the United States was in a deep moral decline, and in December 1996, a NBC/Wall Street Journal poll showed eighty percent thought the nation's morals were much lower than in the 1950s. By the turn of the new century, America became a land of lawlessness reminiscent of the frontier west. Police forces were overwhelmed by their task.

A study by the Home Select Committee on Aging estimated that more than a million elderly Americans were physically, financially, and emotionally abused by their relatives each year, a phenomenon it called "a horrifying national disgrace."[18]

The most distressing and sobering of all of the above, from dishonesty and dropouts to violence, was that much of this conduct was either condoned or became accepted standards of behavior by society. Some attributed this to younger people seeing little change in social conduct in their short life-span whereas the elderly could readily observe decadence after a lifetime of observation of radical changes. In other words, most youth were not aware of any different mode of behavior other than the one they were observing.

Many incidents of permissiveness and indifference occurred. In one example during 1993, a seventy-two year old man was mugged and almost killed. His attacker was shot by a policeman while fleeing the scene of the crime. The courts deemed the policeman's actions wrong because it resulted in paralysis of the criminal and awarded him over four million dollars. Fifty years earlier the approved response, to a person running from a policeman at the scene of a crime, was "Halt, or I'll shoot!" Virtually no public reaction to the verdict occured. Once again, it was the taxpayer who paid the award.

In another case in Los Angeles, an innocent truck driver was pulled from his truck during a riot, beaten with a brick, and nearly killed. The criminal perpetrators were found not guilty on all important counts because it was reasoned they could not be held accountable for getting caught up in mob violence. Since they were Afro-Americans, most felt relieved that they were not severely punished because that may have created another mob protest and more violence. Victims and authorities were paralyzed to react in many crime situations because of fear of reprisals, of being accused of racism, or of overreacting.

Many attempts to explain this dark period were forthcoming, but no one was certain as to the explicit causes except to note that disciplined order in society had collapsed.

John Attarian, a Michigan author, noted that in the mid fifties parents, marked by the Great Depression and World War II, indulged their children with entertainment and materialistic rewards. For the first time parents gave an automobile upon graduation from high school. When children were in trouble, parents often sided with them or quickly bailed them out equating indulgence with love. Discipline was relaxed.

Many attribute the permissiveness of the baby-boom generation to Dr. Benjamin Spock's book, *Baby and Child Care*. It was published in 1946, sold over 28 million copies, and became the bible for child-rearing during that period.

In a joint study, the research departments of Ambassador College of Pasadena and the Los Angeles Police Department stated, "The forty percent of our population still under twenty-one has new standards of conduct. In millions of them the 'Spock marks' are showing through; the results of a permissive age of baby doctors, child psychologists, and the new moralists who have instilled an almost religous dedication to rebellion in youth." [19]

In 1979 Dr. Spock at age 76, admitted that his book helped to create a "generation of children, the majority of whom are arguers" and blamed parents failure to discipline their children. He also castigated the permissiveness in society and the brutalized sex in movies and television for some of their behavior.[20] He speculated that he and other child psychologists may have encouraged parents to evade their responsibilities.[21]

In 1966 social scientists Louis Raths, Merrill Harmin, and Sidney Simon developed the teaching method known as Values Clarification. It was meant to be the ideal way to deal with values without taking sides on a value position. Since by "definition and right ... values were personal things," teachers were instructed not to try to teach children correct values. To tell a student stealing is wrong or that kindness is right, would be to manipulate and coerce a student.

By the early 1970s the teaching of Values Clarification was widespread. Whether intended or not, school children were given the message that parents, the school, and society had no right to tell them what standards of behavior to use. Another result was to "emphatically indoctrinate by encouraging and even exhorting the student to narcissistic self-gratification," said Edwin Delathre, president of St. Johns College. By affirming the complete relativity of all values, they equated values with personal tastes and preferences.

Christopher Lasch, a social historian at the University of Rochester in his book *The Culture of Narcissism,* contended that the youth of the 1970s "saw the world as a mirror of themselves and had no interest in external events except as they threw back a reflection of their own image." He indicated they had abandoned the past and were marooned in an endless present; they ceased to care in any meaningful way about those who would follow them. Earlier in his book, *Haven In a Heartless World*, Mr. Lasch indicated that contemporary children were mainly motivated by self-gratification and bombarded by a culture devoted to consumption. Additionally, he said children found solace in their peer group which regulated their behavior. He observed, never having been given a higher moral order to follow, they yielded to authority only if power was wielded.

Another factor was the growing affluence of a prosperous period that helped insulate the baby-boom generation from the reality of discomfort. Later when confronted with the problems of the real world, they demanded an immediate solution by the establishment. When it was not practical or slow in coming, they immediately rebelled. Some affluent youth claimed they despised their parents but relied on their parent's wealth to support their rebellious lifestyles.

Professor James Wilson, a Harvard political scientist, suggested in 1983 that America's declining public concern with "character training" over the previous sixty years may have played a significant part in the high crime rates of the 1970s and 1980s. He noted in the previous twenty years, cultural emphasis focused upon self-expression, spontaneity, tolerance, individualism and personal freedom. He said rights, not duties, received primary attention. As for public schools, they sharply downgraded character training.

Some experts, who wrote in Soviet journals, portrayed juvenile crime during that period in the USSR as a function of parental neglect; the abundance of alcohol; narcotics addiction; boredom; and what some Russians saw as a profound ammorality among the young, a lack of acceptance of higher values. [22] No doubt, some of this was due to the disintegration of the socialist economic system and all it entailed including the lack of any incentive to succeed.

In America some sociologists faulted the policy of subsidizing irresponsibility, failure, and wastefulness by guaranteeing subsistence to anyone who did not study, work, or save for their own well-being. They believed such a policy eventually carried the seeds of educational, moral, and economic decay. There was no pressing need to finish school, to get a job, or save for a "rainy day."

Most studies, by the 1990s, generally recognized the breakdown of the family institution in America was the primary reason for behavioral disintegration. A study, by the Center for the Study of Social Policy, noted that nearly one-half of families formed in 1990 suffered from one of the following risks on arrival of the first baby: the mother was under 20, hadn't graduated from high school, or wasn't married. Each of the risks increased chances the family would have several insurmountable problems such as poverty, dependence on welfare, or a malfunctioning family. The poverty rate for female-headed families was forty-five percent and six times higher than families of married couples (1988). The principal reason was only half the mothers received child support from fathers.

Economists Lawrence Katz and Anne Case of Princeton, in a survey of young people living in the inner-city of Boston, reported family offspring generally had the same social problems that troubled their parents. They noted that if a family member was in jail while a child was growing up, the child was twice as likely to be involved in crime. He was twice as likely to have drug or alcohol problems, be a high school dropout, or have an illegitimate child if parents had those problems.

"The disintegration of the two parent family through divorce, separation, and out-of-wedlock child bearing is generally harmful to the well-being of children and to the social fabric," said Fred J. Chafee, the executive director of the Arizona Children's Home Association. He noted that three-quarters of juveniles in state institutions came from fatherless homes. He also pointed out that children of single mothers were two to three times more likely to suffer emotional or behavioral problems, more likely to be abused or neglected, do poorly in school, abuse drugs, have babies as teenagers, go on welfare and to commit crimes. He zeroed in on men that no longer assume their responsibilities as fathers, "Men now live in a world that does not tell them that a good man ... does not ignore his obligation to his child and so this person does not have a cultural idea in his head about what it means to be a father." [23]

By the mid 1990s it was obvious that there had been a complete breakdown in the social fabric of the United States due to a gradual decay in disciplined order and standards of conduct. It was so engulfing, most Americans became numb, fast losing their capacity for outrage. Senator Daniel Moynihan warned that citizens had been trying to deal with the growth of crime and other deviant behavior by rationalizing, and thereby, normalizing and decriminalizing much of that behavior partly because the level of violent crime had become so common and overpowering. Society merely stopped recognizing much behavior as deviant and instead redefined its standards.

In addition to the permissiveness that prevailed in society and the concentration on self, most institutions such as government, schools, and family no longer required an individual to take personal responsibility for his own actions. To do so was no longer politically popular; others simply assumed deviant behavior was the result of economic conditions such as unemployment. They blamed everyone else in society for allowing those conditions to prevail.

Lee Kuan Yew, Singapore's Prime Minister, made a remarkable accusation as a distant world bystander in an interview in 1995. He said the United States had "lost its bearings" by emphasizing individual rights at the expense of society. "An ethical society is one which matches human rights with responsibilities."[24]

Some people began to believe the strict, perhaps occasional ridiculous, interpretation of the constitution to preserve an individual's right resulted in the abandonment of the welfare of the greater society. They thought the original authors of the constitution could not possibly visualize all of the problems facing a contemporary society more than two centuries later.

It was not important to point a finger at the various causes, both real and hypothetical, but instead to concentrate on developing a permanent discipline for future human behavior - one that would withstand any tendency for erosion. No real effort was made, however, and the old methods of coping continued to fail well into the future.

By then the social fabric of world society was in an abysmal state. Illiteracy mushroomed. Prejudice and selfishness were rampant. Barbaric incidents were commonplace. Lawlessness and anarchy engulfed large parts of the world.

Decades later sociologists looked back on this period in history and were aghast at the primitiveness that existed. They were incredulous after reading of the enormous gap that developed between the tremendous advancements in science and technology, on the one hand, and the primitive state of human behavior on the other. Even more perplexing, with the intelligence that existed, why was society unable to close the gap?

PART II

TOWARD A NEW WORLD ORDER

"There is nothing more difficult to take in hand, more perilous to conduct, or more uncertain in its success, than to take the lead in the introduction of a new order of things." Nicollo Machiavelli, *("The Prince")*

Chapter 5

DAWN OF A NEW CIVILIZATION

" ... we must keep our planet habitable ... This will involve changes in government, in industry, in ethics, in economics, and in religion. We've never done such a thing before, certainly not on a global scale. It may be too difficult for us. Dangerous technologies may be too widespread. Corruption may be too pervasive. Too many leaders may be focused on the short term rather than the long. There may be too many quarreling ethnic groups, nation-states, and ideologies for the right kind of global change to be instituted. We may be too foolish to perceive even what the real dangers are ... However, we humans also have a history of making long-lasting social change that nearly everyone thought impossible." Carl Sagan, from "Pale Blue Dot"

After decades of gradual social, economic, and ecological decline interrupted by short periods of attempted reform, it appeared that the world had sunk to new depths of primitiveness. Finally in the throes of political and social chaos, a terrible revulsion arose against global institutions and structures. A desperate demand for change was heard around the world.

It was in this environment that a large group of intellectuals,[1] composed of sociologists, economists, and educators from throughout the world, met to discuss what could be done to halt the course of man's destruction. Politicians and government officials were excluded. After considerable analysis and discussion, this group became aware that drastic measures had to be taken if the world was to be saved from this acute and devastating decline. If global society was to become truly civilized, disciplined order and standards of rational behavior must evolve among its inhabitants. At the conclusion of the conference the intellectuals returned to their respective countries to attempt to convince their countrymen to help in this great crusade.

It wasn't difficult for most to agree that a herculean effort had to be made to avert complete anarchy and the eventual destruction of the human race and its environment. No longer were there doubters. Conditions had become so desperate, peasant-farmers as well as many urbanites lived in constant fear of starvation, pestilence, and criminal abuse. Political rulers and other government officials, bureaucrats, and their families were no longer insulated. They were constantly threatened with kidnapping, bombings, and assassination. Protests, rioting, and looting were common. Political violence was unending as urban guerillas carried on permanent warfare with their respective governments. Military force, as a deterrent, was becoming unreliable as many in the armies defected and joined the guerillas.

It was in this environment, politicians and other political leaders began to doubt the prospects of their own future and those of their children and grandchildren. Many thought of relinquishing power to protect their families or to rid themselves of constant harassment and turmoil. Some were altruistic hoping to raise their countries from the depths of despair. Consequently, many of the world's nations agreed with the first conference and sent their most knowledgeable thinkers to convene and devise a revolutionary plan to reverse the disintegration of mankind. The primary goal was to improve the quality of life for all and to formulate methods to achieve that goal. Dedicated representatives from the fields of sociology, psychology, economics and education were selected as well as experts in commerce, ecology, criminology, and in various related fields.

It was further agreed by the participants that a new and radical solution must be found since power-politics, nationalism, and prejudice had to be abandoned. Such a non-political arrangement was, heretofore, unheard of, but times had become desperate; consequently, political representatives were not included. Everyone was aware all nations, cultures, and religions must finally work together to prevent Armageddon.

Many politicians said it would be impossible for a diverse group of intellectuals to meet and construct a plan for a new world order. Yet similar conventions had been held in the past to create an outline of principles to guide social orders. They were reasonably successful for extended periods of time. The Constitutional Convention in colonial America and the signing of the United Nations Charter by representatives of fifty nations were examples. When sincere people can communicate, work, and reason together with an open mind, usually the results are positive.

The members' first objective was to outline the major problems in the world. Then they planned to address them one by one rather than have a random discussion. After much analysis they prepared a list. Each problem was extremely critical in itself and required a definite solution. Nevertheless, the solution of all was contingent on the solution of each because they were all interrelated. Causes were emphasized over symptoms. The list was as follows:

1. The decline of disciplined society. Uncontrolled crime was merely a symptom.

2. The proliferation of weapons of war, and their use in nationalistic, ethnic, and religious conflicts.

3. The massive explosion of the world's population. Symptoms were everywhere from the destruction of the global ecosystem to the reduction in quality of life.

4. The stifling of free-competitive markets. Symptoms were many, but the decline in living standards was most important.

5. Failure of governments to function without power structures, waste, and corruption. The worst symptom was uncontrolled debt followed by rampant inflation in many countries.

After months of discussing these problems, the members began to approach some possible remedies. The number of short-term and temporary solutions were plentiful, but it was abundantly clear none could guarantee to be effective over the long-run.

Finally, a small group began to espouse a new approach. They said, "We can't go back to the old methods of trying to solve our problems. We must discard all of the old theories, prejudices, and selfish-interests and start anew with a fresh approach. We must also concentrate on preventing the causes of problems in human relationships rather than the resulting symptoms.

"At first, it is essential that we do not clutter our minds with specific solutions to isolated problems. Instead, we must concentrate on the kind of society that is desirable and how to achieve it. Also we should recognize from our outline of basic problems, that the control of human behavior is paramount in solving each of them. The main objective should be to create an environment that allows everyone to improve their quality of life. More specific goals and their solutions should only evolve as they appear to help in attaining this primary goal.

"But before we attempt to research serious solutions, we must keep in mind large groups of people will be in opposition to whatever we propose. Youth, for instance, lacking the perspective that comes from experience and education, will see things differently. The masses with their prejudices will fight us all the way. Having said this, we must not distance ourselves from the needs and aspirations of our people. Their aspirations should be our goals, and the solutions must be simple and practical in order for them to work. [2] Those in power will only grudgingly relinquish their status. The politicians, bureaucrats, and one-man rulers will be our most vehement opponents.

"We must also keep in mind that to improve the quality of life for every individual, it must first be determined what is best for all of society. We can no longer put the individual's rights before the welfare of the entire community. Any action by an individual that is detrimental to society can no longer be tolerated no matter what civil liberty may have to be curtailed. This does not mean that the legitimate rights of the individual should not be addressed and adopted into law. Like ants, we must arrange our social life so the unit of survival is the colony.[3]

"Once we adopt the importance of social responsibility, it must be mandated. No longer can it be merely desired.

"If we can develop considerable control over human behavior, then some of society's greatest problems can be solved. Wars can be abolished, crime and fear of others nearly eliminated, and selfish political power can be eradicated. However, this can only be accomplished by taking radical steps."

None of these ideas were new; Sigmund Freud long ago indicated that unhappiness arose from three sources, one of them being human relations.[4] Dr. Alexis Carrel, the great biochemist and philosopher of the 1930s, wrote, "Moral beauty is the basis of civilization, much more than science, art or religious rites." He also noted it established peace among men. [5] Even some civil-rights leaders in the 1990s began to regard deviant patterns of behavior as the basic cause that doomed people to failure in the inner cities. Sociologist, Joseph Wood Krutch, wrote, "Without standards, society lapses into anarchy and the individual becomes aware of an intolerable disharmony between himself and his universe."

The discussion continued as various members came forth with comments and suggestions, "Improving the quality of life through the control of human behavior will be extremely difficult. Since the first moment of organized society, men attempted to build utopias; all have failed mainly because their blueprints for an ideal society were not practical. Most ideologies have attempted to liberate from a purely theoretical pattern, much of it without logic. Kenneth Minigue, author of *Alien Powers,* observed that the ideal ideology is one that focuses not on a single grandiose political structure, as did Communism, but on a menu of many logical and evolving operatives for society.

"Many will say that social reconstruction is a fabrication of idle dreams because 'human nature' cannot be changed. Yet, we cannot be deterred, for we must make every effort to extricate ourselves from this morass of illiteracy, prejudice, and selfishness that has brought us to the brink of chaos.

"We are no longer free to mold ourselves according to our individual likes and dislikes with little consideration for the rest of society. To achieve the most good for the greatest number, we must instead mold ourselves in a scientific manner based on our emotional and physical strengths as well as weaknesses. Fear, envy, selfishness, and prejudice should not be allowed to dominate our thinking. We must make a much better effort to control them. When coupled with illiteracy, they can be devastating. There must also be a greater effort to understand the physiological complexities of the human brain and the rest of the body and how they relate to its behavior.

"A set of principles of individual conduct must be established. These should not be based on custom, prejudice, or religion. The primary concern instead should be how they affect other people. Freedom of conduct should not be constrained unless it brings harm to society or its individual constituents either directly or indirectly. Certainly, laws must enforce specific acts of conduct as they do now, but the crucial factor in controlling behavior will not be laws. It must be *behavioral education* begun in infancy.

"Aggressiveness must be channeled into other activities, such as sports, not crime or war. Acquisitiveness can become a constructive incentive to improve the quality of life if properly channeled. Self-assertion must be directed toward selfless leadership in return for recognition. It must be diverted from the selfish domination of others.

"Youth must be conditioned from the beginning that uncontrolled aggressiveness, selfishness, and domination of others will not be tolerated in the new society. It must be instilled into them from infancy until it is permanently ingrained in their behavior.

"Any temptation to selfishly dominate others in order to satisfy personal greed for political power must be removed in a new society. Citizens have for centuries mistrusted their governments and with good reason. No matter what form of governing structure - monarchy, dictatorship, or democracy - the end result has always been the same - the domination of the majority by a selfish few for the benefit of those few. The power structure usually includes special interests and bureaucracies. These few acquire political power, wealth, and privileges through favoritism, deceit, corruption, and intimidation. This can no longer be tolerated. Some radical structural changes in governance are necessary.

" Nationalism and religious fanaticism must also be eliminated. These are only emotional tools used by rulers to extend their power, through war if necessary. Furthermore, there should be no artificial borders to fan the flames of nationalism and cultural prejudice, to stop the free movement of trade and ideas, and even to prevent the free movement of people and labor. The extensive development of sophisticated communication and transportation technology, finance and trade throughout the world no longer warrants closed communities, or any form of isolation, simply to satisfy ethnic prejudice. We are a world community and must begin to act as one.

"There should be freedom from fear of others. Our children must be taught that any type of criminal activity is abhored and will not be condoned in our society. There should be no permissive exceptions to this demand. Lethal weapons must not be available to allow individuals to execute a criminal act. Physiological reasons for anti-social behavior, such as hunger, must be eradicated. And such things as substance-abuse and sexual drive must be controlled. The treatment of the few remaining criminals must be radically changed to eliminate costly prison systems. It should direct the energies of social offenders to productive labor beneficial to the whole of society as well as themselves.

"In addition to social responsibility and the control of human behavior, other important subsidiary steps must be taken to improve our quality of life. First, it is imperative that adequate food and shelter be created for all by promoting the most efficient productive and distribution systems that can be devised. Second, we must strive to maintain and prolong a healthy and productive life for everyone. Third, a vibrant world ecosystem must be restored that will help improve the quality of life. Fourth, we must respond to the psychological as well as physical needs of each individual. (i.e. early personality and prodigy development ; formative security and love ; sensible sex-drive channels; opportunities in the workplace for creative expression, new experiences, and proper recognition). Finally, we must plan for the survival of our descendents in the universe."

The suggestions expounded by this group made sense to the larger assembly so committees were formed to tackle portions of the general plan. Each committee was composed of experts in that particular subject. For example, one committee discussed how to develop the means necessary to prudently begin curtailing the population explosion. Another committee worked on possible methods to promote behavioral education for children.

Each committee assembled think-tanks to work on more specific issues. Other scientists and technicians from around the world, who were experts in a particular subject, were enlisted to help address some of the more complicated aspects of a problem.

The assembly stressed, that without substantive logic, ideas for solutions by committees would not even be considered for discussion in the larger forum. It emphasized that solutions, based solely on theory, could have little chance of being effective unless the thinkers had experience as achievers in formulating the theory or could rely on the experience of others. Problem solvers and planners had to understand what doers do and need. Otherwise, theoretically perfect plans would be imperfect in execution as was the dogma of Marxists. The assembly also required that the plans of one committee had to be compatible with the plans of all the other committees.

Any radical new idea had to be thoroughly examined and especially tested against all conceivable obstructions found in its practical every-day application. The logic and finality had to be so overwhelming that the sponsoring committee was unanimously convinced of its need.

This took many months, and progress was naturally slow. After arriving at both a practical and logical solution, each proposal of a committee was prepared for its possible incorporation into the articles of a preamble for a world government.

Much time passed before a second assembly convened to hear reports of the various committees. The chairman opened the session with a sober introductory address, "We must recognize in advance that the understanding and solution of the world's problems will encounter massive resistance by most people because of apathy, procrastination, and especially prejudice. But we must persevere acknowledging this is because much of the world's masses are presently illiterate as well as culturally and religiously prejudiced in most of these matters. Their attention focuses primarily on the daily routine of living: working, subsisting, caring for their families, and trying to improve their lot. We cannot fault them, especially those in the less-developed countries, for these priorities since they have little time for anything else. Few of them can comprehend the vast intricate and interlocking sources of their misery and poverty. When profound national decisions are needed, most prefer to have knowledgeable authorities explain what are required."

(It is interesting to note a sociobiologist in the 1970s, David Barash, said, "It is absolutely undeniable that much of the world is in terrible shape. Famine, pestilence, tyranny, and outright savage murder abound. We are rapidly destroying the only planet we have, polluting it and using up its irreplaceable natural resources at an unconscionable rate. We continue to wobble on the brink of thermonuclear destruction. Yet virtually everyone, regardless of circumstance, spends virtually all his or her time and energy attending to intensely personal concerns, centered largely around self, immediate family, and friends. In many ways it is an utterly absurd situation.") [6]

The chairman continued, "It is imperative that the overall plan must be comprehensive. We must be careful not to finalize any one part until all of the others have been thoroughly analyzed, discussed, and meshed into one broad operational concept. In other words, it will not succeed if only some of the elements are adopted while others remain unresolved at that time.

"The control or governance, of these articles for World government, will be the result of this broad preamble of objectives. Let me emphasize, how this is accomplished is very critical if we are to succeed. The government must be a means, not an end in itself. Its formation should, therefore, only be considered after first arriving at all the other objectives and then only with considerable restraint."

With these cautionary admonitions, the assembly began to analyze, discuss, and finally adopt one by one the principles that made up the preamble. After what seemed an eternity, the lengthy and tedious process was finished. This was followed by years of gradual installation and modification of the adopted procedures so that the process was orderly and pragmatic with the least disruption as possible.

The more-developed nations were the first to join the new world government. Countries whose religious and ethnic prejudices dominated the populaces's thinking, were still apprehensive and remained outside for many decades. Gradually third-world nations and finally the least-developed African countries began to participate with advisory assistance from the advanced nations.

***

Many generations later, the results have been astounding. The three great obstacles to human progress have been essentially eliminated - illiteracy, prejudice, and selfish greed for power. There is now a cosmopolitan world without war and internal strife; scientific order and efficient governance has replaced the ineptness of democracies as well as the cruelness of totalitarianism. The basic economic needs of all men are now fulfilled, and the environment has been restored. The quality of life has been greatly improved.

The constructive development of human behavior, that made these goals possible, began with new behavioral education which is explained in the next chapter.

Chapter 6

NEW BEHAVIORAL PATTERNS

"Science has conquered the material world. And science will give man, if his will is indomitable, mastery over life and over himself." Alexis Carrel (from *"Man the Unknown"*)

(Historical Background)
Aspects of human behavior, such as selfishness, have been attributed by sociobiologists to centuries of evolutionary biology. Once called "human instincts," it includes such things as aggressiveness in males, nepotism, intolerance, and exploitation as well as selfishness. These traits probably emerged through natural selection and evolution over thousands of years, a product of environment. They were absolutely necessary for the human animal to survive and evolve under difficult and primitive conditions. Nepotism, for example, merely expresses the inate selfishness to perpetuate one's genes.

No animal, including humans, displays true altruism, a behavioral trait that solely profits another. Altruism usually appears only when individuals are coerced by society or in extremely rare cases of heroism usually when one acts without thought or to impress others. Many times humans help one another when they expect reciprocal treatment or some type of reward. Reciprocity is an important incentive of civilized behavior, but it is not true altruism.

David Barash, professor of psychology and zoology at the University of Washington, in his book *The Whisperings Within* said, "Real, honest-to-God altruism doesn't occur in nature. ... given the fundamental selfishness of evolution, true altruism should never occur since any genes producing altruism should be less fit than genes that produce selfishness."

Later he said, "Genetic selfishness can be expressed directly through behaviors that promote the individual and his or her offspring directly; or less directly through kin selection and its concern for more distant relatives; or, least directly through reciprocity." [1]

Nonetheless, Mr. Barash conceded the significance of environment in molding character and standards of behavior. He said, "It is a profound truth that human behavior is culturally influenced and learned - the product of experience. ... insofar as evolution has made us self-centered, ... it is up to society to make us more tractable. Indeed, if we ever hope to attain real altruism in human behavior, unalloyed by selfish concerns, we had better look to society to drum it into us, because there seems to be no other way it can get there. There is no basis whatever for giving up on someone because 'it's in his genes'. Evolution does not support social inaction." [2]

Even early psychologists and philosophers addressed the importance of cultural environment and human instincts, and most agreed with David Barash's conclusion that mankind must overcome his evolutionary instincts by adopting a selective, behavioral environment and adhering to it.

John Locke, as early as the seventeenth century, believed the human mind to be blank and only furnished with cultural environment. Immanuel Kant believed reason overcame instincts. Sigmund Freud maintained that "civilized society" was founded on the restraint of human instincts. Carl Jung divided the unconscious mind into an individual's own experiences and those accumulated during evolution history.

Mr. Barash sums it up, "Certainly culture is our most important biological adaptation, so let's use it for all it is worth. Doing less would be denying our humanity." [3]

(The New Society)

It is now many decades perhaps a century or two since the articles of World government were compiled.

To preface a discussion of the new society, it should be said that even in this advanced civilization nothing is absolutely perfect. Society is continually improving and amending its way of life especially in light of new technological and scientific advancements.

What is a civilized society? The dictionary's definition of civilize means to elevate in social and individual life, to enlighten and to bring out of a savage state. It further identifies civilized as polite, courteous, not rude, respectful, and a condition of social order. It implies a dignified, sincere, and thoughtful consideration for others.

A truly civilized society must be composed of individuals that utilize a conscious and determined intention of self-control rooted in a learned civil conduct to overcome primitive and deviant compulsions. If they are unable to do this, they will revert to animal-like responses. Unlike non-intelligent life, mankind must consciously design its own evolution.

Since the single most basic problem in molding a civilized society is the control of human behavior, the new society established two broad offenses of law which defines anti-social conduct. In establishing these, it was necessary to balance individual freedoms against the welfare of the rest of society.

The offenses are :

1. Doing damage intentionally or negligently to another person's body or well-being either directly or indirectly.

2. Taking property or service from another person by force, threat or stealth either directly or indirectly.

As can be seen, these offenses encompass many forms of criminal behavior such as theft, robbery, assault, rape and murder. They also include such things as pollution, white-collar crimes, the peddling of addictive substances, enslavement and many more.

However, no amount of laws or deterrents will stop anti-social behavior unless the individual is taught from early childhood to understand and respect civilized conduct upon which the laws are based. Otherwise, laws only work as long as there is a definite fear of being caught and punished. It is futile to rely on laws not backed up by belief in the standards of morality that supports those laws. This was one of the reasons crime was out of control in many countries in the late 20th century.

Children are not born with standards of conduct, so behavioral education taught in both the family and school is one of the foundations of the new society. Children are taught repeatedly that any type of anti-social activity is abhored and not tolerated. They are conditioned to respect the approved standards of social conduct.

In addition, they are taught the importance of compassion and consideration for others and not to violate their well-being in order to further one's selfish aims. This does not mean that competitiveness is not encouraged in the class room, on the playfield, and in the market-place so long as it is confined to the rules of fairness. There must exist ambition to study, work hard, excel, and progress, and thus, contribute to society's as well as one's own well-being. Children are taught that power for selfish power's sake is not one of the rewards. It should be detested as the root cause of many wars and much human suffering in the past.

To enable a child to get along with people in everyday situations, other constructive social traits are fostered. They include courtesy, tactfulness, and cooperation as well as integrity, ethnic tolerance, respect for authority and age (experience and education). By the time a child reaches adolescence, these character traits are so ingrained that anti-social motivation from deviant peers or other outside sources is extremely difficult. A nearly irreversible positive bias has been established.

Behavioral education is taught through a mandatory education system which will be explained in detail later. Suffice to say, the standards of conduct now taught and suggestions for improvement are periodically reviewed by a large group of eminent psychologists, social scientists, criminoligists, and other related experts.

(Historical Background)

Because of the devastating decline in morality during the later part of the twentieth century, eighty-five percent of school parents wanted moral values taught in school and seventy percent wanted educators to develop strict standards of right and wrong (1990 Gallup Poll). Yet at the same time, many parents spent only fifteen minutes a week in any meaningful dialogue with their children (a Baltimore public school survey). The children instead obtained values from television and their peers.

Societies need common values or "Tribalism takes over," said Gary Edwards, then president of the Ethics Resource Center in Washington, D.C. Thomas Lickoma, an education professor at State University of New York said, "We know kids have very little sense of right or wrong. Schools must step into the breach."[4]

But polls also showed that most teachers objected to teaching morality. They were afraid of stirring up classroom controversy, creating family discord by lifting moral standards of students above those of their parents, of taking time away from the teaching of other important subjects, and on general philosophical grounds. Such arguments were termed invalid by others who argued that civilized conduct would never be instilled unless taught. It could not be left to the mere discretion of just anyone. Children could not be allowed the prerogative of choosing their own standards; the result would be anarchy. Of course, it eventually was.[5] During the free individualism of the 1960s, most teachers were instructed that all values were relative and personal. Values Clarification in schools let children try to figure out and embrace their own values.

(The New Society)

Warfare was the most senseless, masochistic, wantonly destructive and genuinely evil of all activities conceived by intelligent life. The founders of the new society earlier concluded they must finally abolish war and its causes. They firmly believed the only chance for human survival was in the development of a cooperative non-aggressive global society. Neither the motivation nor the means to hurt one another must exist. Nevertheless, the banning of war would not be easy, but it was imperative that it be undertaken.

Probably the greatest contribution to war had been the attempts to dominate others politically. When political intimidation failed, military means was used in order to extend or perpetuate the power. Political control is now banned throughout world government. How this was accomplished will be discussed later in detail in the management of the new governance system.

(Historical Background)

For centuries nationalism and religious fanaticism had brought violence and enormous suffering to mankind usually from wars. Most nationalism embodied an ethnic prejudice wherein the people ascribed to a common language, heritage, culture, history, religion, and homeland. Outsiders were looked upon with suspicion, distrust, and even hatred. Intolerance toward other ethnic groups or religions resulted. Barriors were erected to prevent outsiders from immigrating or bringing in strange ideas or goods. Armaments were increased to protect borders. Finally, if hatred was deep enough, wars of ethnic genocide erupted.

How could such primitive behavior continue to flourish as late as the twenty-first century? The answer was each generation was subject to the cultural prejudices taught them. "Children have ready access to a nation's name, its currency, its slogans, its history, its political life," wrote Robert Coles, psychologist and author of *The Political Life of Children*. A narrow, sometimes militant prejudicial outlook became engrained; a very limited view of the outside world was perceived by each new generation.

Examples were manifold, but even in the late 1990s ethnic and religious bigotry was widespread. It was estimated more than sixteen hundred stateless nations existed in a world of only one hundred eighty sovereign states.

During those barbaric times it was difficult to find a country whose minorities were not discriminated or persecuted simply because race, ethnic origin, cultural or religious beliefs differed from the majority. African tribes living in the same country massacred one another in Ethiopia, Somali, Nigeria and South Africa. It was estimated upwards of five-hundred thousand were slaughtered in Rwanda in 1994; most were of the Watutsi tribe killed by the Hutus.

After the collapse of Communism, Eastern Europe was in chaos. Thousands of Hungarians fled Romanian persecution; Turks in Bulgaria were ostracized; the Yugoslav federation broke apart as the ethnic provinces of Serbia, Slovenia, Croatia, and Bosnia each went their own way attempting to eliminate one another in their respective nations. Nationalists of each directed tirades against one another ravaging the countryside and cities, and slaughtering thousands while engaging in ethnic cleansing.

Jewish cemeteries were desecrated in France and Italy as anti-semitism rose once again; immigrant Arab workers in Western Europe were persecuted; Catholics battled Protestants in Northern Ireland; after years of dissention, Belgium split into two separate territorial communities, one for the Flemings and one for the French-speaking Walloons; discrimination against Koreans in Japan was common.

In the former USSR, Armenians and Azerbaijanis killed one another; Georgians and Chechens fought Russians; national fronts were formed in every other part of the former Soviet Union. Hamas terrorized Jews in Israel; Moslem fanatics fanned out from Algeria, Sudan and Iran; Christians and Moslems and even sects within each group fought to the death in the Lebanese civil wars; Hindus fought Sikhs and Moslems in India; Tamils warred on Sinnalese in Siri Lanka.

Nations in South America tended to view one another with suspicion, sought trade elsewhere, and left their borders as unpenetrable wildernesses. Basques tried to separate from Spain using terrorist and guerrilla tactics.

The Islamic religion, especially the Shite sect, fostered intolerance, intransigence and fanaticism throughout the world. They persecuted non-islamic minorities such as the Kurds, Druse, Copts, Armenians, Jews, and Maronites. Fanaticism and political aggression led to conquest by the sword camouflaged as holy wars.

Throughout the world religious and ethnic discrimination was pandemic. In many places it turned barbaric and went berserk slaughtering thousands of innocent people.

(The New Society)

Cultural nationalism and religious fanaticism were the scourge of humanity, the cultivators of prejudice, and perpetrators of war. They had to be abolished by the new society if a world community was ever to exist in peace and prosperity. At first this seemed an impossible task. For centuries these prejudices had been embedded in people and passed from one generation to another. The evolutionary predisposition to hate others, who are not part of the same family or tribal group, had been inherited over thousands of years and aggravated by cultural environment that promoted this hate between ethnic groups. For centuries people tended to avoid those who possessed strange customs, clothes, or language or whose skin was a different color. They avoided the world outside their own enclave and deemed it hostile. The new World government was determined to eradicate this ethnic and religious prejudice no matter how long it took.

Because of the new behavioral approach to education, prejudices associated with culture are no longer taught or tolerated. Ethnic identity in a particular racial, national, or religious group and the observance of that group's customs, beliefs, and even language is discouraged in favor of a new identity with the global community. Once the world government was organized and several generations had passed, acculturation grew in most areas of the globe. This was accomplished with the aid of several developments that linked the earth's inhabitants more closely together.

Foremost among them was the early advancement of video communications via satelites such as the CNN world-wide network and later the World-Wide Web on the Internet. With instant communications people all over the world know instantly and simultaneously what is occuring in any other part of the world. Revolutionary earth-imaging systems four hundred miles above the earth now relay digital images of unprecidented clarity of items as small as a human figure anywhere in the world. The globe is no longer a group of closed strange societies. Using advanced optical and digital technology, networks transfer newsworthy areas into detailed pictures; home video screens receive high-resolution views of current conditions in vacation areas or interesting geograhical spots. Gradually the earth's inhabitants have become more understanding and tolerant of each other. No longer are they duped by nationalist political dogma as the Communist bloc once was prior to its abandonment of totalitarianism. It is now technically impossible for people to be held hostage to prejudicial propaganda.

Another early important development was the spread of trade by multi-national companies to every part of the globe. Products of high quality became standard and were accepted by consumers everywhere. This helped to abolish prejudicial product-idiosyncracies that previously isolated cultural groups.

The adoption of the new world government eliminated border restrictions for both trade and travel. Borders are permitted only to define regional government entities within the overall world governmental structure much as the individual states were in the earlier United States. In most cases these borders are the same as the old national ones except for changes to incorporate similar ethnic areas.

This was not a contradiction. It was thought, despite the ban on cultural nationalism, consideration for equality for every ethnic group could provide a fair and easy transition in the early beginning to a peaceful new world order. This was accomplished through plebicite to determine the wishes of the majority in each small community. For example, large parts of Moldavia, inhabited by Romanians in Russia, are now included in the regional state of Romania. Whereas portions of Hungarian-occupied western Romania are included in the regional government of Hungary. French-speaking Quebec opted to form its own regional government.

The elimination of border restrictions allows the free movement and association of all peoples and ideas as well as free trade. No longer can politicians and bureaucrats restrict the flow of capital, technological information and labor across borders in order to protect a few special-interest groups. Of course, this was accomplished gradually over many decades to prevent the overnight inundation of unskilled labor to technologically advanced countries. Global companies are decentralized so they can produce wherever they can best serve the customer and not a particular national government. This unrestricted flow and co-mingling of cultural groups helps tremendously to dispel ethnic prejudices.

World-wide consumers benefit from free trade since there are no longer border tariffs or quota restrictions to add to the cost of a product. They are able to choose quality at the lowest price regardless of where the merchandise is produced or grown. The economic importance of this, backed by world economists, is detailed later under a *New Dynamic Economy*.

In addition to a global economy, the world government also adopted a common currency regulated by a central world bank with regional offices. All of these improvements aided in the elimination of nationalistic protectionism.

Finally, the adoption of one language for the conduct of government, science, and business was especially important in destroying linguistic nationalism and avoiding misunderstanding in communication. Other languages are not encouraged or taught in schools. Many gradually died out decades later as they became superfulous. English became the universal language because it was already more widespread than others. As early as the 1980s English had become the language of science. Eugen Seibold, president of the West German Research Society, said, "Both for reputation and for recognition in science, English is the common language." Early in global air traffic control, English had been mandated for communication.

Nevertheless, decades after English became official and was taught universally in all schools, several of the dominant world languages - Spanish, French, and Chinese - were still spoken in many homes. Later most parents began to realize that it hindered the progress of their children in school and the work-place. Reluctantly, they did away with their second language.

Because of the abolishment of local borders that benefited no one, the need for territorial aggrandizement by a country in order to acquire natural resources, access to the sea, or more habitable land is unnecessary. Nor does a need exist for a military to maintain closed borders or protect from hostile neighbors. An educated citizenry wants the best goods and services, whatever their origin, and be able to sell its labor at the best possible wage in the world to improve its standard of living.

The above does not mean that all cultures and customs have been eradicated. Many, along with historical museums, draw tourists who are curious to know of early traditions and customs, but they are now sustained primarily for economic benefit. Nationalistic prejudice has long been forgotten much like the cultural American South in the later twentieth century. During that time southern states and their many customs and traditions still existed and were enjoyed by tourists. But the identification by southerners with the entire United States and its economy, instead of with the original Confederacy, helped to eliminate old hatred and prejudices.

Perhaps the greatest contribution to the abolition of prejudice was the eradication of illiteracy through a standardized mandated global education system, one devoid of teaching regional and ethnic bias.

(Historical Background)

In 1979 promiscious sex by unwed teen-agers in the United States rose dramatically resulting in increased venereal disease as well as unwanted pregnancies. Births to unwed teen-agers increased nearly fifty percent over a decade earlier. [7] A disproportionate amount of time was increasingly devoted to pursuing the opposite sex and less to education.

By 1984 most pregnant students were dropping out of school and never returned. Nearly all kept their babies. Because of illiteracy, their ability to qualify for work was impaired. If they married, it seldom lasted, and the fathers evaded child support. Welfare was usually the only avenue left. [8] Sixty percent of mothers receiving welfare (Aid to Families With Dependent Children) were teen-agers according to the Urban Institute. [9] In many cases immature teen-agers, unable to cope with parenthood, resorted to child abuse. The financial cost to the rest of society was enormous.

Teen-age motherhood restricted social and economic advancement for the largely Black and Hispanic population of poor neighborhoods, so poverty escalated. Generations of unwed women lost opportunities for education and jobs because they became pregnant as teen-agers and did not receive financial support from the men who fathered their children. Unlike generations before, most of these men didn't even acknowledge a moral responsibility to help raise their offspring.

A typical situation was an Afro-American mother from Harlem named Juanita. Pregnant at age sixteen, at twenty-two she had five children. She began collecting welfare at an early age. All three of her unwed teen-age daughters had babies before they were eighteen. Many times a mother on welfare resulted in the system being perpetuated by offspring.[10]

(The New Society)

In order to ensure the existence of future generations, males have been endowed, after thousands of years, with a biological agenda to impregnate as many women as possible. The new society realized the sexual drive is one of the strongest physiological needs that motivates humans as well as other animal life. Unless it was controlled in its youth, abuses would continue to grow and retard social progress. The conscious control of sex helped distinguish humans from other animals. After careful consideration the founders arrived at several means to accomplish this.

Sex education is taught early in the home and school to children before puberty. It is also explained that sex is not acceptable until potential parents obligate themselves to accept financial responsibility and are educated in the care of potential offspring.

Upon reaching age ten, prior to puberty, close contact with the opposite sex is reduced through sexual segregation in boarding schools much like the early English system. This helps remove sexual distraction while promoting greater concentration on school activities.

The driving machine is no longer considered a convenience for sex or a toy for the amusement of adolescents where time, resources, and life is wasted. The new society felt certain rewards should come with emotional and intellectual maturity that should not be automatically bestowed on youth simply because of their physical maturity. However, this restriction is generally academic because a driving vehicle is only used in rural areas. Individual vehicles are not used in large towns and metropolitan areas because of the completely revised transportation system.

Should an unmarried teen-age girl become pregnant, she is not allowed the luxury of bearing the child for her own plaything expecting society to pay the cost of medical services and child-rearing. Instead she is required to allow her parents to accept the responsibility for raising the child or have it adopted by another childless couple and then proceed with her education. This serves three purposes. It prevents the distinct probability of a dysfunctional family environment for the child and the subsequent cost to society. It avoids the cost to society of the birth and rearing that the child's parent or parents are unable to bear. It allows the teen-age girl to finish her education and become a productive member of society. More importantly, it supports the decision to curtail the population explosion especially from unwanted babies. This will be discussed later under improving the quality of life within the world's ecological system.

(Historical Background)

Restricting adolescents from driving was not completely new. West Virginia enacted a law in 1988 that revoked the driver's license of students who dropped out of school. They were not eligible to drive again until reaching age eighteen or returning to school. It resulted in the drop-out rate being reduced by one-third. Therese M. Wilson, the state official overseeing the enforcement, remarked, "Nobody has achieved what we have achieved, and it's all because of this law ... we expect our graduation rate to climb steadily from here on out. Ultimately, that means we're going to have a better educated work force with less reliance on welfare programs." [11]

In 1987 a meeting of social scientists concluded that if sexual aggression was portrayed as pleasurable for the victim, it increased acceptance of coercion in sexual relations. Therefore, exposure to violent pornography increased primitive behavior toward women.[12]

In another study by psychologists from the University of California and of Wisconsin, one-hundred and fifty-six male college students were divided into three groups. One was exposed to violent X-rated films, another exposed to non-violent X-rated films, and a third was a control group. It was found that only the first group, exposed to "slasher" films, was eventually desensitized to sexual violence against women. On the other hand, even X-rated films, that were none violent, had no apparent desensitizing effect.[13]

In a 1989 interview just before his execution Ted Bundy, the infamous serial-killer of women, was quoted as saying, " ... I want to emphasize that the most damaging kinds of pornography, and again I'm talking from personal experience ... are those that involve violence and sexual violence. Because the wedding of those two forces is, as I know only too well, brings out the hatred that is just, just too terrible to describe. And it happened in stages, gradually. ... with pornography, that deals on a violent level with sexuality, is, once you become addicted to it - I would keep looking for more potent, more explicit, more graphic kinds of material ... something which, gives you a greater sense of excitement. Until you reach a point ... where you begin to wonder if maybe actually doing it would give you that which is beyond reading it or looking at it.

" ... I have lived in prison for a long time now, and I've met a lot of men who were motivated to violence just like me. And without exception, every one of them was deeply involved in violent pornography."

Interviewer : "The 'slasher' movies is what you're talking about..."

Bundy : "That stuff is, I'm telling you from personal experience, is the most graphic violence on screen, particularly as it gets into the home of children who are unattended or unaware that they may be a Ted Bundy who has that vulnerability, that predisposition to be influenced by that kind of behavior ... "[14]

(The New Society)

Of course, pornographic material brutalizing women as well as glorifying incest and pedophilia is banned in the new society. It is also illegal to make any pornographic material available to juveniles. The later reduces stimuli of the sexual drive in adolescent males. As a result and because of behavioral education, sexual crime has been considerably reduced.

It is also felt that repressing the sexual drive in young unmarried men creates a need for an outlet that does not result in venereal disease, unwanted pregnancy, or worse, in rape. The new society experimented with government-regulated brothels, but their advisability is still being ascertained and are discussed in greater detail in a later chapter.

(Historical Background)

In the late twentieth century, the American media operated under a banner of "anything goes." As a result juveniles were inundated with savage and heinous violence including sexual violence. As early as 1975 a film called *Mandingo* appeared. Roger Ebert, the Pulitzer prize-winning movie critic and a civil libertarian, called it "wretched trash ... obscene ... nauseating ... and excrutiating to sit through in an audience made up largely of children." Following this Bob Greene, a reporter for the *Chicago-Sun Times,* took a survey of children (ranging from second to seventh grade) who had seen the movie. These are excerpts from their response:

"Rosa M. : 'I saw Mandingo ... bit the guy on the chest and a whole lot of blood came out of him. I think you can learn lots of things from movies, ...''

"Tyeta J. : 'My favorite part of a movie is when someone gets killed or torn to bits. The only thing I like in a movie is the bloody parts. I like very gory, gory movies."

"Kim W. (a second grader) : "I like the movie because it was bloody and nasty. He took him in the boiling hot water and stabbed him with a rake, ... he told her to take her clothes off."

"Floyd M. : " ... they wanted to have fun with the girl. ... led her over to the bed and took her clothes off and started beating her with a strap ... It was very bloody and horny."[15]

In the 1990 movie *Wild at Heart* director David Lynch, for no apparent purpose than to shock the audience, depicted a closeup of flies slogging through a puddle of vomit and a scene of a man's head blown off with the brains spilling onto the pavement.

Some of the popular television shows became uncouth and anti-family. In them dad was either a slob or an oaf that burped out loud at the dinner table. He picks his toes and spends his happiest times on the toilet seat. Children were bratty, disrespectful, and one took photos of his mother shaving under her arms. Women in the household were slothful and never did any housework.[16]

Such debasement and ill-manners became common in the 1990s not only on video and in the movies but in pop music and entertainment catering to American youth. Later it became worse dragging whatever remained of civilized refinement into the gutter.

By 1993 it was estimated that daily television watching averaged fifty hours a week for the typical American viewer; the average eighteen year-old would have seen over fifteen thousand murders on television and in movie theatres. A 1991 survey indicated over half believed television had a greater influence on children's values than parents or schools. Additionally, many young children watched the same programs adults watched so the concept of childhood gradually vanished.

TV Guide in 1992 reported, "The overwhelming weight of scientific opinion now holds that televised violence is indeed responsible for a percentage of the real violence in our society. What is new is that psychologists, child experts, and the medical community are just now beginning to treat televised violence as a serious public health issue ..." Some of the early studies supporting this were the National Commission on the Causes and Prevention of Violence (1968), the Surgeon General's Report (1972), the National Institute of Mental Health (1982), and the U.S. Attorney General's Task Force on Family Violence (1984).[17]

The American Psychological Association said, "Since 1955 about one-thousand studies, reports, and commentaries concerning the impact of television violence have been published ... The accumulated research clearly demonstrates a correlation between viewing violence and aggressive behavior ..."[18] The National Institute of Mental Health stated, "Violence on television does lead to aggressive behavior by children and teen agers who watch the programs ... "[19]

(The New Society)

Should selective censorship be employed to prevent the glorifying of anti-social behavior and the thwarting of early behavioral education? "Of course," replied the founders of the new society, "Presenting anti-social entertainment to children, indirectly and ultimately affects the well-being of a civilized social structure."

Censorhip was common when the world was being socialized in the twentieth century under totalitarian governments. Nevertheless, it was met with considerable argument in the new society. The case for limited censorship reverted to the principle that freedom of conduct should not entail behavior that does harm, even indirectly, to others. Activities that subvert the moral development of a civilized society should not be condoned. Those opposed complained that it would stifle freedom of expression; but those in favor pointed out even the First Amendment of the earlier United States Constitution did not necessarily protect all forms of free speech. Instead they showed it was originally intended to prevent congressional acts from interfering with the expression of ideas intended primarily for political, social, and economic change or redressment. It said nothing about the protection of speech which threatened to be destructive to the well-being of the nation. As a matter of fact, the purpose of most earlier laws was to prevent harmful conduct to other citizens or the general society. These laws, initiated by the voters, always restricted individual freedom because individual freedom observed to its ultimate would be anarchy.

Founders of the new society insisted law was a contract among all people to maintain a civilized community. The founders noted censorship had been practiced in all human societies because they agreed on certain norms of behavior. A typical example was the Indonesian Board of Censors that screened movie and other media material for certain standards in the 1990s. No evidence of successful anarchistic societies existed where everyone had the license to do whatever they liked.

On this basis explicit descriptions or scenes of horrible violence is banned in all media in the new society. In addition to the steps earlier noted to help repress the sexual drive in juveniles, scenes or passages of vivid, sexual intimacy are also curtailed in the general media although it probably would have little effect on mature adults. This does not mean that artists cannot intimate violence or carnal love and leave explicit details to the imagination of the viewers as once was done with censorship in earlier times (Hay's Office of the United States).

Planners of the new society argued that in video entertainment it was not necessary to shock children while boring mature adults. Instead they felt well-directed scenes portraying great romantic love stories were far more emotional and fulfilling to audiences than routine bed-room scenes depicted by directors in almost all movies of the late twentieth century. Nor was it necessary to use scenes of explicit brutality and gore to compensate for lack of creative genius. The founders also felt the repetitive use of four letter words in order to receive an "R" rating to entice juveniles was disgusting. Artists in the new society are encouraged to entertain and hold their audiences with artistic excellence in directing, acting, script, music, and photography rather than crudely attempting to shock the audience's sensibilities.

(Historical Background)

It was noted that late in the twentieth century in America, the majority of citizens failed to recognize the cause of most of their social problems. It was not school drop-outs, poverty, teen-age pregnancy, drugs or crime. These were merely the symptoms of the underlying illness. The cause was an absence of guidance and motivation from parents; good parenting was no longer the highest priority of many people. As a result children were being raised lacking a sense of social responsibility and an indifference to anti-social behavior.

Some parents were "flower children" of the permissive sixties and lacked education and job-skills or basic decision-making ability themselves. Others were victims of substance abuse or domestic violence so they had extreme difficulty guiding their children to better lives. Because of these deficiencies many were also unemployed but continuing to beget more children while living on welfare. Some were even homeless living in cars or shelters.

Subsidized by welfare, unwed teen-age mothers gave birth to babies that grew into young men and women who had neither a normal family structure nor productive working fathers to serve as role models. In turn, their own children had little chance to complete an education or receive guidance in social behavior. Instead they turned to the street for moral guidance creating a plague of sociopaths.

The bipartisan National Commission on America's Urban Families reported in 1993, "The family trend of our time is the deinstitutionalization of marriage and the steady disintegration of the mother-father child-raising unit." It noted that unless the family was resurrected, there could not be a solution to the problems of education, crime, or poverty.

A study in 1995 by the Council on Families in America blamed the breakdown of the marriage institution - especially on increasing rates of divorce - for much teen pregnancy, child poverty, and other social dysfunctions. It said, "We as a society are simply failing to teach the next generation about the meaning, purposes, and responsibilities of marriage. If this trend continues, it will consitute nothing less than an act of cultural suicide."

Criminologists Travis Hirschi and Michuel Gottfredson believed that a child's failure to learn self-restraint during early family discourse was responsible for much anti-social behavior later in life. They said more emphasis should be placed on child-rearing and the teaching of self-control rather than on justifications for yielding to impulses; a child must be taught that a civilized adult is responsible for his actions.

"Compulsive behavior and addictions are the bubonic plague of our generation, and I'd be willing to make the thesis that every one of them is rooted in a family that was dysfunctional," said John Bradshaw, Houston-based counselor and author of *Bradshaw On the Family*. He believed, since children idolize their parents regardless of the degree of abuse they experience, they are generally unable to separate themselves from their parents' behavior. If the family's way of dealing with emotions was unhealthy, the child may have incorporated the same behavior to such a degree that the unhealthy behavior was accepted as normal and then perpetuated.[20]

The extent that children became unmanageable, annoyances, and threats to their neighbors was revealed by a marketing-research firm in a suburb of Seattle. It took a survey of over a thousand apartment dwellers in the area. One of the questions was, "If you had a free choice, which of the following groups would you least like to live next door to?" It was frightening to note that children led the list in over half the replies (homosexuals and Afro-Americans were next but were only a small fraction of the first choice).[21]

Typical was the court file and evaluation of a twenty-one year old criminal. His parents fought until he was nine years old; then they divorced. His new step-father stripped and beat him with sticks, boards, and belt-buckles. As he grew older the whippings turned to punchings. When he was eleven, his step-father shaved his head. At twelve he saw his step-father severely beat his mother several times. He began running away from home with increasing frequency and staying away for longer periods. This was followed by truancy, fights, more runaways, and petty thefts. He continued to be punished for running away and not wanting to live in an unfit family.

At fifteen he was sent to a state youth camp as an incorrigible. There he was beaten by the staff and older boys and soon learned to use drugs. At eighteen he was sent to a reformatory for burglary where his drug abuse continued. He checked into isolation to avoid harm from his dope creditors. At twenty he was transferred to a federal prison where he was used as a servant by other convicts; his prison life became a nightmare. When he was paroled, he began drinking heavily and using amphetamines. At twenty-one he was sentenced again for burglary and the cycle continued. [22] And so, a young boy, raised in a dysfunctional family, became an incorrigible misfit and a permanent cost to the rest of society.

Margaret Ronstadt, a Tucson psychologist, said in 1995, "A lot of little girls are in gangs - at age eleven they're in gangs. They'll come in and talk blithely about beating up another girl for initiation. A lot of them have tattoos. They talk pretty freely about stealing, drugs, sex."

Pam Schmidt, a Tucson high school counselor, said, "I've really seen an increase in girls who are actively working on getting pregnant, I've had some tell me they'll kill themselves if they're not pregnant by graduation. There's absolutely no shame." Schmidt continued, "We've bent over backward so much so that people don't feel bad about being pregnant. We've created a monster. We let them be irresponsible too much. We need to hold them accountable." [23]

***

The educational process in schools had deteriorated ominously in the United States during the late twentieth century. Students were not required to study or learn, there was little discipline, and rules or respect for authority were ignored. A high-school diploma no longer guaranteed basic literacy. Seattle School Superintendent, David Moberly, said, "Schools all over the country have been letting students pass on through the grades without having learned their skills."

As a result, a former student sued the Seattle School District for educational malpractice. He claimed he was unemployable because he couldn't read a job application nor take the written examination for a driver's license even though he received both a certificate and diploma from a Seattle high school. Even the Army and Navy turned him down. He had to quit a janitorial job because he couldn't read the labels on the chemical containers. His attorney described his reading ability as "third-grade level." He was unable to maintain adequate comprehension beyond the fifth grade level although his grades did not reflect that deficiency. [24]

Michael Konecky, an eigth-grade teacher in the Tucson Unified School District in 1996, was appalled at the policy of "no retention" and automatic promotion from grade to grade. He remarked, " ... every year we watch students with grades of 'F ' in four and five classes being passed on from grade to grade. TUSD's fifty percent plus high school dropout rate does not indicate promoting kids lacking the skills to succeed is of any value. Students know that they do not need to pass to be promoted, and so they have no incentive to work.

Even some college diplomas meant little in the late sixties and seventies. By 1994 most colleges passed everyone and gave As and Bs to eighty percent of students. At Rutgers only forty percent of the students received As and Bs in the early 1950s. By the 1990s two-thirds received them. At the same time three-quarters were receiving As and Bs at Harvard and ninety percent at Stanford.

"Declining test scores throughout the country, increasing problems of crime, violence and disorder at urban schools; opposition on the part of the overwhelming majority of both blacks and whites to cumpulsory busing; restiveness on the part of many college and university teachers and administrators under the heavy hand of Health Education and Welfare bureaucrats - all this is producing a backlash against the trend toward centralization, bureaucratization, and socialization of schooling," explained Nobel Prize winner Milton Friedman in his book, *Free to Choose*.

Shortly after, the National Commission on Excellence in Education delivered a report titled *A Nation at Risk* describing the many examples of a deteriorating educational system. It estimated twenty-three million American adults were functionally illiterate when measured by basic tests of everyday reading, writing, and comprehension.

The National Adult Literacy Survey, commissioned by the Education Department in 1983 found that fifty million adults could not calculate the cost of a purchase, determine the difference in price between two items, locate a street intersection on a map, or fill out information on a simple form. By 1990 between thirty and forty million Americans could not make sense out of a printed page compared to only three million in 1950! Three-fifths of eleventh graders could not read well enough to do homework. As homework suffered, students fell even farther behind.

The American Management Association reported one-fourth of all job applicants lacked reading or math skills needed for available jobs, and one in nine flunked drug tests so they were rejected. Nevertheless, at the same time, populists were blaming malfunctions in the economy or insufficient governmental help for the permanently unemployed.

Many condemned the growing gap in pay between minimal jobs and higher-paying positions. Few were aware of the reason: an excess of workers without sufficient education or training to obtain better positions and a shortage of educated workers to fill higher-paying positions. The Information Revolution was replacing unskilled workers by the thousands in areas where computers could do the work faster and less expensive than routine manual labor.

In the early 1980s the typical job at a steel mill was routine requiring a minimal education. By the late 1990s a highly-trained and educated employee worked in an elevated, windowed cockpit crammed with television monitors, computer screens, digital displays, and flashing instrument-lights. There was no job opening there for the uneducated and untrained.

Referring to the effects of education on African economies but applicable to any country, Katherine Marshall, a World Bank Africa specialist said, "No country has been successful economically with less than fifty percent literacy." Many businessmen felt if literacy continued to drop in the United States, the ability to compete against such areas as Japan, Europe, and the "tiger nations" would diminish.

Dr. Harold W. Stevenson, a University of Michigan psychologist, after completing a four year study during that period, found that Taiwanese students from Taipei consistently scored higher on reading exams than a group of Minneapolis students. These same Tawainese and Japanese students from Sendai, Japan proved overwhelmingly superior in mathematics than the American students. Dr. Stevenson found that Taipei first-graders were assigned seventy-seven minutes of homework per day compared to fourteen for Minneapolis first-graders. Dr. Stevenson said, "(Oriental parents) ... over and over again emphasize the importance of hard work in hard subjects as the necessary ingredients of success. America's instead, overemphasize school budgets, classroom size, and building modernization." [25]

It was evident that most students graduated from public schools in the United States with less literate qualifications than students in most other countries except those in the most undeveloped third-world.

The Carnegie Foundation for the Advancement of Teaching in a 1988 report said, "In almost every big city, dropout rates are high, morale is low, facilities are often old and unattractive and school leadership is crippled by a web of regulations." [26]

In schools across the United States, educators reported profanity among the very young had become rampant; that vulgarities, once heard in army barracks, were common in classrooms as early as kindergarten. Some school officials believed it signified disrespect for authority, a growing tolerance for public rudeness, and a lack of moral development. They blamed television and movies that exposed children to a steady stream of crude four-letter profanity and said the problem could only be addressed with parental help.[27]

In the 1990s many schools, once islands of safety within an otherwise more-violent adult world, became battlegrounds where discipline no longer ruled. The National Safety Center at Pepperdine University reported three million crimes a year on school grounds in 1987. Another study estimated that on a typical day one-hundred thousand pupils carried guns to school. Most city schools had locked doors. Some used metal detectors and allowed entry only with computerized ID cards. New York City schools operated the eleventh largest security force in the United States. [28]

What were the causes for the decline in literacy? Many explanations and solutions were voiced. For example, many thought additional funds for education and a reduction of class sizes would be the answer. Yet a team of researchers from the Hudson Institute compared the results of identical achievement tests over various periods of time. They showed a consistent decline in all communication studies despite a drop in teacher-student ratios and a near doubling of expenditures per student in constant dollars. Test results were found to decline in all districts, although not as great as in the inner-city.[29]

Total real expenditures per pupil in American schools, after allowing for inflation, rose five-hundred percent from 1930 to 1987. In the 1980s it grew about thirty-one percent after inflation. Expenditures per student in Japan were eighteen hundred dollars compared to thirty-three hundred in the United States reported the U.S. Department of Education in 1985. Yet, Japanese youth far exceeded their American counterparts in literacy.

Eric Haneshek, of the University of Rochester, in sixty-five studies on the effect of educational spending on scholastic achievement, found that there was little relationship between the two. In most cases, what teachers do and whether the student is motivated to learn determines the degree of scholastic achievement. [30] Although American schools had sufficient funds to do the job compared to the rest of the world, many began to wonder why illiteracy was increasing. Still, when educational achievement fell in a school district, the usual solution was to throw more money at the problem; nevertheless, student performance continued to decline.

The National Assessment of Educational Progress earlier blamed the nearly one-half illiteracy in seventeen-year old Afro-Americans on the calamitous failure of the education system to instruct inner-city youngsters.[31]

An example of the thinking by some educators at the time was the Pasadena Alternative School, an experimental public school in Pasadena, California. Students were given a maximum of freedom and a minimum of supervision. Some course options were leatherwork, gourmet cooking, weaving, and "hip lit". There were no tests or grades to measure progress. Creativity was stressed over learning; discipline was kept to an absolute minimum. [32]

Rather than adding more to the curriculum, a better job at teaching core competencies, in order for students to succeed in the job market, was recommended by the National Academy of Sciences in a study in 1984. Such competencies would include "the ability to read, write, reason, and compute; an understanding of American social and economic life; a knowledge of the basic principles of the physical and biological sciences, and experience with cooperation and conflict-resolution in groups." It found "command of the English language" to be the "most basic skill of all" and "essential for success and mobility in American society." [33] Nevertheless, bilingual teaching was still mandated for Hispanic students. Many times it was in direct conflict with parents' desire for their children to overcome the disadvantage of being unable to communicate competently in the work-place.

Some teachers blamed the way they were taught in college. They claimed that education courses were stressed instead of the subjects that would be taught. Many said education courses were stifling and totally without content and should be subordinated to the solid majors in math, sciences, economics, and English.

Rita Kramer, author of *Ed School Follies : the Miseducation of American Teachers*, spent a year visiting educational schools. She found that instead of teaching prospective teachers the importance of achievement or stressing mastery of subject matter in their classrooms, most professors emphasized that competition was distasteful, standards were elitist, and the content of the curriculum was irrelevant. She wrote that one professor told his class of future teachers, "More important than content or thinking is the student's feeling. You are not there to feed them information but to be sensitive to their need for ... self-esteem."

Theodore R. Sizer, formerly Dean of Harvard University's Graduate School of Education and an example of this type of thinking, founded the Coalition of Essential Schools in 1984. His methods, used in over eight-hundred schools, stressed teachers as generalists rather than experts in any one particular discipline. He also emphasized making students feel good about themselves rather than holding them accountable for poor grades; he disdained standardized testing. [34]

Disappointed with the trend away from teaching knowledge, New Jersey launched alternative teaching certificates in 1988. It opened up the field to many talented people in specific fields, with no formal training in education.

Some critics even blamed the textbook publishers. They complained books contained something for every pressure group, a blandness, and a kind of built-in "fairness doctrine" calculated not to offend anyone. Many accused some textbooks of intentionally distorting parts of history or omitting them in order to placate certain groups.

Other critics accused school administrators of not supporting teachers who demanded ordinary disciplinary standards for students. Some said that the relaxation of academic standards in predominate black schools weakened those students' ability to learn "middle class" skills and values necessary to achieve upward economic and social mobility. In addition, they believed innovations such as ethnic studies, Black English, and "relevant" courses added to this inability. These studies also unintentionally fostered ethnic segregation and, therefore, prejudices.

Some critics were even resigned to the idea that cultural illiteracy prevailing in backward ethnic families precluded the effective education of those children in school. They believed, therefore, that it was difficult to argue on behalf of any given curriculum or educational policy to solve the problem.

Dr. E.D. Hirsch, Jr., professor of English at the University of Virginia, wrote in his book, *Cultural Literacy,* " ... the role assigned to our schools is to prepare our children for the broader activities of society and to train them in the literate public culture. Our schools have played this role less well than they should, chiefly because they have followed faulty educational ideas." [35]

He continued, "Supplying ... knowledge to children early is of tremendous importance for enhancing their motivation and intellectual self-confidence, not to mention their subsequent ability to learn new materials. Yet, schools will never systematically impart missing background information as long as they continue to accept the formalistic principle that specific information is irrelevant to language arts skills."

"Every text ... implies information that it takes for granted and doesn't explain. Knowing such information is the decisive skill of reading."[36] In other words, Dr. Hirsch was implying information or working knowledge of certain facts and ideas is absolutely necessary if one is to read and comprehend intelligently. This knowledge or cultural literacy should be garnered at an early age to be effective.

On the other hand, some educators like Rousseau believed the "natural" development of children should be encouraged and adult ideas not taught before they can understand them. John Dewey also believed that adult culture was "unnatural" to young children. Still, centuries before, Socrates said in *The Republic*, "Shall we carelessly allow children to hear any casual tales which may be devised by casual persons, and to receive into their minds ideas for the most part the very opposite of those which we shall wish them to have when they are grown up?" [37]

Statistically it was shown that private schools based on religion, profit, or some other incentive produced a higher level of achievement in students regardless of socio-economic background than did public schools. They attributed this to the stressing of basic academic courses over non-traditional ones and to devoting more time to the task. Indeed, Keith Geiger, the teachers' union president of the National Education Association, on "This Week With David Brinkley" (August 30, 1993) acknowledged nearly half of urban-area public school teachers sent their own children to private schools; yet, they decried any suggestion for those private schools to compete with their jobs. Evidently the teachers knew something the other parents didn't.

In 1988 a California business roundtable called for year-around classes, freer choice of schools, a management role for parents, less district authority, and optional use of private contractors as teachers. Many businessmen argued that there was too much bureaucracy in a centralized and rigid educational structure. They believed it had developed into a massive government-run socialized structure without incentives or the discipline of competition as in more efficient market-oriented services.

Historically, early learning originated in the family. The results depended on several factors : the quality, the attention given, the rewards bestowed for learning, the intensity, and when teaching was started. By the turn of the twenty-first century, these factors had deteriorated in most families to such an extent that the results were disastrous. Contributing to the deterioration were the rising numbers of working mothers, divorces, fatherless families, and teen-age mothers. There was less time for mothers to teach appropriate behavior or motivation, and many families were short on discipline because the strong father-image was lacking. Most teen-age mothers were too immature to teach their offspring. Permissiveness, peer pressure, and time-consuming video took up the void.

Judge Nanette Warner, of the Pima County Juvenile Court system of Tucson, Arizona, in an interview with a local newspaper remarked, "Nobody is preventing crime out there. We're only responding. Some of these kids have never been disciplined and to think that you're going to start disciplining them at age 13 is crazy."

Judge Warner suggested, "We need to teach parenting skills. It's amazing to me that you have to have a license to drive your car, but you don't have to show any level of proficiency to raise children. I'm not saying that we should legislate who can and can't have children, but at some level we need to require or provide adequate training." [38]

In a survey of eighth-graders by the U.S. Department of Education, almost half said they rarely discussed school with their parents. One researcher indicated that when parents failed to stress the importance of education, students tended to do little to succeed in the classroom. The survey reported that students spent an average of twenty-one hours a week watching television (closer to 50 by 1994) but only five hours doing homework. The amount of TV watched by students was rarely or never limited by two-thirds of parents surveyed.

It was estimated the average child would have watched five thousand hours of television by the time he entered first grade (1990). At the end of high school, more time was spent watching television (19,000 hours) than in class. Most teachers and psychologists blamed television for most of the decline in reading skills and general school performance. Jerome Singer, Yale psychologist, found children who were constantly watching television were not only less informed and poorer students but were restless as well probably with shorter attention spans. [39]

Lack of parental motivation resulted in increased school dropouts, so the state of Wisconsin launched a unique program that cut a family's welfare benefits when the family's teen-ager skipped school. This type of intervention indicated the awful deterioration that had occured in parental motivation; society became desperate.

Seventy percent of the students in one high school admitted they had attended classes while high on alcohol or illegal drugs in a survey conducted by the Arizona Criminal Justice Commission in 1989. One senior remarked, "There's nothing to do, and when kids get bored, they experiment ... some kids do it because they think it's cool." The superintendent of the school said, " ... in a sense we mirror the community. We are the sum total of what adults are out there." [40] It was as if he said, "If the parents don't care, why should the students?"

Time after time teachers and principals reported that they did not receive cooperation from parents of students who disrupted classes, threatened teachers, carried guns, or used drugs and alcohol in school. The parents instead would either castigate the principal or just ignore him.

Most educators believed the gradual disintegration of families was the greatest single cause of the decline in student achievement during the last thirty years of the twentieth century. They emphasized it was not better teachers, texts, or curriculum that was needed for lasting school reform, but parental reform.

One educator remarked that New York City had one of the highest expenditures per pupil, and the average teacher's salary was among the most generous. Yet, the high-school graduation rate was below the national average. He agreed that raising teachers' salaries to recruit competent and dedicated teachers was necessary but not sufficient to achieve the best educational system possible. He stressed that the difficulty and complexity of raising educational performance was related to teen-age pathological behavior; the primary factor affecting student behavior was family background. Any education system throughout world history reflected the socio-economic fabric of the community. If that fabric unraveled then the educational system would also decline.

(The New Society)
The disastrous decline of social discipline would never again be repeated. This the founders of the new society resolved after reviewing the disintegration in the late twentieth century. Even if some very radical and controversial educational policies had to be adopted, it was imperative to make changes. Education was the key to the quality of life; good education also contributed to economic equality, which many idealists had been striving. It was the basis of a disciplined civilization and had to be mandated.

With this in mind, the founders further believed that the best educational system depended on the total indoctrination of children into the attitudes and behavior necessary to have a civilized society. Of course, total immersion of the young in a learning process had been recognized as the key in molding humans into any type of social structure. This had been true historically in the successful spread of religions and in the adoption of Marxism.

The new society also believed the control of behavioral conduct in the formative years was closely linked to intellectual achievement.

(Historical Background)
Great thinkers, as early as Plato, believed an effective educational system not only benefited civilization but prevented the growth of lawlessness.

Allan Bloom, University of Chicago professor, in his best selling book, *The Closing of the American Mind: How Higher Education Has Failed Democracy and Impoverished the Souls of Today's Students*, said, "Intellectual virtue and moral virtue are related."

The brilliant and successful educator, Dr. Maria Montessori, early recognized this. She said, "The child must be made to do whatever the adult wishes; the adult will then be able to lead him to the heights of goodness, self-sacrifice and strength, and the moral child will be created. To dominate the child, to bring him into subjection, to make him obedient - this is the basis of education. If this can be done by any means whatever, ... all the rest will follow. The child could not be molded by any other means. It is the first and principal step in what is called 'educating the will of the child."[41]

The attempted control of human conduct has always resulted in a reduction of anti-social behavior. For instance, circa 1840 a significant effort was made to reduce the rising crime rate and high rate of alcohol consumption in America (10 gallons per person in 1829). Professor James Wilson noted that "popular literature emphasized the value of thrift, order, industriousness, sobriety, the mastery of passions" and sought to indoctrinate the young with a regard for their "duties and obligations." At the same time early grade-school textbooks, which stressed moral principles and self-discipline and were known as "readers," were also widely adopted by the public schools. Between 1890 and 1910 about one-third of the articles in ladies magazines dealt with character development in child-rearing. Not surprisingly crime abated and remained so until the 1920s. [37] In contrast Redbook, a leading woman's magazine in 1995, featured "How to Have an Easy Orgasm."

Sanford McDonnell, chairman of Character Education Partnership, described an inner-city school in Washington, D.C., Jefferson Junior High School, which had serious social problems with its 800 African-American students. A comprehensive character education program over a five year period resulted in most of these problems, including student pregnancies, vanishing and the shool recognized for the highest academic achievement in the city. It had a waiting list of over 400 students.

The Victorian moral crusade in England imbued all individuals with the conviction that each individual was morally responsible for his behavior. After World War I it became routine to blame society rather than the individual. Blame was probably due in part to the popular Labor Party's belief the capitalist economy and English upper classes were responsible for the individual's plight. Therefore, the individual was not responsible for his actions.

For decades the low crime rate in Japan was associated with the close social bonds in Japanese communities and strong social sanctions against those who strayed from community values. Japanese ostracized offenders and demanded they not only be caught and punished, but that they apologize and show remorse. Japan had only one-eighth as many thefts and burglaries as in the United States. These behavior patterns had been so engrained, it was even evident in the low crime rates of Japanese living abroad.

(The New Society)

The early founders of the new society were cold realists. They believed that unless taught early in life to do otherwise, most people resort to the inborn tendency to survive through aggressive selfishness. They attempt to take from others what they want for themselves and their offspring. The degree of selfishness determines the degree of anti-social behavior. Humans are merely animals taught and disciplined to use their intelligence to be civilized. Once the control is abandoned, they revert to animal instincts and the chaos that once ensued.

The founders, therefore, decided universal education must be the foundation for an advanced society; mankind must develop the educational process to extend its intellectual power in the universe. Without intense education, civilization could not move forward. Dr. Alexis Carrel wrote in his prodigious book, *Man the Unknown* in 1935, "Intellectual power must be augmented by the habit of precise reasoning, the study of logic, the use of mathematical language, mental discipline and complete and deep observation of things." [43]

Before designing the educational system, the founders of the new society established a research institute to conduct a thorough study of all aspects of human behavior and how it could be molded into the new education program. Only the foremost scientists in their respective fields work at the institute. Later the studies became a continuing process. They encompass physiology and biochemistry as well as sociology and psychology.

If it is determined that some behavior modification would be advantageous following a thorough scientific investigation, the proposal is aired at a meeting of the Committee on Behavioral education. Here they weigh its practicality, its economic and environmental effect, but especially its effect on the freedom of the individual versus its social benefits before it is adopted. Although disciplined order is necessary for the growth of the new civilized society, it cannot suppress basic individual freedoms harmless to the rest of the community.

(Historical Background)

Guy Odom addressed the importance of early character development when he said, "The period beginning with birth and extending through age five has the most sensitive and profound influence of any period on a child's behavior in adulthood. Through age five, attitudes, needs, fears, and behavior that govern the child's later life are instilled in him by the person directly responsible for his day-to-day nurture and rearing, usually the mother. She instructs, praises, rewards and punishes. It is she who demands responses and actions. These are the years that most influence one's achievements as an adult. ... child rearing practices are the root of adult successes or failures and a successful future role or an unsuccessful one ... is established specifically by mothers."

Notables of the past agreed. "The future destiny of the child is always the work of the mother," said Napoleon Bonaparte. Ralph Waldo Emerson noted, "Men are what their mothers made them."

Mr. Odom also stressed the importance of the mother's role in instilling early obedience in her offspring enabling the child to benefit later in school. "A child, of a demanding and encouraging mother, perceives the teacher in the mother's role and responds to instructions as he would at home." Other children benefit less or are indifferent to instruction.

Mr. Odom emphasized that discipline was as essential as love and security when molding a young child, "Discipline is not a euphemism for punishment. A disciplined environment is one in which a disciplined mother exercises her will to limit and restrict unrestrained behavior by the child and guide it in controlled channels. The product of such a mother's organized behavior is an organized, self-controlled adult. An undisciplined mother exhibits little self-control and makes few demands on the child to restrain or regulate uncontrolled behavior. Her permissive child-rearing practices produce an undisciplined adult who has few needs for self-control." Yet he notes that love and understanding of a child's needs are vital in conjunction with discipline to develop an adult with needs to achieve. An equal amount of love and understanding without discipline and motivation for early accomplishments will result in an adult with low motivation to achieve. [44]

Others have stressed the importance of very early education. Many psychologists believed that by the time children reached ten, their personalities were set for life. Therefore, if they could be properly taught before that age, it would prevent most antisocial conduct in later life. "Early childhood, indeed, infant development in the learning processes is ... desirable for all children, regardless of background or ability," wrote Terrel H. Bell, former U.S. Secretary of Education, in his book *Your Child's Intellect; A Guide to Home-Based Preschool Education.*

Barbara B. Baker, president of Challenger Schools of Utah, emphasized that most pre-school programs in the late twentieth century were usually nothing more than day-care programs with a small token of "learning" thrown in. Her school's curriculum, on the other hand, did not underestimate the mental capacity of small children. She taught the rudiments of language to three and four year olds which were fascinated and, therefore, continued to stay excited about reading and learning as they grew older.

Sufficient evidence also indicated intensified teaching at a very early age actually raised the average I.Q. level and increased the speed of emotional and intellectual motivation. The American Medical Association, for example, reported in 1990 that early educational teaching to help develop language and motor skills led to higher I.Q.s and fewer behavioral problems for premature and underweight babies by the time they reached age three.

The brain undergoes enormous rapid development during the first two years of life. Research indicated maximum intellectual growth occured if began during the first three years of life. It also discovered that physical brain development was much greater if there was a very positive environment during those early years. On the other hand, children raised in poor environments displayed cognitive deficits by eighteen months that could be irreversible. Researchers at Baylor College of Medicine found children, who didn't play much or were seldom touched, developed brains 20 to 30 percent smaller than normal.

When children from disadvantaged family environments entered into educational programs by six months of age, the children's incidence of mental retardation dropped eighty percent. This study was according to Craig Ramey, a developmental psychologist at the University of Alabama. He reported that by age three, their I.Q.s were fifteen to twenty points higher than children from the same backgrounds.

The successful Head-Start program in the United States proved that children from backward ethnic groups, who weren't being taught at home, could be taught social skills at a very early age. Other pre-school experimental programs, begun at age four, taught social development as well as basic education. Some private schools, such as Montessori, had children reading, writing, counting, and working simple sums before age six. The consensus was that it significantly altered the child's performance in later life. It put the love of learning into the child at a very early age, and thus, prevented school dropouts later. The ability to succeed in school made employment possible and welfare dependency and crime involvement far less likely.[45]

"In fact, the possibility cannot be excluded that I.Q. heritability is actually zero. What counts is the mother, not the genes," stated Leon Kamin, a psychologist at Princeton who studied I.Q. and the formation of intelligence in his book *The Intelligence Controversy*.[46]

In all studies and research it appeared that the child's intellect developed at the pace at which his mind was stimulated. The earlier it was stimulated, the greater the ability to acquire knowledge and to create the need for more. It was evident that higher intelligence levels were the result of early intensive intellectual motivation.[47]

(The New Society)

Education in the new society is mandatory and begins at infancy. Learning begins whenever there is any apparent permanent change in an infant's behavior which is the result of environmental influences rather than merely physical maturation. Since most studies indicated that intelligence was reasonably stable at age six, early intensive teaching by parents was proposed.

Classes in parenting are required for all couples. A comprehensive manual on desired standards of child conduct is furnished. Mothers are granted an additional three year leave of absence from their employment after the birth of the child for the mother to devote full time to the most important formative years of child training. Periodic calls on the family by a parental guidance expert to ascertain progress and to assist with any problems are also made. These experts have been highly trained in child psychology and pediatrics; they are licensed in the practical aspects of parenting. The cost of such experts to the world community is considerable. Nevertheless, it is deemed absolutely necessary in order to eliminate the vast economic and social waste that resulted from inadequate parenting in the late 20th century. For the same reason it is also important that anyone, unwilling to devote full time to the child during this period, is advised against becoming a parent. It cannot be stressed enough; motherhood is no longer solely an outlet for the ego, a period of adulation and possessive protectionism. Instead, it is a serious all-encompassing endeavor equal to the highest calling in the world.

Of course, child abuse is not tolerated. It was discovered in earlier times that child abuse created a new generation of abusers. If this new generation were unable to abuse their children, they usually resorted to venting their violence against the public and its property such as assaults, vandalisim, and theft.

If the monitors of parenting discover evidence of a dysfunctional family-life, they lose no time in the selection of an alternate environment for the child. Some of the options include adoption, occasionally by grandparents, or placement in institutional homes. These are government regulated and supported boarding schools for children under the age of ten. There they receive an excellent education as well as behavioral instruction. But just as important, they receive regular nourishing meals, decent clothes, hygenic living conditions, and live in a conjenial atmosphere. They are no longer subject to abusive, alcoholic, drug-addicted, or negligent parents. In the long-run, the social and economic savings to society are enormous, and the child is raised to live a normal and happy life.

At age three, the child of a normal family is taken to school for required studies in personality development, social conduct, and more advanced communications (language, writing, reading and arithmetic). The mother is then free to return to her career aided by the school caring for her child while she is at work. Nevertheless, good parenting continues during this early childhood with continued stress on an environment of love, security, and discipline.

School education begun at age three results in many prodigies as well as a running-start in molding personality and behavioral patterns before any adverse environment can affect the child.

In addition to motivating students when very young, the new society endows students with a high valuation of scholastic achievement. As a result, students have come to appreciate that learning takes great effort and requires hard work. Entertainment and leisure time is strictly limited and monitored in order to have maximum time for studies outside of class. Even the very young are not supplied with an excess of games and fun projects in school merely to keep them occupied or entertained. Instead they are impressed with the seriousness of school and devotion to concientious learning. The teaching of social conduct has also created motivation for educational achievement.

(Historical Background)

In the past, teaching guidelines and objectives were fuzzy, nonexistent, or simply not enforced by school administrators anxious to protect "academic freedom" and the jobs of teachers. Educators "covered" courses but never guaranteed that the student had mastered them.

(The New Society)

World-wide learning goals as well as quality controls have been established in the new education system. Teachers help Regional Education Committees prepare standards and goals in general conformance with the rest of the world. Tests are devised to measure how well students are learning. A large part of the tests measure such things as the ability to write, convey thoughts, how to analyze a problem, and estimate its solution. Therefore, teachers no longer "teach to the test". The Regional Committee then monitors each school. Teachers and schools alike are held accountable for students' performances.

Standards of competency in each subject, rather than grade levels, must be achieved by the student in order to progress. This helps insure that the student is not automatically bumped from one grade to the next after merely "covering" a subject but instead has actually learned and developed a reasonable knowledge of it.

No longer is the student left in ignorance of his progress. On the contrary, students need to know early on from their measured progress whether they need to study more diligently. Every incentive possible is used to praise or reward academic progress. Academic achievement is viewed as deserving of equal praise as in sport achievement.

There are no drop-outs and daily attendance is mandatory. Only a very small percentage of students require extra help to reach proficiency. Teachers, whose pupils consistently have trouble, are given help by the school manager or even by other teachers. Those teachers, still unable to maintain the standards either through incompetency, inability to discipline, or laziness, are asked to resign.

A certain amount of constructive academic freedom, within the boundaries of general world standards, is also encouraged. But the standards help eliminate any radical experimentation on youngsters' minds with individual teacher's whims or prejudice as was once the case. However, the World Educational Governing Body and its Institute welcome constructive proposals that are given a detailed and scientific assessment.

The so-called summer vacation has been eliminated so the total time required for education is condensed. Originally adopted when the world was primarily an agrarian society, the "summer-off" was needed by the family to obtain extra help with the production and harvesting of crops. Short periodic vacations are still taken at the convenience of parents; school work is made up on return. This has accomplished the following: costs have been reduced extensively, students are able to enter the work force earlier, and there is more time for a wider curricula. The later two are also augmented by the student entering school at an early age.

(Historical Background)
There were signs in 1990 that competition among schools, through parental choice, was the real answer to the overwhelming problems in the American education system. A think tank of the Brookings Institution released a report recommending the abolishment of any distinction between public and private schools and giving parents the choice of schools for their children. Political scientists, John Chubb of Brookings and Terry Moe of Stanford University, proposed "a new system of public education that eliminated most bureaucratic and political control over the schools and relied, instead, on direct control through markets and parental choice." [48]

Many contended that the school system was being run by entrenched bureaucratic elements: teachers' unions, state education departments, school boards and administrators, and colleges of education. They were accused of perpetuating themselves and growing larger through more control and more financial support from politicians in exchange for strong political support. Most unions contributed generously to the re-election campaigns of legislators who supported the special interests of teachers. In return lawmakers imposed such things as minimum salaries and maximum teaching-load restrictions. They also hindered boards of education from firing incompetents, restricted the use of pay for merit, and looked the other way when teachers went out on strike in defiance of state laws which prohibited teacher strikes in public schools.

The result was that expenditures per pupil, after deducting for inflation, had tripled since 1950 until the mid 1980s, and the average number of students per class had dropped from thirty in 1940 to eighteen in 1986. Yet the drop-out rate rose to thirty percent, average test scores dropped, and employers and colleges complained that high-school graduates weren't being properly educated.

Public schools in those years essentially were run as a government-controlled monopoly, and like any centrally-controlled economic entity, the bureaucrats had little incentive to demand efficiency since there was no competition and the government (taxpayers) was footing the bill. The consumers (parents) of the product (education) had no choice because most private schools were either unavailable or too expensive, and public schools were prevented from competing with one another for students. The public school bureaucracy reached a point where it was unable to improve itself.

Some critics compared the American public school system to an unresponsive socialist economy. "The public school system is America's collective farm," said Lewis Perelman of the Hudson Institute. "Innovation and productivity are lacking in American education for basically the same reasons they are scarce in Soviet agriculture: absence of competitive market-forces."[49]

A professor from Georgetown University zeroed in on the difference between public and private schools at the time. He complained that his taxes supported a system that spent $4900 on each public school student in his county while the tuition for his daughter at a private Catholic school was only $1800. Yet academically, he insisted she received a superior education by any standard.

(The New Society)

A competitive system among schools has now been adopted by the new society. It requires each school operation to not only maintain global learning goals and standard curricula but forces each school to compete on quality for the least cost just as in any successful business.

Quality is achieved by allowing parents to enroll their children in the school which they deem will give their child the best education possible. If they believe the quality of teaching is deteriorating in that school, they are free to move their child to a new school of their choice at the end of the school year.

Firms running the schools must be cost-competitive, as well, because each school operation is contracted on a competitive-bid basis per student for a designated area by the Regional Education Governing Body. Since most are boarding schools, the school does not have to be in close proximity to the student's home.

Firms, whose schools remain consistently and considerably higher in cost per student than other educational firms, eventually lose out to those who are more efficient. If efficiency drops, then either costs rise or quality deteriorates. In either event the individual school must eventually restructure for better cost effectiveness and or quality. If it doesn't improve, money will be lost, student attendance will decline, or both; eventually the school will go out of business. Quality schools are also less expensive because as enrollment increases, the same fixed overhead costs are distributed over a larger number of students.

The result has been the elimination of waste and bloated administrative staffs and bureaucracies formerly prevalent in "public schools," more efficient teaching methods, the use of the latest technology, more modern and easier-to-maintain facilities, and above all, students graduate with learned skills.

***

School curricula for all age groups is broadly divided into: Behavioral Education, Communications, and Life Orientation. A fourth category of Advanced Studies is taught to the oldest group prior to graduation. The importance of Behavioral Education has already been stressed, while Communication is the foundation of all other education and an absolute necessity for employment and participation in the other activities of society.

Life Orientation is an extensive rather than intensive introduction into the world in which we live. It not only gives the student a taste of the subject that he or she may wish to explore more fully, but it prepares the student for broad communications with a literate society. Life Orientation, therefore, includes such things as economic and environmental geography, an outline of world history, contemporary governance structure, and the arts and sciences. In his book, *Cultural Literacy,* E.D. Hirsch stated, "To be culturally literate is to possess the basic information needed to thrive in the modern world." [50] Yet, by the 1990s only two-thirds of American citizens were culturally literate while the teaching of cultural facts was denigrated in many areas.

Exceptional skill in a restricted field does not equate with cultural literacy unless accompanied by a broader background. Communications with literate people or through reading is otherwise impossible unless one shares the same knowledge. Therefore, textbooks in the new society are prepared so they contain as much literate cultural vocabulary as possible for young children.

The Advance Studies encompass such things as advanced orientation in the arts, elective sciences, elective introductory vocational subjects and final preparation for adult responsibilities.

Physical Development is also included in the curricula. It helps refine coordination and reflexes and builds a competitive spirit and cooperation with teamates. Studies have also shown it is mandatory for a healthy long life-span to hone the body against organic malfunctions and diseases.

(Historical Background)

The teaching of Behavioral Education was not completely new. The task of building character finally began to fall on teachers in 1988 when Baltimore extended the school day by twenty minutes for "Character Education," and California insisted new texts emphasize basic civic and personal values. Later by 1994, these studies had been adopted in several other schools around the country. Many people were beginning to believe the task of building character must fall on teachers because nobody else was doing the job.

Sanford McDonnell, former chairman of McDonnell Douglas Corporation and later chairman of Character Education Partnership, an organization promoting the concept, said, "Kids in schools are getting values transmitted to them one way or another, and unless they are taught about values, they get the message that values aren't really that important - or may decide to model themselves on the negative values they see glorified on television or on the streets." Herbert I. London, dean of New York University's Gallatin Division, said today's children have been left "rudderless in a turbulent world." An official with California's department of education remarked, "A generation of kids never learned about the glue that helps this country hang together." An elementary-school guidance counselor said most mothers are in the work force with limited time for thrashing out moral dilemmas. [51]

Studies at the time indicated schools which adopted some "character education" reported a sharp decline in discipline problems, in vandalism, and an increase in attendance.

(The New Society)
The curricula for early ages up through age nine stresses basic standards of social conduct and early character development. It emphasizes actions that are acceptable in the new society and explains why others are not and why the later has a negative impact on others. To young people this approach makes more sense than merely stating rules or laws or some arbitrary premises. Some subjects of early personal development include responsibility, punctuality, reliability, perseverance, hygiene, and intolerance for filth and disorder. Students are also taught thrift - not to waste such things as food, water, energy as well as monetary funds. Anti-crime and drug education are also begun at a young impressionable age.

Basic Communications for this age group are the usual reading, writing, spelling, grammar, and arithmetic. These are augmented with basic Life Orientation subjects: world geography and history. Finally, Physical Development for this age group consists of games for the very young children. Aerobic exercises, swimming, and unorganized playfield sports: group soccer, softball, and touch football are reserved for the older ones - the beginning of competitive group sports.

Psychologists indicate that the average child appears to be psychologically stable up to age ten. After ten the difficult pre-adolescent period emerges. Puberty occurs shortly after age twelve in most girls and thirteen or fourteen in boys. After puberty the stage of adolescence is one where the youth is struggling to become an individual separate from family and other ties. Therefore, the tendency at that time is to become critical and hostile.

Socially detrimental behavior and later criminal activity, caused by poor earlier child-rearing, is difficult to change during this period of adolescence and only at a cost to the individual and society. Otherwise, adolescence is less of a behavioral problem when good earlier motivation is present.

It was thought age ten was an ideal time to move the child away from parents to a government-supported but competitively-run boarding school in a disciplined environment free of any antisocial behavior. Here the love of learning is nourished under a full-time competent professional staff. As indicated earlier, these boarding schools are segregated by gender. Of course, periodic rendezvous with parents are scheduled on special weekends, holidays, and vacations.

During this age period from ten through seventeen, the curricula is expanded, and Advanced Studies are added the last two years. Behavioral Education is broadened to include sex education at age ten, the basic laws of the new society, and later, business ethics. Character development includes creating a good self-image, striving to better one's self, and the encouragement of goals. Basic nutrition, physiology, and first aid are also taught to the older students. It is noteworthy that the purpose of all of these courses, no matter how mundane they may appear, is to provide the graduating student with the ability to cope with every-day problems in adult life.

Communication studies are advanced during this period to include creative writing and its research, public speaking, the use of high-tech communication equipment such as computers, and finally, effective oral communication. The later had been sorely overlooked in earlier societies although research indicated many problems between people and between groups or nations was a direct result of not clearly understanding one another.

Life Orientation during this educational phase is extended to include world governance, and a brief introduction to the various sciences, fine arts, literature, and philosophy as well as practical crafts (mechanics, woodworking, and art). The World Educational Institute felt it was important that students have, at least, a rudimentary conversational knowledge of each subject and are exposed enough to pique possible further interest. The large number of Life Orientation subjects obviously require each to be condensed, or combined with other subjects.

Organized team sports begin at the boarding schools. Physical development and social interaction require that each student select at least one team sport for participation.

Before embarking on the last two years, the student should have matured scholastically and be ready to move into a more defined field of endeavor because of his wide but brief exposure to Life Orientation subjects. So, Advanced Studies are begun two years prior to graduation. These studies are a limited selection of intensive electives as well as final preparation for adult responsibilities. The student is encouraged to enroll only in those courses they find interesting and challenging. Some of these advanced courses include each of the sciences and fine art as well as introductory courses in the professions such as law, medicine, business management, accounting, engineering, architecture, and agri-business.

For those, who have decided to enter the work force upon graduation rather than go on to a three-year professional school, intensive vocational courses are offered during this two year period in all types of mechanical and white-collar categories. This includes valuable on-the-job training as well.

In addition to the electives above, a course in practical personal management is required during the last year. Included in this course are such adult responsibilities as financial and home management, basic food preparation, and finally and very importantly, an introduction to economics and business. The later is brief but taught in an interesting manner so the student can easily comprehend the practical day-to-day effects the economy and business have on an adult's life. This had been woefully neglected in previous education systems.

(Historical Background)

In those early days the student entered the work-world with little knowledge of how the economy operated. As a result many false assumptions and prejudices rose against business management and "the system." Individuals failed to understand the role of government in spending, taxation, in the creation of inflation, and the effects on the free-market system. As a result, they not only couldn't cope with personal financial management but were unable to vote intelligently on important economic matters in elections.

In a test of fifteen thousand students in 1984, only one-half knew the difference between a socialist and capitalist economy. In 1989 the Joint Council on Economic Education tested over eight thousand students. They found only forty percent could answer a series of multiple-choice questions on economics, and only one-quarter could define profit or inflation. Only one-half of high-school social studies' teachers had taken a course in economics. Most felt it an abstraction, too boring to study. Economic illiteracy was rampant.

A typical result was the so-called housewives' revolt against the price of beef in grocery stores in the late 1960s. A "guns and butter" spending attitude without compensating tax increases was fostered by the federal government during the Vietnam war. This created a gradual increase in inflation in the United States. Price increases in food, especially beef, were obviously more apparent because people bought groceries more often than other merchandise. Ignorant of the real economic causes, housewives blamed the grocerystore for the rise in prices and boycotted their beef. They insisted "those big chain stores" were raising prices solely to add to their profits. The housewives were unaware that supermarkets were not only highly competitive but operated on a slim profit margin of only one to two percent of gross sales, and that grocers were also squeezed by rising prices.

How did the government respond to its own inflation-creating follies? It was not by trying to balance the budget with reduced spending or increased taxes. Instead the government placed price and wage controls on the economy. This only camouflaged the symptoms without attacking the cause, but it temporarily satisfied people like those who had boycotted beef. The real cause, of course, was deficit spending and the creation of more paper money to accomodate the deficit. Thus, more money chased fewer goods creating higher prices. This was obvious to anyone with even a cursory knowledge of economics, but few had that knowledge.

Price and wage controls took the pressure off the politicians to "do something," but soon the misallocations of raw materials and labor, shortages, black markets, and a rising pent-up demand for goods resulting from the increased currency in circulation broke the dam of controls; inflation then surged forth stronger than ever. Only raising interest rates by the Federal Reserve Board finally broke the rising inflation rate in the 1970s which then brought on a recession. The politicians then blamed the recession on the independent Federal Reserve Board!

(The New Society)

The last phase of the two year Advanced Studies for students culminates in a one-week survival course in a wilderness area. Survival training fosters self-reliance, self-confidence, and a sense of teamwork while pitting students against a hostile environment in the wild. The student learns the ability to cooperate with and to trust his colleagues in critical situations. He develops a positive feeling in one's abilitiy to overcome tremendous obstacles in simulated life and death situations. The entrance into the adult world is, therefore, helped considerably by this attitude.

Max Singer noted in his *Passage to a Human World,* "An important force in history that has helped shape people's character was personal experience with nature and adversity. Affluence destroys nature's opportunity to discipline character. One of the greatest tasks, therefore, is to find new bases for helping people develop good character that can best discharge our responsibilities as human beings."

All courses, except electives, are designed and taught to have a practical application in life for all students not just those preparing for a career in a specialized category. Even the brief introductory courses in the sciences and fine arts are not abstract because they are taught in a unique manner to attract the student's curiosity to a strange subject and to explain why and how even a little knowledge of those subjects is as important as language to communicate with others.

Because the last two years of Advanced Studies are of such a specialized mature nature, most of the schools that teach advanced studies are separate from other schools and are similar to the old High School or Junior College.

The entire cost of higher three year professional schools, including room and board, is loaned to the student by the government. It is open to anyone desiring to advance his education in the sciences and professions, and who is able to pass aptitude and entrance tests. The student must sign a contract to repay an annual percentage of his income to the government after graduation until the loan is paid in full. Thus, no monetary discrimination results by subsidizing a free professional education for some while others get nothing simply because they prefer to go directly into the workworld.

Religions are not part of the curricula. Instead we have stressed the teaching of standards of behavior and the scientific and psychological control over our lives in a mutually cooperative and compassionate environment. Of course, violent religious fanaticism, a source of much anti-social conduct including war, is now banned.

As a dogmatic way of life or as a dominant drain of time and resources away from the enormous demands in advancing the new civilization, religions are not encouraged. However, many in the new society still find solace and spiritual comfort in the belief of a supreme being or intelligence. This has been a common phenomena throughout thousands of years of history in the most primitive as well as advanced societies.

Still, others believe such a force has been created in the minds of men and yet to be proven. Nonetheless, a genetic intelligence or an architect of a purposeful life, if you will, appears to exist whose origin and explanation has so far eluded the new society's greatest scientists. This will be discussed later when the complex questions about life's place in the universe is posed.

(Historical Background)

The time and wealth expended in the Hindu, Moslim, Catholic, and other religions in most third world nations was enormous. Much of it was used in ceremony, offerings to the gods and in rituals. In some areas like India and Indonesia the greatest part of wealth and time of the poor and illiterate was devoted to rituals and constant offerings to please the dead and their gods. It was also expended in lavish funeral ceremonies to prepare the dead for a fabulous afterlife in the next world. The Western more literate world was not exempt. Elaborate sums were spent on cathedrals and churches as places to worship their god and his disciples. This was common in all previous societies and communities from primitive tribes in the Amazon to slick, sophisticated evangelical programs on television.

Some thought if this time and wealth could be devoted instead to productive endeavors, it could raise the standard of living considerably throughout the world, especially for the poor.

(The New Society)

Some in the original Education Committee thought the proposed new education system was too regimented, but most argued that parents and students would have a choice between methods used at various schools. Furthermore, a little regimentation was far more productive than the anarchy and failure of American schools at the beginning of the twenty-first century and the unemployment and social disintegration that resulted.

The cultural illiteracy throughout the world of less-developed ethnic groups had to be considered before adopting a universal education system. At first the approach to these groups was to modify the general learning goals and curricula. In more remote areas, of course, buildings and facilities were built with this in mind. It was a gradual endeavor, but the basic thrust of the educational program was maintained. As the literacy of an area progressed, the curricula and goals were expanded until they eventually reached the levels of more developed regions.

An Institute of Education was established by the Education Governing Body where proposals for changes in the curricula or in teaching methods are welcomed. Here proposals receive a thorough examination and recommendation before being passed on to the Education Governing Body for approval or rejection. Both groups are composed of eminent professional educators, psychologists, management experts (to appraise the effects on the privately-run administrations of the schools), employers and other experts from throughout the world.

The new society has essentially eradicated illiteracy, ethnic and religious prejudice, and the selfish greed for excessive power. These three dominant human weaknesses has not only retarded the progress of civilization throughout history but has, at times, come close to eliminating it.

Yet vestiges of these three still exist. It never will be a perfect world, so constant vigil is necessary.

The radical control of abusive substances as well as an improved security and judicial system in the new society has also reduced crime as can be seen in the next two chapters.

Chapter 7

CONTROL OF CHEMICAL-INDUCED BEHAVIOR

(Historical Background)
Criminalizing addictive-drug use wrought intolerable results on all members of society because this disastrous policy created infinitely more problems than it solved. For one, the policy was the most insidious cause of crime.

Why? Since it was illegal to use or possess drugs, their purchase and sale became a huge covert activity that demanded exorbitant prices. As a result, it created innumerable and monstrous social and economic problems for the non-users of society.

The insatiable demand for drugs provoked criminal conduct that was far more serious for the rest of society than the addiction of a small number of individuals. Assaults, theft, and robberies committed to buy drugs became epidemic and was uncontrollable by law enforcement. Lawlessness, reminiscent of the frontier West, swept through urban areas. A study as early as 1984, showed that in Manhattan more than half charged with burglary, robbery, manslaughter, and murder tested positive for one or more drugs.[1] Later the Justice Department indicated up to three-quarters of crimes were committed by drug abusers. Most of these criminals tended to be recidivists.

Gerald Smith, head of the retail group for the accounting firm of Ernst and Young, found a growing percentage (41%) of shoplifting and theft by customers and employees was drug-related.

Glenn Ricker, an expert on illegal activity, estimated three quarters of shoplifting was drug-related.

Shooting wars between rival drug gangs killed and wounded many innocent victims including children. The inner cities became war zones creating indescribable terror among its inhabitants.

Joseph A. Califano, president of the Center on Addiction and Substance Abuse at Columbia University and former Secretary of Health, Education and Welfare said, "In 1960 there were fewer than 30,000 arrests for drug offenses; in thirty years, that number soared beyond one million. Today's prisons are wall to wall with drug dealers, addicts, alcohol abusers ... The prison population shot past a million in 1994 and is likely to double soon after the year 2000. Even where civil courts remain open, the rush of drug-related cases has created intolerable delays - four years in Newark, five in Philadelphia and up to ten in Cook County, Illinois. Each year, drugs and alcohol trigger up to $75 billion in health care costs." [2]

**

As early as 1988 drug addiction of significant numbers of Americans became the leading health and social problem in the United States. Addictive drugs had always been available and were even legal in the United States prior to 1914, but never had there been such a demand as there was by the 1980s. Something had gone wrong in American society.

What caused people to use abusive drugs? Most drug users began in their youth. The reasons were many: lack of sufficient parental guidance, the natural curiosity to experiment, adolescent risk-taking behavior and its "glamour" to impress one's peers, boredom due to lack of good work and study discipline, and especially the easy availability to drug supplies being pushed by other users or by those seeking income far in excess of mundane after-school jobs.

A UCLA study by Dr. Geoge Huba followed a group of teenagers from junior high through high school. It found the main characteristic leading to the chain of alcohol, marijuana, and hard drugs was rebelliousness against authority coupled with peer pressure.[3]

Richard H. Blum, a Standford University psychologist, found that children, who habitually used drugs, consistently viewed their parents as permissive and rejective of discipline and respect for authority.

As youths became adults, they perceived the problems of possible addiction. Most recreational users replaced stronger drugs with less abusive ones and with less frequency; some gradually abstained altogether. Most young Vietnam veterans, for example, did not become addicted.

For others, the reasons were less casual. Some were seduced in the early 1970s by the myth that cocaine was a safe, nonaddictive, and clean drug. The media gave tacit approval as it reported cocaine indulgence by rock and movie stars and even athletes. Dr. Timothy Leary of Harvard and others in academia talked of the benefits of recreational drug use. Dr. Peter Bourne, drug adviser to President Carter, wrote, "Cocaine is probably the most benign of illicit drugs currently in widespread use." So, many users ignored moderation and became addicted.

Some studies as early as the 1950s had a darker side which indicated eighty percent of addicts had a history of social maladjustment and were involved in crime before they used drugs. Usually they were victims of parental neglect and broken homes. [4]

Researchers discovered that children, born and raised by alcoholics or drug users, were predisposed to substance abuse. This could have been the result of a genetic connection, the home environment, or both. Some biologists suggested an evolutionary genetic tendency to alcoholism or drug addiction as a result of natural selection. For example, Indians who worked under severe conditions as farm laborers in the high Andes chewed coca leaves to get through the day. This custom continued for many generations, perhaps centuries, so it may have evolved as genetic adaptation.

"We don't see alcohol and drug abuse in the Amish and Mormon communities, regardless of biochemistry and personality," said John Hughes, an addict specialist at the University of Vermont School of Medicine. He was referring to the conclusion at that time by scientists that it was not understandable whether addiction lay primarily in personality or some chemical predisposition.

This led Mr. Hughes to suspect the prime component in addiction was parental and community guidance and environment.

Another interesting observation was that of the National Institute for Drug Addiction. Its researchers discovered many young addicts became involved in drugs or alcohol because some form of clinical mental disorder had gone untreated. [5]

Still, scientists were unsure as to why some users became addicted and others did not. A basic desire for drugs was thought to exist in humans to alter their state of consciousness according to Ronald K. Siegel, a research psychopharmacologist at UCLA School of Medicine and a consultant on the nature of drug addiction to two presidential commissions, the National Institute on Drug Abuse, and the World Health Organization. Mr. Siegel pointed out the pursuit of chemical happiness was in everyday life: caffeine in colas, tea and coffee, nicotine in cigarettes, alcohol in wine with dinner. Dr. Lester Ginspoon, a Harvard psychiatrist and author of several books on drugs, concurred, "I have come to the view that humans have a need - perhaps even a drive - to alter their state of consciousness from time to time." Dr. Andrew Weil of the University of Arizona College of Medicine agreed, "There is not a shred of hope ... to suggest human beings can live without psychoactive substances." [6]

The addiction to any drug, including alcohol or nicotine, is an overpowering desire or need to continue taking the substance and to obtain it by any means. There is also a tendency to increase the dosage and sometimes a physical and psychological dependence on its effects.

In the mid 1980s, crack, a smokable form of cocaine, led to an epidemic. Almost instantaneously it was addictive and released a swift, intense euphoria which lasted about five minutes. This was followed by depression and paranoia causing users to suppress by getting high again and again - known as "chasing the high".

Crack even overwhelmed the parental instinct. More and more social workers began to blame it for the thousands of reported child abuse and neglect cases. A mother of three children in Philadelphia was evicted for not paying rent. For two years she used her entire public assistance to buy crack. Furniture and appliances were sold to buy more crack. Children went without food, stopped going to school, and lived in filth. One mother under the influence of crack, threw her baby against the wall and killed it. Thousands of babies, probably impaired for life, were being born to crack-addicted mothers.

***

Narcotics were legal and enjoyed an open market in the 19th century. In 1890 opium consumption reached a peak, whereas, the cocaine epidemic lasted from 1885 until the 1920s.

Cocaine was produced and widely advertised by reputable drug manufacturers such as Park, Davis and Co. as a cure-all for various medical ailments. It was readily available at the corner drug store in the 1880s. Sigmund Freud made the drug popular in Europe by quoting accounts of its unusual properties from United States medical journals. So it was only natural that its use grew until cocaine's casualties, after prolonged use, began to be recognized. It was no longer perceived as a harmless non-addicting drug. It grew in disfavor from direct observation of victims and from a growing health movement concerned with the effects of alcohol as well as drugs on society. Finally the fear of cocaine reached a peak in the early 20th century creating an environment to pass the first anti-drug laws. The use continued to decline until the memory of its bad effects had been forgotten around 1970. [7]

Dr. Gabriel Nahas, author of *Cocaine: the Great White Plague*, noted that the number of addicts fell from a ratio of one in four-hundred in 1900 to one in three-thousand by 1936. Yet, consumption and sale of cocaine, in 1936 in the depth of the Great Depression with massive unemployment and poverty, was only a fraction of that in 1970 when times were good. Yet, it was just as seductive and illegal. It appeared there was some sort of social restraining mechanism in place that disappeared in the late 1960s; that drug consumption had little to do with despondency that resulted from poverty.

Among those who snorted cocaine habitually, often a lag occurred of several years between the first use of the drug and addiction or other problems. Crack, of course, led to addiction immediately but didn't come into common use until the mid 1980s. Ironically, crack was developed because cocaine became too expensive for widespread use in the illegal drug market. This probably never would have happened if cocaine had been available at modest prices through government-regulated supply clinics.

Because of the delay between use and treatment, cocaine users only began coming in for treatment in unprecedented numbers in 1987. Cocaine-related deaths of several well known public and entertainment personalities accelerated the desire for treatment.

***

The widespread disastrous effect on society resulting from the prohibition of drugs was difficult to imagine. The fact that drugs were illegal to use or possess made them risky to sell. This coupled with the overpowering need of addicts to buy at almost any price created enormous profit for drug dealers. It was this outrageously obscene profit that was the cause of so many social problems during that time. The illegality of drugs bestowed immense wealth on a few while at the same time, bestowing incredible harm on the rest of society. The income was so mind-boggling that drug dealers would stop at absolutely nothing to supply the demand!

The cost to society came from: the uncontrollable crime wave needed to support the habit; from pushers on the streets and in the schools who seduced youth in order to enlarge their market; from the enormous financial costs to interdict the flow of drugs, to prosecute the overwhelming number of cases, to provide more jails and prisons, and to pay for the cost of a growing prison population. The transmission of AIDS through the common use of needles by addicts increased and was one of the principal causes for the deadly disease to spread in America. Society was also harmed from the growing corruption of law-enforcement officials, money launderers in banks, tax evaders, lawyers and judges and even government officials. It cost society in the loss of innocent lives during wars between drug gangs; in increased health-care costs paid by the rest of society for emergency treatment and hospital costs of wounded gang members, crack babies, child abuse, and AIDS-infected addicts. The disastrous effects were unending.

Ironically, the purpose of criminalizing the use of drugs was to prevent many of these problems. The object of the law was to prevent increased addiction, but the easy availability of narcotics had already saturated the market and made them available to anyone wanting them.

At the time, it was estimated one-hundred and thirty billion dollars was spent annually in the United States alone to buy narcotics. This money was being wasted, given to criminal dealers by hedonistic and self-pitying individuals who, unable to cope with life, needed mood-influencing substances. This was in addition to what it was costing the rest of society in billions spent on interdiction, extra law enforcement, and to house criminals for drug-related crimes. Drug Strategies, a Washington based policy organization, estimated $250 billion had been spent for the "war on drugs" from 1980 to 1995. Yet, the effort was a complete failure. Drug use increased and narcotics were more plentiful.[8] It happened at a time when huge government deficits restricted spending for other needed programs.

Most of this enormous sum of money spent for narcotics came from the non-users: the victims of theft, robbery, and assault. Robbery and murder rates were at record levels. Cocaine was found in the urine of most of those arrested in the big cities. Research in 1986-87 of two-hundred and fifty-four juvenile crack users indicated each confessed to an average of eight-hundred and eighty crimes a year. Their average age of first time use was ten; by age thirteen, half had been behind bars. The expensive cost of narcotics was also the cause for an increase in prostitution as young women were forced to support their drug habit. Non-user taxpayers paid an estimated fifteen thousand New York addicts fifty million dollars annually in welfare payments (1971). Most of the money probably went to support their habit.

In order to increase sales, drug dealers stooped to giving free crack to children as young as nine. Once hooked, they were pressured to sell to their friends in school in order to support their habit. Coupled with peer pressure, demand by youth for narcotics became a vicious pyramiding expansion. " ... now a kid can get a vial of crack for three to five dollars. The high is instantaneous, the addiction complete," said Robert Stutman, special agent for the Drug Enforcement Administration in New York.[9] A teacher in Patagonia, Arizona said drug use became so rampant in the schools that one-fourth of the students in her classes were suspected of being "zoned out" on booze or narcotics. In Detroit and on Long Island, ten year old boys were charged with selling crack (1989). In Boston a nine-year old boy offered to sell crack to an undercover police officer.

One of the worst effects of illegal drug trafficking was the final shredding of what was left of the tattered ghetto social fabric. Teenagers were drawn to the fast money, working as lookouts, packagers, runners and sellers. Entry-level positions started at one-hundred dollars a day. As a result, all sense of monetary value was lost, and consequently, a complete disregard for any other values developed except for what money bought. Instant gratification replaced the hopes and goals of the future. Dropout rates increased dramatically in inner-city schools as a result of the high-paying jobs in drugs. Children stole from their parents to buy narcotics, and some parents encouraged their children to sell drugs in order to bring in extra family income. Drug-related crime brought riches and glory as teenagers became dealers and hit men.

In Dallas a fifteen year old was caught carrying fifty pound bags of crack. A police officer was shot down by a sixteen year old in New York and died in front of a suspected crack house. In New York City, Juvenile arrests rose from 386 in 1983 to over a thousand in 1987. Juvenile drug arrests in Washington, D.C. rose from 483 to nearly two thousand in the same period. But juveniles were rarely imprisoned for any length of time because there was no law mandating restrictive custody, so they merely returned to selling drugs.[10]

Organized crime arose to produce and distribute the illegal supply at profits beyond anyone's wildest dreams. Indicative of the obscene drug profits, generated because of their illegality, were those of one woman in Miami. Sheila Arana de Nasser pleaded guilty to drug smuggling and forfeited $150 million she made in the operation![11] No expenditure was too great in order to facilitate the smuggling and distribution. Huge sums of money were used to corrupt law-enforcement officers, judges, and even government officials. Lawyers defended obvious thugs, murderers, and drug king-pins of the lowest calibre for vast sums of money. Accountants and bankers were paid to launder money and evade taxes.

The coke drug lords laundered *billions* of dollars in wealth wrung from the destruction of society, all the result of prohibition. Within forty-eight hours they turned twenty dollar and one-hundred dollar bills into untraceable assets including money-market mutual funds, real estate and legitimate businesses such as resorts and car dealerships. The rate charged for laundering was usually seven to ten percent. This was accomplished by merely carrying the cash out of the United States in luggage and laundering it where the dollar was a favorite black market currency, or into dummy foreign companies, numbered bank accounts and other foreign financial institutions. Then it was immediately moved by wire back into the United States or other investment areas where the volume was so great that it was impossible to monitor by regulaters (i.e. The stock, bond, or commodity markets were examples). As they gobbled up extraordinary chunks of the American economy, it became almost impossible for authorities to trace; the loss in taxes was beyond comprehension. [12]

Outright wars and assassinations broke out between rival gangs fighting for control of lucrative drug-consuming areas. Many innocent victims were mowed down by the ensuing gunfire. Residents of the inner-city were under seige by organized drug terrorists. Shootouts between gangs in Los Angeles alone in 1987 caused 387 deaths. A notorious Jamaican drug gang infiltrated black neighborhoods throughout the country and was responsible for more than fourteen-hundred drug-related murders in a three year period. James K. Stewart, director of the National Institute of Justice wrote, "Crime strangles commerce and industry in the inner-city, and therefore, makes it harder for poor people to get jobs."

Another aspect of the prohibition of drugs was the corruption of Latin-American officials. A criminal empire worth billions enabled it to buy the use of a country's banks, judicial system, access to airports, police body guards, and even a country's military service plus anything else it needed. The motive was greed, but if that didn't work, fear did. Bribery, kickbacks, money laundering, arms trafficking, kidnaping and murder proliferated. Nothing was too despicable to satisfy the greed for so much money. [13]

The Columbian drug cartel threatened to kill ten Columbian judges for every drug lord extradited to the United States. After the threat, about five-hundred judges resigned. The drug lord's money-power bought countries and threatened to replace elected governments. Their power was mind-boggling.

El Dorado Airport in Bogota was the busiest airport in the Andes for drugs. Colonel Leonel Mendoza Aguirre, in charge of policing the facility, was arrested on charges of running a police ring of officers who charged thirteen-hundred dollars for each kilogram of cocaine that was allowed to pass through X-rays or past American-trained anti-drug dogs.[14] Even Columbia's president, Ernesto Sampler, was accused of taking money from the cartel for his campaign.

By 1994 fully two-thirds of South American cocaine was smuggled through Mexico into the United States. Referring to Mexican drug cartels, Eduardo Valle, former head of an elite anti-drug unit of the Mexican attorney general's office, declared, "These people are very dangerous, very powerful, immensely rich people. It's not just police chiefs who are involved in drug trafficking. It's politicians, financiers, people from many circles of the country's economic, political and social life."

Mexico's major drug cartels infiltrated many government offices: supreme court judges, federal judges, state governors, the police, and army as well as the ruling Institutional Revolutionary Party (PRI). Even General Jesus Gutierrez Rebollo, Mexico's top anti-narcotics official, was arrested in 1997 for collaborating with the drug cartel. Assassinations of leading reform-minded political candidates in the party were attributed to some corrupt members of the PRI in collusion with drug traffikers. By 1994 the Attorney General's Office, in particular, was heavily involved with drug traffickers. Mexican officials acknowledged the problem, but said it would never be wiped out until the demand for drugs at any price in the United States was eliminated.

Interdiction of drugs coming into the United States was a failure. Millions of dollars were spent to help eradicate the sources in other countries, to stop the flow at the border, and to apprehend drug bosses. But drugs continued to pour in unabated. The profit was just too enormous. "All the interdiction efforts do is to keep profit margins high for the cartels." This was a statement attributed by *Time* (12/3/90) to David Kenner, a Los Angeles defense attorney, who was reported to have defended many alleged drug traffickers.

The drug epidemic was not only in America; it was worldwide. Europe was being overwhelmed via shipments from Columbia through Spain and Portugal. Britain was saturated with heroin and Sweden with amphetamines. Southeast Asia supported a huge market in narcotics.

***

After many years of uncontrolled drug traffic in the United States and the complete failure of prohibition to prevent it, people began to look for alternatives. Some felt more prisons, more police, harsher mandated sentences for drug pushers and users, and the use of the military to interdict in foreign countries was not the answer. Instead, they believed such methods were creating an even worse situation. For one thing, they recognized that public resources for such activities was limited. No matter how many drug dealers were apprehended and put away, the tremendous profits would recruit others to take their place. As a result, the courts were continually swamped and jails were exploding with arrested drug dealers and users. 44,000 were arrested in Washington, D.C. alone over a two year period.

They recognized the core of the problem was prohibition, not drug use. Prohibition made drugs extremely valuable, and thus, fostered obscene profits, corruption, and crime. The entire social structure was collapsing because the temptation of easy wealth in drugs was corrupting sheriffs, police, the border patrol, judges, bankers, lawyers and others associated with the illegal drug trade as well as the underprivileged youth of the inner-cities. In 1989 it was estimated a pusher on the streets of Washington, D.C. grossed twenty-five hundred dollars a day!

A United States District Judge, Robert W Sweet, who was a former federal prosecutor and a deputy mayor in New York City advocated the legalization and dispensing of drugs by the state.

He said, "The war on drugs has failed to stop the traffic, or to alter the social patterns which produce the phenomena."[15]

Others believed it was totally unfair to force the majority in society to be ravaged by crime in order to support the habit of a minority and thus, the profits of drug dealers; to tax citizens for the costly but failing interdiction, or the enormously expensive apparatus used to apprehend, try, and incarcerate thousands of drug users for actions that harm only themselves.

Many thought taking drugs, like alcohol or tobacco, implied no malice toward others; it was, therefore, a vice and not a crime. They believed those acts were not crime against society unless they resulted in harm to others such as accidents caused by driving under the influence. The vast majority of users did so peacefully and harmed no one except, perhaps, themselves. Besides, they argued, millions of users believed they were doing nothing morally wrong against their fellows so they continued to ignore the laws. They felt the laws impinged their personal freedom; this prevented the war on drugs from ever being successful.

Still others believed, once the government was authorized to protect a mature adult from his own foolishness, other encroachments would be advanced to curtail his freedom to pursue activities that did not hurt others.

Advocates for the decriminalization of drugs presented a formidable case. Those in favor claimed society would save billions of dollars once the profit was eliminated, and drugs were administered at near cost through government auspices. They listed the following economic gains: a tremendous reduction in burglaries, muggings, and robberies to support the habit, a reduction in law-enforcement costs to apprehend users and dealers, a rapid easing of the over-burdened judicial system, the sudden reduction of the exploding prison population and the end of the need for more prisons and costly support of the drug-offending inmates and finally, the saving of billions of dollars to interdict drugs from across borders. Even the overwhelming medical costs, associated with intensive hospital and emergency care of addicts from overdosing or the treatment of drug-gang members and innocents suffering from gunshot wounds, would be eliminated. This was one of the major causes of rising health-care costs which many overlooked while blaming others.

More important, they claimed, lifting prohibition would eliminate the loss of life and the wounding of innocent citizens mowed down during shootouts between drug gangs or the senseless murders and bodily harm during robberies to support the habit. A staggering blow would be dealt corruption of law enforcement, government officials, and all others reaping profits from the sale of illegal drugs. Moreover, they believed disadvantaged youth would no longer be lured by the prospect of sudden riches so it would help get them off the streets and back into schools. Here they would receive, at least, a rudimentary education enabling them to qualify for basic employment. And finally, the incentive to seduce school children and other youths, in order to widen the market for the sale of drugs, would vanish.

Those in favor of decriminalization said none of the above benefits would occur while attempting to enforce prohibition. Instead they believed the carnage to society would continue unabated until prohibition had ended. As early as 1972, Milton Friedman, the Nobel prize winner in economics, asserted that the elimination of drug prohibition would accomplish more for law and order than any other conceivable measure.[16]

Those in favor of continuing to categorize the use and sale of drugs as criminal, based their belief on two main arguments : (1) decriminalization would result in many more addicts and (2) the use of drugs was not a victimless crime.

Would an unacceptable increase in addiction be the result of decriminalization? Some reasoned, that under prohibition, anyone wanting illegal drugs already had no difficulty finding them for sale. This was especially true considering they were pushed for profit to everyone including schoolchildren. It was difficult to imagine drugs being anymore accessible. Furthermore, there was a difference between selling drugs for profit and merely having them available at cost from regulated facilities. They, therefore, concluded it was far from clear it would increase the number of addicts, especially if narcotics were dispensed to hard-core addicts through government-monitored clinics. They claimed it already was a public-policy disaster so how could it get worse! Indeed,

Lee P Brown, "drug czar" in the Clinton administration, noted, "We haven't seen any change in the chronic drug user." In fact, the 2.7 million hard-core addicts did not decline. They consumed three-fourths of street drugs and committed most of the violent crime to support their habit.[17]

Nevertheless, others pointed to the increase of addiction in Britain and the Netherlands after the relaxation of prohibition. Although the arrests of users was relaxed, possession still remained a serious offense under Netherlands law, thus perpetuating the profit for drug dealers so the problem persisted. In Britain the program to prescribe methodone for heroin addicts, proved to be a failure and addiction increased. This was due mainly to the continued sale of illegal drugs. However, the return in the 1990s to prescribing a weekly heroin supply by clinics to addicts allowed many to return to normal productive lives. After complete failure using the American system of handling addiction, the Swiss government in 1995 also set up clinics for hopeless addicts dispensing drugs at cost.

Some asked if it was fair to penalize all of society in a failing attempt to protect a small minority from harming themselves. They admitted it was a personal tragedy for addicts, but criminalizing the use of drugs added to that tragedy by creating a disaster for the rest of society. Which needed the greatest sympathy - the self-chosen victims or the innocent?

Others reasoned that it was time for the government to stop denying the reality of personal responsibility; it was time to empower individuals to feel responsible when they create their own problems. To the extent it was an individual decision and an exercise of one's free will, addicts should accept the consequences; it should not be society that is held responsible. After all, they suggested, if provided the proper educational background on the subject, most people would make the right choice.

Furthermore, it was argued more users died from using alcohol and tobacco than were killed by drugs. According to the Department of Health and Human Resource Services: fetal alcohol syndrome was one of three top causes of birth defects, eighteen million adults were either alcoholics or had alcohol abuse problems, and nine of ten teen-age auto accidents involved alcohol.

Tobacco was generally accepted as a means to shorten life. Yet, both alcohol and tobacco were legally regulated abusive substances and were generally accepted by society. But, their problems were treated as personal and social rather than criminal. The sellers of tobacco and alcohol couldn't be blamed for the demand for their products, nor could drug traffickers. The demand and responsibility lay only with the user.

The advocates of prohibition also claimed the use of drugs harmed many others besides the user - that it was not a victimless crime. They pointed to such things as the the enormous loss of productivity while at work or because of absenteeism, the birth of crack or alcohol syndrome babies, driving under the influence, and the destruction of families. An extreme example was the case of a Detroit woman who allowed her thirteen-year old daughter to be raped in order to settle a crack debt. This would not have happened if drugs were available at near cost through government-regulated clinics.

Of course, these same things happened during the prohibition of illegal drugs and the legalization of alcohol. It didn't matter whether they were legal or not; it made little difference. Without early guidance and education in standards of morality and the consequences of drug use, people continued to not only abuse themselves, but to also abuse others.

(The New Society)
Sociologists of the new society look back on those horrible years with disbelief. In the new society there are few of those problems. The use of mind-altering drugs is no longer criminal so their cost is not kept artificially high by the high risk formerly involved in their sale. This, in turn, had previously resulted in gigantic profits on their sale and thus, created many problems. Now the profits are gone, and the corruption, violence, and vast economic costs to society, associated with drug prevention, has ended. In their place we now have intensive drug education, adequate rehabilitation facilities, and government regulated dispensing centers. Drug and alcohol addiction is treated as an individual physiological and medical problem.

The promotion of good parenting and the adoption of Behavioral Education, as earlier explained, has helped instill a discipline to adhere to certain standards of conduct - standards that in former times were ignored in a more permissive society. This has assisted in the elimination of many drug-related problems.

Decriminalization has allowed funds to be redirected from law enforcement to prevention. An intense education program has been mandated, beginning at age seven, on the personal costs of abusive substance use.

The child is conditioned to reject narcotics throughout life regardless of their legality. Additionally, the sale or giving of tobacco, alcohol, or other abusive drugs to minors carries very harsh penalties, and this fact is well-advertised. Research indicated, for example, that unless one started cigarette smoking before age twenty-one, he or she seldom started at all.

Our close supervision and restricted movement of students within our boarding school system has eliminated any possibility for the black-marketing of alcohol and other drugs to our youth, so there is no pressure from peers to experiment. The debilitating effects of abusive drugs including the potential for brain damage and death are taught; youth is instilled with a sense of responsibility and integrity to make their own decisions, to use free will and behavior when they become mature adults. As part of our education program, a mass-media campaign portrays the use of drugs as dangerous, stupid, and scorned by peers and important persons. Yes, the media is censored and all advertising for tobacco, alcohol, and narcotics is prohibited.

Since the use of narcotics has now been decriminalized, their sale is regulated by the government's Pharmaceutical Division in licensed clinics, hospitals, and pharmacies. There is very little black-marketing now because the inordinate profit potential is gone, and demand is mainly from a diminishing number of addicts who are supplied at minimal cost and treated as medical cases.

After consultation and the patient's computer record is checked for previous visits, dosage, and degree of addiction, the correct dosage is administered by a professional. Sales are restricted to mature adults just as they were for alcohol and tobacco in earlier times. (When the minimum age for drinking was raised in the 1980s from eighteen to twenty-one and accompanied by aggressive enforcement, teenage drinking declined considerably. "Drinking simply goes down when drinking age goes up," said Dr. Alexander Wagenaar, professor of public health at the University of Minnesota.18) To thwart unregulated trafficking, all types of mind-altering drugs are available at the clinic including any newly-designed ones. But new non-addictive drugs, that have been developed, are always recommended.

In spite of the intensity of the new anti-drug and Behavioral Education at home, in the school, and in the media, there are always a few who can't resist the temptation to experiment. The price is low enough to prevent black-marketing, or stealing to support the habit, yet, costly enough to discourage curious or casual usage. If some insist on trying abusive drugs for the first time, knowing full well the disasterous results that are brought upon themselves, then that is their decision. The results are their responsibility, not that of the rest of society.

Because the purchase and use of previously illegal drugs is now allowed, there no longer exists a tantalizing forbidden fruit that is glamorized as in early days. It is no longer socially acceptable, and peer pressure has disappeared. Instead, it is now associated with a medical or physiological problem as illustrated by sanitized clinics attended by people in white medical gowns. As a result, we have few first-time users and practially no recreational users.

The largest group to purchase from government regulated sources is, of course, addicts holding prescriptions to purchase weekly supplies. Unlike casual or first-time users, they are free of any stigma to feed their voracious demand.

Black-marketing of drugs has not only lost its lucrative profit margin, but its principal demand, which was from addicts, has vanished. Addicts can now get their supply at cost whenever necessary and without hassle. The remaining market is now so small as to make it unprofitable for unlicensed dealers, especially in light of the severe penalties for selling unregulated drugs.

Addictive drugs are not administered or provided in unlimited quantities because some addicts would be tempted to take an overdose. It had been shown when the price was exorbitant as in the old black-market days, users couldn't buy unlimited amounts and so made do with what they could afford.[19] Of course, any one showing severe signs of distressful withdrawal because they have used up their weekly allocation, are not turned away.

The cost of narcotics includes a small surcharge to finance rehabilitation facilities, medical research on addiction, and pharmaceutical research for mind-altering but non-addictive and less abusive drugs. Centers for rehabilitating addicts, whether for alcohol, tobacco or narcotics, are available to any addict desiring treatment at no cost. As in any addiction, only the user can make that decision. Because they are no longer confessing to criminal activity, more have volunteered for treatment. Ample facilities are available unlike in the early days before decriminalization. Then, most government funds went to fight the sale of illegal drugs instead of for drug education, rehabilitation, and the research of addiction.

Nevertheless, rehabilitation becomes mandatory when the user is unable to live a normal productive life or is a threat to the well-being of others. Examples include women who are pregnant, airline pilots, train engineers, those who have required drug-related emergency-room treatment at the expense of the health-care system, and those who are no longer able to hold a job because of their addiction. If the individual can no longer meet those responsibilities, the person is committed to a rehab facility rather than risk the lives of others or impose problems on the rest of society.

(Historical Background)

Risking the lives of others while under the influence was not a victimless activity. Take the case of a twenty-five year old mother in Indiana in 1988 who was taking cocaine at the time she padlocked her nine year old daughter in an unheated attic for three to five days without food or water. The young girl suffered frostbite and had both lower legs amputated.

During the drug epidemic of the last half of the twentieth century, little was known of effective drug treatment. Ninety percent in rehab returned to drugs. It was fairly certain in the United States, that addiction started primarily but not exclusively in youth who dropped out of school, were unemployed, and were frequently from dysfunctional families. Most were Afro-Americans or Hispanics. Many were not interested in rehabilitation, and those who were, returned to the same vulnerable inner-city environment and eventually to welfare or crime.

In 1994 China adopted a law offering addicts a choice between voluntary detoxification or forced "cold turkey" in labor camps because voluntary and compulsory detoxification centers were failing.[20]

(The New Society)
Because of early anti-drug and Behavioral Education and elimination of black markets in the new society, drug addiction is no longer a major problem. Regardless, treatment for addiction is taken seriously and is comprehensive. Several means of controlling it are now used and there is a constant search for new methods.

Still, one of the most effective methods is empowering individuals to feel responsible for their own lives and for their own problems, not to blame third parties, and to overcome through organizations such as the original Alcoholics Anonymous and Narcotics Anonymous. These had proven highly successful. The new society believes general socio-economic conditions do not prevent individuals from helping themselves. It, no longer, blames the suppliers of alcohol, tobacco, and drugs for their consumption.

Since a small fee was added to the cost of abusive substances, including alcohol and tobacco, there are now funds available to pay for new methods of treatment. It encourages pharmaceutical companies to spend more for research in molecular and cellular biology of the brain in order to more thoroughly understand the basis for addiction, and thus formulate chemical antidotes. Pharmaceutical companies have now developed many ways, including catalytic antibodies to thwart the craving of addicts. Antibodies are designed to trigger chemical reactions with the addictive drug molecule in the bloodstream causing it to become inert and unable to reach the brain.

At various times, the majority of humans prefer some mind-altering substance or one that causes a feeling of well-being. A survey in 1989 indicated seventy percent were against the prohibition of alcohol. This explains why making a criminal offense of the use of these substances has always failed. The problem is to keep it under control so harm is diminished in the new society. This is why drug companies are encouraged to spend more to research and develop non-addictive euphoric drugs to replace the more abusive ones. One of the first drugs of this type, fluoxetine, was developed in the later part of the twentieth century. We have now developed many more sophisticated ones, which are now sold in pharmacies as well as clinics.

The sale of alcohol, tobacco, and less addictive drugs such as the mild version of marijuana are sold only in licensed regulated restaurants and stores. Once again, it is a criminal offense to sell or distribute any of these abusive drugs to minors.

The production, shipping, and distribution of all of these products is handled by private companies (wineries, distillers, breweries, cigarette companies, pharmaceutical manufacturers) much like it was done in the twentieth century. Pilfering is no greater than for other merchandise because people have not only been thoroughly programmed with Behavioral Education, but the profit margins on narcotics, like alcohol and tobacco, are no longer lucrative. The products can be obtained by any adult at reasonable cost.

Following the decriminalization of drugs decades ago, the effect on the new society has been miraculous. The enormous illegal profits disappeared. Drug cartels, gangs, and peddlers have been put out of business just as occured following the repeal of alcohol prohibition. Corruption associated with drug sales evaporated because there was no longer a need or way to support it. Gangland wars suddenly stopped. Crime in the streets, robberies and burglaries dropped sharply because there was no longer a need for addicts to pay exorbitant prices to buy drugs. School children were no longer being enticed to use or sell crack. Easy money was no longer available to inner-city teen-agers. They returned to school to prepare themselves for the work-world. Latin-America and Southeast Asia governments began to function for their citizens and not for the drug lords. Billions of dollars were saved by society for productive needs.

Nevertheless, there were still other areas of criminal conduct to address by the early founders of the new society as outlined in the next chapter.

Chapter 8

SECURITY

(Historical Background)

By the 1990s crime in America was completely out of control. Crime not only increased, but the percentage of criminals apprehended declined. The criminal court system became intolerably bogged down in postponements and delays. Miscarriage of justice due to harranguing the jurors with legal double-talk was common as was improper sentencing. Incarceration was a joke. It cost the taxpayers more money to house, feed, and care for one prisoner than it cost the noncriminal citizen outside. And the convicts were running the prisons! Rape, murder, drug consumption, riots, and hostage taking were common. Yet, additional prisons couldn't be built fast enough.

Between 1960 and 1975, the crime rate in America soared two-hundred and thirty percent.[1] By 1981 there were thirteen million serious crimes reported annually but only two million arrests.[2] Yet, only one-hundred and sixty thousand felons were sent to jail. In other words, ninety-nine percent of all serious crimes were committed with impunity.[3] Furthermore, a study by the Justice Department indicated two-thirds of inmates released from state prisons were arrested for a serious crime within three years, a damaging report on recidivision.

Justice Chaies Wettmer summed it up when he said, " ... a person who has been through the system and is contemplating a crime probably views things as follows: (1) if I do it, I won't get caught, (2) if I get caught, I won't get prosecuted, (3) if I get prosecuted, I won't get convicted, (4) if I get convicted, I won't go to prison, (5) if I go to prison, it won't be for very long."[4]

Typical. was a case in New York . A man, serving a 45 year-to-life sentence for murder, drug and weapons possesion, was stopped and his van searched. He consented to the search after troopers, who had been stopping cars to check for illegal game during hunting season, found a murdered body, guns, ammunition, and cocaine inside. An appeals court threw out his conviction claiming state troopers had no reason to ask to search his van.

So many despicable and heinous crimes were perpetrated on humans, most people became numb to the onslaught. Juveniles killed for a few dollars or just for the thrill. Children shot one another in school with handguns. Most parents exercised little control over their children, especially those in the inner cities. When confronted with a criminal charge of their child, the response of many parents, as well as community leaders, was to blame it on the economy, racism, police harassment or just, "Not my kid." They could never accept lack of parental guidance as the real cause.

Most were aware of the costs for police protection, property loss, security devices, medical treatment of victims, and lost income when incapacitated by assault. They were not aware of the enormous cost of crime in lost time by society. Loss of valuable time by the community included locking and unlocking doors and windows to automobiles and homes, transporting children to school by car to avoid perverts and kidnappers, being monitored with metal detectors at airports and schools, planning by women to escort each other or avoid certain urban areas, assisting prosecutors with their cases against the criminal and many more.

The first responsibility of government was to protect its citizens. Unfortunately, government appeared powerless to prevent lawlessness from spreading. Politicians could always take enough tax money from some and give to others and to experiment with new welfare programs but never enough for adequate police protection, more judges, and enough courts to handle the increasing load of criminal cases. Billions were spent for a highly-trained professional military force used to quell riots, civil wars, and to secure peace in some remote part of the world, but never to protect Americans in the war zones of inner cities.

The primary social institutions of the time: the home, school, and church became inadequate in the task of producing law-abiding citizens. It, therefore, fell increasingly upon the government to control society through increased apprehension, sentencing, and incarceration. Coupled with a more complex society, the maintenance of public order inevitably became more technical and difficult even when funds were available.

The result was a near breakdown in the criminal justice system. The rate of apprehension fell behind the growing number of criminals at large. Prosecution was delayed by increasing technicalities in the legal system. Sentencing was influenced by the growing need to shorten trial time through plea-bargaining because of the burgeoning number of pending cases. Judges also felt compelled to reduce or eliminate prison sentences because of the lack of sufficient prison facilities. The sentence was no longer based solely on the optimum detention or punishment needed.

***

One of the worst problems in the criminal justice system was the extreme leniency shown toward youthful offenders. The early system was designed to function as a benign and wise rehabilitation of children under seventeen with the optimistic belief the child would revert to a normal law-abiding person with proper social guidance. In the words of the New York statute, the person was considered "not criminally responsible ... by reason of infancy."

Rita Kramer, author of *At a Tender Age: Violent Youth and Juvenile Justice,* wrote that this philosophy had not changed even though juvenile crime in the 1990s "had taken on a character unthinkable when the present justice system was set up ... "

"Between 1987 and 1991, the fastest-growing crime by juveniles was loaded gun possession. Cases of violent group assault - 'kids' causing serious physical injury 'for fun' - had increased dramatically."

A particularlly sordid example of the ineptness of the judicial system was the case of an eighteen year old New Yorker convicted of murdering a taxi driver. During the trial, police revealed that he had committed at least four other slayings before he was eighteen! By the time he was fifteen he had been arrested some twenty-five times for purse snatchings, muggings, stick-ups, assaults, and threats. He simply avoided prison for these crimes by not showing up for trial after which "everybody forgot about it" according to the judge who finally sentenced him to fifteen years.[5]

Conduct which was criminal for normal adults was not crime, legally speaking, when it appeared as juvenile delinquency. Take the case in the mid 1980s of Robert, one of three boys who raped and sodomized an elderly bag lady in New York's Central Park. Afterward he beat her to death with a stick and was given a sentence of eighteen months! This was the maximum penalty provided by New York law for any act - even murder - committed by a person twelve years of age or younger.

Mrs. Kramer noted, "Eighty percent of chronic juvenile offenders (five or more arrests) go on to adult criminal careers." Peter Reinharz, chief of New York City's Family Court Division, reported eighty-five percent of juvenile offenders were charged with felonies. He remarked, "We hardly ever see the non-violent anymore. These are dangerous people."

Nevertheless, Mrs. Kramer indicated the general approach was to use civil rights, minutiae of procedurial technicalities, and anything else to "get the kid off." Even when sentenced for a serious crime, the punishment was mild. "Eighteen months in a facility, that usually has TV, a basketball court and better food and medical care than at home, is the worst that all but the most violent repeat offenders have to fear in New York." All of this was at a cost of eighty-five thousand dollars a year per inmate paid by the taxpayers of New York state. [6]

It was also important to note when assessing this problem, in all stages of civilization throughout history, a pattern prevailed that young males committed the most violence and crime. Psychologists still did not have a clear reason for this.[7]

***

Another problem was the treatment of hard-core repeat offenders. Most research and studies supported the view that a hugely disproportionate share of crime was committed by a small number of predator criminals.

In the early 1980s the Rand Corporation published a study by Jan and Marcia Chaiken entitled *Varieties of Criminal Behavior*. Using data from a survey of twenty-two-hundred prison inmates, they determined a small group of criminals developed a similar pattern of behavior. "They began taking drugs as minors, committed violent crimes before they were sixteen, were eventually addicted to multiple drug use, and committed an inordinately high rate of robberies and other crimes of property, as well as assaults, to feed their addictions ... such convicts admitted to committing an average of one-hundred-fourteen robberies, burglaries, and thefts per year. Whereas, convicts who had never been on drugs committed an average of thirteen per year."

One study by Temple University established that 237 individuals committed over five-hundred thousand crimes during an eleven year period. Another study, by Professor Marvin Wolfgang of the University of Pennsylvania published as early as 1972, showed that seven percent of a young male age group committed sixty-two percent of the crimes as well as eighty to ninety percent of violent crimes. All were repeat offenders that had committed at least five crimes.

It was common for police officers to risk their lives arresting criminals whom they rearrested again after a few days for another crime. In Seattle, a criminal wrestled the gun away from a policeman, jammed it under the officer's bulletproof vest and tried to fire. The officer thwarted the attempt and with another officer's assistance, brought the man to jail. Eighteen months later the same officer arrested the same criminal after a car chase. He hadn't even received an eighteen month sentence for trying to kill a policeman!

The U.S. Government Accounting Office reported that two-thirds of repeat offenders were placed on probation. Worse, many were allowed to remain free even after they committed crimes while still on probation! Some observers thought this was the core of the crime problem. Many predators were nothing more than savages with absolutely no sense of moral values or how to live without hurting others. Some people felt they should be banned permanently from any semblance of civilized society. Why it was allowed to continue was beyond common sense. On closer examination, it was evident that crime victims were unorganized and, therefore, unable to bring sufficient pressure on their elected officials as did other special interest groups such as the American Civil Liberties Union and the National Rifle Association. It was true that politicians periodically postured and passed a so-called "crime bill," but it was always ridiculously ineffective so the problem continued.

***

The theory of retribution had declined much earlier at the beginning of the twentieth century in place of reformation. Preventive detention continued in use with new methods to deal with recidivision. The success of reformation was still being debated when a crisis was reached in the prison system. The number of criminals being sentenced had simply exploded and overwhelmed the capacity of containment.

All resources were spent finding new methods of detention or building new facilities for containment with little left over for reformation. Even the parole system degenerated in order to reduce the overcrowded prisons rather than parole based on merit. So, thugs and murderers were once again released to prey on society.

Some socialists believed an unequal distribution of wealth in a capitalistic economic system evoked crime. But on study, it was noted that serious crime was also prevalent in socialistic economies such as the Soviet Union and China before they adopted free-markets.

Many emphasized the lack of economic opportunity and unemployment as the major cause of high crime rates. Although this theory was deeply entrenched, once again, a historical comparison of crime rates with unemployment in periods of hard times showed the opposite.

For example, homicide as well as property crimes since 1900 rose through the prosperous 1920s until it reached a peak in the early 1930s. It then declined through the Great Depression and by 1940 had dropped forty percent. It remained fairly level until the early 1960s when it increased sharply reaching a peak in the mid seventies. The crime rate nearly doubled from 1961 to 1969 while unemployment dropped from 6.6% to 3.4%. Conviction rates for men between twenty-five and thirty were also only one third that of juveniles between fourteen and sixteen. Yet economic hard times created more difficult problems for older men with families to support than for young boys.[8]

Still, others believed crime was morally justified as a protest of inequitable laws. It was true that many inequitable laws had been passed by politicians for the benefit of special groups to the detriment of the majority. Although some of the laws were bad, the problem with that reasoning was all laws theoretically represented the will of the majority as passed by their duly-elected representatives. This, of course, was one of the principal problems in a democracy. Often laws were passed for political advantage rather than on the basis of scientific expertise and equity. At other times, the majority was in favor of a law although the minority thought it inequitable. Once again, this was one of the problems with a democracy. But, if one was to follow these democratic rules, disobedience in the form of criminal acts was wrong.

Earlier sociologists blamed increased crime on racism as well as economic inequality. Later, an analysis of this theory concluded the gap in income and wealth, especially between ethnic groups, was principally due to the behavior and attitudes of the particular ethnic culture and not the economy or attitudes of the greater society. It appeared the lower the family and community moral and work standards of an ethnic group, the greater the potential for a lower standard of living and for criminal activity. It was true as previously mentioned, that race discrimination existed toward many cultures throughout American history: Jews, Chinese, Japanese, Irish, to name a few, but they had disciplined family and community standards resulting eventually in economic prosperity and adversity to crime. This was not true, however, of such cultures as the American Indian and Afro-American.

An interesting reflection was made on this in 1986 by James Payne, chief of the Corporation Council in New York City's Family Court dealing with juvenile offenders, (equivalent to a district attorney in adult criminal system). Mr. Payne, an Afro-American, a product of a broken home, and a Vietnam veteran who put himself through law school, said of his childhood, "We didn't have a middle-class income, but we had middle-class values."

Mr. Payne was blunt, "There are too many people around here bleeding over these kids, encouraging them to believe they got a raw deal. And as long as you believe society is to blame for your problems ... Hell, they're standing on the corner of 125th street and Eighth Avenue right now, blaming the white man for all of their problems. But if you go back and look at their individual histories, where they had an opportunity to do something for themselves - they didn't go to school, they didn't want to look for a job, or it wasn't a good enough job - they always had an excuse. And we reinforce it. Academics, sociologists, psychologists, want to blame anything but the individual himself.

"You can't say it's poverty that causes crime," he continued, "Of the millions of people living below the poverty line all over the country, only a fraction ever commit a crime. But it's the same fraction, over and over again. And jobs programs don't stop crime. These kid's only responsibility is to go to school, and they don't even do that. What makes you think they're going to get up at seven, put in a full day's work? They're not out there committing crimes to pay the rent, or feed themselves, or take care of a sick mother. They're not buying milk for the baby. They're either putting it in their arm or up their nose."[9]

An interesting psychological study was made in 1970 by Doctors Samuel Yochelson and Stanton Samenow; they developed a typical personality of a hard-core criminal. From an early age the child was hyperactive physically and mentally and addicted to "excitement." He was chronically restless, irritable, and dissatisfied. The tendency was to lie, cheat, steal, and fight. He rationalized by blaming his parents and environment. He shied away from giving or receiving affection.

By 1972 Doctors Yochelson and Samenow arrived at one simple conclusion: the criminal freely chooses his way of life in his quest for power, control, and excitement. Furthermore, he can choose to change if he musters courage or the will to endure the consequences of responsible choices. This remarkable study did not necessarily indicate rehabilitation worked, only that it was possible for a criminal to change. A prior seventeen-year federally-financed study, The Criminal Personality, came to the conclusion that nothing worked in rehabilitating most hard-core criminals.[10] Some people chose deliberately what made them feel good (drugs and alcohol) or the easiest way (theft, robbery, and hustling) rather than what was right or wrong or best for themselves. The unbridled self-gratification of all desires raised primitive animal-like behavior in humans that differentiated the uncivilized individual from the civilized.

Several excellent studies indicated there was a physiological correlation between criminal biological parents and their criminal offspring. Other studies showed genetic transmission may have created a predisposition to alcoholism. In either case, only the propensity existed, not the finality to become either a criminal or alcoholic.[11]

In most studies the percentage difference was not great, and later studies of alcoholism found no such connection. These studies instead suggested that environment, especially the family environment, played a much stronger role than many previous researchers believed. If the parent was a criminal, then it was usually obvious that offspring would be brought up in an atmosphere that did not differentiate between right and wrong.

(The New Society)
The early Committee on Security analyzed studies on heredity but decided they were inconclusive at the time. Nevertheless, scientists of the new society have expended considerable effort today in the research of genetics and its correlation with various behavior. It is hoped that someday this research will contribute to the control of crime.

Other physiological drives created from environment, that could tempt one to a criminal response: hunger, the sex drive, and drug and alcohol addiction have been either eliminated, diverted, or reduced to a negligible cause of crime in the new reformed society.

Criminalizing the use and sale of narcotics, no doubt, contributed more to the explosion of crime during earlier times than anything else. As explained previously, this problem is solved so the concentration can be directed to preventing other crime. As with alcohol, tobacco and narcotics, the new society felt it unreasonable to penalize individuals or otherwise control their conduct for activities which harm no one except, perhaps, the person engaged in it. It may be helpful, therefore, to reiterate the two broad principles of criminal law that has been established:

(1) Doing damage intentionally or negligently to another person's body or well-being directly or indirectly.

(2) And taking property or services from another person by force, threat, or stealth either directly or indirectly.

(Historical Background)

Gambling and prostitution as well as the consumption of abusive substances were essentially victimless activities, but because they were illegal, an inordinate profit potential was quickly exploited by the greedy and ruthless criminal element. Illegality unleashed many criminal activities. Cheating, tax evasion, pimping, corruption, racketeering, gangland wars, debasement of morals, and murder were only a few.

Prostitution existed for centuries, acknowledged if not condoned or accepted. In the ancient world of tribes, promiscuity for hire was unnecessary because of the existence of polygamy and the accepted tradition of sexual communism among men and their wives. In fact, some groups did not recognize marriage or barely tolerated it as an infringement of communal rights. In many communities men bought their wives. As late as 1995 some inhabitants of New Guinea practised this, purchasing wives with pigs. In some countries it was customary for young women to sell their sexual favors in order to earn a dowry or as part of a solemn religious duty at the sanctuary of a goddess.

In all of these customs, including marriages in earlier times, it appears that love, as understood in the twentieth century, was significantly absent and evolved later in history. Love, as distinguished from animal sexual fulfillment, seems to be a product of a human's unique ability to assess another's personality, character, and other human factors. It appears to be a sign of intelligent civilized life. Even when Christianity first accepted marriage as the voluntary union for life of one man and one woman to the exclusion of all others, love was probably absent in many cases. Women, regardless of their rank, were essentially salable properties. It is, therefore, understandable that some became prostitutes.

Both Greek and Roman civilizations accepted and regulated prostitution. During the Middle Ages prostitution was a recognized function of social life. It was not only licensed and regulated but constituted a source of public revenue and was protected by law. It wasn't until the Reformation that Christian condemnation of extra-marital activity occurred. At the time, it appeared that prostitution was condemned primarily on the grounds of infidelity in marriage but generally condoned for other reasons.

In more modern nations, abolition was tried and usually failed because prostitution then went underground increasing venereal disease, fostering rape, and other sex crimes. In order to sell their favors in a prohibitive environment, prostitutes sought out pimps who promoted them to other males in return for much of the earnings. Many pimps were vicious; they seduced young girls in order to exploit them, and beat them mercilessly if they held back their fees or in any way did not obey them. Some countries, like Argentina in 1954, rescinded their laws on illegal prostitution because of the problems they created and authorized the reopening of brothels.

A woman or man who married for money was, in fact, a prostitute. The giving of money or bestowing of gifts in exchange for companionship or sex also involved women as well as men. The wealthy nymphomaniac, who bought sexual favors, was an example. But these activities, in most cases, hurt no one so long as both parties were satisfied with the relationship and were unharmed.

Most men drawn to prostitutes were usually: students or other youths experiencing the peak of the sexual drive; military personnel, lonely travelers, salesmen and others without a sexual outlet; married men whose wives were unable to have intercourse; men who preferred more erotic sex.

(The New Society)

After careful consideration, the new society experimented with legalized government-regulated brothels. These operations are carefully monitored by medical and government authorities. Women independently set fees and conduct business as a cooperative commercial entity retaining all proceeds less their contribution to the cost of running the facility including attendants, security guards, and the cost of medical and regulatory inspections.

Young women voluntarily enter this business because the financial rewards are exceptional, and the stigma of illegality and pimp exploitation has vanished. Some women enjoy the excitement and attention of many men, but after a few years most look elsewhere for a more normal life, eventually marry, and have a family or live as respectable spinsters.

As a result, venereal disease and unwanted pregnancies in our youth has been considerably reduced. Equally important, we have reduced criminal activities such as rape and sex crimes, violence and economic parasitism associated with pimps and organized crime involved in prostitution when it was illegal. Law enforcement officers are no longer corrupted by bribes from pimps and prostitutes.

(Historical Background)

Christian, Jewish, and Moslim religions have for centuries generally forbid gambling and held it to be sinful and wasteful. The long record of legislation prohibiting it has been attributed mainly to this philosophy but also on economic grounds. Generally, in England and the United States gambling was illegal if some skill was not involved (i.e. horse racing in place of slot machines).

Historically most people enjoyed some form of gambling and were in favor of more liberal laws. It appeared that most gambling in the later half of the twentieth century was of a recreational nature. Only a very small percentage (3%) of gamblers were compulsive and addicted.

(The New Society)

To rid itself of the crime associated with illegal gambling, the new society has legalized all forms while licensing and regulating its operations. It emphasizes the recreational aspects by stressing games or activities requiring some skill or judgement rather than pure luck. As a result, activities such as lotteries and slot machines are access-limited to licensed casinos in restricted locations rather than spread in every store and commercial outlet.

Licensed gambling casinos are closely regulated to prevent "skimming" and to insure a liberal payout to customers. Mathematical odds are posted for all to see. As a result, profits are not as lucrative as in the early days. Profit margins are now similar to other businesses. There is little incentive for organized crime or corruption of law-enforcement officials. It is, now, merely another form of recreation.

In addition, permanent internal auditors are hired by the government to peruse receipts, odds, and general gambling operations. The government charges a small percentage of net receipts to pay for this as well as for rehabilitation of compulsive gamblers.

Race tracks and other sports events involving gambling are also licensed and regulated. Card games, sport pools, and similar recreational gambling prevail in most communities but are not licensed or regulated unless they assume a significant commercial size.

Generally, gambling is viewed by the new society to be a victimless activity except where the small percentage of compulsive gamblers are involved. Mandatory rehabilitation is required if compulsive gambling results in severe deprivations to one's family, the embezzling of funds, or the inability to hold a productive job.

***

After careful consideration while forming the articles of World Government, the Committee on Security agreed with the Committee on Behavioral Education; the primary cause of rampant crime in the twentieth and twenty-first centuries was the complete breakdown of social conduct and that it was due to a gradual disintegration in disciplined order within social institutions. Changes in apprehension and in the criminal justice system, although badly needed, would have only limited influence on the rising crimerate. To seriously reduce it, the committees backed fundamental changes in social behavior. Their main objective was to prevent crime, not punish it.

The Committee on Security then began to outline solutions in the prevention of crime. First and foremost was the adoption of Behavioral Education as previously discussed as well as mandatory parenting and education requirements. It was correctly assumed that this in itself would reduce the crime rate to such a level that other changes would be less significant.

A large segment of the public participated in illegal gambling, prostitution, and the use of abusive substances throughout most of the 20th century. As a result, the public tolerated corruption in law-enforcement officials in order to overlook its indulgence in such pleasures. Because of this attitude, the overwhelming evidence was conclusive that the terrible toll of related crime on society was far greater than the occasional detrimental effects on individuals who were unable to control their own behavior. Thus, the decision to decriminalize these victimless activities was adopted early by the founders, and it helped to reduce crime significantly. It was not easy to enact decriminalization because of age-old prejudices and emotional arguments involved.

Another important proposal designed to reduce crime was the abolition of all lethal weapons.

(Historical Background)

In countries where guns were banned, such as Japan, assaults with fire-arms were nearly unheard of during the later half of the twentieth century. Yet, in the United States by 1992, the Justice Department reported that crimes committed with handguns had soared almost fifty percent from the annual average of the previous five years. (931,000 handgun crimes in 1992). Several years later, homicide and assaults with guns of every description overwhelmed the populace. By 1995, 16,000 people were shot to death in one-year in the United States compared to 38 in Japan! Even adjacent Canada had few incidents of gun violence. Why the difference?

From colonial times people used firearms for hunting game to feed their families, to protect them from marrauding Indians, and later in opening the frontiers of the West. During the Revolution it was necessary that every man be part of the armed rebellion. So Article II of the Bill of Rights specified, "A well-regulated militia, being necessary to the security of a free state, the right of people to keep and bear arms, shall not be infringed."

On close observation some said the original concept, written immediately following the throes of the Revolutionary War, was designed primarily to help defend the nation. It would be accomplished with militias from the various states to thwart future alien foes. This occurred when many states mustered their respective militias, composed of ordinary self-armed citizens, during the War of 1812.

Nevertheless, many scholars of that ammendment to the Constitution agreed in principle that the right to keep and bear arms was a fundamental concept of democracy. Later, any effort to ban firearms to curtail crime, was held by many as a way to disarm lawful citizens leaving them unprotected from the criminals who would obtain guns unlawfully.

This permissive environment appeared to be unique in the world. As social conduct deteriorated, guns proliferated. Accidents abounded; family members mistaken for a prowler or in domestic squabbles were shot more often than criminals breaking into their homes. Automatic weapons were used, not only by organized gangs and other criminals, but in psychopathic massacres of numerous innocent people. There were cases of drivers being shot in traffic for offending another motorist. Adolescents, immune to the violence on T.V. and in the movies, thought nothing of shooting one of their peers in a dispute; some were as young as eleven. Schoolgrounds became battlegrounds, and even young children, playing with their father's loaded gun, would turn it on their playmates.

(The New Society)

The banning of all lethal weapons evolved naturally after the world disarmament conference which prohibited the manufacture of all arms or the raising of military forces. All individual firearms were then collected and destroyed. Subsequently, if anyone was seen brandishing a firearm and did not surrender it immediately, they were subject to being shot on sight by a member of the new Security Force. Later of course, firearms used initially by security forces were also destroyed and replaced with non-lethal ones. Today anyone in possession of or attempting to manufacture firearms or any lethal weapon is subject to the most serious of punishments.

The main objective of the new society is to prevent crime. The methods adopted have been so successful that crime no longer is significant. In turn, this has reduced the needs and cost of security, judicial, and detention systems.

Another aid is the identification system. Everyone throughout the world has an optical card utilizing advanced technology to store individual data; it is the size of a standard credit card. The individual's history is stored in a world computer bank that can only be opened with this card. Its contents are released through a password, fingerprint, voice print, or by identifying the person by the photo image released on the reader.

It includes any criminal history and how the individual compensated society. This aids security people in apprehending detainees awaiting trial or leaving detention areas. It alerts potential employers because everyone must possess an identification card in order to secure employment.

Some members on the original Committee for Security protested that an identification system was too radical or an invasion of privacy. But most on the Committee responded that any of the above information is already a matter of record (i.e. medical history on file at a health organization, apology for criminal conduct already divulged publicly, credit and employment records, and many others). Furthermore, divulging the information to restricted, authorized persons should not be a source of embarrassment unless the individual has done something wrong. In fact, it is that sort of stigma which acts as a deterant to crime because it is well known to everyone that criminal activity will appear on one's permanent record. But more important, identification prevents criminals, still serving time in World Resource Camps, from leaving and returning to a job in society. As soon as the absentee uses the I.D. card, his criminal record is divulged and the authorities notified. There are no prisons or physical barriers in the camps except for lifers. Lifers are the only criminals incarcerated.

As Behavioral Education took effect, less crime locally and world-wide occurred and the need for extensive security forces to maintain order was less. At first many thought such a situation was impossible to achieve. Upon closer reflection of several earlier societies, such as Japan, it was found to be an entirely reasonable expectation.

(Historical Background)
In 1981, for example, a Japanese was twelve times less likely to be murdered than an American. For each rape in Japan, fourteen occured in the United States, and for each property crime in Japan twenty in the United States! Yet, the population of the United States was only about twice that of Japan. In the United States in 1984, 580,000 inmates were imprisoned compared to only 50,000 in Japan including pre-trial detainees.[12] This resulted primarily from a very early constructive behavioral pattern.

(The New Society)
The mere presence of Security Forces acts as a deterant to temptation since everyone already has a common knowledge of the repercussions of anti-social conduct. Periodically the media runs public notices outlining briefly the usual sentences prescribed for common crimes and other adverse results associated with criminal conduct. These include the stigma of permanently recording the crime in the individual's computerized file; publication of the convicted criminal's name, crime and his apology in all of the local media; the cost of repaying the victim for all loss or damages as well as legal and court costs out of future earnings. A convicted person is required to apologize to the victim in court following the verdict, and this helps the victim psychologically to overcome the trauma of the crime.

The principal purpose of the Security Force is to work as an investigative body. One area of particular importance is to investigate and abort planned manufacture of lethal weapons of any kind. They also inquire into and apprehend those involved in planning of either organized crime or insurrection against the world community. On rare occasions members of the Security Force are needed to apprehend a dangerous suspect.

Since lethal weapons are outlawed, the Security Force is armed only with non-lethal deterrants. Although harmless, they completely incapacitate individuals for a limited period of time. One of the methods used, an offshoot of earlier Soviet military experimentation, is a chemical that puts people to sleep without knowing what is happening. The United States military had earlier developed various methods of destroying arms and armament without hurting humans. These are also used when needed.

Most crimes are misdemeanors, and suspects are merely notified to report for trial on a certain date. Failure to appear invalidates their I.D. cards for purposes of employment and receiving various benefit vouchers that are needed. Consequently, jails are used only to detain the few charged with the most serious felonies.

(Before the new society, if the docket was overly conjested, prosecutors would not sort out serious repeat offenders. No mandatory order of precedence existed. Usually the docket was overwhelmed so cases sometimes backed up for months.) Now, not only has the number of cases diminished, but those, charged with serious allegations as well as repeat offenders, are prosecuted first. Plea-bargaining is no longer used to expedite cases or to reduce prison sentences for lack of prison space because prisons have been abolished.

(Historical Background)

Many times in the later twentieth century jurors became confused by the torrent of legal gobbledygooks. Feeling inadequate to judge a case and fearful of making an error, they would absolve themselves by not convicting a defendant the judge overwhelmingly felt should have been convicted. Some jurors, after being verbally harassed and intimidated by other jurors, would go along with a unanimous verdict only to recant their mistake later. Many confessed to not understanding their instructions. Some made procedural mistakes such as checking off "involuntary manslaughter" when they really meant justifiable homicide (self-defense). After a prolonged trial and long deliberations, others would rush to a verdict in order to get back to a normal life, making serious mistakes in the process.

Predominantly Afro-American and Hispanic juries in the inner cities had a tendency to strongly favor criminal defendants and civil plaintiffs. For example, plaintiffs in St.Louis won eighty percent of the verdicts where personal injury was involved but only forty-eight percent in the suburbs. In the Bronx they won seventy-two percent, and damage awards averaged $1.2 million versus only half that in suburban and affluent Westchester County. Such juries naturally identified with those in the underclass that brought claims against deep-pocket business and government or defended themselves against criminal charges brought by police perceived as abusive and racist. [13]

The juries in complex commercial cases, conscripted from the general population, were hopelessly inadequate to cope with the intricacies associated with accounting, contractual law, and economics of large businesses. Opponents of the jury system called it an amateurish ritual that had long outlived its usefulness. Ninety percent of the world's jury trials were held in the United States. England and most other developed countries long abandoned this practice, but in the United States the jury system was enshrined in the Seventh Ammendment to the Constitution.

(The New Society)
Today in the new society there is no trial by jury. A random group of naive citizens, with no sophisticated knowledge of law and experience in the field of criminology, is not expected to arrive at a prompt and equitable verdict. A judge has the education, training, experience, and capacity to understand the law better. In the past the selection of juries contributed heavily to delays in the judicial system. Additionally, excessive court costs and the interruption of citizens' lives associated with a jury are now eliminated. This has reduced case-backlogs giving both the defendant and plaintiff the benefit of a speedy trial.

One knowledgeable judge usually presides over less-serious uncomplicated cases, where there is overwhelming non-disputable facts, or the suspect has already pleaded guilty. Any case of a very serious or complicated nature requires a panel of three judges expert in trying that particular criminal category. The defendant also has the right to a three judge panel should he prove the circumstances warrant. Bear in mind, all court costs must be paid by the defendant if convicted even if that means periodic deductions from any future salary.

No longer are trials delayed or postponed for months or years. We have adequate, intelligent, and experienced judges. They are no longer appointed by political cronies or elected by voters whose knowledge of judicial expertise is minimal; they are selected, instead, through competitive examinations.

(Historical Background)

Punishment of criminals did not encompass imprisonment until the late eighteenth century. Prior to that, official punishment consisted of beatings, branding, slavery, torture, mutilation, or death. True, jails were used to make debtors pay their debts and to insure the presence of the accused at trials, but even dungeons were only used to remove those who threatened monarchial power.

Nevertheless, as late as the 21st century, some countries in the world continued some of these practices. Malaysia, for example, being a predominant Moslim country, punished theft in some cases with amputation of the hand while robbery was punishable by death. At the same time in Singapore, a Confucian society, caning was common for many crimes, and trafficking in drugs or use of handguns in robbery received the death penalty. Most of those countries had very little serious crime.

Deprivation of freedom by imprisonment as punishment was considered far more humane than the above when it was first adopted. Nevertheless, inmates, as late as the nineteenth century, who violated arbitrary rules while in prison, were chained, flogged and tortured with such things as stretching, sweat boxes, and water cannons. They slept on stone floors in unheated cells without toilet facilities, and food was meagre and unappetizing. Once released, inmates were strongly motivated not to return.

By the late twentieth century prison conditions in the developed countries, especially the United States, were almost luxurious compared to earlier times. Comfortable beds in heated cells with flush toilets were standard. No one worried about going hungry, as in parts of the third world, since plentiful meals consisted of good wholesome food. Abundant recreation was available to keep prisoners from getting bored: liberalized visits from friends and relatives, access to telephones, libraries, hobby shops, movies, television, weight rooms, gyms, and mail privileges to name a few. Some were even granted weekends or vacations outside the prison for so-called "good behavior!" Vocational and educational programs, health and dental care and other amenities were also paid by society.[14] Such standards of incarceration did not come cheap. The cost per prisoner in most cases exceeded the annual income of many taxpayers. This did not include the cost of building the prison or about one-hundred thousand dollars per inmate bed.

Prisoners were not required to do any hard labor as in the chain-gang era. In fact, they were not required to do any work even to help pay for their subsistence. Labor unions, in most cases, pressured politicians to eliminate such requirements to prevent a competitive labor source.

In addition, legal aid grievance procedures, human rights protection, and press interviews were furnished. Law libraries were mandatory. Prisoners were considered indigent and could be represented without cost by a court-appointed attorney. As a result, the courts were clogged with frivolous grievance cases or appeals costing taxpayers millions of dollars. Cases in Arizona were brought because TV rights had been taken away from offending prisoners!

Convicted of vicious crimes, some would sue their victims who had to pay large attorney's fees to fight these frivolous suits. One prisoner, who was serving twenty-five years for stabbing his wife eleven times and destroying her voice box, sued her over visitation rights and even the validity of their divorce. It cost her seven thousand dollars in attorney's fees to fight the suit.[15] In another instance a prisoner filed a claim against the county for clothing and other belongings he left in the vehicle he stole while commiting robbery, assault, and weapons violation. The items had been given to charity.[16]

Nevertheless, as early as 1974 Robert Martinson, a New York researcher, after compiling all available information, concluded that prisons did not work. They did not rehabilitate nor reduce recidivism. More astounding, he further concluded all rehabilitation methods used at that time were failing: probation, parole, halfway houses. He was not alone; prison administrators, including the director of the federal prison system, renounced rehabilitation as a realistic solution except in isolated cases.[17]

In 1990 there were over 700,000 people imprisoned in the United States; by 1995 over one million. Prisons bulged because of the dramatic increase in arrests for drug-law violations, longer sentences, as well as the increase in overall criminal activity. Still, the system continued to fail.

Considering the comfortable living conditions, recreational facilities, and liberal amenities void of work, how could inmates become worse instead of better? Incarceration had become a complete failure for many reasons; some were obvious.

Prisoners were allowed to congregate and roam about threatening other inmates and shouting obscenities at guards. As a result of the prohibition of constructive work, inmates spent their days in idleness and turned to drugs, building arsenals of weapons, gang formations, violence, murder and rape. The chief activity was talk - long discussions about the best way to fence stolen goods, where to buy guns, or whether theft was easier than robbery. Rule enforcement was extremely lax. In some instances, prison officials shared power with gang leaders because correction officers were afraid of inmate reprisals. Riots and hostage-taking was commonplace. It appeared that prisoners were running the prisons!

In *Mothers, Leadership and Success,* Guy Odom said,"Criminals have in turn interpreted public softness and compassion as fear and weakness. (They) express little anxiety about arrest, conviction or prison. The inability of the current system to prevent or curtail criminal activities will have serious consequences in the future as the social structure continues to decay." [18]

In most instances discipline fell by the wayside. Some attributed this to a continued interference in the administration of prisons by human-rights activists. Others complained that bureaucratic inertia had taken over. Consequently, many citizens called for competitive privatization of prisons. Others called for employment of inmates on constructive and worthwhile projects, even building additional sorely-needed prison facilities. They said, "We cannot afford useless members of society."

Prison guards and correction officers in the United States had a bare minimum education so couldn't properly cope with the many complex problems. Two things were uppermost in their minds, their paycheck and their own safety from the inmates. In contrast, two-thirds of the guards in Japanese prisons were college graduates, and the results were exemplerary.

Former inmates ridiculed the manner in which prisons were controlled and suggested much tougher prisons. [19]

Many criminoligists believed prisons were useless in curtailing crime. They reasoned criminals had little self-control, and most reverted to their old ways when freed. Their studies indicated criminal aggressiveness peaked at age eighteen and only diminished as the criminal aged.

(The New Society)
Finally, after careful consideration of previous incarceration systems, the original Committee on Security decided to completely abolish prisons and replace them with World Resource Camps.

In the late eighteenth and early nineteenth centuries, the major deterant to crime was the stigma attached to criminals. By the late twentieth century a considerable amount of crime was no longer universally stigmatized. Shoplifting and employee theft were examples. Instead, apprehension became the main deterrent. In the new society, due to early Behavioral Education programs, we have reverted to stigmatizing all criminal activity and we no longer glorify any part of it.

Now, most crimes are lesser and non-violent such as fraud, theft, vandalism and non-support of fathered children. Historically, most law-enforcement officers repeatedly stressed that crime was especially impacted if certainty of punishment existed. Therefore, today the punishment is a standard mandatory one for first time offenders and for non-violent offenses.

First, if found guilty of a non-violent crime, it is permanently noted on the individual's personal computer file. Second, he must publicly confess and apologize in a paid local advertisement. (Singapore experimented in 1995 with a similar retribution. It televised convicted molesters' confessions and placed their photographs in newspapers accompanied by graphic descriptions of their crimes.) Next, he must attend evening classes in behavioral re-education, make monetary repayment to the victim for all damages and loss as well as court and legal costs. Unlike crime in the twentieth century, the convicted criminal is held financially responsible for the complete and total costs of his crime no matter how long it takes to fulfill those obligations. This can require automatic deductions from the criminal's salary. Finally, he must face his victim's monitored interrogation and repent. The later helps the victim immeasurably to recover from the shock by being able to inquire and vent anger. On the other hand, the criminal has a chance to find out, first hand, the human consequences of his act and apologize.

Following a second offense in addition to the above, the offender must serve a one-year sentence at hard labor in a World Resource Camp. As can be seen, we are more lenient in our sentencing. This is because our criminal laws are now universally respected and severely enforced; deterrants are far more effective.

Our child-support laws are vigorously enforced against a father whether married or not. The new society refuses to assume the cost of raising children that have been indiscriminately propagated by transient fathers. Because of the use of ID cards, it is easy to track them down and force them to be responsible for the children they have fathered.

Suspects involved in misdemeanors and other nonviolent crimes are not held in jail but must appear in court at the time of trial. Failure to appear results in an automatic conviction, the voiding of their ID card, and the immediate notification of the individual's employer who must then suspend him from work and access to subsistence vouchers. It must be pointed out, that any convicted criminal at large, without a valid ID card, will not be granted employment anywhere. Therefore, he does not have access to minimum subsistence vouchers from his employer. (This will be discussed in detail later.) The criminal's survival depends on our societal structure. Therefore, no-shows at trials or convicts who have left World Resource Camps before completing their term are rare.

More serious crimes include violence such as assault with intent to kill, robbery with threat of bodily harm, and rape. Also included in this more serious category are three or more repeat offenses of a non-violent crime, dispensing of unregulated abusive substances, and serious intentional and harmful pollution. Suspects of these more serious crimes are held temporarily in jail pending trial. In addition to the usual sentencing requirements already mentioned, criminals of these crimes must spend five years in a World Resource Camp at hard labor. Probation and reduction of sentences are prohibited by law. As can be seen, sentences are much shorter than in the twentieth century. Studies have shown that long prison sentences in early days, by themselves, did not appear to deter inmates from returning to crime.

Sentences are to insure that offenders repay society by contributing labor in the world's more difficult and shunned work environments. It is still important that the offenders repent, relearn society's acceptable behavior, and return to the fold as productive citizens. As with lesser crimes, this usually consists of confession, public apology and restitution to victims as well as re-education.

The early Committee on Security, with the assistance of the Economic Committee, was aware that certain environments and types of production were avoided by most workers especially where hard physical labor was involved. They concluded that such occupations could be more readily and justifiably filled by convicted criminals. This also allowed the offenders to participate in constructive work while supporting themselves and their families. Those, with families, were encouraged to bring them to join the local community, albeit in a harsh and isolated environment in most cases. Many, who were serving only one year, were allowed to take jobs in their community but only as janitors, street cleaners, garbage collectors, menial seasonal, and other similar jobs that few wanted. The eventual return to normal society was made easier by these approaches. This was a far cry from the uselessness of the old prison system.

Guards or restrictive barriers are not present at World Resource Camps except for a normal Security Force as is present in any community. However, rehabilitative facilities such as educational classes and psychiatric clinics require mandatory attendance. Adequate food, shelter and basic amenities are obtained in return for labor. Escape into a hostile environment, where survival may be extremely difficult, is not a viable option. Anyone refusing to work or deciding to leave can not survive for long in most cases. It is extremely difficult to return to large populated areas because transportation and new employment is impossible without an ID card.

Minimum subsistence vouchers are not available unless one is employed or disabled.

World Resource Camps are actually organized and administered by private companies like any other productive business. The only difference is that convict labor receives basic subsistence vouchers but are not allowed to participate in the profits as do other workers and supervisory help.

Some are construction camps in hostile environments such as the Arctic and Antarctic, jungle, or desert. Others are located in wilderness areas for logging and mining the far north or the jungles of the Amazon. Parts of the program include fishing and canning vessels operating under adverse conditions in the North Atlantic and North Pacific for months at a time.

Working and living in such conditions is harsh and lonely so no one looks forward to returning after their sentence is completed. Everyone tries to avoid a life sentence which is the penalty for a second offense of a serious crime. These lifers, repeat incorrigible offenders, are in isolated locations far away from others and usually in more hazardous and confining endeavors such as coal and hard-rock mining at deep levels. Lifers live in sparton barracks, without their families, without recreational amenities, and are surrounded by lethal high-voltage fences, guard dogs and a few guards. These Camps are reminiscent of the old prisoner-of-war camps of the twentieth century. Lifers must construct their own facilities. If they damage or destroy any, they must repair them or otherwise, be at the mercy of the weather.

The most serious crimes of all are, such things as, the manufacture and distribution of lethal weapons, the attempt to forcibly overthrow the lawful world government, premeditated and animal-like murder, heinous assault and torture with complete indifference to civilized behavior. (An example of this occured in the late twentieth century when a man brutally raped and then cut off the arms of a fifteen-year old girl. He was later released into society on parole where he raped and killed a young woman!) Such crimes are now practically non-existent.

The early founders of our new society debated at length on what to do with these few individuals. It was felt they were too dangerous to ever return to society. Some felt their criminal acts were so serious they forfeited all right to live in a humane community.

The Committee on Security had already elected to eliminate prisons and the costs of associated problems. Therefore, prisons were not the answer for the most serious crimes. Instead, the Committee proposed that convicted criminals of capital crimes would, indeed, be banished for life from the society for which they had no respect. One of the harshest penalties, learned from criminology, was to be shunned from the rest of society. Accordingly, it arrived at a unique solution, one that appeared to fulfill the needs at a small cost. The chance for these serious criminals to return and, once again, threaten society would not be possible.

Instead, they are exiled to large remote polar islands above the Arctic Circle and north of mainland Canada and Siberia. They are landed with nothing but rudimentary survival equipment including harpoon and fishing gear and a small amount of provisions. In winter when the ice freezes over the surrounding seas, escape is highly unlikely because of the extreme temperatures and rudimentary travel gear available. In summer the islands are patrolled by boats of the Security Force to prevent anyone attempting escape in an open boat.

Life is hard and a constant battle just to survive. No civilized society exists there. Most exiles isolate themselves, afraid of others who are also vicious predators like themselves. The result is a very lonely and harsh existence in a vast empty world. Even worse, is the perpetual thought that they will never be able to return to the companionship of any society, never to read or hear of that society, and with no hope of ever making contact with the outside world again. This is truly the greatest punishment of all.

Let us summarize our new system of crime prevention. It consists of mandatory Behavioral Education as well as regular standard education at an early age, mandatory parental guidance and training, followed by boarding school, the abolition of lethal weapons, and the decriminalization of victimless crimes. The judicial system has also been streamlined, prisons have been eliminated, and criminals punished and isolated in several unique ways. Penalties and punishment are certain as well as common knowledge to everyone. People are made accountable for their behavior rather than allowed to blame their environment or the rest of society.

Chapter 9

A RESTORED ENVIRONMENT

(Historical Background)
Secretary of Commerce Stans in an exceedingly grim warning to the nation in 1970 predicted the following. Population could reach 300 million in America by the year 2000 and most would be living in a "vast megalopoli." Sharp increases in conjestion, pollution, crime, and youthful alienation would create frayed tempers and mutual hostility in an anthill society.[1]

***

Jacqueline Williams, a welfare mother of fourteen and pregnant with her fifteenth child, told the black mayor of Washington, D.C. "Why don't you all find me a better place to live?"

He replied, "Why don't you stop having all these babies?"

"Until God stops me," she said. "I don't want to mess my body up with birth control." The city paid $10,000 a month to house and feed her family including her second husband.[2]

Sixty-two year old Leontina Albina, her husband, and their remaining eighteen children lived in a two-room wooden shack. The shack, with no running water on the edge of a slum, was located in Colina, Chile, a rural community twenty miles north of Santiago. Married at age twelve, she gave birth to fifty-nine children; several were twins and triplets. Albina was asked at that time if she would continue to have children. She shrugged, "If God sends them to me, yes."³

Across the world in Africa, Christiana Nzeakor contributed to her husband's twenty-five children along with two other wives. She was extremely proud to be initiated into the Society of Those Whom God Has Blessed, a Nigerian club limited to women who had at least ten pregnancies.⁴

In Keton Village, Rao Changain, refusing an abortion, gave birth to a third child in defiance of China's one-child limit. "I had to keep trying until I had a boy," she calmly told Communist Party officials.⁵

A man named Denja, in Kenya, boasted he had fathered 497 children.

Grace Agbonna, a family planning coordinator in Nigeria, said, "The number of children one has is something to show off. It is a status symbol."⁶

The average African woman had seven children; the average Kenyan had eight. Africa's population doubled every twenty years! The World Bank in 1985 called population growth "the single greatest long-term threat to Africa's economic development."⁷

Nearly all rapid population growth occurred in the developing countries of Africa, Latin America, and Asia; those areas already supported seventy percent of the world's people and were the least capable of absorbing the increase.

"A high birth rate usually accompanies a culturally low civilization and a low birth rate for a culturally high one," wrote Guy Odom in *Mothers, Leadership and Success.*

In *Ethnic America,* Thomas Sowell indicated studies showed Mexican-Americans had much larger families than either whites or blacks. This accounted for a great deal of poverty and lack of education of the females who married at an early age. As Hispanic women obtained more education, they bore fewer children to support. Incidentally, hispanics, whose mother-tongue was English, also completed high school about fifty percent more often and went on to college about seventy percent more often than those whose mother-tongue was Spanish.

Generally, women, with more education, married later than those with less education, had higher rates of contraceptive use, had smaller families, and had lower child mortality rates. A World Resources report for 1990-91 indicated the following:

Adult Female Literacy Rate	Total Fertility Rate
Singapore 79%	1.7
Canada 93%	1.7
Sudan 14%	6.4
Afghanistan 8%	6.9

***

As early as 1976, India added one million people every twenty-eight days. By 1987 the world's population doubled in thirty-seven years and passed five billion. It was predicted to double again in another forty years. The world added eighty million people each year, a population equivalent to all of Mexico. The population in undeveloped countries grew even faster with a growth rate of two and one-half percent, which doubled every twenty-five years.

The United Nations released a report which indicated increased demands of the world's expanding population damaged the basic natural resources on which all life depended. Tropical forests shrank at a rate of twenty-seven million acres a year. Topsoil was lost at the rate of twenty-six billion tons. About thirteen million acres of deserts were created each year; half the world's irrigated land was in danger.[8]

By 1990 it reported that population growth outstripped all previous forecasts and increased at the rate of a quarter million people each day! The United Nations' Population Fund's annual report in 1991 estimated ninety-five percent of the increase in population came from the poorer developed countries, with Africa leading the way. Yet, in the industrial nations of North America and Europe, population increased only slightly through births. Eighty percent of the world's population lived in the developing countries where environmental damage and economic hardship became monumental. The Population Fund predicted the developed nations would be severely pressured with immigrants fleeing poverty and environmental problems from this Third World.

Lester Brown of the Worldwatch Institute noted that forty thousand babies died each day from malnutrition and disease. Many occured in regions where the population explosion destroyed ecosystems necessary for human survival.[9]

In the agrarian society of the developing world, farms had to be carved into smaller and smaller plots when handed down from parents to offspring. As life became impossible to sustain on such meagre farms, people turned to the big cities for work. A mass exodus began from rural to urban areas, such as Narobi and Mexico City. Here people piled up by the millions and created huge sprawling slums. In the case of Mexico, the explosion blew northward and ignored all borders and immigration laws as people scrambled for survival.

In Bolivia ninety-seven percent of its rural peasants lived below the poverty level. They migrated in droves to towns and cities hoping to find a meagre method of survival. "It's less urban pull than rural push," said Rafael Indaburu, an official of the United States Agency for International Development's Bolivian Office. "In the countryside, when you run out of food, you starve," said Gomercinda Valdez de Sajama, who moved to El Alto with her young family of eight. "Here, whether you're rich or poor, there's always something."[10]

El Alto, Bolivia was typical of Third World cities, an urban conglomeration of rural immigrants. Its population in 1976 was 95,000; by 1994 it reached a half million! Its dirt streets spilled a mixture of garbage and raw sewage. Laundry was done by many in a nearby river filled with refuse and dead animals. They used the same water to drink, cook, and wash. Most used the public toilets when available or the streets and rivers. [11]

It was estimated at the current rate of population growth, by 2500 A.D. only 1.13 square feet would be available per person. An enormous human tragedy was unfolding. Historians discerned a dramatic distinction from societies of the past: massive overwhelming numbers. More people required more cities, more homes, more farms, more factories, more transportation, more of everything! "We have never seen this growth rate in the history of mankind before," said Alfred Saury, a leading French demographer. [12]

Takashi Sato, Japan's minister of Agriculture in 1988 cautioned, population growth will result in shortages of food, resources, and energy ... and environmental destruction beyond national boundaries."

Dr. Louis Hellman, Deputy Assistant Secretary for Population Affairs for the U.S. Department of Health, Education and Welfare early in 1977 warned, "No country, however far sighted it may be in controlling its own population, can escape the consequences of the failure of others to moderate population growth. For population growth has reached the stage where it is a threat to world stability and to national security."[13]

Dr. Hellman was proven correct when the immigration of illegal Mexicans across borders of the United States was no longer controllable by 1994. When better methods of control were suggested, the steady growth of Hispanic-Americans and their increasing political force fought their adoption. The tail began to wag the dog as Mexicans illegally swarmed into the American southwest and began to overrun the European-Americans.

Many sociobiologists believed that a close relationship existed between available land resources and the degree of human aggression shown. If land resources could not properly support a growing population, war or other aggressive and destructible efforts for adjoining resources often resulted.

The explosion of population in the developing world caused thousands more to enter the job market each year and created widespread unemployment. New jobs could not be created fast enough to meet the demand. Education fell far behind in these areas because of the lack of facilities. The standard of living dropped rapidly; infant mortality climbed; hunger spread. It was estimated that sixty percent of the population was undernourished. As early as 1979, UNICEF estimated more than thirty million children under the age of five died of starvation the previous year. Abject poverty in Third World countries was a direct result of exploding population in the later part of the 20th century.

No matter how much food production continued to rise, people produced babies faster. Moreover, even the smallest decline in world harvests, due to the vagaries of weather, resulted in widespread famine.

Food donations by developed nations could no longer sustain the world. They had to be rationed. As early as 1977 Senator

Sparkman, the then chairman of the Senate Committee on Foreign Relations, concluded, "I would urge (us) to establish a direct correlation between economic assistance and effective population control programs. This may seem severe, but our resources are limited and priorities must be established. It seems to me infinitely more humane to direct our aid where it will really help people rather than to places where it will be quickly buried in the avalanche of uncontrolled population growth."[14]

More mouths to feed required more marginal land for farming. As a result, deforestation and soil erosion escalated. An example was the monumental erosion on the tropical island of Madagascar off the east coast of Africa. Streams and rivers, red with silt, created a huge red ring around the island that could be seen by astronauts far above the earth!

The combination of soil erosion, drought, and overgrazing caused desertification. In 1993 the United Nations Food and Agricultural Organization said land degradation, coupled with demands from population growth, could wipe out the agricultural value of areas equivalent to the size of Alaska in two or three decades. An additional area, larger than Australia, would need restoration.

Technological advances in fishing, to bring in more seafood for the hungry multitudes, depleted ocean fisheries, created imbalances in the marine environment, and extinguished species. It was estimated by scientists in Southeast Asia that the area lost one-third of its coral reefs by 1994. In the Philippines, for example, renegade coastal villagers harvested fish by dynamiting tropical reefs thus destroying the ecosystems for other marine life.

In tropical waters throughout the globe, coral reefs were being extinguished. Cyanide fishing, harbor dredging, coral mining, deforestation, coastal development, agricultural runoff, shipwrecks and careless divers, according to Time (Sept 20, 1996), were contributors.

Mineral and fossil fuel reserves were rapidly depleted by the voracious demand. The price of oil skyrocketed in the early twenty-first century as reserves ran low, and the rising demand for energy permeated the price structure of all goods creating hardships for vast numbers of inhabitants.

World-wide demand for water began to double every twenty-one years. Communities fought over insufficient water resources. Because up to three-quarters of water consumed by humans was used for agriculture, shortfalls in water due to weather also meant shortfalls of food with periodic famines. Without adequate drainage, continuous irrigation of farmland destroyed thousands of acres through salinization. Deforestation set forces in motion that severely reduced the amount of rainfall where trees once grew.

Dr. Norman Myers, a consultant for the World Bank and author of *Ultimate Security,* wrote, "With water there is surrvival. Without it, there is no food nor sustenance of any sort." He predicted the water supply per person in some countries such as Nigeria and Kenya would shrink by one-half in less than ten years. [15]

Residents, of over eight thousand villages in India in 1990, were forced to hike long distances to the nearest well or river for water. Much of the water was contaminated with sewage and industrial waste. One-third of Beijing's wells went dry, and in Mexico thirty million people had no safe drinking water. In Cape Verde and Barbados, water was nearly depleted. Human populations outstripped the limited amounts of fresh water, the most precious life-sustaining fluid.[16]

The harvest of dwindling supplies of firewood denuded the landscape in vast areas of Africa and Asia. To satisfy the demand of the world's hordes, great swaths were logged in the hardwood forests of areas such as South and Central America. The *Jakarta Post* reported in 1994 that seventy percent of the original forests of South and Southeast Asia had been lost.

The *Jakarta Post* also emphasized that tropical forest destruction would eliminate much of the world's plant species, including many used for medical and other human purposes. They quoted A.Z.M. Obaidullah Khan, regional representative in Asia for the United Nations Food and Agricultural Organization, "And what we have before us is the prospect of irreversible mass extinction of species." He estimated at the present rate of deforestation, up to thirty-five percent of tropical species would be extinct by the year 2040.

Kunda Dixit, author of the *Post*'s article, said, " Indonesia has more types of plants than the entire African continent. Nepal has nearly as many bird species as North America. And more than half of the world's marine life is found in the seas surrounding Southeast Asia. ... impoverished people (in these and other undeveloped areas) desperate for food are destroying natural habitats, causing irreversible biodiversity harm."[17]

As people, desperate for farm land, pushed deeper into and denuded the tropical forests of Africa and South America, the earth's greatest source of exotic microbes, they contacted horrific diseases, such as Ebola and AIDS, that had circulated there for eons among various animals. African poachers, desperate to feed their growing families, killed off large herds of elephant, not only for their ivory but for meat and brought rhinos and other animals to near extinction.

Excessive pollution of the earth's atmosphere by too many inhabitants caused forests to die from acid rain, possible destruction of the protective ozone layer, and the gradual increase in carbon dioxide and methane. These gasses trapped solar heat that radiated from the earth's surface and re-radiated it back. Whether this would gradually increase the earth's average temperature was controversial because it wasn't certain all other factors would remain the same. Nevertheless, most felt it prudent to endorse the concept of slowly reducing emissions.

Technological advancement added to the problem of pollution, not only in earlier years of the developed nations, but later in the Third World especially in Asia.

Excessive toxic waste polluted the soil and water. The disposition of nuclear waste became a serious problem. At times, noise pollution was deafening in the large cities.

Even tourism became a problem as thousands overran exotic fragile ecosystems and infrastructures. Ecuador set a limit of twenty-five thousand tourists a year to the Galapagos Islands. Bermuda imposed a limit on cruise ships that could visit. The growing amounts of garbage from tourists, even in Antarctica, renewed demands to limit visitors. The fragile countrysides of Nepal, Bhutan, Tibet, and Africa were threatened by hordes of tourists. Visitors generated twenty-five thousand pounds of garbage daily in Yosemite National Park. Campgrounds and picnic areas in popular National Parks and Forests in the United States were overbooked, and the government limited the number of hikers on certain trails and offtrail camps. Robert Redford, a dedicated environmentalist, asked, "Is it right to deny our citizens the right to enjoy the beauty of Yosemite? And how then do we manage this resource?"[18]

Large cities were overwhelmed with the rising deluge of garbage and sewage. Some began polluting the oceans by dumping the excess there, and beaches were strewn with all types of garbage including refuse from hospitals. Land-fills for garbage were rapidly disappearing. Others used incineration and merely transferred the waste from the soil and water to the air.

Thousands were killed in so-called "natural disasters" such as floods in Bangladesh. But the problem was not an unexpected flood; it was thousands of people being forced to live in marginal areas: marshlands and those slightly above sea level because no other land was available for the exploding population.

It seemed as soon as one problem was addressed, a new crisis evolved. The overrunning of the earth's surface by millions of exploding humans was comparable to the destruction of a tropical forest when it was overwhelmed by an explosion of army ants devouring everything in sight!

The seriousness of the situation was aptly summed up by Dr. Cat Tiedcke, "Like any life-support system, man's ecosystem has finite ability to sustain human lives ... Unless population growth is brought under control the inexorable increase will reach a point where it is stopped not by a controlled decrease of the birth rate but a disastrous increase of death rate." [19] One could have added that in the meantime the quality of life would continue to degenerate until there was only one objective: survival.

Perhaps the perfect example of a ravaged land by humans was the nation of Haiti. From the air in 1997 one could easily define the border of Haiti with its island neighbor, the Dominican Republic. Verdant forests of the later stopped suddenly and gave way to the abrupt barrenness of Haiti. When Columbus saw Haiti in 1492,he marvelled at its luxurious forests. By 1997, less than two percent of Haiti was covered by forest.

Thousands of acres of forest were destroyed to make room for growing sugarcane. Many trees were logged and shipped to Europe to make mahogany furniture.

Haiti had one of the fastest growing populations in the world: Haitian women averaged five births each. As the population increased and pressed for income, farmers chopped trees to make and sell charcoal or to carve out meagre farm areas. As farms were passed on to offspring, they were cut in smaller parcels so each could have a farm. But families of seven could not exist on half acre farms, and malnutrition, then, became commonplace.

Without rainforests, which exude water vapor, less rain fell, the water table dropped and desertfication accompanied by erosion began to occur. Sea water turned brown from the runoff and killed the plankton needed to feed the island's fish. It was an example of the ultimate environmental disaster.

***

Most people were unable to understand the vast problems created by their personal reproductive decisions. This was clearly illustrated in a 1989 report by Harold Olmos of the Associated Press when he interviewed a typical mother, Maria Ruiz, in Venezuela. She and her family lived in a squalid tin-roofed shack in a slum on the outskirts of Caracas. Her husband worked ten to twelve hours a day at a brick plant one-hundred miles away for about twenty-five dollars a week. This allowed Maria to feed her children corn bread for breakfast, black beans and spaghetti for lunch and dinner, and a little meat on Saturdays. Maria said, "I was blessed with twenty children, but my triplets and another three died in the sixties from dysentery."

As early as the 1970s some said the carrying capacity of the world had already been passed which meant death rates would rise until population growth stopped. They assumed this could only occur through starvation, pestilence, and war. Was AIDS nature's answer to this problem? What about the undiscovered deadly virus released from the depths of the Amazonian jungle through deforestation? Or could a nuclear exchange between two countries trigger a nearly simultaneous missile launch throughout the globe and end in the obliteration of all but a few?

These were not some horrible assessments of future destruction millions of years away when the sun eventually burns out. This catastrophe was rushing down on the earth's inhabitants in the later part of the twentieth century. But only a few were concerned with attacking the cause head on rather than merely the symptoms. Most, like Maria Ruiz, were not even aware of the cause.

Ironically, the real cause of the explosive growth in population was not an increase in the birth rate. This had remained fairly constant for many decades. The culprit was *death control,* the rapid decrease in the death rate through technological advances in medicine, agriculture, improved sanitation, and other life-sustaining improvements while maintaining the same birth rate. Death rates had been cut to less than half of what they used to be; longevity increased without a compensating reduction in birth rates.

Even the abolishment of the slave trade and the suppression of tribal warfare by colonial powers aided in Africa's population growth. Infant mortality rates in the Third World declined significantly after World War II.

The average length of life in the more advanced countries in 1838-1854 was about forty years. By 1937 it had risen to sixty years. In the 1990s it was close to eighty! The result was a runaway growth in population.

***

Urban sprawl had been blamed on developers, pollution on industry, species extinction on human insensibilities, soil erosion on over-use, depletion of natural resources on greed, and hunger on the richer nations' unwillingness to share. In a narrow sense and to some degree this was true, but most industries were merely attempting to supply what people needed and demanded. These were not the causes. Instead, they were simply the symptoms of an insatiable demand of growing hordes to use and inhabit the earth. Everyone seemed ready to address the symptoms but afraid to face the real underlying cause: population explosion.

The truth was most individuals believed birth control was a personal decision, based on religion, morality, and their own need and desires. They believed it should not be forced on them. Most either did not associate nor want to associate growing world problems with this personal decision.

Finally, nations especially effected such as Egypt, India, China, and Indonesia pushed for world-wide birth control education and its adoption spear-headed by the United Nations as occured at the Cairo Conference in 1994. Yet even at this late stage, religious groups such as the Vatican representing the Catholic religion and fundamental Moslims vehemently opposed efforts of the conference.

In Nigeria, one of Africa's worst examples of exploding human proliferation, a man's prestige depended on the number of his offspring. Newspapers with full-page obituary advertisements listed all the children, grandchildren, and great grandchildren sometimes with photos of family members. Moreover, Nigeria had a strong Moslim area in the north and a strong Catholic sector in the south. Both favored large families and opposed contraception.[20]

Mohammedanism also allowed polygamy and since it was a widespread religion throughout the world, the problem increased. Moslim fundamentalists fought against national family-planning efforts in such places as Iran, Egypt, Bangladesh, and Pakistan. As a result, Moslim countries were some of the densest populated areas in the world. President Mubarak of Egypt said in 1989, "If people did not have eight, nine or twelve children, there would not be a food problem (in Egypt)."

Roman Catholics have created the same problem in countries like Mexico, Kenya and the Philippines. When Pope John Paul II was in Brazil, Latin America's most populous nation, he attacked widespread birth control programs and accused officials of undermining the Brazilian family by promoting them.

Developing nations had a problem creating capital surplus to purchase agricultural and industrial technology to pursue economic growth. Instead, everything they produced was consumed by a growing population. Lacking economic growth they could ill afford funds for any form of social security. Therefore, people continued to produce more children to assist them in their old age as well as to provide their own personal labor force; typical, was India.

***

Most nations lacked any sort of population stabilization program. Some attempts were made to limit the family size, but to most Third World families, this usually meant after the desired size of four to six children was reached. Of course, this did not reduce the birth rate.

Third World parents welcomed good public health and all types of death control, but they also wanted lots of children. Many used contraceptives only to space births and to limit their families after the desired number had been reached. This would not change even if a "perfect" contraceptive was invented. So, most national birth control programs were only fractionally successful - even in China and India where the greatest effort was made. People would not conform against their will unless educated or forced to do so. Dr. Julia Ojiombo, the assistant minister of housing and social services in Kenya said, "It's no use forcing birth control on people before they are themselves ready to accept it."[21]

Still, most people in developed nations and many in undeveloped ones paradoxically wanted to see population growth curbed. A Gallup poll as early as 1976 showed that eighty-seven percent in the United States did not like to see their country's population grow. It was also true that a substantial forty percent of married women in the developing world wanted to avoid further child-bearing but didn't have available contraceptives (World Bank study 1993).

Bruce Wilcox, president of the Institute for Sustainable Development, said fundamental changes in society were necessary to solve the problem of exploding population. Cultural attitudes that promoted high birthrates had to be changed. The former president of the World Bank, Robert McNamara, declared in 1991 that the world must act immediately to hasten the reduction of population growth in the 1990s. "Family planning is simply a basic element in a poverty-reduction program," cautioned Rodulfo Bulatro, senior demographic specialist at the World Bank in 1993.

But stabilizing population failed for lack of political will. Even though most scientists were in agreement that draconian measures were necessary to reduce the birth rate for the survival of future generations, politicians could not instigate such means against the will of their constituents. This was a classical example of why political democracy could not properly cope with the serious problems of society.

(The New Society)
After carefully reviewing the history of the disintegration of the environment, the original Committee on Environmental Controls was well aware that population explosion was the source of many of society's problems. Unless the founders of the new society acted to curtail it, the future of mankind would be in jeopardy.

However, some on the Committee questioned whether any type of voluntary program could possibly succeed. If it couldn't, how could they press incessantly for even better death control in the future knowing it would only end in catastrophe? Such things as the advancement of medicine, increased farm production, and better sanitation would only further expand the population and merely allow survival. The crowded conditions of an everyday living world would accelerate with all the accompanying socio-economic problems, and the aesthetic quality of life would continue to get worse.

Should food and medical relief, therefore, be curtailed in areas that refuse to help themselves by limiting family size? Could children, thus, be punished for the ignorance of their parents? The Committee agonized with the moral and ethical considerations involved in such a drastic step and decided against it.

(Historical Background)
In China couples were fined for having more than one child, but many merely paid the fine and had another baby. Mass sterilization on a voluntary basis failed earlier, but later it became more popular in scattered areas. By 1989 ninety eight million women and thirty-five million men had requested it as a permanent solution. Later a new law required abortion or sterilization to prevent births of children with disabilities. (In 1927 the United States Supreme Court, in Buck vs Bell, upheld a Virginia law allowing ster-

ilization of retarded people living in institutions.) Family planning had only partially succeeded earlier in India, so later more drastic measures were suggested such as compulsory sterilization and abortion.

Some seventy percent of Thailand's couples practiced family planning. In the Singapore area, one of the densest populated areas in the world, the growth rate was cut to 1.3 per family. After the second child, full medical and educational costs had to be born by the parents. In addition, family tax deductions were eliminated.[22] Eventually a small family became socially acceptable as in the United States.

Many studies indicated children in smaller families were healthier, more secure economically, and also achieved more education and a higher I.Q. The World Bank reported that with good family planning, it took only twenty years for the average family of a region to decline from eight children to two. Polls showed that when women definitely wanted to limit their children, they preferred a simple fool-proof method: sterilization over oral contraceptives or other methods.

(The New Society)
Finally, after considerable review and analysis of historical data followed by intense debate, the Committee was convinced only draconian measures would work. Population control, for the sake of future civilized society, must take precedence over reproductive freedom.

In order to reach a stabilization point where the birth and death rate were in balance, it was decided to permit each family (woman) a maximum of two children. After that, it was mandatory for both the man as well as the woman to be administered long-term contraceptives, such as the popular Norplant of the 1990s and the later-developed male birth-control pills. A third child would be automatically placed for adoption by couples without children. If a fourth child were born, the mother would be required to have compulsory sterilization.

Once the world population stopped growing and small families became acceptable to everyone, the final population-control program was undertaken. This final program limited each woman to one child until the total population reached the ideal point. Then the new society returned to the two child limit.

The world's inhabitants finally returned to a level of population where all live in comfort and dignity without fear and without destroying the environment. They live in a world whose population resembles that of decades before when pristine wilderness areas were frequented by a few instead of hordes, and a renewed quality of life has become a reality.

***

After formation of the world government, another problem became evident with the free movement of people. Those from poor undeveloped regions would migrate immediately to more prosperous developed areas in order to raise their standard of living. In so doing, enormous problems could develop as occured during the rush of rural inhabitants to Mexico City and other Third World cities in the later twentieth century.

Accordingly, it was decided to make it an orderly transition. Until new generations were on the same educational level as the more developed regions, migration was restricted to those who were qualified to fill jobs in open positions. Those, who could successfully pass competitive examinations, were accepted. In the meantime, everything was done to raise the living standard in the undeveloped areas as quickly as possible through birth control, education, and economic development.

(Historical Background)

Prior to the population explosion in the mid-twentieth century, little thought was given to pollution and depletion of resources. During these earlier periods adequate resources were available for consumption. The small amount of pollution was easily absorbed without detrimental effects. The first statesman to seriously consider the environment was the American President, Theodore Roosevelt in 1908. He remarked, "We have become rich through the lavish use of our natural resources and we have just reason to be proud of our growth. But the time has come to inquire seriously what will happen when our forests are gone, when the coal, the iron, the oil and gas are exhausted, when the soil has been further impoverished and washed into the streams, polluting the rivers, denuding the fields and obstructing navigation." [23]

(The New Society)
Even after the world's population growth had stabilized decades later, there was still a real need to conserve remaining resources and control pollutants. The founders of the new society did many things to retard pollution. As mentioned earlier, it was a criminal act to deliberately pollute. It is now required that all mining and industrial facilities create processes that recycle by-products in such a way that they are either chemically neutralized and disposed as harmless, or processed, sold, and used in other industries where those toxic products are needed. The cost of neutralizing and disposing of waste products is passed on in the price to the consumer who requires the product; it is not passed on as a waste disposal cost or pollution tax to the general public.

In order to reduce emissions and the possibility of the so-called "greenhouse" effect, an orderly phase-out of fossil-fuel combustion was adopted. This included the abolition of most gasoline-operated individual driving-vehicles (more about this later when the new transportation system is explained). In the meantime, most people relied heavily on clean-burning natural gas which was in abundance over much of the world for a long period of time. New more-economical fuel-cells have also been developed, similar to the ones used as a source of electricity on the earlier space flights.

A crash program to develop new inexhaustible energy sources such as hydrogen and nuclear fusion was undertaken with vast financing from the world community. Hydrogen is abundant and comprises about ninety percent of the universe. Hydrogen fusion, the process that fuels the sun, is essentially an inexhaustible energy supply. It produces one-millionth of the nuclear waste and a ten-millionth of the radioactivity of earlier nuclear power plants.

Although substantial research was done to turn coal into a clean-burning fuel, it still remains a primitive source of energy. Instead, before their depletion, fossil-fuel resources are reserved for the manufacture of petro-chemicals. Solar energy, merely the transfer of hydrogen-fusion from the sun, was found difficult to transport from our reflectors on the moon and uneconomical compared to the potential of fusion.

***

Some biologists said the crisis in species extinction in the previous centuries had not been equaled since the mass disappearance of the dinosaurs. Therefore, the new society set aside large animal parks and stocked them with endangered animals and birds in order to preserve the species. The eventual reduction in world population allowed the world government to reestablish these species in many parts of the world such as reforested tropical areas. These areas were made permanent wilderness for the enjoyment of future generations and the preservation of ecosystems.

As late as the twenty-first century, nuclear waste accumulated with no serious plan to rid the environment of this dangerous toxic material. It became a serious threat to future generations. Today, all nuclear waste is transported beyond the pull of the earth's gravity to be lost forever into deep outer space. Propulsion is now quite reliable, simple, and less expensive partly due to new fuels. Nevertheless, in spite of this rather radical method and its cost, it is absolutely necessary to rid the earth of this pollutant that could contaminate the soil and water for centuries in ways we could not imagine.

(Historical Background)

By the early twenty-first century, waste and garbage was innundating the world especially in the more developed areas. For example, America alone was generating one-hundred and sixty million tons of solid waste each year by 1988. Land fills had become inadequate and were contaminating drinking water. Incineration, even with scrubbers and filters, was uneconomical and had many problems including the production of toxic ash. Recycling helped but was far from complete. Sewage plants were often inadequate, and excesses were dumped into rivers, bays, and oceans.

A Restored Environment

(The New Society)

The early Committee on Environment studied the normal composition of household and commercial garbage in the United States to find about forty percent was paper and containerboard followed by yard vegetation of eighteen percent. Food wastes, metals, glass, and plastics, about equally divided, comprised the balance.

Many reasons arose why recycling hadn't worked too well in earlier times. It was difficult for most people to relate to the problem as long as garbage was picked up frequently and at an insignificant fee. Most consumers valued products of convenience: disposable diapers, throwaway pens and razors, plastic bags, disposable packaging. It was also uneconomical and impractical for many apartment complexes and commercial enterprises to recycle. Extra time was needed to sort waste; this usually meant additional labor costs.

Paper and cardboard products, the biggest portion of waste, were many times uneconomical to recycle because regional differences existed between the amount of paper consumed versus mill recycling capacity. Paper mills also had difficulty using hundred percent recycled material. Additionally, no price advantage existed over new paper in most instances.

Nevertheless, the procedure of dumping all waste into a "garbage" container to be hauled away and dumped in a huge landfill was primitive. Worse, the custom prevailed in most undeveloped countries of not even attempting to dispose of waste - any kind of waste. The Committee realized, in spite of the problems, a mandatory waste disposal program must be instigated wherein all waste is processed and reused. It had a twofold purpose: to stop waste pollution and to conserve natural resources by reuse.

All homes are now required to have organic disposals that pulverize food waste into the sewage system. Sewage is now treated, processed and sold for use in agriculture.

Garden refuse must be machine-pulverized and set aside in special bags for pickup. Automated composting plants decomposs the waste in large vats without odor. The cost is a tenth that of burying or incinerating. After processing, it is sold for mulch and soil conditioner to help rebuild eroded soil areas

Other recyclables are more difficult. The Committee on Environment standardized all packaging and hardware parts and discouraged the use of materials that are unrecycable. Bulk mail now is no longer a big chunk of homeowner's waste. The postal system is now run by private competing companies, and junk mail is not subsidized so it is only a fraction of its previous volume.

The new multi-story living complexes have a chute for paper products which lead to a dumpster. Plastics are now truly biodegradable similar to Biopol and Vertix used in the late 1990s. Glass bottles and containers are no longer manufactured. Cans and other glass are bagged separately by tenants. and deposited into separate dumpsters. Any misuse by tenants is subject to an expensive sorting charge against the entire complex. All recyclable pick-ups are free in exchange for the recyclable product. Because decomposition or spoilage of recyclables is no longer a problem, pick-ups are less frequent and, thus, more economical for recycling companies. People wanting pick-ups of such things as old furniture, large appliances, video sets and other large items, or books, magazines, and clothing need only place a call to thrift stores. It is then picked up at no charge during a regular periodic pick-up for this material.

All other trash, not recycled, is picked up on a fee-per bag basis. Special empty bags are purchased from the recycling company to pay these fees. Therefore, the expense of billing for this purpose is eliminated. The cost of bags is substantial and are specially marked to prevent use of other bags. When consumers must pay for this extra trash, they generate less. It has become a strong incentive to recycle as much as possible. In the old days when flat monthly fees were charged, those who generated a lot of garbage paid the same fee as those who generated little.

This small, remaining, unrecycled waste is easily incinerated without significant pollution and generates electricity as its by-product. All the methods of recycling appear adequate, but we are constantly coming up with new and improved ideas emphasizing a monetary incentive to recycle.

People soon became accustomed to the advanced recycling, and it became routine like anything else. To process recyclables economically was more difficult. However, the Committee on Environment knew it could be done because Japan, as early as 1988, was recycling sixty-six percent of its cans, fifty-five percent of its bottles and fifty percent of its wastepaper.

Automated recycling and incinerating plants are integrated. Metals and glass are sorted by computer for color and chemical composition to meet quality and contamination specifications. Because recycling is mandatory, reclamation plants are more abundant reducing transportation costs from the recycling centers. As a result, even processed waste paper is now economical and competes readily with raw wood. No longer is there a problem of price volatility in the newsprint market because of fluctuating prices of wood pulp. Furthermore, wood pulp is no longer a reasonably cheap resource and is used mainly to supplement recycled waste paper,

Industries neutralize much of their toxic waste with the use of specialized bacteria created primarily through genetic engineering. The toxic substances are eaten and then metabolized into such harmless things as carbon dioxide, water and protoplasm. Other companies cut waste generation by using fewer toxic substances, reusing some wastes, and substituting alternative materials. This has also resulted in large savings. Keep in mind, any method that reduces the cost of protecting the environment, can be passed on to the consumer in a more competitive price.

The reduction of population results in a corresponding reduction in livestock necessary for food markets and personal pets. This in turn, has reduced the generation of methane from manure. However, through laws, we have eliminated the primitive custom of allowing tons of pet feces to be deposited at random throughout large populated towns and cities while human feces were disposed into a sanitary sewage system. On an average day in 1995 Berlin, crews collected forty tons of dog manure from the streets!

Strict marine conservation has been adopted to protect ocean ecosystems while, at the same time, encouraging the development of large fish hatcheries and vast aquaculture farms. These farms have been developed to grow trout, catfish, crawfish, and newly developed species. Salmon, lobster, crab, oysters and other saltwater seafood are grown and harvested in gigantic sea farms.

***

Before population was reduced, fresh water became critical and expensive. To alleviate shortages many conservation measures were adopted. These included faucets with mandatory automatic shut-offs, recycling of waste-water for garden and agricultural purposes, and automatic "drip" systems for landscaping to prevent run-offs. Water lines, basic plumbing and water filtration systems are present in previously undeveloped regions. But the greatest accomplishment in this area was the improvement, of seawater desalinization plants. They are now cost-effective and located in many parts of the world.

(Historical Background)
In the ninteenth and early 20th century when available land became more valuable and difficult to find in heavily populated areas, people merely migrated to new virgin areas: the American West, Australia, Canada, and the Matto Grosso of Brazil or expanded the suburbs of their cities. By the end of the twentieth century there was no more virgin land to appropriate. It was no longer thought to be an infinite resource.

Later, land became polluted with toxic waste, ravaged for mineral resources, destroyed by salinization when irrigated, its water contaminated and wasted, and top-soil relentlessly lost. Over-farming and fire-wood gathering resulted in treeless landscapes causing soil erosion during torrential rains until all that remained was sand and rocks in many areas.

Typical was the erosion in Spain. Santiago Marraco, director of the Institute for Preservation of Nature in Spain, said in 1988, "Thirty million acres, or one fourth of the country, are affected by severe erosion that could turn them into a desert unless it is checked."[24]

In Iran, near the ancient Persian capital of Persepolis, a large beautiful forest once stood that helped retain the area's moisture. Then the inhabitants gradually deforested it until only a barren desert remained. So the problem had been longstanding and ongoing.

The over-use of natural resources was also closely associated with pollution. For example, the rapid depletion of tropical forests reduced the absorption by trees of carbon dioxide from burning fossil fuels.

Urban sprawl removed valuable cropland from the world's resource bank. In the United States, alone, it was estimated that one million acres of prime farmland had been urbanized every year in the 1980s.

Shorelands and other recreational areas were no longer unlimited and accessable to everyone. Most had long been appropriated for residences or other private uses. Those, which remained public, were extremely crowded and overused.

In some instances these lands were utilized efficiently, by using a market economy for their most economical and practical purposes. Most were, therefore, used for the long term. Nevertheless, in other instances, the uses were temporarily exploited or planned within the lifespan of the owner. Little thought was given to how it should be left or used by future generations. At other times, it was misused for the wrong purpose (housing development on prime farmland) by someone ignorant of its more valuable long term potential. Often, especially in third world countries, the land was ravaged due to ignorance through overgrazing and erosion. A great demand existed by nearly everyone to exploit land, many times for the short term, which resulted in environmental and resource problems.

(The New Society)

The depletion of the world's limited land resources and the resulting destruction of the environment was a problem around the globe when the Committee on Environmental Control first met. They recognized the obvious solution was to limit population. Additionally, it was decided the earth's limited land resources must be strictly controlled if the needs of future inhabitants were to be fulfilled. It was necessary to insure land was not wasted but instead, put to the most efficient use to benefit the greatest number of people then and in the future. The Committee realized land is the world's most valuable natural resource. Its allocation and disposition could no longer be jeopardized by an individual's decision.

Ignoring the affect of inflation, the cost of owning land in the past was generally so high that land utilization was pursued for any economical purpose as quickly as possible to help compensate for its cost. (i.e. Raw land had to be developed, within reason, as soon as possible to bring in income.) In contrast, large estates frequently could afford to keep large chunks of land out of use or in inferior use for very long periods although it had a more superior potential use. Economic waste also resulted from changing its utilization too soon or too late. It required many scientific and professional minds from all fields associated with land use to evaluate and make the correct long-term decisions.

After months of research, and heated debate, the Committee on Environmental Control arrived at a radical decision. Everyone on the Committee was pressured by their own prejudice and society's centuries of tradition of owning one's own land. But after a thorough analysis of the pros and cons, they realized it was for the good of posterity to accept a radical but brave decision. The Committee decided that all land and its natural resources should be owned, controlled, and leased long-term by the world community. It firmly believed a strict hands-on control over land use and classification by a regional land board consisting of many professional experts was far better than mere zoning codes that were constantly revised or modified to please politician's special interests.

Government ownership of land was not a new idea. It had been advocated and adopted by the Marxists. There the similarity ended. They used it as a method to control and eliminate class wealth whereas the new society is interested primarily in scientific land use and development.

***

All commercial and agricultural land is now leased on a long-term basis, usually for a lifetime, in the case of an individual.

Its use-classification is predetermined and closely monitored by the regional Land Use Board. It is required that each regional Board include the following: civic planners and engineers, architects, economists, business and industrial managers, attorneys, financial analysts, experts in the field of retail marketing, agriculture, forestry, mining, and outdoor recreation as well as scientists (biologists, geologists, ecologists). Each is called upon for input when a new proposal is made for classification or zoning so that nothing is overlooked.

Generally, the main functions of the Board are to classify the use and zone land, to select private professional leasing agents through competitive bids, oversee their execution of leases, and monitor the use of land.

At first, it seemed this number of professional people on each Board would incur considerable cost to the government, but the total rentals received in each region reach enormous amounts. The costs for the Board, its staff, property-leasing agents, and other overhead is a miniscule fraction of the revenue. As we shall soon see, land rentals have become the major source of income for the government so it is very important that it be handled by highly qualified experts in their respective fields.

In addition, each regional Board's leases and activities are periodically audited by private independent auditors who report the results to the public. Terms of Board members are limited and staggered.

***

If the tenant should decide to leave before the lease has expired, he may sell his leasehold-improvements to a new tenant who must renegotiate a new long-term lease. The renegotiation is much like that for leases of commercial property before the new society. In other words, the Land Use Board only leases the land and does not own or sell the improvements, and its leasing agents handle all aspects of the leasing much like it was done in earlier times.

The only exceptions to this arrangement are parks, recreational areas, wilderness areas, and civic improvements. Even these are maintained by private competitive firms that are far more efficient than intrenched government bureaucracies.

The policy of leasing land does not inhibit desirable economic growth because the result is similar to the former lease-back procedure adopted by many businesses in the late twentieth century. In that procedure, companies sold the land on which they had improved with buildings, plants, and other structures to another party. Then they leased the land back in order to put the funds from the sale to a better use through additional expansion of their primary business operations (the things they do best, not real estate investment).

Leases, with options to renew, are handled by professional property-management experts hired by the Land Use Board on a competitive basis. The object is to obtain the best possible return available to the community while closely monitoring the use of the land. Most leases are based on a percentage of sales or income and are renewable on that basis. Should there be a dispute at that time on a fair rental, the lease is put up for auction to the highest bidder. All leases must be publicly advertised to give anyone interested a chance to bid. Nonetheless, land-leases and the sale of leasehold improvements are handled much as they had always been for commercial establishments.

Of course, mineral, water, and logging rights, as well as farm and grazing lands, are also leased and monitored.

The most concentrated job of the Land Use Board is the continued monitoring of the proper use and non-despoiling of the land. A leasee found in violation for the first offense is fined and must restore and pay for any resource or pollution damage. A second violation results in lease forfeiture as well as payment for additional damages. Of course, if any charge is thought to be unjustified, the accused may appeal it in court. More serious premeditated violations are still subject to criminal prosecution.

***

The transition from private land holdings to common land was immense and had to be accomplished in an orderly manner. To prevent major economic disruptions, land-use classification for the most beneficial purposes proceeded very gradually. It took decades before this was accomplished.

Any change from current use is given considerable thought and planning by the many professionals on the Board so nothing is overlooked in their final decision. It also welcomes input from current occupants or other interested parties who may suggest a more productive use. However, the Board acts quickly in some areas. This is to prevent further deforestation in critical areas of the tropics, to stop serious erosion of top soils, and to give immediate attention to other areas requiring it.

The transfer of private land to the world community is effected by merely deeding all land parcels to the common pool. Buildings and other improvements remain the property of their owners. New leases are granted to the original owners at zero rentals for their lifetime. In the case of corporations and partnerships, leases are at zero rent for the next fifty years before the lease is renegotiated on a competitive basis. No exchange of money occurs and the former owners continue to use the land as before for their lifetime.

In the meantime, of course, owners can still sell this new leasehold along with any improvements to a new tenant. If, however an outstanding mortgage or loan exists on the land, the debtor is required to continue making the payments until his death or sale of his leasehold. At which time, the Board or the new tenant assumes the payments until the loan is paid in full.

In the meantime, if the property is reclassified for a more efficient use, and if the original improvements to the land no longer abide by the new classification and have to be dismantled or modified, then the owner is fairly compensated by the Land Use Board.

***

Another very important benefit of government ownership of all land is the elimination of practically all taxes because the income from leases is more than adequate to cover the reduced cost of the new government.

At first, however, no income came from leases. Income gradually accelerated as property improvements were sold, death came to the original owner, or land parcels were reclassified, and leases were signed with new tenants. During this short interim, a small consumption tax was imposed to meet the government's needs.

The direct control of land by the world community has become an important factor in the control of the earth's environment, but it also has led to the abolishment of the income tax in the new economic system.

At first, the very idea of not owning one's own land seemed to be a loss of a basic right. But, the Committee on Environment reasoned that this was merely a custom enshrined in a prejudicial mentality. All of us are brief transients here on earth; individuals should not hold it in perpetuity. It is for all humankind now and in the future to use and enjoy.

As the new system of leasing instead of owning took hold, nothing really changed very much from a business standpoint. Ranches and farm enterprises continued to lease grazing and crop lands. Businesses built plants and office buildings on leased land similar to the former lease-backs. Yet, commercial and urban sprawl gave way to attractive, orderly and more efficient growth. Parks and recreational areas were still owned but not run by the government. Eventually, business people and ranchers became accustomed to it. Homeowners were essentially not effected as will be seen in chapter 11, *Freedom of the Individual*.

Chapter 10

A DYNAMIC NEW ECONOMY

(Historical Background)
The collapse of the wealth-making process had led to economic dark ages and the virtual annihilation of civilized society at various times in history. A case in point was the extinction of Roman civilization in western Europe in the fifth century A.D. The commerce and trade (market-economy) of the Roman Empire was one of its great sources of strength. The devastations, by the Teutonic and other warrior societies that brought the fall of the western Roman Empire, ended most of this trade and commerce. It was followed by centuries of considerable poverty and economic stagnation identified by nomadic tribalism and feudalism. Average French families, even in the late 1700s, spent most of their income just to buy bread to stay alive. Finally, industrial capitalism came to western Europe in the nineteenth century during a period of minimal government intervention. [1]

This, the factory system, brought forth the Industrial Revolution that was rugged and ruthless. Harsh as it may have been, it was the road to freedom for millions of farm peasants who abandoned rural land owners. Even in the late twentieth century, countless people in third-world countries moved to free labor markets of towns and cities to escape the poverty and hopelessness of rural living.

The first capitalist societies were primitive and cruel, but the value of profit and loss as a measurement of efficiency did not lie in its clumsy origin but in its future potentiality.

Did it work? The answer is that by 1976 the leading capitalist nation, the United States with only six percent of the world's people and only seven percent of the world's land, produced half of the world's farm crops. It also produced over two-thirds of the world's computers, most of the passenger aircraft, one third of the world's paper products, farm machinery, and electrical power. The American standard of living had the greatest advance in the history of the world during the preceeding thirty years. Disposable income in the United States rose 170 percent even after deducting for the rise in price inflation!

In the late 1970s and early 1980s the United States deregulated finance, telecommunications, and air and ground transportation (i.e. It removed onerous government interference in the market mechanism of these industries.). It also drastically lowered tax rates across the board. These policies led to an increase in the formation of many new small-businesses from 270,000 in 1978 to 640,000 by 1985 resulting in many new job openings.

In the early 1990s Israel's socialist economy had declined to an abominable stage. Economic stagnation with unemployment of ten percent accompanied a debt that was thirty times that of Mexico on a per capita basis caused by subsidizing kibbutzins. [2]

Shimon Peres, the Labor Party leader, and at that time finance minister, began rapidly privatizing state-owned companies such as El Al airline. He explained, "I tell my friends in the labor movement that if we want to spend money like socialists, we have to make money like capitalists."

Mexicans, in a 1993 survey, said they believed the sale of state-owned enterprises was good for the average person in spite of their long exposure to socialist rhetoric. Nearly all of the one-thousand one-hundred government-owned and operated companies in 1982 were sold to private firms. The proceeds were used to reduce the national debt, and the interest saved raised social spending. The expense of bureaucrats to run the social programs was reduced by furnishing the products, equipment, and professional supervision directly to needy communities to build schools, streets, water and sewer systems. Citizen participation nearly eliminated labor costs and waste. Oscar Espinosa, head of the state development bank said, "We want to build a strong base of support for free-market policies that Mexico never returns to the old paternalistic way of doing things." [3]

The real eye-opener was Chile. From the Marxist government of Salvador Allende in the early 1970s, Chile developed from a wretched economy with shortages of basic necessities, runaway inflation, and state-run business confiscated from the private sector into the most vibrant economy in Latin America.

After a bloody military coup in 1973, General Pinochet's government returned six-hundred expropriated companies to their owners and began the long and difficult process of returning to a market-economy. After nine consecutive years of growth, the gross national product more than doubled, and inflation declined to twelve percent by 1992 from four digit levels. Unemployment dropped to less than five percent, and the government was running a surplus instead of a deficit. The extraordinary ten percent annual growth was not a consumption boom but a healthy one based on exploding exports and investment in new plants and equipment. Chile even had a trading surplus with its leading trade partner, Japan. It continued to sell off state owned companies to private investors, deregulated the economy forcing companies to adapt to competition or go broke, and lowered important tariffs. Inefficient industries had no protection.[4]

***

New product and service innovation from the assembly lines of capitalism freed American women from daily drudgery and heavy manual labor expected of them in previous decades. No longer did American women have to grow gardens for food, gather wood for fuel, tote water, spin textiles, and sew clothing. Their counter parts in many other places in the world continued these chores decades later.

Later, food spoilage for lack of refrigeration was also eliminated. Heating water on wood stoves, washing clothes and dishes by hand, and inumerable other chores were abolished. Finally, convenience foods purchased at supermarkets and fast-food restaurants further enabled women to be as free as men in seeking career employment. The dynamics of a competitive free-market economy had contributed greatly to the liberation of the American woman. In 1990 the contrast with the average Soviet woman living under a rigid non-competitive and inefficient government-run economy was difficult to comprehend..

Many capitalist specialists were necessary to help in this change: savers, investors (risk-takers), inventors, producers, distributors and retail merchants. Without them, American women would have been on a par with their socialist equivalent in the former USSR, years behind in standard-of-living improvements such as hot-water heaters, automatic washing machines, dishwashers, refrigerators, freezers, electric grills and ovens, and microwaves because governmental bureaucracies had fundamental incapacities for performing economic tasks. In addition, competitive markets gave women improved products and the best quality at the lowest possible price.

(The New Society)
It was obvious to the early Economic Advisory Committee, after reviewing the historical evidence of the many catastrophes of centralized economies, the efficient-market was, without a doubt, the logical economic mechanism for the world. But before it was unanimously recommended, the Committee decided to review the pros and cons to be certain nothing was overlooked.

(Historical Background)
As early as the 1970s before the collapse of socialist economics, the *Reader's Digest* reminded its readers of the incredible complexity of a free-market economy. For example, it meshes an assortment of skills, wages, resources, and prices with the consumer's needs and desires. Yet, it leaves the actual choice to the individual consumer to control the merchandise he purchases.

The socialist economy, on the other hand, could not operate with this freedom of the consumer. In the centralized economy the ultimate decisions, about what products to produce and make available and at what prices, are taken away from the consumers in the marketplace and are placed in the hands of a political bureaucratic authority.

The onetime chairman of General Motors, T.A. Murphy, brilliantly summed it up, "There are really only two ways to allocate resources in a society: by consumer choice or by government edict ... the consumer speaking through the marketplace or the economic planner speaking through the ... administrative process. Comprehensive national (economic) planning must ultimately involve coercive powers of vast federal agencies which we must expect will be as remote from the influence of ordinary citizens as those which exist today."

In his best-selling book, *Free to Choose,* Milton Friedman, the Nobel prize winner in economics, said, "Wherever the free market has been permitted to operate, wherever anything approaching equality of opportunity has existed, the ordinary man has been able to attain levels of living never dreamed before."

In a free market, the "market test" eliminates inefficiency and promotes product and service development which enables the standard of living to rise. Specifically, consumers choose between similar products and services. The quality and price offered, helps the consumer vote at the market place.

At some point if the price of a product rises or the quality declines more than what the consumer is willing to accept, the demand declines. The result affects future prices, quality, and production volume of those items, which in turn, affect future sales and profitability. If the producer is to succeed, it must offer goods and services that consumers want at the right price.

If the sale of goods declines far enough that it ends in a loss, the business may eventually go bankrupt and disappear eliminating an inefficient producer. On the other hand, if the demand is so great that sales and profits rise, not only does an efficient producer continue in business, but others are induced to try their hand at the same business. This increases the output to meet the rising demand for a particular product. The increased competition eventually causes the price to drop and quality to rise benefiting the consumer and incidentally, reducing any excess profit of the first business enterprise. The end result is that the free market finds the level of activity which produces the greatest satisfaction for both consumers and producers. It helps to discriminate between wise and an unwise use of capital, labor, and other resources in a bewildering variety of possible uses. On the other hand, the bureaucracy necessary in a socialist planned economy to provide thousands of these decisions was enormous, and they were usually wrong.

Although agreeing with most of the above, early advocates of the planned-economy suggested several reasons why the free-market test was not always justifiable.

They readily admitted that the consumer had a choice in a free market, but they believed, from a practical standpoint, the consumer had no choice when it came to what type of store was to open for business and where, so central-planning was necessary. That argument was invalid because what, where, and when a store is opened depends on the potential demand of consumers if the store is to be profitable.

Another argument was that a possible demand may exist for some products and services that may never become available. Still, if there was enough demand, it would be profitable to open a business to supply that particular service or merchandise; sooner or later it would happen. Furthermore, it was this entrepreneurial spirit to create and develop new businesses and products that created the large gap in technological innovation between the early Soviet bloc and the West.

Some said free markets resulted in a stream of frivolous products. Needless to say, if consumers don't want the product, they usually have enough intelligence not to buy it, and the product is discarded (i.e. The product must have elementary utility, or it is soon shunted.) Besides, what is frivolous to one is not to another. The consumer should have the freedom to decide for oneself rather than be told by a distant bureaucrat.

Some suggested that if several markets in the United States were already centrally-planned and controlled in a free-market economy, such as education, postal service, passenger trains (Amtrack), and healthcare (Veterans Administration medical system, Medicaid and Medicare), then why not have the government run the rest? Others responded, because there was no competition in these government-run markets, they were constantly in a state of turmoil and losing money or far-exceeding their estimated expenses, and the quality of service was poor. Progress or lack of it seemed to be inversely related to the degree of governmental interference in the market process.

Still, others contended money could not be a measure of an equitable exchange between two parties whose income and wealth differed considerably. In other words, a specified amount of money in return for a service or product may seem large to a person with a small income, whereas it may seem small to the purchaser living on a relatively large income. Therefore, it was believed it would not be an equitable trade although the transaction occured as a free exchange.

Most people believed this argument could be refuted for two reasons. First, if the individual with a large income derived it from earlier sacrifice and more productive work than another with a smaller income, then it was still an equitable transaction.

More important, was the relative value placed on the amount of money received by a seller with a smaller income and wealth. If the payment was considered fair and adequate within the seller's own community and living standard, then it should be considered an equitable exchange. It would only be inequitable if the seller considered it to be. For example, governmental price-controls which mandated a sale below a free-market value could be considered inequitable to the seller.

Living standards were relative. For example, a shocked American tourist asked a Peruvian guide about the people living in squalor and primitive conditions along the Amazon waterfront in the city of Iquitos in the late 20th century. "Don't worry mam," the guide responded, "These people are Indians recently from out of the jungle. They now consider their living conditions much improved and most are very happy about it." This, of course, in no way means that a society should not strive for a higher living standard.

Some said there was no such thing as a truly free market. In some markets this was true because governments had always interfered with free-markets for various well-meant reasons. The interference had created public monopolies such as the postal service and public schools, artificial prices caused by tariffs, quotas, and subsidies, and at times, price and wage controls. Any of these attempts to reduce competition or stifle free exchange inevitably ended in dislocations and distortions in the free-market that were eventually detrimental to the consumer.

A typical example of governmental interference in the market place occured in the 1970s in the United States. For years congress had set price controls on oil whereas in the rest of the world, oil sold at the much-higher free-market price. This resulted in Americans paying only fifty cents a gallon for gasoline when it was selling between one and a half to two dollars per gallon in Europe and Japan.

Foreigners, therefore, demanded much earlier that their auto manufacturers respond by developing and manufacturing smaller cars that consumed less gas. At the same time American drivers continued to demand large gas-guzzlers from American manufacturers because American gas was cheap.

Suddenly, after many years of this distortion, the OPEC oil cartel raised the price of exported oil significantly. Since the United States was dependent on much of that foreign oil, congress was forced to abandon the price controls on oil resulting in a sharp rise in the price of gasoline to over $1.50 per gallon.

Immediately, American drivers sought smaller cars, but none were being manufactured by U.S. companies. So instead they bought foreign cars. Everyone then blamed the U.S. auto manufacturers for not having built smaller cars to compete with smaller foreign models although there was no demand earlier in the United States. The new changeover and retooling took several years. Few realized that government interference in the price of oil had created the problem.

But the media was quick to lay the blame on "greedy" auto manufacturers as were most people who had little understanding of the real world of marketing and business. Many were also quick to denounce the economic motives of businesses that made a profit. Not much was ever said about those with losses or those who went bankrupt because they could not compete efficiently. Most criticizers were not interested in how the competitive market system actually functioned. It was easier to assume that any business making more money than them, must be doing something either illegal or unfair.

It was interesting that many in those times, who disdained the free-enterprise system, worked in the centrally-controlled system of government from the teacher working for the school district to the bureaucrat working for the federal government. Most of them lived in a riskless world, guaranteed of a lifetime job, generous pensions protected with COLAs, automatic pay increases, many paid-holidays, and generous vacation and healthcare. Nevertheless, there was little incentive to get ahead as in the real workworld of business. For many it was a riskless dead-end, and maybe this was reflected in their resentment toward business.

Another example of government interference in the free-market was the savings and loan debacle of the late 1980s and early 1990s. Savings and loans and banks required a bailout by taxpayers of over $150 billion, which added to the already burgeoning national debt.

After the failure of many banks during the Great Depression of the 1930s, congress established the Federal Deposit Insurance Corporation to insure the deposits of small savers (up to $2500) should a bank or thrift fail. This was later raised to $10,000 and then to $40,000. By 1980 it had reached $100,000 and covered multiple accounts in the same bank so there were many deposits by wealthy individuals which were insured for over a million dollars. Big depositors moved vast sums quickly to the riskiest S & Ls because they offered the highest interest rates, but were fully insured by the government (taxpayers).

Many S & Ls speculated with these taxpayer-insured funds by loaning to extremely risky real-estate developments, by buying junk bonds, luxury-car dealerships, and investing in expensive art and other collectables. Many of the thrift executives drew obscene salaries, and several fraudulently embezzled funds for their own personal use, or at best, took large personal loans at interest rates far below the average. They did this by attracting huge amounts of deposits with above-average interest rates and insured by tax-payers. "Thrifts were essentially printing money through deposit insurance," said William Seidman, former chairman of the Federal Deposit Insurance Corp.

If private insurance had been bought from insurance companies, intead of from the government, this disaster would never have happened. The premiums, S & Ls would have paid private insurers, would be based on the prudence of their loans. Any risky, inefficient S & L would have been charged very high premiums. Therefore, they would have had to make less risky loans or see their costs rise and profits decline. Those, who failed to get insurance, would have few depositors willing to risk their savings.

Even if the free-market system was deemed the most efficient and most equitable economic system yet devised, there were some who castigated speculators in the commodity pits as the parasites bred by this same system. They could see no value, whatsoever, in speculating on the rise and fall of the price of wheat, oil, or copper for pure profit (or loss). But here once again, it was the lack of knowledge of how the market system really works, that created this disdain.

Victor Niederhoffer, chairman of NCZ Commodities in 1989, explained succintly, "When a harvest is too small to satisfy consumption at its normal rate, speculators come in, hoping to profit from the scarcity by buying. Their purchases raise the price, thereby checking consumption so that the smaller supply will last longer. Producers, encouraged by the high price, further lessen the shortage by growing or importing to reduce the shortage. On the other side, when the price is higher than speculators think the facts warrant, they sell. This reduces prices, encouraging consumption and exports helping to reduce the surplus." Of course, if some speculators were wrong in their assessment of the market, they lost. Unlike common stock investing, for every dollar profit made in commodities, a dollar was lost by other speculators.

***

Free trade among nations or regions was merely the free-market system expanded geographically. For years there was virtual unanimity among economists, regardless of their political leanings, that free trade between countries was good for all consumers and workers living in those countries. The opposite effect occured when two countries imposed protective duties on one another.

For example, one country would protect a small group of sugar-beet farmers by adding a twenty cent per pound tariff on imported sugar from another country whose main agricultural forte was a very efficient cane industry. The second country would then retaliate by adding a twenty cent per pound tariff on imported apples from the first country which grew top-grade fruit in abundance. The result retarded efficient production in both countries while it protected the inefficient. The tariffs raised prices on each side of the border causing demand to drop. So production declined and unemployment rose in each country.

In addition, since sugar costs more in one country and apples more in the other, consumers could not afford to buy as much thus slightly reducing their standard of living. But, the accumulated effect of all tariffs on all merchandise reduced considerably the standard of living.

The net effect was for unemployment to be greater, standard of living to be lower, and a wasteful use of resources consumed in the protection and production of inferior and higher priced merchandise.

Yet, invariably, politicians throughout the world sought protectionism (higher tariffs and trade barriers) rather than free trade in order to protect small but very vocal special interests. Each of these minority groups had such a strong interest in preserving their inefficient businesses or farms that they created enormous pressure on politicians to protect them.

In 1930 the Smoot-Hawley Tariff bill was passed by congress in spite of the protests of 1028 leading American economists. It raised the basic American import tariff to fifty percent, brought rapid retaliation from Europe, and helped intensify the Great Depression. Yet, generations later, politicians were still threatening to restrict trade because of another country's "unfair" trade practices. The tit-for-tat eventually led to retaliation, and everyone suffered.

On the other hand, to consumers or potential new job recipients, the detrimental effects did not appear obvious, so little organized opposition occured against protectionism. It was purely a case of economic ignorance for most. In essence, politicians robbed consumers and workers to buy votes of certain unions, businesses, and farmers that couldn't compete efficiently in world markets.

Later the creation of the Common Market, the abolition of tariffs and trade barriers in the European community, created an economic boon to all nations within that organization. Other countries clambered to become a part of it. It was an excellent example of the benefits of free trade.

The United States Treasury Department estimated in 1994 that a global trade agreement, negotiated under the auspices of the General Agreement on Tariffs and Trade, if ratified by Congress, would be equal to a saving of $744 billion to the world's consumers in a ten year period.

(The New Society)

The original Economic Advisory Committee came to a unanimous decision to adopt the freedom of economic choice. They reasoned it was, by far, the most efficient economic system.

So, today the new world society has a competitive market for goods and services that is completely free of government interference. No longer are artificial distortions and dislocations in the economy created by politicians and bureaucrats. Furthermore, no function operated by the government exists which private enterprise can do more efficiently.

Now freedom to offer competitive products and services, freedom to choose between these competitive products and services, freedom to patent and market one's inventive skill and research, and freedom to apply one's best skills and to sell those skills and labor exists anywhere in the world. In other words, we now have complete freedom in competitive markets which has resulted in the most efficient methods of production and distribution known todate.

Former multi-national companies have integrated small businesses in undeveloped countries and provided them with capital, technology, management, and access to world markets. Such labor-intensive industries as the production of raw commodities and assemby-line manufacturing of less-sophisticated merchandise have grown in the undeveloped countries because they have the labor pool whereas developed regions require workers for more sophisticated technical work. These developments are diametrically opposite to the policies of Third World countries in the past which many times inhibited "foreign investment" because of overriding nationalistic and cultural prejudices.

Certainly, we have regulations that prevent monopolies and keep markets competitive, educate consumers, and set minimum standards to protect health, body, and environment. Aside from that, governmental influence no longer impedes the market mechanism.

In addition to creating the best choice for consumers, competition has also stressed the importance of profit and loss as a measurement of efficiency. An example is the choice for parents between competitive schools. No longer is the student restricted to only one monolithic government-operated school system.

***

After the efficient market was recommended as the logical economic mechanism and in light of the above historical evidence, the Economic Advisory Committee spent months analyzing such things as the distribution of profit and loss, capital formation, taxes, inflation controls and the zoning of commercial, industrial and agricultural land.

Aside from the statistical measurement of effectiveness, the Committee pondered what was in the profit and loss incentive that motivated individuals to do better than in a profitless society. First, they found a much greater pride and sense of achievement in an individual who is able to better his life and living standard through his own initiative in contrast to one who merely accepts the benefits common to all in a welfare state.

Second, many individuals are inclined toward various degrees of laziness, and some to dishonesty when involved with large institutions. These and other characteristics prevent workers and managers, in a vast governmental bureaucracy, from operating at optimum efficiency when not disciplined by the profit and loss incentive.

The possibility of receiving greater reward than would be received otherwise, also motivates the individual to better education, harder work, and sacrifice.

(Historical Background)

Steven W. Mosher in his book, *Broken Earth, the Rural Chinese*, queried a team leader on one of the collective farms in Marxist China on why the farm workers worked so little. "There's nothing to be done (about it). It is useless to have them work longer hours. They just rest more in the fields. People aren't lazy all the time, just when they do collective labor. When they work on their private plots, they work hard."

A new policy in the 1970s in the Soviet Union had the same result. Members of giant collective farms were alloted small plots of about one and a half acres to farm for themselves. The yield was kept for their families and any surplus could be sold. These tiny plots amounted to only three percent of the Soviet's cultivated land, yet they furnished nearly one-half of its vegetables and meat!

Also, the absence of risk of an individual's own savings invested in a business, either as an owner or employee in stock, as well as the absence of profit and loss discipline, bred indifference and waste in government owned and run enterprises.

Typical of the indifference from governmental employees was an incident related by a customer at a Seattle post office. He approached the customer service window to cash a fifty dollar U.S. postal money order. The clerk announced that they didn't have enough money on hand to cash an order that big on Saturday and advised him to come back on Monday. Trying a different approach, he inquired if the clerk would write a money order for fifty dollars, but the smallest bill he had was a hundred dollar one to pay for it. The answer was, "Yes, if you buy a money order." The customer inquired why he couldn't cash the fifty dollar order if the clerk was willing to cash a hundred dollar bill. The clerk said they didn't cash money orders that big early in the morning.

The customer compared his treatment to a hypothetical case in a bank imagining the furor that would erupt if it announced, "We don't cash our own cashier's checks this early in the morning."

(The New Society)

If a business operation yields a profit, then it is worth continuing. If it does not, it usually is rectified by cutting costs, improving sales by raising the quality of merchandise and service and reducing the price, or simply by discontinuing the business. Profit, therefore, is the statistical measurement of efficiency in business.

Since the Committee agreed that efficiency could only be effectively measured by profit and loss, its next important decision was to determine how profits were developed and who should receive them.

Profit, of course, is what remains after deducting all costs of operating a business from the sales receipts. In addition to the raw material costs of the product, other costs include such things as rentals of buildings or land and equipment, interest on money borrowed, general overhead costs such as utilities, but especially management and labor. Management and labor account for the biggest portion of total costs. If costs exceed monies received from sales, the difference, naturally, is a loss.

In a non-competitive market monopolized by one company or a government-run business operation, the profits are essentially meaningless in controling efficiency. This is because the price structure is artifically higher than in a competitive market. So, the consumer suffers unless the private company's prices are regulated as are certain utilities.

On the other hand, the degree of profitability of a firm in a free, competitive market is affected by such things as:

1. The efficiency of management, workers, property, and finances.

2. The quality, service, and price compared to competitors. (If price is lower, more is sold; if too low, profits are erased.)

3. The uniqueness of the product or service (If in very high demand, competitors will quickly copy it and reduce the share of sales to each producer and possibly the price.)

The Economic Advisory Committee also analyzed what purpose profits had in addition to a measurement of efficiency. (In the 19th and 20th centuries, profits, derived from small businesses, were considered compensation for the use of the owner's land, buildings, machinery, and his savings invested in the business. It was also a salary, if you will, for the personal services of the owner in managing the business and perhaps, participating in the actual physical labor of production.)

The Committee believed, that if the return for the above purposes seemed fair, no logical argument could be made that the profit was unjustified. Only when profit exceeded a fair return for these purposes, that an argument ensued over the justification of the excess.

Nevertheless, after considerable debate, the Committee determined any excess was equitable for several reasons. First, it was an additional return for risking the owner's life savings. They could be totally lost in bankruptcy arising from the uncertainty of changes in the business world which could not be foretold in advance with any degree of accuracy. In other words, profit to compensate for risk had to be considerably greater than, for example, interest received on a riskless savings account.

Any excess also acted as an important incentive to work harder and be more efficient, in contrast to effort expended when the income is guaranteed in advance as in a fixed salary. Unlike work for a government bureaucracy, an incentive also existed to, not only increase sales and profits, but to prevent them from declining. Any drop could result, not only in lower profits, but even a cut in worker's salaries, or worse, in lay-offs.

If there are losses, both management and employees work harder to increase productivity. Failing this, the company could eventually go bankrupt, and all would lose their jobs and any savings invested. This did not occur in government businesses. The losses, instead, were subsidized by taxpayers, and inefficiency and indifference usually continued to the detriment of the consumer as well as the taxpayer.

The Committee felt incentives should apply to workers as well as managers and owners of businesses, as a reward for their ability and extra effort to create a profit. Without incentives, the economic system could not operate at its maximum competitiveness, and therefore, its maximum efficiency to benefit the consumer.

It was easy to accuse profits of serving the rich who had scant regard for ethical precepts or public sensibilities. Some truth existed in these accusations, but upon in-depth study, the Committee found these cases were the exceptions rather than the rule. As in all activities, those who lied, cheated, bribed, and were extremely selfish in order to succeed in life were prevalent. But, they were the minority in the thousands of businesses which operated each day. Now much less of this conduct is displayed due to our early Behavioral Education.

Furthermore, under the earlier capitalistic economic system, often huge concentrations of wealth passed from one generation to another. The behavior of the inheritors in handling this wealth was sometimes abusive. Yet, no correlation existed between inheritance and the early accumulation of the wealth from the profits of business. (This was another problem that the Committee researched and later resolved.).

The Committee also addressed the question of whether one business should make far more profits than another. If buyers had a free choice to select between competing products or services; if a company competed against other efficient businesses; if it served its customers better; the Committee concluded a company earned the right to higher profits. By keeping expenses lower than its competitors, it was able to lower prices or give better quality. Higher profits allowed it to continue doing this.

It also served its employees well by being able to give them better benefits, working conditions, and employment security when profits were higher than its competitors. It is the company which can offer the best opportunities for advancement and for new jobs because it will have more capital available for growth and investment.

Stockholders of companies also benefited when higher profits allowed for higher dividends and a greater appreciation in the value of their stock. This benefited nearly everyone in the new society because of the widespread stock investment of workers as we shall soon see. (Even in previous generations, the majority of stock was owned by pension funds of wage earners and by mutual funds of small investors. Of course, individual investors with vast stock holdings existed, but most of the wealth, in the form of stock in U.S. corporations, was held indirectly by the nation's workers and small business owners. Many were not aware of this "socialization" of American business.)

Retained profits in businesses as well as savings generate investment capital for economic growth and causes the eventual rise in living standards. They are fundamental to the economy and, thus, to everyone. In short, the most profitable companies are the best of all possible companies.

***

The Economic Advisory Committee, then delved deeper into motivation in the work place. They wanted to know if incentives really were basic to increased productivity and, thus, a benefit to society by increasing living standards.

During their investigation the Committee found a great misunderstanding regarding productivity and its influence on living standards. Generally, productivity refers to the number of units or services produced per man hour. Any increase naturally results in more goods produced for the same effort. As a result, any business able to increase productivity, is also able to sell at a lower price than a competitor. This results in the consumer able to use less income to buy these goods. The savings can then be used for other purchases resulting in better living standards. Therefore, it is extremely important for consumers when businesses increase productivity. Some on the Committee said, "What if increased productivity is not passed on to benefit consumers?" Others replied, "If it, instead, increases profits excessively, competition will quickly move in to take advantage of a lucrative situation, and the price will then drop."

When more automation is used which requires less workers, productivity is increased. This is facilitated by such things as new software programs, better computer networks, and more powerful micro-chips. Other techniques include work teams, pushing decision-making authority as far down the organization as possible, and training workers in multiple skills so they can do more than one job. Reorganization of assembly lines and offices to simplify and speed the flow of work also contributes to more productivity.

The common complaint, then, is jobs are lost. This is true initially, but over the longer term job openings not only increase but become more interesting and challenging. Every technological advancement in automation opens up new fields and jobs to support that advancement. Additionally, consumer purchasing power from the savings of increased productivity creates demands for more products and, thus, the need for more workers. Some labor mobility is, of course, necessary as innovation alters production and demand shifts from one product to another. Nearly all economists agree, however, that increased productivity eventually brings about faster economic growth, greater global competitiveness, higher real salaries on average for the work force, and vastly improved living standards.

An example was the extraordinary prosperous economic period in the later 1990s in the United States and the world, mainly the result of the earlier computer-driven "downsizing" and greater world-wide adoption of the market-economy after the collapse in socialist economies (more competition and thus, rising living standards).

***

A well-known fact to psychologists on the Committee was that rewards led animals, including men, to put increased effort into their activities. Experiments with hungry rats showed those, rewarded with food at the end of a maze, made significant progress in mastering it; those, not rewarded, showed little progress. Controlled experiments of competition among children resulted overwhelmingly in faster learning among those receiving either monetary or recognition awards compared to those who received neither. [5]

Animals appear to be motivated to the greatest degree by food, water, and other basic physiological needs. Well-fed humans, on the other hand, are greatly motivated by material rewards and recognition.

This observation led the Committee to the conclusion that some direct link between effort and reward definitely should exist. Difference in rewards was a fundamental distinction from one of the original premises of socialism. Furthermore, in order for incentives to be based on profit or loss, it was absolutely necessary for them to evolve in a free-market environment where equality of opportunity exists.

The Committee then began to study inequality in rewards - what caused it and why it was needed by both individuals and society.

(Historical Background)

Many idealists in the 20th century believed that income and wealth should be distributed more equally. This was an important element in socialist idealogy. Typically, they viewed taking from the "rich" and giving to the "poor" as being fair. Most did not have a logical or moral justification of why it was fair. Perhaps, it was the belief that the poor needed or deserved part of this wealth or that there was some sinister reason inequality existed, that it must have been acquired in an unfair manner. True, some acquired wealth through inheritance or by devious and unethical means, but this was the reason for laws regulating such practices. Rarely did the proponents include themselves in the group to give the most to the "poor." Usually, they assumed there was always someone else with more wealth and income who should share with the "poor."

In *Free to Choose*, Milton Friedman pointed out it was one thing for ninety percent of the voters to elect to tax themselves in order to help the bottom ten percent. But he suggested it was not only unfair but antiethical to liberty for the majority to force the top ten percent to pay to help the bottom ten percent.[6]

Was it reasonable to assume inequality was unfair? An example of two typical life-styles in the 1990s may explain why inequality existed.

Assume two individuals started out in life equally. Neither inherited wealth, both were physically unimpaired and did not encounter debilitating sickness or accidents, neither were inclined to cheat, and both had equal opportunity for a good education and employment. Yet, one's income and accumulated wealth eventually surpassed the other by a wide margin. How could this have possibly occured?

One studied diligently in school and excelled. The other "got by" prefering "fun" activities. One was ambitious and devoted himself to long hard work on his job. The other preferred to do the bare minimum to hold a job without being fired.

One refrained from spending on expensive luxuries and entertainment. He took his recreation in less expensive areas while the other indulged. One postponed spending for luxuries and built up considerable savings. The other even borrowed at high interest rates to satisfy his desires. One began to invest his savings in a small business or in investment vehicles such as mutual funds or real estate to build a larger income. The other continued to borrow and spend for expensive cars, vacations, and material things - living from paycheck to paycheck.

Just one of these differences would ultimately make one poorer and the other richer. Is it then fair for the richer one to distribute a share of his income and wealth to the other? Most governments thought so and enacted taxes, subsidies, and welfare to enforce it.

In his *Principles of Sociology*, Herbert Spencer, the early English philosopher believed that some people in any society would always be "poor" or less productive members. He also heartlessly and coldly calculated that society "constantly excreted its unhealthy, imbecile, slow, vacillating, faithless ... (and) incapable members." He argued against social welfare because he believed impoverishment was nature's decree for the inability to survive as others did - a sort of evolutionary natural selection.

The great emancipator, for equal opportunity for Afro-Americans, believed inequality in wealth, promoted incentive for progress. Abraham Lincoln said, " ... property is the fruit of labor. That some should be rich shows that others may become rich, and hence is just encouragement to industry and enterprise. Let not him who is homeless pull down the house of another, but let him work diligently and build one for himself, by example insuring that his own shall be safe."

Wendell W. Gunn, an Afro-American in his mid-thirties, in a letter to the editors of the *Wall Street Journal,* wrote that Afro-Americans must be free of racial discrimination so they and all Americans have equal access to America's wealth. But he also said, "Individuals in a free society strive to produce above the average because of the prospect of reaping benefits which are also above the average. ... individuals specifically strive toward inequality. To promise equality of reward regardless of contribution ... is to destroy the prime incentive of the potentially productive. Inevitably, society would lose the benefit of the enormous pool of energy, ingenuity and drive."

Will and Ariel Durant in *The Lessons of History*, wrote, " ... only the man who is below average in economic ability desires equality; those who are conscious of superior ability desire freedom ...,"

Milton Friedman also talks of inequality in the pursuit of life. "(Peoples') different values, their different tastes, their different capacities will lead them to want to lead different lives. Equality of opportunity ... is an essential component of liberty (but) the use of force to achieve equality (in income & wealth) will destroy freedom." [7]

To strive by rising above equality is one of the most basic instincts of everyone. It is as Adam Smith wrote, "The uniform constant and uninterrupted effort of every man to better his condition." [8]

Alex Tocqueville, the great French sociologist of the early 19th century, believed passionately in liberty. He believed the world was moving inescapably toward democracy but discerned equality was incompatible with liberty.

For decades politicians redistributed income from taxes to the inefficient elements in society professing a humane attitude toward the poor, the elderly, and the distressed in return for these special-interest votes. Yet, their efforts failed miserably to solve the problems of these "underprivileged."

(The New Society)

It became necessary to overcome the inclination to divide the rewards of efficient producers with non-efficient ones in the name of compassion. In no way did the Economic Advisory Committee interpret this new approach to mean indifference to society's responsibilities for the very young, the ill, and disabled. These were dealt with in a specific manner by the Committee on Individual Rights and Freedoms.

In addition, the Economic Advisory Committee recommended that labor and management participate in a plan for incentive rewards.

(Historical Background)

In the earlier capitalistic societies, accumulated wealth in a family was passed on from one generation to another. As a result, inordinate concentrations of affluence and power grew over the years in most countries. In 1985, for example, *Forbes* magazine stated that nearly one-half of the four-hundred richest fortunes in America were mainly or entirely inherited. In some areas of the world, they virtually held a monopoly on economic and political life. This was especially true in Latin America where early Spanish land-grants helped create vast family-owned estates and business conglomerates. This negated the efforts of the masses to better themselves when born less fortunate. By 1989 the richest twenty percent families of Latin America enjoyed a more extravagant lifestyle than the upper class in highly developed countries such as Japan and the United States while other citizens were approaching the poverty level of Bangladesh.

The problem did not arise from incentive to make profit, which helped amass wealth, but with conduct of those who inherited the wealth. If the wealth had been invested in ventures to create more jobs and to raise living standards of all through more efficient production, then it was beneficial. On the other hand, if the inheritors hoarded this wealth or used it to gain economic or political advantage with which to exploit others, then it was detrimental to society. Additionally, many times the heirs were either inept or ignorant in the proper management of vast inherited enterprises, and the economy eventually suffered. Even Andrew Carnegie, the immigrant steel tycoon, believed that parents, who left enormous wealth to their offspring, generally inhibited their ambitions and drive and encouraged less useful lives.

(The New Society)

The subject of inheritance was a particularly difficult one with which to deal for the Committee. Many creaters of wealth claimed that, if they earned it, they should be able to dispose of it as they pleased. To do so before death made sense. After death was the critical point of argument. Instinctive parental protection of offspring as well as a method to bestow gifts on loved ones created strong feelings among most to preserve this age-old custom. In spite of this emotional nepotism, the Committee realized overwhelming evidence indicated many reasons why large inheritances had to be eliminated.

They reasoned that, in addition to eliminating large concentrations of economic power in the hands of a few who didn't earn it, everyone in the new society should have the same equal opportunity from birth until they die. A few pampered heirs supported in luxury and leisure, incapable or unwilling to work, made no sense in a society devoted to improving the quality of life for everyone.

They reasoned that every able person should be a producer. Parasites living on inheritance or who inherit an unfair advantage over others could not be permitted. The prudent use of time was required to affect maximum productivity in the new society. Furthermore, they reasoned a desire and a challenge for a productive life must be instilled. Inherited affluence tended to invalidate these desirable goals.

After considerable debate, the Committee agreed to permit individuals to grant gifts of a reasonable but limited amount to their relatives or friends during the donor's lifetime. A surviving spouse, as co-owner, may inherit an undivided estate. If no surviving spouse, personal property, except as noted below, may be willed to relatives, friends, or charity. Inheritance tax does not exist in the new society. Extremely valuable non-productive property such as rare art work, collectables, jewelry, gems, and gold may only be willed to museums. Otherwise, unclaimed personal property is merely auctioned and the funds retained by the government.

Reasonable, limited amounts of investments may be liquidated and passed on to family heirs or others. The Committee decided the balance of vast investment holdings should continue their purpose as invested capital to create future growth for the economy.

This was accomplished by merely leaving these large investments with the institutions in which they were already invested. Continuity was, therefore, assured in enterprises that the deceased had substantial interest without the problem of forced liquidation at death. Stocks and bonds of large corporations were merely liquidated and the proceeds plowed back into the respective companies. Pension and mutual funds were handled in the same manner. Even the liquidation of savings accounts were moved into a special fund at banks to be distributed annually to the other depositors. This benefited remaining investors and, thus, was another incentive for young people to invest.

There were some on the Committee who argued that certain individuals, who had accumulated substantial wealth during their lifetime, may begin wild spending sprees to use their fortunes as the end of their lifespan approached. But, the Committee agreed that if an individual labored over a lifetime to accumulate wealth, it was his right to spend it as he pleased. In fact, most agreed it might be a good idea to indulge oneself as the twilight of life approached.

The founders of the new society realized that equal opportunity necessitated this radical elimination of vast inheritances including private land ownership. Yet, the new society recognized the competitive character of this economic playing field and the importance of individual acquisition as a necessary economic stimulus and reward for one's own achievements instead of relying on those of one's parents. Today every individual begins on a level playing field to develop his or her native capacity without either artificial stimulus or obstacles.

***

As previously mentioned, the competitive market-system was adopted as the most efficient allocation of resources required in the production of goods to meet consumers' demands. Management and labor, even land leased by the government was allocated in this manner. Capital, the physical as well as financial assets used in production, also must seek the most lucrative return comensurate with the degree of risk involved.

(Historical Background)

During a distant time in history, a gatherer of wild grain discovered if he did not eat all he gathered, he could save some seed to sow for his own crop. Much later, farmers realized if they grew more grain than their families needed and saved the remainder, it could be traded for a rudimentary plow which, in turn, would help to grow even more grain.

Early on, people realized personal consumption was the end result of most productive effort. But, economic progress always depended on a society foregoing some current consumption by saving and investing money in the tools that improve the quality of life through more efficient production. In short, economic progress depended on capital, its lifebood, from savings. Without savings, living standards could not improve. Current savings created the jobs and income of tommorrow.

Ironically the net national savings rate in the leading industrial country, the United States, continued to drop gradually from about eight percent of the gross national product in the 1960s to two percent by 1986. That was one-fifth the rate in other major industrial nations and only one-eighth that of Japan. [9]

As a result, investment in new plants and equipment fell gradually in the United States while its foreign competitors experienced stunning productivity advances that enabled them to rapidly increase living standards. The standard of living in the United States slowed considerably. At the same time in some industries, workers were cut drastically to increase productivity and competitiveness worldwide. Many companies simply fell behind unable to compete in international markets.

How could savings fall so dramatically in an advanced industrial nation?

Many reasons appeared that contributed to the problem. Rising Social Security and pension benefits partially negated the reason to save for old age. A gradual rise in appreciation of the dwindling supply of real estate and a long-term secular appreciation in common stock, in companies whose capital assets and earnings continued to grow with long-term inflation and population growth, contributed to the wealth of many. During the 1960s and 1970s automatic wage increases, cost-of-living adjustments, and the pressure of labor unions in a world market that gave American companies little competition, left many apathetic to saving.

Additionally, politicians provided many health and welfare services at government expense. Some benefits were so generous that many people were addicted to them and saw no reason to fight for a job with less income, let alone, save money for a rainy day. Rapidly ballooning welfare spending by government demanded ever higher taxes which helped reduce what was left for savings by other individuals. Increased social spending also created larger deficits financed in competition with business borrowing, thus many times squeezing out the private sector's needs for funds to buy new equipment and production facilities.

Some thought the most important cause for a shortage of savings was the tax on interest and other income earned from savings and all other forms of investment capital needed for business to grow. At the same time, spending was rewarded by reducing taxes for all interest paid on loans to buy such things as vacation homes, recreational vehicles, pleasure boats, and other types of luxuries and consumerables. Furthermore, the tax on savings often resulted in a net loss of purchasing value after deducting for inflation; so, as people grew older, the life-savings of many bought less.

In Japan, on the other hand, interest on savings up to $58,000 was tax free (1987). Capital gains taxes didn't exist; whereas in the United States, they were taxed as ordinary income. Many times, these gains on investments merely represented appreciation due to increased inflation compounded over a period of time, and the risk was sometimes much greater than insured savings in a bank. In Japan interest paid on purchases of luxuries or other consumerables was not tax deductable; therefore, Japanese had far less incentive to look for the biggest house with the biggest mortgage for a tax shelter as Americans did.

Many economists felt the difference in taxation, between Japan and the United States, was the main reason for the decline in capital investment in the United States and a sharp rise in Japan. The result was a gap in the trade deficit that widened between the two countries in the 1980s as the United States imported more from Japan but were unable to increase its exports. This was due, in part, to aging production and less-competitive facilities which resulted from less savings to invest.

When people saved less and borrowed more, the result was not only less investment capital for business to meet the demands of consumers, but a larger demand was created for borrowed funds by those same consumers. When the demand for more funds were added by the government to finance a growing deficit, the result was each borrowing group had to bid against the other for the dwindling supply of funds. Interest rates therefore, rose. Added to this was the necessity of savers to demand that the cost of inflation and taxes be added to their net return from interest (real interest rate). This too increased interest rates.

As higher rates forced the U.S.Treasury to pay more interest on government bonds, it pushed the national debt even higher requiring ever more bond sales from savings to finance it.

A more unique result, of higher or lower interest rates, was the effect it had on bank loans. For many years after WWII, the prime rate set by banks was very small, and therefore, the profit margin was also small. So, banks required borrowers to provide large down payments on property before loans were made and would not finance speculative undertakings. As a result, people had to save more to buy a home or other large purchases.

In later years as interest rates on loans became higher and the bank's margin of profit became greater, banks were anxious to make more loans. They were willing to make riskier ones with smaller down payments. Consequently, savings suffered even more since saving for cash down on real estate, business, and other assets were needed less. Banks loaned for speculative business buyouts and even bought "junk" bonds. As interest rates rose and became costly, demand to borrow for new plants and equipment to improve productivity was curtailed, and economic growth stagnated. Disincentives to save not only reduced funds available for future business investment but increased interest rates for everyone adding a multitude of problems.

For many economists, it was difficult to understand reasons behind a detrimental taxing policy that penalized savers and rewarded spenders. Some realized that the makers of tax laws, the American Congress, had opted to benefit consumers with tax deductions because all consumers were voters and would, thus, support their reelection at the polls. When the combination of federal spending programs and tax deductions for spenders required additional taxes, it became easier to tax savers and investors because they appeared to be in the minority.

Little thought was given to the long-term detrimental economic effects of such a policy on the country. After all, politicians were not economists. Furthermore, once the policy had become entrenched over a long time period, it was politically impossible to change. Congressmen, then, blamed everything else for the myriad of problems that arose instead of going to the source of the difficulty.

(The New Economic Society)

The use of computers and other advanced technology has reduced business inventories which, in turn, reduced storage space (i.e. buildings and land) and necessary raw materials. This has reduced capital needs, but as the new civilization progresses, the demand for investment capital is still great. The reason is, as world population stabilized with family-planning controls, labor, as well as land, is now limited. Therefore, the only way, the new society can continue to progress, is to increase productivity by becoming capital-intensive in the Information Age.

More capital investments are now made in advanced technological equipment, robotic machinery, computers, and artificial intelligence in all industries as well as agriculture. The wasteful use of land, labor, and capital has been eliminated through their continued allocation in sophisticated markets unlike in the old centrally-planned economies. The shift of these resources from the previous less-productive to new more-productive ones has been unending. Marx believed the collapse of capitalism was inevitable because of the diminishing productivity of capital. Yet, in capitalistic countries from as early as 1860 through the 20th century, productivity rose except in the most severe periods of depression.

Risk-capital is merely the life-savings of workers, management, and others invested in an untried endeavor in the hope it will be well-received in the competitive market and, thus, become profitable. It is used to enable entrepreneurs to start out in business with the incentive to make above average income (profit) in exchange for risking their life-savings to possible loss as well as long hours of effort. If the profits are plowed back into the business, then it is additional risk-capital.

In most cases risk-capital is necessary to form a new venture before banks are willing to loan additional funds. Usually, banks believe loans are less risky when investors have already invested their own savings. The borrower will then strive harder to make a business successful in order to prevent the loss of his life-savings.

The Economic Advisory Committee looked at the usual sources of capital financing: depreciation reserves built up to replace existing but deteriorating and obsolescing plant and equipment, bank loans, profits reinvested in business, and especially savings of individuals (direct business loans, direct and indirect business investments, stock, and bond investments).

For the Committee, it was imperative to devise means to increase savings available for risk and investment capital in order to research and develop new or improved services or products and, thereby, improve mankind's future; new challenging job opportunities could also be created.

First, it decided to encourage the most advanced financial markets in the world. It was vital to efficiently match up capital needs with funds to be loaned or invested. Tax policies had to foster saving and investment and inhibit the consumption of non-necessities and luxuries. Fiscal governing policies were required to prevent inflation which, in turn, would contribute to low and stable interest rates. Risk incentives were encouraged to stimulate investment in new entrepreneurial enterprises, not only by investors, but by management and labor as well.

A mandatory witholding of a small percentage of all supplementary bonuses and profit-sharing is invested in regulated bond and common stock funds. These investments are administered by employer firms much as pension plans were in the past. It is a forced savings program just as Social Security once was.

Dividends are paid quarterly and become additional supplementary income for the individual. However, the principal can only be withdrawn for other investment purposes, including the formation of one's own business. After twenty years, portions can be withdrawn for any purpose.

This program accomplishes the following:

(1) It helps finance the productive system through mutual funds enabling a better living standard for all.

(2) It adds extra income for the saver-worker.

(3) It provides an opportunity to open one's own business.

(4) It enables the saver-worker to participate in the appreciation of stocks evolving from the growth of various businesses.

(5) In effect, it socializes industry through the participation of worker-investors without the malfunctions of government-run bureaucracies.

In addition to the above and as earlier explained, vast sums of some estates were kept invested in productive industries instead of forced-liquidation by heirs. This helped immensely to retain capital investment without disruption to productive enterprises.

(Historical Background)

Income taxes were not an incentive to work harder, to save, or to better one's-self through education and ambition. Instead they penalized the worker who abstained from buying luxuries in order to save and invest one's income. It penalized the corporate manager who worked fifteen hour days sometimes six and seven days a week in order for the business to succeed and thereby boost his success. It penalized the small businessman who risked his life savings in order to produce more than others? Were these people guilty and needed punishment for some sinister activity by having large chunks of their income taken from them?

In England under the Socialist government in 1977, the highest tax rate was eighty-three percent of income. Pollsters found that half of managers considered taxes to be the cause of less efficiency in their positions, and many admitted they didn't work as hard as they once did.[10] As late as 1996, the president of Belarus, a former Communist head of a collective farm, put into law a ninety-two percent income tax on private business profits hoping to eliminate free enterprises in favor of government-owned ones.

The American Congress passed a bill imposing a one percent income tax in 1894 which was declared unconstitutional a year later by the Supreme Court. It ruled that taxes would have to be levied in proportion to population to be fair and not by income level. The *Washington Post* earlier described it as a tax that. "... punishes everyone who rises above the level of mediocrity... "[11]

Yet in February 1913, the Sixteenth Amendment authorized an income tax; it was passed in October by Congress in order to bypass the Supreme Court, and was ratified by the states. The *New York Times* opposed it, "When men get the habit of helping themselves to the property of others, they are not easily cured of it."

In the 17th century, John Locke, the famous English philosopher whose governing ideas were apparent in the Declaration of Independence, wrote in *The Second Treatise on Government*, that man had a right to property because he commingled his labor with it (in reference to confiscatory taxes by kings).

The out of pocket cost to tax payers and the expense to national governments in collecting income taxes was enormous. In the united States the original 1913 tax law was sixteen pages. By 1989 it encompassed 36,000 pages! It was estimated 577 million man-hours annually were consumed in filling out U.S. tax forms during the 1980s. By the 1990s, the laws were so complex that most taxpayers were forced to pay experts to compile their tax returns.

It was calculated in 1990 that for every hundred dollars paid in taxes by America's small businesses, three-hundred and ninety dollars were paid out to compile and comply with those taxes, primarily for accounting costs. The total expense of compliance, not the tax, for large corporations (Fortune 500) exceeded one billion dollars in 1992 in a study by Professor Joel Slemrod of the University of Michigan and Professor Marsha Blumenthal of the University of St. Thomas. These funds were essentially wasted on non-productive labor and passed on to consumers in the price of services and goods.

Hobbled by outmoded computers, obsolete technology, and personnel problems, the Internal Revenue Service was unable to collect billions of dollars in back taxes. They also had difficulty appraising what was legitimately owed in new taxes. The governmental cost in enforcing tax laws was outrageous.

Worse, taxing wages had the effect of increasing unemployment. Steep increases in unemployment in Canada and Europe in the 1990s was primarily due to big increases in payroll and personal income taxes. When workers taxes were raised, businesses then had to raise wages to compensate by restoring the same take-home pay as before. In order to do this, many businesses had to resort to trimming their work force because they could not afford the additional labor expense.

If a large portion of income taxes was used to finance welfare programs, as was the case in Canada and Europe, net wage earnings became even less attractive. Then in order to retain good employees, wages had to be raised sufficiently above welfare benefits. This resulted in increased costs to businesses that could not be passed on to consumers so the work force was further trimmed. Additional unemployment, required more welfare which resulted in a vicious cycle.

Most taxpayers felt they were paying their fair share, but doubts always lingered that others were not. In fact, some did not bother to file an income tax form.

Many said, "If the 'rich' paid more taxes, a big portion of the deficit could be eliminated." Yet, the Tax Foundation estimated if the United States Congress passed a law confiscating all personal income above the fifty percent top tax rate in 1980, it would only be enough to run the government for eight days! Another estimate figured seventy million taxpayers were paying for government benefits for eighty-one million who paid no taxes.

Before income taxes were indexed for inflation in the late 1980s, tax payment not only increased with every increase in salary (salaries rose to keep pace with rising inflation), but the tax rate also increased when individuals were then pushed into a higher tax bracket, creating a veritable money machine for Congress. By 1996 the average American paid more in taxes than for food, clothing, and housing combined reported the Tax Foundation.

Other major inequities in the American income tax also existed. For example, the tax fell twice on savings - once on income as it was received and placed in a savings account and again on the interest it earned in the account. Profits earned by corporations were also taxed when earned and taxed a second time when they were distributed to their owners (stockholders) in the form of dividends.

(The New Society)

The Committee noted they had eliminated class discrimination and promoted equal opportunity for all by eliminating the inheritance of vast wealth, but were adamant in not depriving efficient producers of wealth from their labor during their lifetime.

Moreover, vast sums from burdensome taxes are no longer needed. The largest expenses of the world community are education and the care of youth. The cost of security enforcement, welfare for the disabled and handicapped, regulating and governing boards, special research institutes, and some minor miscellaneous functions make up the balance. These are easily financed from commercial land rentals.

As earlier explained, no longer does a need exist for expensive armaments and defense. Social Security and pension funds are also eliminated because people continue in their occupation until they are no longer productive, albeit at a gradually reduced degree. Everyone is expected to help produce and in return, be guaranteed adequate food, housing, commuting transportation, and health care based on a minimum salary. Therefore, welfare does not exist except for education and the disabled and handicapped. (more about this later).

After adopting the efficient-market system, subsidies have been discontinued for agriculture, postal service, transportation and any other business because no longer are government-run or subsidized businesses maintained. All are private, extremely competitive, and efficient.

No longer is it necessary to make huge payments of interest on government debt because no debt exists - only surplus.

User-fees also help eliminate the need for taxes. It is reasoned, anyone using a specific recreational facility, should help pay for its management and maintenance since it is not considered a basic necessity. Furthermore, it is considered unfair to tax those who do not or can not use such facilities. All land for such recreational facilities is leased on a competitive basis and run by private companies in the most efficient manner possible. Leases are negotiated by professional agents to guarantee a fair rental to the government based on gross receipts. (In the later part of the 20th century the leasing of concessions, grazing land, and forests were at fees that were grossly inadequate - another example of bureacratic indifference and ineptitude.)

Entrance fees are charged for such things as wild animal and wilderness parks, botanical gardens, community beaches, and camping areas. Fees are also charged for museums, libaries, and other civic attractions. Children, students, handicapped, and disabled are allowed free access.

(Historical Background)

User fees had been common to gain entrance to National Parks and Monuments in the United States in the 20th century. However, this income went into the general fund for all government expenses - never directly to maintain or improve the parks. As entrance fees grew over the years, appropriations for the parks became miserly. The entire National Park system degenerated to the point where some National Monuments had to be closed for lack of sufficient funds to maintain them. In 1994, National Park Service Director, Roger G. Kennedy, told Congress a $5 billion backlog of physical needs existed in the parks, and still no money was appropriated - a typical example of a government-run enterprise by bureaucrats and politicians.

In the 1990s Congress added an additional twenty-five percent tax (fee) to airfares to be used for airports which were in dire need of enlarging and improvements. Instead, the money was used for other programs while the airports continued to worsen. If airports had been owned or managed by the airlines or other competent private businesses, this would not have happened.

(The New Society)

User fees, also, pay the cost of rehabilitative facilities of specific activities such as compulsive gambling, alcohol, tobacco, and narcotic addiction. The fee is paid by an addition to the price of the above services or goods.

Regulatory bodies protect all citizenry. Some are for consumer product and service protection, anti-monopoly, and environmental control. These are financed from general government funds.

Occasionally there is a need for massive financing to fund a major project. This is accomplished by a one-time tax which has a mandatory expiration upon completion and financing of the project.

Since it is believed economically prudent and more equitable to tax non-necessity consumption rather than productive labor and savings, a small percentage tax on all consumerable goods, except necessities, is used for this purpose. Furthermore, a consumer's tax is simple to administer and collect. It results in considerable saving to the government and in the elimination of a citizen's tax preparation.

If the project is regional, such as massive infrastructure, the tax is restricted to the region which would benefit by the project. If instead, it benefits the entire world society, the tax is worldwide. The later entails items so expensive that even a consortium of many corporations cannot finance, or would not find profitable - expensive research projects similar to the search for super-conductivity, advanced energy resources, and space exploration.

(Historical Background)

Inflation confronted the world for centuries reaching nightmare excesses in many lands. Roman emperors repeatedly debased their coinage and inflated prices. The French revolutionary government printed such a flood of assignats, they fell to one five-hundredth of their former value. In America the Continental Congress issued so much paper money, it was "not worth a Continental."

Hyper-inflation ravaged Europe following World War I and in Latin America in the later half of the 20th century. In Germany the wholesale price index rose from one-hundred in July of 1922 to 726 *billion* by November 1923! At the heighth of the inflation two thousand printing presses were running both night and day to turn out currency. Prices doubled in a few hours. Workers were often paid three times a day, but wages couldn't keep up. Their wives would meet them, take the money and rush to the stores to exchange it for goods. Shopkeepers could not obtain goods fast enough to hedge against the cash taken in. Farmers finally refused to bring produce into the city in return for worthless paper; food riots ensued; workers marched to the farms and looted gardens.

Businessmen abandoned their legitimate occupation in order to speculate to maintain the purchasing value of their cash from becoming worthless. As businesses closed down, unemployment soared. People sold everything: furniture, clothing, jewelry to buy food. The economy completely collapsed.

It seemed at one time or another every country in the world experienced severe inflation. In 1974 it reached 25 percent annually in Italy, 25 percent in Great Britain, and 900 percent in Chile in 1976. Brazil's inflation reached 30 percent a month in 1989 and by 1994 an inconceivable rate of 7000 percent annually! In Russia the ruble was worth forty-two cents for a dollar in the fall of 1992. By May 1993 it had dropped to ten cents as the printing presses worked day and night to feed runaway inflation.

In the United States, the inflation of the late 1970s and early 1980s forced poverty on many or necessitated the wife to work outside the home to maintain the family's standard of living. In 1963 sixty percent of young men earned enough to keep a family out of poverty, but by 1984 only forty-two percent could. Many were not aware this was a significant cause of women entering the work-world.

In Brazil and Argentina the indexing of wages, taxes, and government bonds to inflation merely perpetuated inflation and more speculation to keep pace with it. Businessmen frenetically speculated in real estate and the stock market ignoring the business of producing and selling merchandise and services. The middle-class rushed to buy black-market dollars or gold. Strikes increased as higher wages were sought, schools closed, stores were looted, and trains were burned. Without tangible property, the poor were completely exposed to the scourge of rising prices and in desperation turned to Marxist activists for a solution.

During inflation, those living on fixed incomes or competitive salaries suffered most. Whereas, those with large property ownership or cost-of-living escalators, were hurt the least.

Businesses tended to hedge against rising prices by buying huge stocks of raw materials and machinery or to build new factories. As a result, inflationary periods, at first, appeared to be prosperous. But much of the new capital expenditures proved unnecessary or inefficient. Inventories skyrocketed and became a burden at the higher interest rates. Labor became less productive as workers became preoccupied with strikes for higher wages, bought durable goods before prices rose, and generally tried to stay ahead of inflation. There was enormous waste and inefficiency throughout the economy.

The Federal Reserve and some other central banks in the world usually stopped rapid inflation by the curtailment of credit as occured in the late 1970s and early 1980s. With credit available only at very high interest rates, it was no longer feasible to increase inventories. Instead, high interest expense necessitated their liquidation. Speculation became costly, and the purchase of raw materials, new machinery, and plants dropped precipitously. Because of the resulting decline in purchases, business fell off; unemployment rose. The inevitable result was a recession which had vast social consequences.

The alternative was to allow inflation to continue to escalate until money became completely worthless. It was then repudiated by establishing a new stable currency backed by reserves that represented tangible assets such as land, industrial plants, or gold. Speculative credit also could be restrained by requiring repayment of loans in tangibles equal to the original value of the loan. The social consequences were always enormous as savings and fixed incomes were wiped out. But a new stable currency brought confidence and finally an end to inflationary expectations and economic chaos.

Most economists regarded runaway inflation as one of the most destructive events ever devised against mankind outside of war. It not only misallocates economic resources and production but warps basic social conduct and moral values by affecting incentives, thrift, work ethics, and reasoning. It redistributes wealth in a chaotic fashion, primarily hurting the poor and elderly - those least able to protect themselves. It creates great social unrest among all of society when it reaches its worst stage because everyone becomes desperate to salvage something out of the economic chaos.

The important question, of course, is "What caused such devastation and how could it be prevented ?"

Many laymen and politicians blamed rising prices or shortages of some commodities for inflation. These, however, were merely the symptoms and not the cause. It is true that shortages of certain products will temporarily increase the price until new producers quickly respond to fill the demand. Inflation also rises from wage costs rising faster than productivity; once again, this is a symptom and not the cause.

It is also true that governments create gradual price and wage increases by: raising taxes, adding expensive and unecessary regulatory red-tape, making foreign imports expensive to consumers by raising import tariffs, allowing excessively generous jury awards against businesses that are merely shifted to consumer prices, putting upward pressure on all salaries by arbitrarily raising minimum wages for some, and increasing the price of farm products through government-induced shortages due to crop misallocations from subsidies.

Nevertheless, economists generally agreed that the principal cause of extensive inflation was as follows:

(1) an increase in demand that exceeded the supply of goods and services

(2) when that demand was artificially stimulated by an increase in the currency supply or credit

(3) and neither is restrained by reserve backing in tangible assets or commodities sufficient to liquidate them.

In other words, inflation is increased when governments print excessive amounts of paper money or flood the credit markets (banks) with easy money at artificially low rates of interest. This increased buying power, in turn, bids goods to ever higher prices.

To put it another way, a government's central bank controls the quantity of money. If it is increased, potential demand for goods is increased; when demand exceeds the supply of goods and services available, prices rise. Probably no other economic statement is as well established as this. [12]

***

Many believed that the real culprit for an excessively expanding money supply by governments was their economic malfunctioning. Once again, one of the main problems noted were dislocations in the efficient-market mechanism because of government interference.

Typical, were tariffs added to the cost of imported goods into the United States (protectionism). It was estimated that American consumers paid up to twenty-five percent more for clothing, five percent for cars, and thirty percent more for sugar to protect less-efficient businesses and workers from foreign competition. The total cost in one year exceeded 14 billion dollars with the greatest burden falling on lower income people.

The biggest problem, however, were politicians' attempts to satisfy an exploding population's demands in excess of what their economies could produce. They could not understand that, in the long-run, such efforts were an economic disaster. In the short-run, they appeared to make their constituents happy who, in turn, voted to extend their tenure in office. Some of the worst cases occurred in third-world countries. There, subsidies for food, gasoline, and many other items were financed by printing nearly worthless money and by placing price-controls on those products. The result was a reduction in output and eventual shortages, black-markets, and hyper-inflation in all of the economy.

Interference by governments resulted in mushrooming government spending that required: higher taxes, more borrowing (creating more dubious paper currency), and the transfer of funds from the productive business sector to non-productive government. Thus, productivity was reduced instead of raised. To make matters worse in the United States, higher taxes were directed at savers and investors further curtailing investment in new plant and equipment which would have increased productivity and helped retard rising prices. Even the increased taxes on workers had the effect of reducing their output and/or causing them to demand higher gross incomes to maintain after-tax income: this increased labor costs and finally prices.

It was, therefore, obvious to many economists that rising levels of taxes to pay for government spending did not increase productivity and reduce inflation. In fact, they believed it had the very opposite effect including eventually increasing unemployment.

F.A. Hayek, the 1974 Nobel Laureate in Economics, argued for years that in search of full employment, Western governments

A Dynamic New Economy   271

had pursued inflationary monetary and fiscal policies. Then, to counteract the inflation, they introduced wage and price controls that prevented the market system from operating, thus creating more untold economic problems. Hayek firmly believed governments must be prevented from inflating the money supply in order to promote political aims.

(The New Society)
Looking back historically, the Economic Advisory Committee believed it had solved some of the problems of inflation through their earlier decisions. These were to eliminate government interference and distortions using the efficient-market mechanism and by adopting tax policies that increased savings and investment, rewarded society's productive element, and inhibited consumption of luxuries. It helped to abolish inefficient government-run businesses that could be operated more productively by the private sector. As outlined earlier, the limited need for government spending eliminated the need to borrow vast sums and inflate the money supply.

After the official adoption of the above methods, the Committee set up a special permanent board to monitor and enforce these principles throughout the world economy. The Board works closely with the World Central Bank. Between the two, financial resources are carefully perused and made available on an equitable and sound money basis. This is done through regional central banks throughout the world resulting in subdued inflation. Our Consumer Price Index hovers between zero and one percent annually. Interest rates are low, assisting our capital-intensive world economy.

Of course, there is only one international currency in the world which eliminates the various problems of former days with foreign exchange, especially the instability of some currencies. Paper money is always reedeemable in gold coin and the World Central Bank freely buys and sells gold. Nevertheless, after a half century of stable currency and no inflation, little buying or hoarding of gold exists except for jewelry or industrial purposes. [13]

With our new form of governance void of undisciplined politicians, there is no longer a problem maintaining a sound currency.

Therefore, gold is hoarded by only a few since it is an asset with no income.

(Historical Background)

The European Community's common agriculture policy was called the "crazy agriculture policy." It subsidized European farmers and was not only costly and complex, but it resulted in the production of mountains of excess butter and lakes of wine. It cost nearly two-thirds of the E.C.'s budget.

In the United States, Congressmen and bureaucrats were reluctant to let go of the political monster created by farm subsidies and regulations. By 1991 the half-century old price support program for milk required five-hundred bureaucrats merely to administer. The dairy surpluses were so large that the government induced farmers to reduce their herds by paying the farmers more than one million dollars to slaughter excess cows.

Regulations promoted production of twice as much milk as consumers could drink. Critics claimed the system stimulated inefficient production and discouraged new processing technology. It was estimated that in some years it cost consumers and taxpayers $1.7 billion annually.

The Justice Department and the General Accounting Office of Congress urged that the government's role in dairy subsidies be gradually reduced. Yet, one of the most powerful lobbies in Washington, the dairy lobby which included big corporations like Kraft and Bordens, opposed deregulation. Unfortunately, the regulations were so complex and innumerable that it was impossible for Congress to even debate the issue. [14]

The United States Commerce Department reported in 1988 that sugar subsidies added $3 billion a year to consumers' grocery bills. The price of twenty-three cents per pound in 1990 had been set by Congress. The world price was twelve cents! Congress received large campaign contributions from the sugar lobby while grain farmers complained that subsidy-rich sugar beet farmers drove up land prices squeezing them out.

The silliest subsidy was to tobacco farmers. The government was buying tobacco and guaranteeing tobacco loans to support the price. It also supplied free government grading of tobacco crops.

Meanwhile, the Surgeon General was exhorting the viles of smoking to the American people.

During these bygone times, farm subsidies, costing nations billions of dollars, were commonplace. The reasoning was twofold. First, there was the fear a nation would be left vulnerable in times of war or other catastrophe if they didn't protect their own farmers no matter how costly and inefficient they were. Secondly, most citizens wanted to insure an uninterrupted source of farm products by guaranteeing farmers a higher income regardless of the cost to subsidize them.

(The New Society)
Today under the world community government, void of wars and national trade borders and with population controls, no country or region is vulnerable to a food shortage even in times of a regional catastrophe.

Moreover, all operators of farms and ranches have access to commodity reports which keep them constantly informed of potential shortages and surpluses in the world. Consequently, it enables them to make more accurate and profitable planting decisions. Additionally, all operators are educated to use commodity future contracts to hedge these decisions. In other words, if an operator plants wheat when the price is three dollars per bushel, he can guarantee that price against a future drop. Farmers are able to do this by selling wheat at that price in the commodity futures markets and agreeing to deliver wheat later at harvest time to offset the earlier sale.

All farm operators also carry special crop insurance against natural disasters such as drought, storms, flood, and disease.

Most farm operations in the new society are large, sophisticated, and scientifically operated like any other business and take the same risk like other businesses. Small inefficient family-farms of previous times have long been replaced by large corporate agribusinesses, some being franchised operations to individuals or partnerships. Subsidies are no longer paid. If an operation is inefficient and can't compete in world markets, it may go bankrupt like any other business, making room for more efficient operators. This has been of enormous benefit to consumers.

Most work requires sophisticated computer-operated machinery, highly educated managers, and technically trained workers. One example is global-positioning-satellite technology which help control costs and boost crop yields. Computer-equipped agricultural machinery pick up satellite signals that indicate such things as soil acidity, fertilizer and herbicide requirements, and harvest yield for specific areas of a large field of hundreds of acres where walking the entire field would be impractical.

However, some of the more seasonal and menial labor is done by those, awaiting openings in more advanced occupations, or by first-time offenders of less-serious non-violent crimes. The later are required to work a year at these operations.

All farm and ranch operators are encouraged to buy stock in a regional commodity-surplus corporation. These firms buy surplus farm products when prices are abnormally low. They then process, store, and sell them during shortages when prices are high. This accomplishes several things; it helps stabilize prices for the farm operators; profits from the corporation help offset losses of individual operations during bad times; the surpluses act as a hedge against a natural regional disaster and benefit the entire region.

***

There were some who described the new economic system as a merger of capitalism and socialism, but both systems were crude when compared to the new advanced economic order. In truth, it represented improvement over the best of the old economic systems and eliminated the worst.

Chapter 11

FREEDOM AND RIGHTS OF THE INDIVIDUAL

(The New Society)

Throughout the world, the individual is now free to make life decisions and to plot his future without fear or restraint as long as those decisions do not harm others. Nevertheless, individuals are responsible for their choices and cannot blame the rest of society if those choices are wrong.

The individual now has an equal economic opportunity at birth, an excellent government-funded education, equal employment opportunity through mandated competitive examinations, freedom from income taxes, and guaranteed basic economic security in return for industrious labor. Additionally, the individual's right for protection from criminal harm is the government's first priority.

In spite of the need to adopt methods of social behavior that protect and benefit the entire community, the place of the individual in the new socio-economic structure is extremely important. Unlike the old Communist governments, freedom and well-being of the individual in the new society are not subordinated to the development of the state. The end result cannot justify the elimination of basic individual rights. Throughout history, the great majority of ordinary people have been treated as an undistinguishable mass by authorities seldom recognizing individual needs.

Laws now establish broad-based freedoms and rights. An individual's liberty is the right to settle his own destiny in complete freedom from outside influence. Individual rights, however, are no excuse for non-compliance of laws and regulations that protect society. In contrast, beginning in the 1960s freedom of the individual had been extended to unparalleled extremes in the United States with little regard for its effects on others. It mattered little if it conflicted with the overall good and structure of society so long as it did not conflict with the interpretation of the Constitution.

Today the individual and society have a mutual responsibility. In order for the individual to receive the opportunity to achieve his full potential, he must, in return, cooperate in contributing to the full potential of society.

The new society has established the following economic freedoms and rights of the individual:

1. Equal economic opportunity at birth without the distortion of vast inherited wealth.

2. The right to own property (except natural resources).

3. The right to basic economic security in return for labor.

4. Freedom from taxation of all income.

5. Equal employment opportunity through competitive examination free of any bias.

6. Freedom to choose one's occupation, place of work, and to choose between competitive goods and services.

7. The right to compete for a job or in commerce anywhere in the world without trade barriers or government interference (except reasonable regulatory standards). [1]

Some of the social freedoms and rights of the individual are as follows:

1. Life, property, and freedoms shall not be unlawfully infringed.

2. The right to governmental protection from criminal harm (including environmental).

3. The equal right to a government-funded education and behavioral development.

4. The right to petition local and regional governing boards for serious non-judicial grievances and suggestions and to obtain a fair and prompt resolution.
5. Without detrimental effect on society:
   A. The right to privacy.
   B. Freedom to communicate.
6. The right to a fair and speedy trial.

The Committee on Individual Rights and Freedoms believed mandated education and behavioral development was necessary for the growth of civilization. Without it, the individual would be impeded and on an unequal foundation to cope with life. Therefore, no child is deprived of education and behavioral guidelines needed to get along with others as in earlier times when many young children were without proper parental guidance and motivation; the result was disasterous for all of society.

Probably no single factor contributes more to the well-being of the individual and, therefore, society than the freedom to choose. Additionally, equality of choice makes each person responsible for his actions. Each is judged on the results of his choices through life. Errors by individuals can no longer be blamed on society.

It is this freedom to choose that differentiates every member of society; it molds each person. Ironically, no matter how equal one is treated throughout a lifetime, each will show different results as he chooses the degree of effort and life-style preferred. This also determines one's economic level.

(Historical Background)

Without freedom of choice, the individual could not achieve the potential to create, challenge or invent, but had to accept whatever employment a government offered. Under many socialist economies, the worker was assigned employment. This was especially true in the Soviet economy. No one could choose in the marketplace but had to buy whatever the government produced. People could not accumulate assets. The incentive to save and invest was absent. Most American children were not sent to a school of their choice but had to accept government-run schools. With closed borders or emigration restrictions, most were not free to choose where to live and work in the world. The list goes on.

(The New Society)

To maximize individual potential, the Committee was determined to see that everyone in the new society had an equal opportunity throughout life. It was imperative each had a fair chance in the workplace to meet challenges, to compete for the job of their choice, and to express creativity,

If the job of choice is unavailable at the time, the individual has the opportunity for temporary work in exchange for economic security (minimum salary). This type of work, although less desirable, is always available. It is advertised in world-wide computer data-banks.

A small percentage of the labor force is always looking for better positions. But there is no idleness, no unemployment, and no welfare because people are always employed even if temporarily. Unless one has sufficient savings for living expenses, every able-bodied person works in order to receive, at least, basic necessities from a minimum salary. (More about that later.)

(Historical Background)

In early times, jobs were often obtained through bias. Gender, race, age, fraternal and political affiliation, favoritism, and the influence of wealth and power more often determined who received a position rather than ability. In many cases, this determined who held political office as well. Education, impressive experience, proven ability, and other good credentials were not as important as the "right connections", attendance at the "right" schools, member of the "right" fraternity, lodge, religion or social class. This was unfair to the individual and a hindrance to society's progress.

(The New Society)

There was unanimous agreement in the Committee that a more equitable means should be used to fill job positions. They, therefore, mandated through law that every individual have the right to equal employment opportunity based solely on competitive examinations.

All job openings, including government, are now filled on this basis. These exams include tests and appraisal of aptitude, reasoning ability, education, previous experience in that particular field of endeavor, records of proven ability in allied areas, as well as physical examination for certain jobs and psychological tests to determine the individual's ability to work with others in that particular position.

Most tests are conducted by computers. One of the tests includes simulated tense confrontational problems with other employees or customers wherein the applicant responds with a microphone on a recorded tape which is later reviewed and graded. Computers tell applicants explicitly what the job involves eliminating the usual hesitancy of applicants to ask. Computer interviews save time and personnel, weed out unqualified people, and reduce turnover. This saves the government as well as private employers large sums of money. Most important, computers are not judgmental.

Job openings are also computerized in regional data-banks. All job openings are required to be advertised through these banks to enable anyone equal access to compete. Bias of any type is forbidden, criminal, and subject to severe penalties. Computerization also assists in moving labor forces rapidly from areas of oversupply to areas of undersupply.

(Historical Background)
During the later part of the 1990s in the United States, Canada and Europe, groups arose with chronic unemployment or with salaries far below those of others. Yet, this occured when there was not a shortage of job openings as evidenced by pages of "help-wanted" ads in metropolitan newspapers. In a Dun and Bradstreet survey in 1993, eleven percent of small business said finding qualified and motivated employees was their most pressing problem.

Many, at the time, were puzzled by the growing gaps in income and the growing rate of structural unemployment (unresponsive to vigorous economic growth).

Low-paying jobs requiring few skills were some of the toughest to fill by employers. High-paying positions requiring education and considerable technical skill were also difficult to fill. So why the problem with structural unemployment?

Some employers of low-skilled jobs, who were willing to train an untried applicant, found some simply unemployable. These people were physically and mentally competent, trainable, and said they needed the job - meaning they needed money. Yet, they were not dependable to be on time or to even come to work some mornings. They could not follow instructions or work at a reasonable pace. Most had scant job history usually going from job to job or on welfare in between. Many were lazy, undisciplined, or on drugs.

Some thought unemployment was the result of too many perks. By 1995 employers became over- burdened by laws, passed by politicians to garner favor with workers, mandating the payment of benefits. The cost of American employees' rising unemployment compensation, industrial insurance, workman's compensation, one-half of social security, parental leave, the accounting cost of witholding employees' income taxes and others were forced on employers in increasing amounts by the government. When all of the above was coupled with other fringe benefits such as health insurance, vacations, pensions, paid-holidays, sick leave - some mandated by unions and others from voluntary enticement - the costs more often exceeded the base salary of the employee. Therefore, these additional labor costs negatively influenced hiring new workers. Many employers opted to pay overtime to existing workers to avoid paying fringe benefits to new employees. Firms were also reluctant to hire new applicants because each required the open-endess of potential benefit-costs in the future. Others used part-time workers from contract service companies such as Manpower, Inc.

Other economists noted governments, especially in Europe and Canada, paid unemployed workers generous income (from employers contributions) in addition to other welfare benefits. Consequently, many unemployed refused to accept less desirable or lower paying positions; they merely chose to remain unemployed. Workers also wondered why they should work at these types of jobs in order to pay onerous witholding taxes when they could receive more tax-free income by not working. The government's generosity was too much for many competing firms needing workers. Several of these governments' outlays for welfare exceeded one-half of their gross domestic product. In Sweden it reached seventy four percent!

A typical problem occured in West Germany in 1989. While unemployment was widespread, economists estimated between 500,000 and 800,000 jobs were unfilled because of lack of skills, little education, or those who simply opted to take advantage of West Germany's generous unemployment benefits. It was felt these categories comprised most of the long-term unemployed.

Some, who analyzed the widening gap between salaries, were convinced the cause was lack of education in the low-income group. A big demand for educated workers in highly technical, demanding positions went unfilled. On the other hand, large groups of poorly educated workers fought for the few decent paying jobs that did not require high technical skills. Those, who dropped out of high school or graduated without reading and writing skills and a reasonable degree of ability to comprehend, were doomed to either seek the lowest-paying undesirable jobs or go on the dole.

Other economists blamed the new computerized Information Age for much of the disruptions in the labor market. As computerization and other advanced technical equipment, such as robotic machinery, replaced repetitive and simple tasks, manual labor jobs, especially in factories, began to disappear. Those remaining required more education and technical training but paid higher wages in return.

Expanded foreign trade by multi-national corporations was also thought to reduce wages in developed nations but raise them in Third World countries through competitive labor. Overall, however, this reduced prices and increased quality and made available innovative products for consumers everywhere. This resulted in lifting the standard-of-living just as pay raises would.

(The New Society)

The gradual increasing gap in salaries was eliminated long ago. Certainly, there are differences but nothing like those existing in the 1990s. In the new society everyone receives a competent education, as earlier explained, and many go on to more advanced studies for more challenging positions. School dropouts have been eliminated. Everyone has an equal, unbiased opportunity to compete for job openings. Welfare is unavailable for a person physically able to work.

As more educated workers become available, advanced, technical, and skilled jobs are more easily filled; salaries become less inflated. On the other hand, increased automation in the lower-paying job sector overcomes the lack of job applicants. It also results in the need for higher pay for these employees who are now skilled in the use of automation.

If a desired job opening is not available or if the applicant cannot successfully compete for a particular position, he must, of course, compete for one less-demanding or less-desirable. This is necessary to receive minimum economic security. This may mean temporary routine work or simple physical labor. These jobs are transitory until a more challenging or desirable position is obtained. Again, a job opening always exists to anyone able to work. As a result, there is no unemployment. This is because openings for physical labor or routine work are always available in such areas as basic maintenance, cleaning, farm and construction labor, fishing, logging, mining, and simple assembly-line jobs.

It is important to keep in mind, although there will always be jobs requiring this type of work because employees want to move on to more challenging jobs, many have been eliminated as sophisicated robotic machinery and computerization replaces them. This results in positions requiring more technical expertise and education, and jobs that are more interesting. Each technological advancement also opens up new fields and improves the standard of living for everyone. More important, the Information Age is releasing more workers for more advanced fields of endeavor - fields required for mankind's survival in the exploration of the universe and to address the other purposes of an advanced society which is later explored in the final chapter.

Minimum economic security, regardless of occupation, covers health care, commuting transportation, shelter and food. In exchange, anyone able to work, must fill a productive position in society.

Any able-bodied person, unless able to live on his savings, who is unable to hold a job or refuses to work, is not allowed to become an unwanted parasite or a vagrant in society. Instead, the Security Forces send the person to a Natural Resource Reserve. There he must work or perish in a hostile environment.

Whether executive, entrepreneur or janitor, each is guaranteed a minimum base salary that covers these vital living necessities. The amount is determined from regional cost-of-living indexes compiled periodically by averaging prices and fees of these necessities.

It provides necessary but not luxurious economic security. However, further improvement must come from the individual's own efforts in the form of incentive compensation and not from the distribution of other's income (welfare) nor from vast inherited wealth.

The base salary establishes a safety net which insures that no individual goes homeless, hungry, or without medical attention. There is no need for costly and wasteful government bureaucracies to administer welfare to a large portion of the population through innumerable inefficient agencies.

Yes, a few require assistance such as the elderly too feeble to work, orphans, and those suffering from a debilitating sickness or accident. They are provided with basic necessities by the government.

Base salary is not paid in cash. Instead, the employer pays for the employee's monthly commuting pass, premium for his health maintenance organization, and fee for the home-owners' cooperative association (for maintenance and amortization). The remainder pays for a "smart card" used for groceries.

The " smart card" represents a deposit of a specified amount of money, and each time it is used, the amount of the purchase price is automatically deducted by an electronic reader. When empty, the card is void. These cards were used in the 1990s for pay phones and some U.S. transit systems. It can only be used in food stores for the purchase of groceries. The amount deposited for food purchases each pay period helps the individual to closely monitor his purchases. In no way does this mean the individual isn't free to buy expensive gourmet foods and wines with his supplementary income.

This very unique way of handling the base salary of an employee helps insure that the employee's family does not go hungry, homeless, or without medical help. There is never a need to supplement wages with various public welfare programs. The method of handling is not a great departure from the variety and methods of bestowing employer benefits in the late 20th century.

A reasonable minimum salary appears to be fair for the employer only if there is a job for every able-bodied person and each works, as is the case now. It is not fair when unemployment prevails and some employers are still forced to pay minimum wages raising their labor costs excessively in a depressed economic environment as was once the case.

In retrospect, the great economic conflict, prior to the new society, was not between business and labor unions. It was between a wage that allowed a business to produce competitively and a wage that covered the living costs for the worker. This duel was because both the employer and employee were fighting to survive. Both were right. No longer do we have this problem.

Individuals spend their salaries much like in previous times. Income, in excess of the basic salary, is spent on such things as a better home, travel, dining out, recreation, or even obtaining medical attention outside his HMO if desired.

(Historical Background)

The problem of achieving quality health care at reasonable costs began near the end of the 19th century. It gained momentum through the first half of the 20th century as the complexity of medical science developed, and a greater demand arose for hospital care. By the 1950s the financial burden became so great it necessitated an increasing demand for some type of financial protection against excessive medical costs.

In addition to private medical insurance, various forms of socialized medicine arose, initially in continental Europe, the Soviet Union, and England. Near the end of the 20th century it had been adopted, in one form or another, by nearly every developed nation on earth.

Two great problems evolved. First, medical care, provided directly by government-owned medical facilities including hospitals and government-employed doctors and medical personnel, degenerated to the point where most patients, who could afford it, opted for private care. Second, the phenomenal advance in medicine prolonged life of the very old at a tremendous medical cost to the rest of society. In the United States the government insured most of the cost through Medicaid and Medicare and did not actively hire medical personnel or own medical facilities except Veteran's Administration health care. Yet, a survey in 1989 indicated ninety percent of adults thought the system needed a complete overhaul.

Nearly one-half of Canadians said their health-care system, admired by other countries, needed significant change. And nearly three-fourths of Britons indicated their government-run system needed radical changes. [2]

Britain's system of socialized medicine was once the envy of the world because of low-cost to taxpayers, and because it was free to everyone. By 1988 it was in chaos. Government employees (unions) in the system became a formidable special interest group because of the impact of their numbers (over one million). They demanded ever higher salaries and benefits. Costs of rapidly advancing medical technology also rose dramatically. Because of a lack of cash and incentive, facilities were in disrepair, wards closed, and equipment was lacking. Surgery was delayed for desperately ill children while others were placed on long waiting lists.

It was reported in the 1990s that more than a million people were waiting for admittance to hospitals, and a quarter of them had waited a year. Often people with serious conditions were placed on a waiting list to obtain a CAT scan. Less serious but similar problems occured in the Canadian system.

The outpatient surgery unit at the Churchill Hospital in Oxford, England was typical. It squeezed beds side by side in a disintegrating ward. Overhead glaring fluorescent lights, unheated halls, and unpainted concrete ceilings greeted patients. Women, receiving adverse Pap-test results, had to wait another two months before another test could be taken to confirm the results. If still adverse, they had to wait another three months before treatment.

In a typical cost reduction attempt, an administrator in Birmingham proposed letting a private firm build and run a hundred and sixty-bed-pychiatric facility for half the cost required of the government. But under pressure of the unions, he was forced to abandon the idea.[3]

The Soviet system was even worse creating a health crisis on a scale unknown in any other industrialized country. Infant-mortality rate was two and a half times higher than in the United States and ranked fiftieth in the world. Life expectancy for males declined from sixty-six in the 1960s to sixty-two by 1979 compared with seventy-two in the United States. One-third of rural hospitals had no hot water, one-quarter no sewage system, and some lacked running water. By the early 1990s many hospitals did not have enough nurses so family members took over the care of relatives.

Pravda reported administrators tried to hide negligence and lack of sanitation in maternity wards that led to the death of many mothers and infants. Even Premier Gorbachev exposed the failures of the health system and requested its overhaul as a top priority. [4]

By 1994, France's socialized health care system had a record $10 billion deficit. Yet, employers contributed an amount equal to one-third of an employee's wages, and the employee paid an additional fourteen percent into the loss-ridden system.

The Veteran's Health Administration, the largest health care system in the United States and one of the largest in the world, was analogous to a socialized health care system. All of its medical facilities were owned and operated by the government. All personnel were government employees.

After sixty-three years of operation, it was ridden with redtape and regulations. Each employee was governed by volumes of codes, regulations, and policy restrictions. More than four-hundred attorneys interpreted obsolete procedural provisions and defended thousands of malpractice suits. All of this was destructive to quality patient care and staff conduct.

More than half of patients with routine medical problems waited hours, sometimes all day, to be seen for only a few minutes by a doctor. Often those with urgent medical problems waited up to three hours. Specialists couldn't be seen for two or three months, and if surgery was required, a patient waited for months. These malfunctions were reported in a study by the General Accounting Office in 1993. [5]

In the United States, escalating health care costs rose from seven percent of the gross national product in 1970 to over fourteen percent by the early 1990s. Between 1980 and 1991 average family income grew ninety percent, but health-care costs rose one hundred and fifty percent! Many cited astronomical jury-awards for medical malpractice suits which caused doctor's medical liability insurance to skyrocket and its costs passed on to future patients. Others blamed rising health care costs on a cumbersome medical insurance system, government red-tape requirements, as well as the increased use of expensive high technology in medicine.

But Dr. Leoy Schwartz, the president of Health Policy International in 1991, pointed out that the United States was paying for its behavioral problems in health costs that far exceeded those in other developed countries. Victims of violence overwhelmed many emergency rooms at considerable expense. One fourth of the nation's spinal cord injuries were the result of assault, and the lifetime cost of treatment and rehabilitation was estimated at $600,000 per patient.

Borrowed needles for drug abuse and promiscious, unsafe sex were associated with an estimated one million people infected with AIDs. The rate of infection was three times that of Canada and six times that of West Germany. Some thought it was because those countries were without large populations of blacks since blacks shared disproportionately as victims. The lifetime cost to treat AIDs was approximately $85,000 a year per patient or $6 billion annually. The cost of treating about 375,000 drug-exposed babies was $63,000 a year per baby for the first five years (about $25 billion).

Crack-babies cost as much as a quarter of a million dollars each to warehouse in hospitals' intensive-care units. The cost was paid by other hospital patients or taxpayers. The expense of treating AIDs babies was also high and usually born by everyone except the parents.

Other health-care costs which were usually levied against all but the perpetrators, included drug overdoses requiring expensive emergency treatment; costly medical problems with deliveries because the mothers were too ignorant or lazy to avail themselves of free pre-natal care; babies born to an overwhelming increase of unwed teen-age mothers. Most unwed teenage mothers, especially low-income minority women, ignored pre-natal care. Then if birth was premature resulting in organic damage to the baby, Medicaid picked up the tab amounting sometimes to $2500 per day.

In the southwest United States, thousands of Mexican citizens illegally invaded the United States and hid from immigration officials. Yet, border states were forced by federal law to offer free health-care to these felons adding millions of dollars to the states' costs.

Despite the overwhelming evidence cited above, many people still blamed the medical industry for most of the rising costs and campaigned for a rigid government-run health-care system.

Another reason costs were out of control throughout all countries was the industry was generally immune from competition in the marketplace. In addition, where the system was socialized and run by the government, the quality degenerated for the same reason - noncompetitiveness.

Medicare, itself, was a symbol of inefficiency. It financed hundreds of thousands of unnecessary operations, yet, refused to pay for simple inexpensive preventative measures such as physical examinations and most immunizations. It paid for highly sophisticated medical technology to keep a mind and body alive that had hopelessly degenerated. Many of these very old would have opted to die with dignity.

Additionally, most people in the United States were covered by some form of prepaid health-care benefit by their employer, an insurance company, or the government. Consequently, they made little effort to carefully utilize these benefits. After all, it wasn't their money being spent.

(The New Society)
In the beginning, the Committee on Individual Rights and Freedoms created several subcommittees - one of which was the Committee on Health Care. Its function was to analyze how to cope with health problems and recommend suggestions to the newly formed society.

Many costly problems, that previously had seldom been addressed such as emergency treatment of violence victims, drug-overdoses, crack babies, and AIDs patients, were nearly eliminated. New standards for behavior, behavioral education, decriminalization and proper monitoring of drug use, has helped unburden our health-care system.

After lengthy analysis from many health-care experts, the Committee decided, that although medical service availability was socially mandated for everyone, competition in the health-care field was imperative. This was necessary to obtain the best quality care at the least expense - just like all other industries. They realized this was particularly difficult to attain during a medical crisis when there is no time to shop around to compare quality or cost.

Health maintenance organizations compete for members in the competitive market place. Employers attempt to select the best possible HMO for quality care at the least cost with the assistance of employee and management representatives.

Employees are concerned about cost because the premium paid from their basic minimum salary cannot exceed their region's average medical costs compiled in the current cost-of-living index. Furthermore, if the premium is less than the average cost, any difference is required to be paid to the employee in cash - because it is still a part of their minimum salary. This acts as an incentive for employees to select cost-effective HMOs.

Most HMOs today are non-profit *cooperatives* run by the member-patients from many firms. Each has a vote at the annual meeting, helps select a board of directors, and votes on any change in the monthly premium or policies involving patient care. Members' decisions keep quality high and costs down.

The cooperative hires its own administrative staff, primary-care- physicians, nurses, and support help. Members are organized to monitor and exert pressure for quality care when needed, whereas in former HMOs they were not. Many have an ombudsman empowered to review complaints of those who feel they have been the recipients of excessive cost-control or improper care.

This method proved highly successful for Group Health Co-operative of Puget Sound, a cooperative HMO formed in the 1930s that blossomed into one of the largest HMOs in the United States during the 1980s and 1990s, a huge enterprise with its own hospitals.

Managed health-care facilities are generally well-organized and coordinated to streamline treatment of patients, eliminating waste and inefficiency. The patient has immediate access to everything needed for quality medical care.

Most HMOs in the new society are regional. They consist of health clinics with their own X-ray, laboratory and other testing facilities, pharmacies, dental, and optometry departments. Each clinic handles routine medical problems. It, also, requires preventive care such as routine physical examinations, immunizations, pre-natal care, and cancer screening which benefit, not only the member, but in the control of costs.

Deductables or co-payments are not charged. It is felt an unnecessary visit is a small price to pay for a possible early diagnosis of a chronic disease. Left undetected, it could be extremely costly to the HMO as well as to the patient. The use of physician's-assistants for such things as first-aid, colds, and other routine maladies reduces the cost of office calls.

Each HMO has computers available to members that tap the medical libraries and databases for current information on any ailment including diagnostic decision trees. They also tap the Internet where discussion of ailments with other network users is possible. The result is a patient informed of services and treatments available worldwide for a specific illness, and he becomes nearly as knowledeable as the primary physician - not about how to practice medicine but about what medicine has to offer.

More serious medical problems are passed to specialists and hospitals which are contracted in each community or area on a competitive basis. Contracts are made with hospitals, skilled nursing facilities and services, ambulance companies, and physician specialists. These firms and people compete intensively in quality and price for the business from HMOs.

Quality of each entity is determined through annual ratings systems. Such things as a summary of care as measured by selected outcome indicators by classes of illness severity, descriptions of quality assessment programs, average wait for non-critical surgery, and specific advanced medical technology currently used for various illnesses. These standards for comparing quality and performance are the same worldwide. One can obtain a true picture of how each measures up to competitors. Periodic inspections are also made by representatives of the HMOs. Prospective members can also compare each HMO with their competition.

If a serious and expensive operation or treatment is needed, the patient, with help from his primary physician, still has freedom to select the specialist or specialist-clinic outside those contracted by the HMO. The cost is then negotiated and paid by the HMO. However, the member-patient is required to pay a reasonable co-payment. This is necessary to control excessive expenses outside the HMO contracts.

All HMOs and other medical facilities are required to use standard simplified medical forms and records to reduce unnecessary paper work.

The fixed premium removes any excuse to provide wasteful and unnecessary services. It also is an incentive to keep people well by appropriate preventive care.

Each member selects a primary physician within the HMO and is free to change. If a patient is not satisfied with a diagnosis, he may ask for a second opinion or a specialist.

Competitive hospitals have reciprocal agreements. A patient can be taken to the nearest one in an emergency and is covered until transferred to the one contracted by his own HMO.

Intrusion of government into the health-care system no longer creates waste and inefficiency under a maze of regulations that adds expense and stifles innovation. No longer are patients insulated from the true cost of medical care. An open-ended reimbursement system which rewards excessive hospital admissions or excessive, inefficient use of expensive technology and equipment has been eliminated.

Health-care benefits are all inclusive. No eligibility exclusions are mandated, and the coverage is universal. Those too ill or disabled to work have their medical premiums paid by the government (this is explained later). Those, who can afford to be more independent in the selection of their physicians and medical care, are free to do so.

(Historical Background)
As early as the late 20th century, the National Health Service in Great Britain restricted coronary by-pass operations to patients under age fifty-five. The state of Oregon's Medicaid program also restricted certain medical procedures that were thought wasteful or not critical.

Nevertheless, in most areas during this period, the very old (above age 80), the brain-dead, and terminally ill had their lives prolonged at any cost without consent. Some were so degenerated as to be unaware of their condition. Elderly patients, with chronic debilitating diseases that destroyed the mind and wasted the body, were given such ridiculous treatment as cataract surgery, kidney dialysis, or even open-heart surgery to prolong their life. Many were tube-fed, inserted with urethral catheters, and injected with antibiotics at the first sign of infection. And for what purpose? Many wanted to die, felt they were being punished, and did not want to end their days in a vegetative state. But the primitive philosophy of the day insisted on prolonging a life of incurable wretchedness simply because it was felt everyone was entitled to live regardless of their age, circumstance, or cost. Yet, a 1985 poll found eighty-five percent endorsed a terminally-ill patient's right to have a doctor cease trying to extend life. [6]

A typical case was that of Edward H. Winter, who had a heart attack in May of 1988 at age 82. Shortly after, he instructed his doctor, should his condition worsen, he did not want to be resuscitated. Three days later while experiencing fibrillations that signalled sudden death, a nurse revived him through electric shock. Two days after being revived, he suffered a debilitating stroke that confined him to a nursing home. He could speak only a few words before beginning to cry in despair. After two years, his medical bills exceeded $100,000. His doctors said he could live for years with only a scant chance for improvement. [7]

To keep the very old alive, an insatiable appetite developed for money because the cost was enormous. Two-thirds of the total cost of health-care in an average person's lifetime, occured during the last two months of life. It was estimated the health care costs of people 85 and older was double that of even 65 year olds. As the elderly's average age increased in the early part of the 21st century, a substantial portion of gross national income was spent prolonging their lives to the detriment of younger age groups.

(The New Society)
It was obvious to the Committee on Health Care that funds for this purpose were not limitless nor was it always desirable. So, drastic steps were taken to set up guidelines for withdrawal of costly life-support procedures. These are individuals whose productive life is over and whose quality of life is intolerable. The Committee believed quality was as important as the length of life. It believed dying should not be prevented with herculean artificial efforts when it is obvious that the time for dying has arrived. Instead, the patient is kept comfortable and attended with love and compassion through the dying process.

When such things as dignity and a personal sense of value to society is gone and one is completely dependent on others to merely exist indefinitely, the quality of life is gone. The Committee emphasized how and why we live is of primary importance. Existence, by itself in a civilized society, cannot be considered a value. Life is only a necessary mode to the attainment of values. Dying is merely a stage in the metamorphous of life. Death in the terminal stage should be viewed as a natural and appropriate end to a satisfying life. With this in mind, the Committee came to a radical decision. It set guidelines for assistance in allowing one to quickly end their misery and futility just as one would compassionately put their suffering pet "to sleep."

***

As indicated earlier, a portion of basic minimum salary provides shelter for every employee and their family. Homelessness does not exist.

In the 20th century, indiscriminate sprawl of free-standing homes used up scarce urban land. In the new society during an advanced planning stage, parcels of land are zoned by the Land Use Board for multiple-story dwelling complexes and incorporated into a diversified community. High-density construction conserves land for other more useful purposes. The complexes are surrounded by community gardens, parkland, and sophisticated recreational areas.

The Land Use Board contracts to have housing complexes built with government funds on a competitive basis. Once the Board zones a parcel of land for home construction, competitive biding is open to contractors. The bid must include plans, upgrades, options, amenities, recreational facilities, and an amortization schedule. Models of units and samples of upgrades and options are available for all prospective home-owners.

The first contractor to receive fifty percent or more home-buyer applications is selected. This procedure insures the best quality at the lowest price without bureaucratic favoritism or interference. Upon completion, the contractor is cashed out by the government, and payments to the Land Use Board by the new home-owners begin.

Minimum standard complexes are built for those living primarily on a basic minimum salary. No deposit is required; only an application indicating permanent employment is necessary. The affordable monthly payment is minimal because it is based on an eighty-year amortization with no interest. Payments directly to the Land Use Board are made by each cooperative home-owners association.

Larger more luxurious units are available providing one has sufficient income in excess of a basic salary and is able to submit a deposit.

Each new complex is managed by a controlling cooperative of owners. Ownership of the land is still retained and controlled by the Land Use Board, but there is no rental on the land. Buildings and facilities are owned and managed by the cooperative.

The cooperative hires a manager and assistants who handle vacancies, maintenance and improvements, contract and pay for insurance, utilities, and monthly amortization payments. To pay for these expenses, it collects monthly payments from each home owner's employer deducted from minimum salaries. Additional amounts are collected directly from the home-owners of more luxurious units.

Home units are treated by the occupants in the same manner as condominiums and free-standing homes were in the past. They add improvements, renovations, and furnishings to their taste while enjoying all the surrounding ammenities of the complex. Some complexes are designed for the elderly and some for young singles as well as families. However, there is total integration and no class distinction. Every owner has a vote in the governing of the complex and chooses how to live there providing it does not detrimentally affect neighbors.

Anyone, creating a shabby, untidy, or unclean area detracting from the homes of other members, is required to rectify the problem or move. Filth and disorder that once prevailed in the inner-cities is not tolerated. This prevents a few from ruining the neighborhood ambience for the rest.

Each owns his home indefinitely. Should he die or decide to move, the unit is then taken over by the cooperative and allotted to a new occupant. Aside from the payment for any extensive inside improvements, no other funds are needed to buy a home. The transfer of equity as in former times has been eliminated. If a home has been amortized, monthly payments are less expensive. But, the home is also older, may be in need of more frequent repairs, and may be obsolete in some other respects. Most homes of this type are adequate and easily affordable for those living principally on a minimum salary.

Essentially a home-owner still chooses the home he wants at the price he can afford. The unique method of buying a home without paying for equity reflects the actual structural value of the home and not the land underneath as in previous times. It prevents the escalation of home prices due not only to inflation of building materials and labor but primarily to inflationary aspects of diminishing favorable home sites. This prevented many from buying adequate housing in the past.

In the new society there is a home for everyone because the new economic system has held inflation in check, and the Land Use Board stands ready to make land available and finance residential home complexes as they are needed. Much less land is required as in the days of single-home construction. For all these reasons, homes are much more affordable relative to other living expenses.

(Historical Background)

In the later part of the 20th century a spirited debate ensued over the pros and cons of welfare. Because welfare benefits were tax-free, some states offered benefits equivalent to $36,400 in pretax wages, far above the poverty level. This left little incentive to work. "People actually perceive they're better off going on welfare than working," said Donna Shalala, Human Services Secretary in the Clinton Administration.

Two-thirds on welfare had been there for eight years, and three-quarters said they were not looking for work. Families were weakened; incentive to work, save, and be ambitious was reduced; the freedoms of all were constricted. Swedish economist Assar Lindbeck noted that when a welfare state, such as Sweden, gives too much to those who are idle and takes too much from those who are not, the incentives to work and produce are destroyed.

Many advocated more taxpayer funds, not less, to be spent for various welfare programs. Some proposed those with higher incomes should contribute more to those with less. Any problems within the welfare system were the result of inadequate funding, they claimed.

Others argued that waste and inefficiency in the bureaucratic administration of welfare programs was horrendous. Widespread corruption and cheating in the system stirred public anger. Much of the money was not going to the poor, but instead, was drained off by administrative costs supporting a massive bureaucracy. One of the most ironic examples was a job training program in Cincinnati for welfare recipients wherein many could only land jobs administering welfare.

In the United States, the welfare system had more than one-hundred different programs that evolved piecemeal and haphazardly over the years. Eligibility standards, benefits, and responsibilities were complicated and counterproductive. For example, in 1974 the Supplemental welfare portion was only one-twelfth of Social Security. Yet it required one-half of the total administrating costs for the entire Social Security system and indicated the tremendous waste in the welfare portion.

Some even advocated large direct cash payments (negative income tax) to the working poor so all but one agency could be eliminated. The expense saved in bureaucracy could be devoted to the recipients.

Welfare also caused disruptions in the labor market. Labor mobility was reduced because many laid-off workers prefered to draw unemployment benefits rather than look for work elsewhere outside their local community.

Unemployment compensation, food stamps, Medicaid, housing and cash benefits were, many times, greater than net income from wages after witholding taxes. Therefore, many workers preferred to go on welfare. So without sufficient job applicants, business swapped automation or other substitutes for labor. The result was less job opportunities and still more unemployment. This was particularly true in the European Community because of their massive expansion of social benefits.

It was estimated that U.S. state and federal governments spent more than $5.5 *trillion* on welfare programs since 1965, yet the level of people in poverty had remained virtually constant. By 1994 over five million families in the United States were receiving welfare checks in addition to food stamps, medical care, and other benefits. This was a thirty-four percent increase in just five years! One in ten Americans received food stamps. Teen-age mothers headed nearly one-half of these families, and two-thirds of them lacked a high-school diploma. Hispanics and blacks received about sixty percent of the welfare checks, yet accounted for only about twenty percent of the population.

Britain under the Labor Party and socialist Sweden began welfare programs that not only bankrupted both countries but led to untold human social problems. Once the government was thoroughly embedded in the economic distribution of income, it became almost impossible to diminish its role, let alone void it.

Sweden's taxes became almost confiscatory. There was an enormous system of welfare subsidies. Investments slumped; growth and productivity lagged. Savings became non-existent, and investments went abroad. All types of government services degenerated, particularly medical care; poverty increased.

In Britain in 1992, an unemployed couple received free rent, medicine, school meals, plus one-hundred and sixty dollars per week and additional cold-weather payments. Total benefits were equal to about $300 per week. Since most jobs available in the poorer areas paid about $150 to $250 there was little incentive to get off welfare. Most unemployed in these areas were not educated enough to take higher paying jobs, and the early home environment placed little emphasis on learning. Both Britain and Sweden rewarded welfare and unemployment at a higher level than working and productivity.

(The New Society)
The unique method of providing basic necessities for families through minimum salaries negates huge bureaucracies to provide welfare.

Nevertheless, when people are not working, they may be vulnerable unless they have sufficient savings. It is required that anyone, discharged from their position, receive a minimum of two months severance basic salary from their employer. This allows time for the employee to find some type of work, even if menial, because temporary job openings are always available. Few quit their job without planning their next employment.

The "smart card" provides food for each child in a family and a wife who cannot work because she is either pregnant or rearing a child under age three before she returns to work. Additionally, when the child reaches age ten, he is enrolled in the government-supported boarding school for higher education and is no longer a significant financial responsibility to the parents.

Welfare for teen-age mothers no longer exists. Teen-age pregnancy has been virtually eliminated for several reasons. First, teenage girls have been explicitly warned they have only two options: (1) The baby may be raised by her parents or adopted by another couple, or (2) the pregnancy aborted. A second pregnancy would result in the consequences of population control.

Secondly, teen-age pregnancy is no longer a serious problem. Boys and girls attend separate boarding schools, and cars are no longer driven so the opportunity for sex is diminished. Government-regulated brothels are also an outlet for the young male sexual drive.

In more primitive times, many people were born mentally retarded and physically handicapped. Some could not control simple body functions and existed in a vegetative state. Most required full-time help from others and existed without the slightest hope of improving. In many cases they were simply warehoused in institutions at tremendous cost to society.

In the new society, prenatal testing is mandatory to determine if any genetic abnormalties exist that could cause a baby to die at an early age or to live seriously retarded or handicapped. DNA tests have now been developed that identify any number of inherited diseases and disorders. Should a test indicate a serious and incurable genetic or chemical defect, the fetus is automatically aborted.

Still, individuals, due to illness or accident, become vegetative. In such cases with guidelines from medical authorities, the family must decide to either cope with the care of the individual on their own with limited community assistance or to withdraw life-support systems.

Those individuals who are only somewhat mentally or physically impaired are sent to special schools to improve their ability to cope with routine everyday tasks and placed in the labor market working up to their level of capability so they may be self-supporting.

This leaves only a small percentage of people in need of welfare: the very-old who are feeble and those, due to a debilitating accident or sickness, are unable to work and handle routine problems. These people are placed in government-funded care-centers. If the person can reside at home with limited care, their monthly medical premium, home owner's fee, and "smart" card for food purchases is paid by the government.

(Historical Background)

In the late 20th century there was a serious problem of people living on the streets. Most had substance-abuse and mental problems. Many had been deinstitutionalized. Several doctors and specialists at John Hopkins School of Medicine made an in-depth study of several hundred homeless in Baltimore. They found most displayed mental disorders such as phobias, major depression, dementia, and schizophrenia. The majority were alcoholics. These people were generally dismissed from mental institutions, never admitted, or never rehabilitated. They ended up on the streets.

***

By the end of the 20th century many nations adopted some form of retirement pension or security. In the United States, it was originally devised in the 1930s to supplement individual savings for retirement. Half the cost was paid by the employer and half was withheld from the employee's salary.

By 1980, so many new benefits had been added that the system was in serious financial trouble. Supplemental Social Security (SSI) for the poorer retirees, Medicare, disability insurance for anyone whether retired or not, and annual cost-of-living increases had been added over the years until the program was no longer a pension system, but a giant welfare entitlement.

Benefits increasingly went to people who had not contributed through wage deductions. As both benefits and the average age of the population increased, the dependency fell heavily on younger workers whose Social Security tax on their wages exploded. The escalating burden became so great for employers that many delayed hiring new workers. More important, younger workers could not look forward to a funded system for their own retirement. Instead it eventually became bankrupt and was funded out of general taxes.

An inequity in the system was the provision that penalized those who wanted to continue working past the program's retirement age of 65. Another inequity was the taxing of payments to some retirees although income tax had already been paid on their income from which the Social Security was originally deducted.

The American system also demanded that funds paid into Social Security be invested in government obligations. The requirement became a prescription for permanent inflation as it released these funds to politicians to spend indiscriminately for special interests. Furthermore, if the funds had been invested in common stocks and commercial bonds, as in private pension funds, they would not only have been secure from being squandered on government spending schemes, but the system would have been well overfunded. This would have paid for higher retirement payments as well as reducing deductions from the salaries of younger workers.

On the other hand, private pension funds during this period were highly successful appreciating rapidly in the 1980s and 1990s. They eventually became the principle source of retirement income. Unlike Social Security funds, private pension funds were diversified into stocks, bonds, and real estate of many companies and professionally managed to seek the highest yield and appreciation with safety of principal.

Unlike Social Security in the United States, Chile adopted a system where ten percent of every worker's paycheck was witheld and deposited into an individual savings account managed by a private fund selected by the employee. The private funds averaged an annual fourteen percent return. Chile eliminated the possibility of free-spending politicians using the social-security monies. The government's only role was to regulate the private funds to ensure a minimum pension upon retirement. The workers were happy, and the funds served as a foundation for a growing capital-market of stocks and bonds that supported the expansion of industry. Nations throughout the world sent representatives to Chile to observe and adopt the innovation.

By the late 1980s, private pension funds became the largest stockholders in American industry controlling over one-half of the largest corporations. Therefore, profits and growth from these corporations increasingly went to the American wage-earner in the form of appreciating pension funds for retirement. As Peter Drucker so aptly emphasized, "Thus, the worker and the capitalist had eventually become one and the same person." Most people were unaware that the majority of corporate profits (dividends) went to employee-pension funds - indirectly to wage-earners. Ironically, this ignorance by many of the electorate, therefore, led to the advocacy of higher taxes on corporations or other anti-business lawmaking to the detriment of most employees.[8]

One of the big problems with any government retirement program during the 20th and early 21st centuries, was the rapid growth in an aging population. In the United States in 1935, one in ten were over the age of sixty-five. By 1975 the ratio was one in four.

By the year 2000, it was much worse. Coupled with rewarding early retirement in some industries and an optional early retirement with Social Security payments, the labor force was considerably reduced. Even if a retirement at age sixty-five was realistic in 1940, by the early 1990s, it should have been raised to around seventy-five based on life expectancy.

Most industrialized economies faced a common demographic problem. Unless something changed, governments eventually would have more older people to care for, and the cost was going to be staggering. Production in the work-place fell on fewer people reducing the standards of living for all. The transfer of payments from young workers to the rapidly growing older population was the principle underlying cause.

Some felt early retirement was an anachronism and rewarding early retirement a folly. They reasoned, why should productivity diminish and living standards decline for all simply to retire a growing portion of the population to an unproductive existence?

A study by Lou Harris polsters in 1991 found two million retired Americans were ready, willing, and able to go to work. Further studies in both the United States and Britain revealed workers above age fifty-five had forty percent less absenteeism, stayed on the job three times longer, were often better sales people, and could be trained in new technologies such as computers. [10]

Furthermore, there was increasing evidence that most retirees were not happy with their circumstances. These were people forced to retire or opted to retire because Social Security or a pension were available. Some had financial problems making ends meet. After dropping out of the work force, nearly all felt left out of the mainstream of society. Having contributed in the work-world helping customers, fellow workers, employers, or society in general, they felt no longer needed or wanted. This was devastating to their self-esteem. Many developed no other interests other than their earlier work or profession. So they became bored and searched desperately for something to do. Some merely existed as useless members of society filling time with golf or bridge.

(The New Society)
The Committee on Individual Rights and Freedoms was well aware of the provisions that the Committee on Environmental Controls was formulating to curtail the population explosion. As the birth rate dropped, longevity continued to increase as medical science prolonged life. The discovery of cancer-causing genes that control the division of cells and pharmaceuticals that normalize those genes has now eliminated cancer as a major cause of death. This contributed greatly to our longevity. The Committee, therefore, realized employing older workers to fill some of the jobs would be required.

In addition, it was obvious from historical research that monetary retirement systems of any type were not in anyone's best interest. Generally, it was thought an individual must be allowed to live a productive life and continue to work in a self-supporting role as long as he is physically and mentally able.

Of course, if an individual prefers to retire to pursue some avocation or other interest or even to take a lengthy vacation trip with accumulated savings, that is his perogative.

As the worker ages in a physically or mentally demanding occupation or in positions of great stress and responsibility, periodic physical examinations assist in evaluating whether a less-demanding position or reduced work hours should be substituted. Professional sabaticals are given as well as longer vacations. Nevertheless, it has been shown that regular mental and physical activity retards the aging process.

If the individual becomes feeble and is unable to work and care for himself, the government provides the funds for a comfortable environment to live out his life. This overall approach to the problem of aging is far less costly to society and better for the individual than earlier retirement programs. Especially, when meshed with our procedures to end the prolongation of misery in the terminal stages of the very old.

(Historical Background)
Large cities expanded in the 20th century because of the completion of access transportation to the workplace. Yet, this very access exacerbated the problem of commuting until some office

and factory employees put in eleven to twelve hour work days but actually worked only eight. This was not only a waste of an individual's time but a waste of productivity for society. Large sprawling cities, such as Los Angeles, Mexico City, London and New York reached gridlock during heavy traffic periods in spite of billions spent on public transit.

Another problem at that time was the large concentration of uneducated and unskilled workers living in inner-city ghettos that steadily grew in land-scarce metropolises. Living expenses were forced higher in areas where real estate was generally scarce and transportation conjested than in rural and suburban areas or small towns. Paying for the higher living costs required residents to be even more highly skilled and educated than small-town residents. Many professionals living in skyscraper-apartments met that challenge, but the opposite was true of people living in ghetto areas so life continued to deteriorate and poverty increased.

(The New Society)

After the government took control of land and scientifically planned its use through Land Use Boards, towns and cities are now designed and zoned for the most desirable livability for the individual rather than haphazard expansion and conglomeration.

Big cities of the current century are radically changing. One of the better plans that has been tried is for headquarter cities. Each is composed primarily of heavily condensed operations which are located in close proximately to each other. Many contain the regional headquarters for governing boards, governmental research committees, senior industrial and commercial management, dispersion centers for economic, medical and scientific data, and for other similar headquarter operations.

People with specialized skills needed to assist or complement these headquarter functions are also in this location. Included are attorneys, accountants, financial analysts, investment bankers, and advertising agencies. Top education, economic, and scientific coordinators, and environmental consultants as well as other specialty consultants are all located in headquarter cities. Facilities for the more elaborate cultural events are also located in this area.

No longer are there problems associated with masses of humanity living in our largest cities. No longer are uneducated and untrained people living in large poverty-stricken ghettos because now education and training is mandated for all. A mass exodus of those former residents to satellite towns has occured where all industrial and most office and commercial work is done.

This has been made possible by the technological advancement in communications. All work in satellite towns is quickly linked with administrative, research, and other offices in the headquarter cities. Many early innovations have contributed: advanced telephone and video technology, fax machines and electronic mail. Even more advanced and sophisticated, computerized methods now make it unnecessary to centralize almost any type of work. An increased amount of work is done at homes or while traveling. Even complicated medical diagnosis is performed or checked by computer networks from vast amounts of data originating in the research libraries of headquarter cities.

Large cities are relieved of the necessity to house and otherwise accomodate the former hordes of working people. It is true, some professionals prefer to live and work there. But most prefer to live in the relaxed environment of the smaller satellite towns. A rapid transportation system makes this possible without spending excessive commuting time. Consequently, the need for accompanying retail, service, medical and delivery system workers in the headquarter cities has declined significantly. As a result, these cities are smaller and more concentrated.

Assisting in this is the absence of conjested transportation and parking problems. Helping to accomplish it are subterranean deliveries of all merchandise and the total exclusion of vehicles except for emergencies. Promenades between buildings are enjoyed by pedestrians. Noise and air pollution has been decidedly reduced.

***

Underground high-speed subway systems connect with satellite towns as well as a few selective points within the headquarter city. Completely automatic, computerized " people movers," requiring no attendants, fan out from the various subway stations and speed people to their destination. This has eliminated the need for excessive stops in the high-speed subway system creating a more convenient and much-faster mode of transportation than in former times.

Access above certain levels in our skyscrapers is by high-speed limited-stop elevators. Helicopter pads atop most buildings provide direct rapid access to hospitals, airports, bullet-trains and nearby cities. Because this is a custom service, the cost is commensurate.

Since the largest portion of the work-world has been diverted to satellite towns away from the headquarter cities, workers live in close proximity to their place of employment. This negates the need for extensive and time-wasting commuting. Another benefit for the individual is a more wholesome living environment in a smaller community. Parks and other recreational areas are nearby. People have a greater sense and pride of belonging, friendliness, and cooperation among neighbors. There is less stress, noise, and very little crime and pollution.

***

The regional Land Use Boards have carefully zoned land keeping factories, office complexes, and energy facilities equally distributed among satellite towns so that too great a concentration does not evolve and negate the benefits of decentralization.

Individual industrial plants and office complexes are relatively small in size, clean, well-landscaped, and part of a larger industrial park. It was found that smaller factories, with educated work forces of not more than two hundred, were far more efficient than the dinosaur plants of yesteryear.

These factories are very responsive and able to change production schedules or switch to another product quickly. They require less movement of supplies and materials and less inventory. Some don't carry inventory of finished goods but produce items as ordered. Because of fewer layers of employees, management is more efficient and able to respond faster; workers' suggestions easily surface. The small size of each facility also enables management to be more selective in obtaining good workers.[11]

***

Generally, industrial parks or work centers are surrounded by a greenbelt and then by living complexes. These include multiple story home developments as earlier discussed, schools, commercial centers, and cultural centers (libraries, museums, galleries, auditoriums, and theatres). Living developments are surrounded by outdoor recreational and sport facilities as well as parks and green spaces.

Shoppers enjoy the convenience of the multi-storied commercial centers such as Hong Kong and Jakarta developed in the 20th century because of lack of land. This allows shoppers easy access to many stores without having to be transported over large areas as in earlier times. Frequent-shopping stores, such as large grocery markets, drug emporiums, cafetetrias, and fast-food restaurants, are on ground level for convenience. Located on other floors are less-frequented specialty shops and services, medical clinics, and necessary government offices. Some take an entire floor. Dinnerhouse restaurants with magnificent views are usually on the top floor.

***

Transportation in satellite towns is similar to the headquarter cities. All vehicles, except those used for emergency purposes, are prohibited. Their noise and pollution is gone. Thousands of square miles of land are saved for other more useful purposes by eliminating paved freeways, most roads and highways, parking and garage areas, and by condensing urban areas

Merchandise and raw materials are delivered in large containers to a depot outside of town by railroad. Trucks pick up the containers and proceed underground to their destinations within the town. Actual deliveries are at subterranean unloading docks at the base of the multiple-story industrial and commercial complexes. Subterranean access is also used by emergency, ambulance, and security vehicles, as well as by smaller trucks to deliver large merchandise items such as furniture to a shopper's home complex.

These underground access routes through the towns are limited. They are cut out just below the surface and covered over by concrete for pedestrian mall-walks or for a green belt. This makes them relatively inexpensive to construct.

High speed subway transit moves people to headquarter cities and to limited exits within town and the work-center areas. This system is profitable because, unlike former times, there is no competition with automobile transportation. Yet, with automated "people movers" and condensed high-rise living and work complexes, transportation is actually more convenient than before. Prior to the 1920s before wide use of automobiles, American transit systems accounted for most urban commuting. Furthermore, the tremendous costs of automobiles are gone. Hundreds of thousands of lives are saved annually from highway carnage. The financial savings for fuel, insurance, maintenance, and depreciation is in the hundreds of billions each year.

" People movers" transport riders at high speeds for shorter distances such as from subway exits or from one building complex to another. All transit systems are standardized throughout the world to eliminate confusion and to expedite traffic. Again, high-speed express elevators to upper levels of various complexes also help expedite commuters and shoppers.

***

Surrounding the multi-story living complexes are outdoor recreational facilities. Swimming pools, tennis and volleyball courts, playing fields, picnic areas and children's play grounds proliferate. Interspersed are man-made streams, waterfalls and small lakes using recycling pumps to capture natural serenity and for boating and fishing in the fish-stocked lakes. Small flower beds or vegetable plots are available for use by home owners.

Each of these recreational areas is required to be built by the original developers and included in the cost of the home. The land is donated by the government. Maintenance expenses of these areas are shared equally by each home-owners cooperative.

All homes have large balconies to enjoy the outdoors at close hand. Here one can garden with potted shrubs and flowers, barbecue, and allow small children to play. Each home overlooks the park-like setting of paved paths or mall-like walks and plazas, bordered by trees and greenbelts, which link the various home, commercial, cultural complexes and recreational areas. These paved areas are used by walkers, joggers, and cyclists. All motorized vehicles are prohibited. The entire environment is serene and esthetically pleasing. Pollution, traffic noise, graffiti, and untidiness is no longer a problem.

***

Most shopping is done with small collapsible carts for holding packages. These are transported to homes within minutes from convenient first-level stores in the living complex or via "people movers" from a more-distant commercial complex.

Those requiring faster or longer distance- transportation still have access to helicopter service atop one of the complexes.

Just outside most headquarter cities are bullet-trains that travel extremely high speeds to another nearby headquarter city, comparable from Paris to Berlin in bygone days. These trains run on magnetic levitation at speeds close to three-hundred miles per hour and more. Passengers ride on a cushion of air and move about comfortably at top speeds. The ports of these trains are serviced by subway systems for each city.

For longer distances, airports are located in rural areas convenient to headquarter cities and their surrounding satelite towns and are accessible by the rapid transit system. For extremely long flights, quiet super-sonic airlines travel half-way around the world in a few hours.

In remote areas, rental vehicles are available for sight-seeing or visitors. Tour vehicles are also available to help vacationers experience wilderness parks or remote sightseeing and recreational areas. Farm and ranch operators and other rural residents have individual vehicles for mobility.

Transportation today uses new sophisticated energy sources so there is little need for vast reserves of oil. Remaining oil reserves are used primarily in the manufacture of petro-chemicals.

Pollution from the burning of gasoline no longer exists and, therefore, can not effect the temperature of the earth's atmosphere.

In satellite towns, a common sight is people leisurely weaving their way on bicycles down paths to and from the nearest recreation or cultural center. They do this, not because it is more convenient than "people movers," but because it is healthier and esthetical in the park-like environment. It is also fun in an atmosphere free of automobile hordes.

It must be noted that the construction of new towns, cities, and transportation systems and the restructuring of many older ones did not occur over a short period of time. It took many decades and a few centuries to complete. Earlier construction began in the more developed countries and much later, spread to the less-developed ones. Work is still progressing in some of the more difficult areas. The process has been slow and gradual with the least amount of disruption as possible. The only comparable historical task was the building of huge freeway systems through large heavily populated urban areas in the mid-20th century. Although those efforts were insignificant in comparison, it did prove it could be done.

It is interesting to note that as early as the 1970s, a state-wide land-use law emerged in Oregon that allowed Portland to discriminately channel growth rather than halt it. Developments outside a boundary ringing the city were banned to preserve farmland and forests. Therefore, developers began redeveloping inside the city with more high-density housing such as condos and apartments all within walking distance of retail and civic centers. They overlooked parks, bike trails and broad sidewalks. New regulations required high buildings to devote large portions of first floor to retail space. Parks replaced some existing or potential freeways. Light rail transportation developed within the area. By 1996, seven states adopted planning laws modeled on Oregon's, and others were studying them.

***

In addition to remunerations, an even more important motivation for being productive prevails in the individual. Probably foremost is the need to build and maintain a strong sense of self-esteem in the workplace because that is where the individual spends most of his wakeful life. It is no longer enough to merely make a living. Work should provide non-material, psychological, and social satisfaction as well. Without it, productivity also suffers.

Employment satisfies the need to belong to a group and to have a significant relationship with others. In the early 20th century, Sigmund Freud suggested the individual required four principal psychological needs: security, recognition, emotional relationships, and variety in life. These should be met in the work-world.

(Historical Background)
Historically, well-run organizations made their employees feel needed. They also offered them challenges, new experiences, and most importantly, responsibility by promoting actual participation in the decision-making process. In addition, by tapping the knowledge, experience and creativity of the individual, organizations were helped on the way to success. In return for successful contributions, employees were sincerely praised and given recognition as well as additional monetary compensation.

In most organizations in the past, however, the potential of individuals was the least utilized of all productive resources. Tom Peters in his book, *A Passion for Excellence* said, "We got so tied up in our techniques, devices and programs that we forgot about people - the people who produce the product or service and the people who consume it." [12]

Peter Drucker in his book, *Management: Tasks, Responsibilities, Practices* aptly remarked, "Management of employees to be successful must not encompass paternalism nor adversarial relationships. The purpose of good management is to make the strengths of employees productive and the weaknesses irrelevant. ... we have to move from 'managing personnel' as a 'cost center' and a 'problem' to the leadership of people." [13]

Some believed employees wanted responsibility so they could achieve, be innovative, and feel needed. The delegation of responsibility could result in new challenges and new experiences. To take responsibility requires productive work, feedback of information for measuring and directing oneself, and continuous learning as well as specific areas of authority. They must also be trusted if given the responsibility in order to foster self-confidence and self-motivation. It was interesting in 1990 when workers were asked in a survey, for the factor that caused the most stress on the job, the most frequent answer was, "Not doing the kind of work I want to."[14]

Once again, Mr. Drucker elaborated, "The worker and his group must be responsible for their own jobs and for the relationships between individual jobs. They must be responsible for thinking through how the work is to be done, ... for meeting performance goals and for quality as well as quantity, ... for improving work, job, tools, processes and their own skills." In some cases, worker's teams controlled nearly everything that the boss formerly did in their work area. This was effective because management made use of the worker's knowledge and experience in the one area where the employee was the expert. In effect, it became an entrepreneurial environment. It helped to create individualism and its accompanying creativity.[15]

(The New Society)
The Economic Advisory Committee set up a sub-committee on management. Its function was to formulate broad management principles which could be recommended in the teaching of business administration and other administrative categories in school.

The Sub-Committee, in addition to recommending giving more responsibility to employees, advised setting up internal competition where feasible. Successful work teams are rewarded so they develop a sense of pride and dignity. Constant communication exists between management and employees. Initiative is promoted, even though organized discipline prevails. Each employee has a stake in the results because of incentive rewards. Despite management's authority, creativity of employees and their teams is stimulated.

The need for variety in life requires that there be variety in the work-place. Time limits on most jobs are recommended and most employees are moved periodically from one position to another to avoid a job becoming routine and boring. The efficiency of the worker transferred to a fresh environment more than offsets the small cost of indoctrination. As the worker's diversified experience grows, he also becomes more suitable for promotion. This, in no way, restricts anyone from taking competitive examinations for any position that becomes open, as required by law.

Routine jobs are rarer than in the 20th century. Whenever the work becomes mechanical, automation usually follows. Today, manual assemby-line production is nearly obsolete. Computer control has resulted in cost effective and flexible mass production. A large variety of products from a standardized process is the result.

This, in turn, requires a more-educated work force. The "knowledge" worker of the Information Age has replaced the manual one.[16] Peter Drucker once forecast that the central social problem of a new society was to make knowledge the productive force and to make the knowledgeable-worker achieve it.

In addition to using computers, faxes, e-mail, cellular phones, networks, and satellite uplinks from the past, workers today have added still more sophisticated methods to cut time expended, boost quality, and slash costs. Workers now take responsibility for results. The top-down command-control bureaucracy is obsolete.

Another important factor in sustaining self-confidence and self-esteem in the individual is to feel secure from being discharged. As Mr. Drucker put it, "Employment is an extension of personality. It is achievement. It measures the employee's worth and his humanity. Unemployment creates severe psychological disturbances, not because of economic desperation, but primarily because it undermines self-respect."

Several methods to help insure secure employment have been adopted by business. Generally, if an employee performs satisfactorily, he is assured indefinite employment with that firm. The result is an employee dedicated to the welfare and profitability of the firm, knowing that if the business succeeds so will he.

If a job is eliminated, most businesses retrain if necessary, so the person may compete for other openings within the firm.

Most larger firms constantly research and develop new and improved products and services in order to insure continued profitability. This helps maintain stable or growing employment as well as benefiting consumers.

It was earlier discussed, that in addition to a basic minimum salary for the purpose of insuring economic security, managements are encouraged to develop plans for incentive rewards. It is believed that a direct link between effort and reward will improve productivity and, thus, improve the living standard of everyone.

The individual now works in an environment that is not only challenging and invigorating, but the rewards are related directly to performance. This in turn, fosters self-motivation and a sense of achievement.

Since the individual worker's contributions in the workplace are not equal, apportioning incentive rewards are also unequal. Some still feel such a system is not fair. But it is this inequality that makes it function and create a better life than that within a socialist economy.

(Historical Background)

The success of sharing in the profits of very large companies had become a debatable point in the 1990s. The process was much more successful in smaller companies. Many reasoned that profit-sharing had been tried in large companies with little result. This was because profits, even in good years, seldom exceeded one-tenth of workers' regular income. In other words, straight salaries were ten times as important as profits. It was believed profit-sharing seldom worked as an incentive and was only of secondary importance to a living-wage.

Even one-hundred percent employee ownership and control of a large company had little effect on industrial labor relations. The uncertainty of steady income under such an arrangement and the ineffectiveness of one individual in controlling the outcome of profit and loss appeared to be the reason. This was especially true if void of other incentive and workplace motivations. [17]

Yet, after examining five-hundred publicly traded companies, Douglas L. Kruse, a Rutgers University economist and author of *Profit Sharing: Does It Make a Difference*, found that generally profit-sharing firms had greater productivity than companies without it. He pointed out that smaller companies, with fewer than eight-hundred employees, saw productivity gains substantially higher than companies without profit sharing. This was probably due to employees being able to see the relationship between their work and the bottom line.

(The New Society)
Instead of straight profit-sharing, various incentive methods are now used based on factors that each individual worker can help control. One incentive reflects a distribution of the difference between current labor expense and a normal one. For example, if normal labor costs are about sixty percent of sales, and the current costs are lower because of increased efficiency, the difference would be distributed seventy-five percent to employees and twenty-five to the company for its part in contributing to labor-saving efficiency.

Another incentive is based on accumulated bonus points allotted for approved suggestions for improving efficiency as well as other non-tangible contributions such as quality control. For instance, if a defective product is overlooked by a worker, bonus points are deducted from his total.

There is no limit to the types of bonuses wherein the individual has a degree of control. This is especially true in small organizations. In very large ones, it is broken down into divisions and teams. The allure of a fat monthly incentive bonus clearly increases the efficiency of the workers.

Piece work is a strong incentive because it motivates the employee to increase his efficiency and productivity in order to increase his income; it becomes an entrepreneurial effort. A worker can actually see his income build. But piece-work incentives are only a part of the total system and may not be applicable to many businesses. Furthermore, quantity by itself, can be detrimental if not offset by quality bonuses.

***

Today it is universally recognized if supervisory and management people think like owners (stockholders), they will consider the impact of their actions on the price of the stock. If they actually own large chunks with their own money at risk, they will be even more cognizant of those actions. So, in most large companies in the new society, these people are encouraged to take out personal loans from a bank with which to purchase stock valued at several times their normal annual compensation. As a result, they benefit considerably if the stock rises due to good management, and they stand to lose if their decisions are poor.[18]

The law of industrial patents, developed earlier in England, made it possible for an individual to be rewarded for his inventive and creative skill and time expended in research. This was a notable victory for incentive compensation for gifted and industrious individuals. This has been taken a step further by the new society. Even workers in large organizations, who have invented new products or processes, benefit from patents by receiving a portion of any royalties that the organization receives.

There is nothing to prevent increasing a flat salary to the employee and some prefer it. Nevertheless, the great majority prefer incentive compensation, and organizations also prefer it because it stimulates increased productivity while creating satisfaction in the workplace.

All of these forms of supplementary income are in addition to the required basic minimum salary Supplementary incentive income raises the individual's living standard commensurate with the effort expended.

Another incentive is the freedom from taxation on income. In previous times a point was always reached where many workers felt that any increase in salary or income was not worth the extra effort. Progressive taxation confiscated such a large portion, that the initiative to produce more was eroded. No longer is this a disincentive.

However, once economic needs and material wants are satisfied, it becomes less satisfying for the individual to obtain more income. It, therefore, diminishes as a motivating force. Other desires become more important at that point such as job security, more leisure time as a worker ages, and the freedom to move to where the greatest contribution can be made to society.

Psychological demands also become more important. Self-esteem is raised through an important relationship with other workers; new challenges and experiences are offered; respect and recognition are bestowed. The employee is welcomed as an important part of the organization by assuming responsibility, participating in decision making, feeling needed and wanted, and developing a comradeship with fellow-employees and managers, not only at work, but during company sport, gym activities, and in dining rooms.

A strong need throughout history has existed for the individual to become truly free to participate in the decision-making process in a meaningful way. In the new world community, this is not only possible in the work-world, it is equally true in the immediate community where one actively participates in the neigborhood and home-owners' associations in order to control and maintain an enlightening and comfortable life-style.

Most important, the individual not only has the right to petition serious grievances and suggestions to local and regional governing boards and to obtain a fair resolution, but he has the practical and physical means to do this. This will be discussed in the next chapter. Even in those democratic governments of the 20th and 21st centuries, this was seldom possible except in theory. Politicians, then, only acknowledged and acted when it appeared in their own political best interest. Most of the time it was for the benefit of highly-politicized special interest groups rather than for the benefit of all of society.

In the next chapter, the old methods of governing and politicking are gone. In the new society the individual finally controls and is held responsible for his destiny. This freedom is without restraint except for laws which protect the rest of society.

Chapter 12

A NEW GOVERNMENT THAT WORKS

(Historical Background)

Kill or be killed! Most mammals form communities for mutual protection. Some are created for the purpose of bringing down prey that cannot otherwise be killed by a single animal. Many animal communities are also controlled by a dominant member, usually the oldest and strongest male. We can probably assume that the first community of humans existed for the same reasons and was also dominated by a single or even several males because of their aggressive brute force.

These communities were probably small, some being only family groups. Like many other mammals, some of the family groups may have consisted of a number of females, children, and only a few of the strong resourceful males. The weakest males were probably driven off. Therefore, propagation was polygamous and resulted in strong survivable offspring. When the dominant male became weak, he probably was killed or driven off by a stronger marauding male.

As human knowledge increased so did the functions of living and survival until it became beneficial to form tribes. The larger group could more easily repel aggressors. In turn, it could overwhelm other smaller tribes and thus, take what they wanted including their women for breeding and children for slaves.

The imagination of these earlier people began to create spiritual significance in their life surroundings. So, the need for a more sophisticated community structure evolved and was, again, led by the most dominant male, a chief, with the help of spiritual leaders. In most cases the office of chief remained in the same family and was passed down from one generation to another.

Life became more complicated with the great transformation from hunting and gathering to the domestication of plants and animals. Tangible wealth also began to accumulate when the nomadic life gave way to a more permanent one. This required an even more sophisticated governing structure especially as the population grew. Nevertheless, the dominant member of the community continued to rule; his will was the law.

Absolutism, the form of government in which all of the power was concentrated in a single individual, continued for centuries in one form or another. In most instances, self-determination by the subjects was non-existent. Even when democratic methods of governing appeared as in ancient Greece, the rest of the world was under autocratic rule. This took many forms such as dynasties, empires, monarchies, and sultanships. Control was usually maintained by force, not by leadership which fostered the needs of the governed. When a ruler coveted the wealth of a neighboring country, he merely ordered his armies to invade and took it.

When it became clearly intolerable to the governed, a stronger or perhaps alien leader obtained the support of the people in order to overthrow the current ruler. Nevertheless, the result was eventually the same, the absolute domination by a single individual.

After the Industrial Revolution, the need for more sophisticated governments became apparent. Yet, most of them were still ruled by selfish groups of leaders in the name of nationalism or religion. Even the dedicated ideology of social justice through socialism resulted in governments that became tyrannical like Stalin's - corrupt and eventually for the benefit of an elite few. Whether it was the Maoists of China or the ruling PRI party of Mexico, the result was always the same. True, lip-service was paid to ideals but was always overrun by the selfish interests of the ruling minority.

***

A New Government That Works

Man's inhumanity to man has been chronicled throughout the history of governments. Well into the 21st century inhuman totalitarian governments continued unabated especially in undeveloped countries. Probably one of the most barbaric episodes to occur during this period and one that happened as late as 1978, occured in Cambodia.

A Khymer Rouge Communist leader, Pol Pot, after years of revolutionary warfare, finally controlled Cambodia in the 1970s. His objective was to follow the Maoist principle of returning to "point zero" - to rid the country of all mental and physical vestiges of the past prior to programming it for socialism. All traces of history, culture, and industrial civilization were to be eradicated in a conscious pre-meditated plan of annihilation.

Economic life was brought to a standstill. Money was abolished "once and forever," and the national bank was blown up. Industrial enterprises were demolished, machines destroyed, and electrical cables cut (electricity- enhanced consumption of appliances which was considered detrimental to the socialist philosophy). Bikes and motor-scooters were broken and littered the streets. The only railroad was destroyed beyond reconstruction. Even surgical instruments were piled up and burned with gasoline; hundreds of pounds of drugs and medical supplies were broken, urinated upon, thrown out windows, or burned. Rice paddies were deliberately destroyed; food supplies were reduced below starvation levels.[1]

To rid the country of any intelligence of prior-society, the Khymer Rouge completely abolished the educational system. They burned all books, printed matter, and entire libraries. Teachers were banished to hard work on farms. The Buddhist clergy was exterminated. Anyone with a profession or education was assigned to the most degrading work possible. As a result, the illiteracy rate skyrocketed from about sixty percent in 1975 to ninety-five percent by 1979. Persons evacuated from towns were forced to throw away all personal documents, snapshots, and souvenirs of any kind. All personal history, including marriages, was abolished, and husband and wife separated; new vows were forbidden. Any contact between a man and a woman was punishable.[2]

The Polish reporter, Wieslaw Gornichi, who documented the above said, "I am a journalist for thirty years. I have seen five wars, lived through the hell of Nazi occupation in Poland, witnessing many atrocities, much human suffering, probably too many ravages of war. Yet, after the overthrow of the Pol Pot regime, never have I seen anything comparable to Cambodia. What happened in Cambodia was clearly beyond any accepted scale of values. I was listening to stories so monstrous that they cannot be retold in a newspaper report."[3]

"I have seen scores of schools turned into torture chambers, their floors even now covered by clotted human blood and large pieces of dehydrated scalps ... human leg bones are still chained to iron beds. Next to them one finds those infamous hoes and iron bars used by the Khymers for slow killing of their prisoners ... I saw many skulls bearing large nails in the temples, in eye-holes, in the forehead ... " It was estimated that in four years the population of Cambodia had been reduced by one-fourth or approximately two million exterminated in the killing fields.[4]

Another horrible example of despotic totalitarian rule was the terrible period in China from 1966 until 1976 called the Cultural Revolution. Mao Tse-tung, then Chairman of the Communist party, was believed to be responsible for the deaths of sixty to eighty million people because of his economic mistakes and political vengeance. He knew little about economics.

During his Great Leap Forward of 1958-60 he mandated an absurd industrial campaign where farmers were forced to leave their fields and become steel workers. Having no skills at this, the metal was of poor quality, and much of it was useless. After three bad harvests, the country was plunged into starvation, and about forty-three million people died during the famine. People were forced to ration food, steal, and scavenge for roots and rodents.

Many others were killed and tortured because they were intellectuals, landlords or business people like in Cambodia. Zheng Yi, who was involved in the Tiananmen Square uprising, wrote the *Red Memorial* telling of the horrors of those times. In the province of Guangxi, he secretly photographed police files of some of those attrocities.[5]

A New Government That Works 323

He told of one instance during a Red Guard frenzy in which a twenty-year old "class enemy" was hunted down, carried back in a bamboo cage, and beaten and poked with hot iron rods until he passed out. Yi Wansheng, a member of the Red Guard at the time, was interviewed by Zheng and freely admitted that he slit the young man's chest while he was still alive, reached in and pulled out his heart and liver. He then divided up the organs to be eaten. Zheng said, "Because he was a class enemy, it wasn't enough to kill him. You had to eat him. It was a symbol of loyalty to the party." He documented over sixty-four people eaten in Wuxuan county, fifty-six were hearts and livers, thirteen were sets of genitals consumed, and seventeen people were disemboweled while still alive. It was unprecedented and called political cannibalism.[6]

***

Many people began to believe that a democratically elected government was finally the answer to their search for an equitable system, especially after the United States had survived and appeared to prosper under democracy for two-hundred years. Because of overwhelming pressure from its citizens, many Communist governments relented and adopted pluralistic political systems with several parties competing in elections. This began in 1989 in Hungary and Poland.

Under the American Constitution, the greatest power in government was delegated to the elected legislative branches of the Senate and House of Representatives. These two bodies were given enormous and exclusive power to impose taxes, borrow money, provide for the common defense and general welfare, and to pay for those expenditures. They were also given the exclusive power to regulate commerce, control the value of money, impeach, set up judicial tribunals, and to declare war. These were enormous powers and responsibilities.

The President, representing the Executive branch of government, could disapprove by a veto the laws that Congress passed. Nevertheless, the objection was meaningless if his veto was overridden by substantial votes in the legislative body. The Executive branch functioned primarily as an administration to carry out the desires of Congress. True, the President was allowed to make treaties but only with a two-thirds approval of the Senate. Even the President's appointed heads of departments were subject to approval by the Senate. So in essence, the Presidential office was designed to carry out the wishes of Congress, to administer the various bureaucracies set up by it including military forces, and to be an important symbolic head of state. To further restrict the powers of the Presidency, Congress in 1951 passed the twenty-second ammendment to the Constitution prohibiting more than two terms as president. Nevertheless, some presidents forcefully recommended new laws and policies on Congress and were successful if a large part of the Congress was of the same political party.

Most citizens thought this was an ideal situation wherein the legislative branch, the democratically elected representatives of the people, controlled the government. They felt there were too many instances in the past where concentration of power residing in a single person was detrimental to the governed. It was true that even under this system, some Presidents attempted to obtain greater power through devious means. Franklin Roosevelt attempted and failed to "pack" the Supreme Court with additional justices to a total of fifteen from the original nine in order to obtain "constitutional" approval of some of his unconstitutional programs. He was accused even by members of his own party of attempting to destroy the independence of the judiciary,

For the most part in the early days of the United States, the Legislative branch honestly represented its constituents. In a small-populated agrarian country the needs of the electorate were simple and few. "Citizen-statesmen" met each year in Washington to handle governmental needs and then returned to their plantations, businesses, and professions. Their primary interest was their community, work, and family. As representatives, their legislative work was merely a voluntary interruption to serve their community. They saw their terms as temporary, and there was no particular incentive to be reelected. The remuneration was meager, and few areas existed to corrupt the decision-making process. Democracy seemed to work well.

***

By the late 20th century, this changed dramatically. The agrarian society gave way to a sophisticated and highly industrialized one. The boundaries of the nation expanded, population increased, and communications and travel made everyone aware of governmental functions and problems.

As population expanded, states were alloted additional representatives to the House of Representatives until finally an unwieldly body of nearly five-hundred debated complicated bills. With increasingly diverse issues, the chance of important individual contribution was small. How could one committee, that large, arrive at an intelligent decision? Therefore, hundreds of committees and sub-committees were created to analyze problems. Some members couldn't remember all of the panels they were on, let alone what they could intelligently contribute.

The proliferation of committees also resulted in much overlapping of issues. Many times, ten or more committees and subcommittees would hold hearings on one proposal. With so many involved, legislative action during the year was seldom reached.

As bills and laws increased and became more complicated, members of Congress increasingly forfeited their duties to larger staffs and assistants. Congress gradually abdicated their responsibilities and dumped more of their jobs onto the backs of staff to draft, negotiate, and rewrite the nation's laws. Americans were unaware that staff aides, unaccountable to the voters and growing in influence, were developing powerful relationships with lobbyists and special interest groups. Some were even paid thousands of dollars consulting fees by these groups. In many cases they were running things on Capital Hill.

Congress had thirty-one thousand employees on their staffs compared to only one-thousand for the British House of Commons by 1988. These staff-employees analyzed, contributed, and created an even greater number of more-complicated laws. Bills became so numerous, voluminous, and complicated that they were never read by most Congressional members before they were voted on. Moreover, many of the staffers who wrote the laws were young and had little or no experience working in the every-day practical environment of the private sector. This explained why so many laws created didn't work well in the real world. The truth was some were very bad laws.

Congress also created more bureaucracies to administer these laws, at the same time becoming more overwhelmed with the many details of bureaucratic functions. Consequently they granted wide and unwarranted powers to some bureaucracies to formulate their own laws under the Executive branch. Occasionally, even Congressmen were unaware of some of these laws or their ramifications until brought to their attention by constituents. Such large bureaucracies became not only difficult but impossible to monitor by Congress resulting in vast waste and corruption.

***

A major contribution to growing government agencies was a gradual but consistently rising transfer of responsibility from the individual to the government. As social morality declined, more problems confronted the family and community. Child abuse, juvenile delinquency, school dropouts, and unwanted teen-age pregnancies were dumped on the rest of society. Alcoholism, drug abuse, and crime increased. Victims of many of these became unemployable, homeless, and their poverty increased. When these problems became uncontrollable and a crisis reached, they were transferred to the government. It was believed throwing money at any problem and giving it to the federal government was the solution.

In his book *Governing America,* Joseph Califano Jr. who was head of the Department of Health, Education and Welfare in the Carter administration, wrote that the department is "charged by law to solve human problems that other institutions - the family, the schools ... had failed to solve or even to address."

The dependence on government bureaucracies to solve problems that arose from malfunctioning individual and family behavior created a false sense of well-being while ignoring the underlying cause. Governments superficially treated the problem by increasing rehabilitation facilities, more law enforcement, more prisons, and stiffer sentences. To handle unwanted pregnancies, youth were furnished condoms and instructed in safe sex. When that failed, they were furnished obstetric and pediatric care, welfare, and child support. When students dropped out of public schools, more funds were granted for special education and job-training courses. If dropouts still could not qualify for a job, the government supported them with food stamps, public housing, Medicaid, and other welfare programs. All of this, of course, was paid out of the incomes of taxpayers who did not commit crime, did not have children when they were still children, and did not drop out of school.

Of course, such efforts by the government had little impact, and in many cases, failed completely. The rising trend of these problems escalated because the symptoms not the causes were addressed. For an individual, six months of confinement or intensive counseling couldn't erase fifteen years of family abuse and neglect.

***

As Congress's responsibilities increased, it became readily apparent that a large body of people educated and experienced in only one field (the vast majority were lawyers) could not adequately solve the problems of the day. Most problems were economic and required the expertise of economists. Others required experience in such fields as psychology, criminology and the sciences. Yet all of these fields had only a miniscule representation in Congress that passed laws concerning those subjects.

To get around this, the legislative body created more committees. Each specialized in a particular field where experts could gather to testify. The problem was: who selected these so-called experts and on what qualifications? Were they the best or were they selected for their bias toward the interest of the majority's party? Then after listening to the testimony, much of which was either not comprehended or misunderstood, the politicians had to make an expert's decision and formulate a law. Even then, the law reflected the pressure of special interests, the news media, and the uninformed general public rather than less-biased testimony of experts on the subject.

Typical was the paradox of Congress's lip service in favor of increased savings by Americans to invest in modernizing industry.

This was for business to compete more effectively against Japan whose savings rate far-surpassed that of the United States. At the same time, Congress penalized savers by retaining high taxes on interest and other income derived from savings. Meanwhile, they gave tax deductions for the payment of interest charged when borrowing money for consumption. This contradictory policy made absolutely no sense and illustrated the absence of unbiased economic planning by legislators in favor of what was politically acceptable.

***

As the numbers of house members increased, lawmakers began to find it more advantageous to champion a narrow cause at the expense of the larger interest. This resulted in greater difficulty in passing important legislation for the entire country. By 1989 filibusters in the Senate for one year totaled more than between 1919 and 1960! This tactic was previously reserved only for momentous divisive issues such as war, slavery, and the civil rights bill.

Charles Ferris, a top assistant to Majority Leader Mike Mansfield during the 1960s and 70s, remarked in 1989, "The Senate has become close to a pure democracy, which some people say is pure chaos."

"There's a sense that the whole system is breaking down," said Senator Daniel Evans, a former college president and governor of Washington State, whose frustrations led him to retire.[7]

"Congress has greater difficulty in legislating. There's more gridlock, more frequent intransigences," said Richard Fenno, a University of Rochester political scientist whose specialty was Congress.[8]

In any government where the politicians have such great powers as outlined in the Constitution, it became inevitable they would become captive to powerful special interest groups as well as to their own voter-constituents. This was especially true as the nation became more wealthy and able to grant more subsidies until its practice of doling out still more subsidies became so widespread that its morality was seldom questioned.

Alex Fraser Tytler, a well-known Scottish judge and a professor at the University of Edinburgh in the late 18th century, made an interesting observation at the time, "A democracy cannot exist as a permanent form of government. It can only exist until the voters discover they can vote themselves largesse from the public treasury. From that moment on, the majority always votes for the candidates promising the most benefits from the public treasury, with the result that a democracy always collapses over loose fiscal policy ... "

This was true in both the Athenian Republic and the Roman Empire. In the later days of Rome, members of the Roman Senate occupied most of their time dispensing subsidies and currying favor with constituents.

In earlier times the majority of elected members of the United States Congress were statesmen - in the sense, that above all else, the general welfare of the entire country was considered. Most Congressmen voted for what was right for the greatest number of their countrymen with only cursory efforts to promote narrow self-interest groups or themselves. By the middle of the 20th century, this changed. There arose an effort among politicians to build political strength at the expense of the country's best interest. The attempt by political office holders to deliberately use the legislative process to perpetuate tenure rose gradually until the 1990s when this motivating factor appeared all-consuming.

The principal means of maintaining tenure indefinitely was by amassing large blocks of votes and financial support from self-serving groups in exchange for special and discriminating benefits. These benefits were many and varied but usually were in the form of financial subsidies, tax deductions, or the easing of regulatory laws. All resulted in little or no benefit for the country as a whole and many times to its detriment. The welfare and good of the vast unorganized electorate was sacrificed to many small well-formed groups which were organized around narrowly-focused interests; often they wielded the real power in Congress through highly efficient lobbyists promoting programs to serve those interests.

The *Government Assistance Almanac 1989-90* detailed 1,117 domestic assistance programs! It appeared no interest group went unsubsidized by the federal government. The funding of special interest projects became imbedded in the political system and could not be abolished.

Examples were: grants of as much as hundred thousand dollars helped teachers understand the Constitution; the Forestry Incentives Program provided up to ten-thousand dollars to plant trees on an individual's property; the Fishing Vessel and Gear Damage Compensation Fund paid up to one-hundred and fifty thousand dollars for damage to a fishing vessel if hit by a foreign vessel.[9] Even larger subsidies were for: dairy farmers which cost taxpayers seventeen billion dollars in the 1980s and an additional forty billion dollars in higher prices, the Market Promotion Program that subsidized multinationals' foreign advertising cost one-hundred and ten million dollars annually, the Rural Electrification Administration which originated in the 1930s to provide electricity to farmers and had long outlived its purpose. It spent two billion annually in subsidized loans to private utilities. Hundreds of other utterly wasteful and useless subsidies were made into law.

Huge amounts of money were expended by lobbyists and trade associations to wine and dine, pick up tabs for all sorts of personal gifts and expenses even sex, and to contribute vast sums to the politicians' campaign chests for the next election. In addition, members of these political groups promoted letter campaigns to write and call their respective congressmen individually. The pressure on the selfish interest of the politician to be reelected was unrelenting.

State legislatures were not immune. A typical example of campaign contributions to a New York state legislature in 1993-94 were:

New York State Teachers $3,300,000
Public Employees Union $1,000,000
Civil Service Employee Union $1,000,000
Healthcare Associates $1,000,000
Trial Lawyers $900,000
State Bankers $800,000

The end result were lawmakers that sponsored narrow self-interest legislation at the expense of the majority. The general tax-paying public, was such a large group that organizing an effective resistance was next to impossible.

In the 1980s Congress railed about the burgeoning federal deficit but continued to include pet projects into spending bills and special breaks for small groups into tax measures. For years the process became so frequent and biased that lawmakers were unable to finish appropriation measures. These were needed to finance the federal government in time for the new fiscal year - Congress's most basic task!

Until 1995, all types of suggestions to control spending from line-item vetoes proposed by several presidents to a constitutional amendment to force the balancing of the budget fell on deaf ears. Politicians did not want to eliminate their most important means for reelection, the ability to spend to obtain votes. Some people believed such laws were unnecessary because lawmakers had only to vote the required appropriations to balance the budget. But, that never worked because Congressmen were unable to muster the will to cut unnecessary spending. Others said, "Throw the rascals out." if they couldn't balance the budget, but replacements soon fell into the same patterns of spending for special interests.

There were untold examples of catering to economically detrimental legislative issues. For instance, in June of 1974 Congress, concerned about rising inflation, publicly accused the administration of not doing enough to restrain it. Meanwhile the legislature was preparing laws to guarantee price-support loans for beef and to restrict its importation in order to keep the price up for a group of cattle growers. At the same time American consumers were complaining about the rising cost of beef.[10]

In 1987 Americans paid more than twice the world price for sugar. Congress had passed a law guaranteeing sugar growers eighteen cents a pound by having the Secretary of Agriculture stop the importation of sugar over a certain quota.[11] So the entire population paid subsidies for a few. Yet, all economists were convinced quotos bore more heavily on the poor than the rich. They also agreed they had the effect of diverting supply from less costly to more costly producers to the detriment of all consumers.

In most cases the benefit for a narrow constituency required lawmakers, who supported a bill or amendment, to agree to support like measures of other Congressmen in exchange for their supporting votes. This method of pushing through a measure, that would normally have very limited support, became quite common. In an election race politicians also promised legislation that would lavish more benefits on their constituency than an opposing candidate. The benefits, of course, were eventually paid by borrowing more money or increasing taxes; politicians bought support with the voters' own money. An even more popular method was to increase taxes on those with higher incomes because they were in the minority and represented fewer votes. Either way, it was almost a sure method of getting votes from the majority.

***

Once Congress created a government bureaucracy to fulfill special interests, the bureaucracy grew until it became entrenched and wielded political power of its own. The vast number of bureaucrats employed in a particular program or agency, in turn, became a special interest group which influenced politicians in the same manner. They insisted on larger appropriations for their agencies and fought strenuously against any budget cuts. They cried out for job security, higher salaries, perks, pensions, and salaries indexed to inflation - the same inflation they helped to create by contributing to an unbalanced budget. Congressmen, regardless of their ideological persuasion, seemed powerless to break the strong grip that these elite barons of bureaucracy had over them. Consequently, the bureaucracies became self-perpetuating.

Innumerable reports, over the years to cut unnecessary costs in government bureaucracies, were put forth, but each had been consigned to dusty library shelves. Finally in 1983, a commission consisting of over a thousand businessmen-volunteers, financed by two million dollars from businesses and an additional fifty million dollars donated in time, travel, and living expenses, was formed at the behest of the Executive branch. This was for the purpose of only cutting inefficient waste in the management of programs but without making cuts for policy reasons in programs themselves. They recommended an estimated sixty billion dollars a year of cost cutting which involved three-thousand recommendations. The implementation of the Grace Commission findings would have helped tremendously in the budget-balancing process.

Cash management alone was estimated to save billions. For example, because of the government's sometimes tortuous way of handling incoming checks, large amounts of interest was lost because days passed before they were deposited. Another example was one-hundred and thirty incompatible accounting systems that could have been reconciled. It also recommended fewer but more efficient computers so information would flow in a more efficient manner. Some of the computers were so obsolete they were no longer serviceable by their manufacturers.[12]

At the end of 1982, three-hundred and one billion dollars was owed to the government but little was being collected. If private business debt-collection methods were used, it was estimated over eight billion dollars could be collected within three years. This also would have resulted in the saving of interest needed to carry that amount of debt. Mistargeting benefits to the poor resulted in misuse of billions. The Social Security Administration made fifteen billion dollars in erroneous payments between 1980 and 1982. Before the amounts were recovered, one-hundred and twenty million dollars in interest was lost. Military commissaries cost seven-hundred and fifty-eight million dollars annually. Yet, they originated in the 19th century to serve soldiers on frontier outposts miles from the nearest cities or towns. In 1983 there were five in San Francisco alone. The commission chairman, J. Peter Grace said, "The amount and variety of waste we found were incredible, but we just scratched the surface."[13]

Their report was later substantiated in 1990 when the Comptroller General of the General Accounting Office estimated one-hundred and fifty billion dollars annually could be lopped off the budget deficit if waste, corruption, and mismanagement could be eliminated in governmental bureaucracies.

The overall result, of this intensive investigation, was a complete failure to heed the recommendations, except for a few. This should have been expected because bureaucrats didn't want changes to disrupt the "easy way." They especially did not want cost-cutting which might keep the bureaucracy from growing or worse, a lay off of uneeded government employees. The screaming was heard by the Executive branch as well as Congress which didn't want to lose the votes of thousands of government workers, so little was done.

Even when the Executive branch was in favor of overhaul of a program or agency, the closing of those offices in a Congressman's district may be considered inappropriate if the administration wanted that Congressman's vote on a bill crucial to it.

Waste was rampant in government programs. For example, the Federal Crop Insurance program was bled with claims that were underwriting blunders, errors, or were fraudulent. A Florida tomato grower collected three-hundred thousand dollars in frost damages from the program after a big freeze. He actually harvested most of the crop approximately forty days before the freeze. The General Accounting Office discovered drought claims of eighteen million dollars paid to farmers in error because the crops were irrigated. A Montana farmer was allowed to buy government crop insurance after his wheat crop had been lost; it cost the taxpayers seventy-thousand dollars. Compounding the problems, the Agriculture Department didn't bother with recovering overpayments made in error to farmers after ninety days [14]

Most waste was the result of sloppy management, and it seldom mattered if a subordinate brought it to the attention of his boss. Furthermore, if one spoke out to the public, he usually was shifted to a dead-end job, transferred, or asked to take early retirement. It was nearly impossible to fire a government employee. Waste on a massive scale usually meant one of two things: either the bureaucrat in charge was a poor manager, or some bribery was going on.

The Department of Agriculture with its sixty-seven billion dollar annual budget (1993) and one-hundred and thirty thousand employees was perhaps the worst example of bureaucratic waste and inefficiency second only to the old Soviet bureaucracies.

Karen Elliott House, a staff reporter at the time and later promoted to Vice-president of the *Wall Street Journal*, uncovered tremendous waste in the Agriculture Department in a feature article in 1977. She reported there was one full-time employee for about every ten farmers. As the number of farmers declined, the Agriculture Department turned to self-promotion, continued doing obsolete jobs, and creating new ones to keep busy. It became a monster-bureaucracy engaged in dubious tasks and without direction. Thomas Foley, then chairman of the House Agriculture Committee said, "No Secretary of Agriculture runs the Department. It's too big."[15]

It performed many out-dated tasks including the Rural Electrification Administration begun in 1935 to provide electricity for many farmers and ranchers. Although all farmers had electricity by 1993, it was still going strong and getting larger. The Farmers Home Administration was created during the Great Depression to make loans to help farmers from losing their land. By 1993 these low-interest loans were made to anyone in small rural towns who was considered poor.[16]

The Department spent four million dollars each year on peanut research including ways to increase yields. Yet it spent another one-hundred and ninety million dollars to buy surplus peanuts. Consumers were then forced to pay higher prices as well as the cost of subsidizing peanut farmers. Once again, the unorganized majority was being penalized to benefit a well-organized minority special-interest group. At the same time the department paid for a research project aimed at producing oranges of uniform size in order to make packing easier. It spent thousands of dollars on a study to determine how long it took Americans to cook breakfast, lunch and dinner.[17]

In 1993 fifty-three county offices nationwide cost the Agriculture Department more to administer subsidies than the cost of the subsidies themselves. Some offices were desperate to find someone to subsidize for fear of having their offices closed. An office in Connecticut paid an exclusive equestrian sport club thirty-five hundred dollars as a conservation subsidy to help pay for a loading dock to dispose of horse manure. Yet, the affluent members paid twenty-thousand dollars annually for membership in the club.

Hundreds of department employees milled about corridors in the Washington office or lingered in the cafeteria at all hours. A memo to supervisors from the Secretary of Agriculture warned, "Tardiness, eating breakfast immediately after reporting to work, extended coffee breaks, excessive lunch periods and early departures convey a poor image to the public." Many high-salaried assistants had little to do all day. A Miss Rodgers, who was interviewed, said, "I've answered the phone a couple of times this morning. That's about it. It's a normal day." She was paid thirty-four thousand dollars; in 1977 this was a relatively high salary. Nearly everyone was given a merit increase whether they deserved it or not. In 1976 only forty-four did not receive them.[18]

In 1979 the Joint Economic Committee of Congress sharply criticized the performance of federal workers. Hourly output of work lagged behind that in private business, and no relationship existed between pay raises and productivity. The Committee reported government employees responded poorly to incentive rewards and instead stole, wasted, or mismanaged ten percent or more of federal expenditures. The Postal Service had the highest increase in yearly salaries and one of the lowest increases in productivity. The study estimated that if productivity were increased ten percent, approximately eight billion dollars could be saved without cutting programs. Furthermore, the report said the Justice Department estimated fraud took as much as ten percent of total government expenditures, and mismanagement raised the total much higher.

The Agency for International Development was another example of an overpaid mismanaged bureaucracy. The head of A.I.D. working in Vietnam in the late 1960s was paid five thousand dollars more than the Chief Justice of the Supreme Court. Ten of his assistants received more salary than members of the President's cabinet, Senators, or Congressmen. They also received an additional twenty-five percent hardship allowance, three-thousand dollar maintenance allowance, and many other fringe benefits. Many sold post exchange and commissary goods (access was another fringe benefit) to the Vietnamese on the black market to further enrich themselves.

As late as 1996 government employees continued to waste taxpayers' money. Some things observed and reported by an anonymous bureaucrat were - attending social or political events during work periods (Earth Week, Women's Equality Day, AIDs Awareness Day, and others), expensive entourage of agency heads (example: a scheduler paid $70,000 annually), running private businesses from government offices (a real estate business "on the side"), publishing book-size reports no one reads, playing "solitaire" on computers, and thousands of *Washington Post* and *New York Times* subscriptions for government employees (to prevent boredom?).[19]

The complicated regulations governing the civilian work force in all bureaucracies was another factor preventing efficient operation of government. In 1977 the regulations filled twenty-one volumes - some five-feet thick! Jule Sugarman, then the vice chairman of the Civil Service Commission which wrote the regulations and oversaw their administration said, "The Civil Service system makes managing government very difficult. We must simplify the system." But, Congress was reluctant to make changes in the many Civil Service laws for fear of losing the voting support of federal worker's unions.[20]

There simply was no way to get rid of inefficient or incompetent government workers. Any management decision to create more efficiency could be challenged in a lengthy process by workers lasting sometimes months or even years. A case in point was that of an economist employed by the Department of Housing and Urban Development during the Carter administration. He admitted doing nothing on his job, but warned they could not fire him. "I'll spend whatever time it takes. I'll wait you out like I did the others."[21]

State, county, and municipal employees were also relatively safe from dismissal. The American Federation of State, County, and Municipal Employees union filed innumerable civil-service appeals and grievances and gridlocked most disciplinary measures. Jack Gallt, staff director for the National Association of State Personnel Directors (1994), said that civil servants had a relatively secure job compared with those in the private sector.

The only way a federal worker could lose his job was through a budget cut that affected his program. So as an agency grew older and its initial purpose was fulfilled, more of its manpower and energy was devoted to obtaining funds and fighting off any budget cuts. The result was an unproductive bureaucracy that was overstaffed. Actual firings were at the rate of one person every seventy years![22]

Ninety-nine percent of all eligible federal employees received annual merit salary increases. In addition to their "automatic" merit increases, federal employees received annual raises to maintain "comparability" with private industry. This comparison emphasized high-paying positions in large corporations rather than those in small businesses. Salaries were also indexed to inflation. Fringe benefits exceeded those in private enterprise. Paid holidays averaged 3.6 days more, vacations twenty-five percent more, and pensions and insurance benefits twenty-eight percent higher. Sick leave and health care was extremely generous (1992).

Pensions, as well as salaries, were indexed to inflation. So, some government employees and retired elected officials received more in pensions than their full-time counterparts. Federal retirement programs cost the taxpayers over five billion dollars in 1970. By 1993 it had reached sixty-five billion dollars. As early as 1986 unfunded pension liabilities had reached nearly a trillion dollars! This was in addition to the national debt - money that someday would have to be paid.[23]

After twenty years in the military, members could retire on a lucrative indexed pension. Double-dippers would then take another federal position as a civilian. They were also allowed to count their years in the military on their civilian as well as military pension. During the recession of 1975 with large numbers of unemployed, one-hundred and forty-one thousand of these double dippers were employed in the government.

A former Congressman from Massachusetts, Hastings Keith, said he was receiving four separate government pensions - civil service, military, widower's, and Social Security. He claimed that in twenty years it had increased over six-hundred percent to a total of about ten thousand dollars a month. It was due to "double-dipping" and the compounding cost-of-living adjustments.

Thousands of government employees' ranks and salaries were higher than their required work level resulting in seven-hundred and eighty million dollars each year in overpaid salaries. Embellished job descriptions, such as "vertical vehicle controller" for elevator operator, produced higher salaries. Bureaucracies had not only become lethargic and self-protective, but government civil-service employees had become the new barons of society. It was impossible for politicians to break the powerful grip that these new barons had over everyone's daily life.

American bureaucracies had grown by the mid-90s to become larger than the entire economy of any country in the world except Japan. The number of government employees had surpassed those in the entire manufacturing sector. A Gallup Poll in 1995 found two-thirds of Americans saw big government as the biggest threat to the future of the country.

***

Subsidies to farmers became one of the worst drains on the government's financial resources not only in the United States but in Europe and other developed countries. In the United States subsidies were implemented during the Great Depression in the 1930s. They were well-meaning to supplement incomes of needy farmers and to protect the nation's food sources. Yet, by 1990 the average full-time farmer had a net worth far in excess of the average taxpayer, while the number of full-time farmers - many were corporate - had significantly increased. It was true that part-time farmers - hobby, for tax deductions, and those with other jobs - had shrunk, but these were not the full-time commercial enterprises on which a nation depended for food. The average income was $168,00 for full-time farmers in 1988 versus an average family income of $38,000.

James Bovard, author of *The Farm Fiasco,* noted that during the 1980s farm subsidies cost the taxpayers $20 billion a year and another $10 billion in higher food prices. He wrote, "And there is nothing to show for these outlays except idled acres, polluted groundwater and richer farmers." [24]

In 1986 it was estimated farm subsidies were costing every American non-farm household $680 annually. In Europe less than three percent of the economy was farming. Yet, European Community consumers and taxpayers shelled out $93 billion in subsidies resulting in huge surpluses of cheese, wine, and other delights.

A subsidiary of Con Agra corporation, the mammoth food processor, was receiving price supports from the government merely for shearing wool from lambs that were already destined to meatpacking plants; it totaled $480,000 annually.

The extravagance to peanut farmers was one of the worst examples of government subsidies. This boondoggle dated from the 1940s. It limited the number of peanut farmers eligible to receive subsidies to 44,000. The price of peanuts was propped by subsidies about fifty percent above the world market price and considerably above production costs. Those who held these lucrative monopolies from the government, usually inherited them. Many holders leased them to other farmers for a nice profit. It was estimated the cost to consumers for artificially high peanut prices was close to $400 million above what they would pay in a free world market. This was in addition to the cost of the subsidies paid by the taxpayers.

***

Robert Shrum, a former speechwriter for President Carter, later wrote a series of newspaper articles exposing the perks and elitism of Congress. He aptly called it "The Imperial Congress." Congressmen and Senators had gradually added non-taxable perquisites that finally reached a level of obscenity. A partial list of their less expensive perquisites was - private subsidized barbershops (one fourth the going rate), free massage and sauna, private gym and pool, full-time employees to wash and polish members' cars, license plates allowing illegal parking, private luxurious and subsidized dining rooms, free fresh plants from government subsidized nurseries, free customized furniture and free loan of paintings from the National Gallery of Art, and free travel trunks. [25]

The Congressional Reference Service of the Library of Congress wrote ghostwrite articles, partisan speeches, entire books, and sometimes term papers for the children of Congressmen. The House bank negotiated loans on generous terms from private banks in Washington, D.C. Members frequently overdrew their check acounts without penalty. Although Congressmen were not allowed to hire relatives, this was easily circumvented by exchanging job openings with other Congressmen's relatives.[26]

Years before health-care became a common employee benefit in the private sector, the Congress and Senate provided themselves with a generous subsidized health plan, life insurance, and death benefits. Salaries and pensions were extremely liberal even after serving only six years.

Although legitimate foreign travel by members was necessary, its blatant misuse to provide free vacations for a legislator's spouse and family became commonplace. Approximately two-thirds took these trips annually. A generous per diem allowance was granted without the necessity of expense records. Large overseas purchases were ignored by United States customs on returning to the United States. Although illegal, many foreign governments paid for some of these excursions for lobbying purposes, but no one ever investigated or prosecuted.

Lawmakers not only granted themselves innumerable tax-free perquisites but also exempted themselves from virtually every regulatory law passed. For example, they were exempt from the Civil Rights Act and the Equal Pay Act in the employment of their staffs. Some of these abuses were rectified in 1995. After leaving Congress, they were not required to abide by the Ethics in Government Act although this act was strictly enforced against anyone leaving the Executive branch. Congress also defeated attempts to include themselves in the special-prosecution law, yet vigorously applied it to anyone in the Executive branch. [27]

Congressmen and Senators became powerfully influential. Senator Cranston, who was reprimanded by his colleagues for his questionable influence in one of the savings and loan scandals, remarked, "Everybody does it." He was referring to the common practice of exerting pressure on government agencies to give special concessions or accomodations to special-interest constituents. In return the constituents rewarded a legislator with campaign money and various other non-taxable rewards and largess. The question then arose, "Where does fund-raising and constituent service end and bribery begin?"

It became even more questionable when a "grandfather clause" was passed that allowed all members of the House elected before 1980 to convert campaign funds to their personal use on retiring from office. Unspent campaign funds totaled millions of dollars which Congressmen had available for their personal use.

The powerful influence of Senators also enabled them to obtain privileged information from constituents who had benefited from this influence. The opportunity to participate in lucrative real estate, business, and other investment deals enabled Senators with long-terms to retire as millionaires.

In addition to exchanging benefits for votes and largess, incumbents, through various and ingenious laws, also established a system of insuring reelection. One of these methods included the huge tax-payer-paid staffs who turned their attention and energy to reelecting their boss when a challenger appeared.

Probably Congress' most useful reelection devise was the free mailing privelege. It put opponents at a devastating disadvantage by swamping their election area with thousands of letters touting the abilities of the incumbent. In 1986 Congress sent out twelve-thousand letters for every incoming letter! The incumbent's name was constantly before the electorate; the challenger had little chance to thwart it. In addition to the free mailing privilege, the House even provided each member a $5000 allowance for newsletters paid by the tax-paying voters.[28]

Photos for such newsletters were provided by special photo shops at taxpayers' expense. Additionally, a private television and recording studio featuring state-of-the-art technology and equipment, make-up and professional sets for members was also paid by the voters. The typical resulting tape was about fifteen minutes and mailed free to the voting areas' television stations. The stations then ran them free as "public service" programs, effectively promoting the incumbent.[29]

Political Action Committees gave large amounts of money to incumbents in hope of favorable treatment but rarely gave to challengers. Individuals, on the other hand, were prevented by law from donating more than $1000 to challengers.

Gerrymandering was the method of altering election district boundaries to obtain the largest plurality of partisan votes. It insured the reelection of the incumbent by dramatically shrinking the number of competitive districts.

Until 1994 the House reelection rate of incumbents hadn't fallen below eighty percent since WWII and reached ninety-eight percent in 1986. Those who won garnered an incredible three-fourths of the vote in 1988. Eighty percent were either unopposed or faced only token opposition. By 1990 two-thirds of potential voters didn't even bother to go to the polls. This gave incumbents another advantage when running for reelection. Most House incumbents enjoyed a de facto lifetime tenure. Edward Zorinsky, after becoming Nebraska's new Senator, said, "Obviously the whole system seems geared to reelection."

In 1963 Representative Thomas Curtis of Missouri recommended legislation to limit the number of terms for members of Congress. He admitted that it was "legislation least likely to succeed." Senators Hayakawa from California and Danforth of Missouri proposed it in 1977; Senator Armstrong of Colorado suggested it again in 1990. Finally in desperation at the futile attempts in Congress, several states adopted it in 1992 only to be declared unconstitutional in 1995 by the Supreme Court.

Federal grants amounting to hundreds of millions of dollars annually went to innumerable organizations. Many times this money found its way into public advocacy, political campaigns, and organizing efforts for various lobbies to block budget cuts that threatened the programs of these very same organizations. In other words, taxpayers were paying to prevent spending cuts in government expenses - cuts that would benefit the taxpayers!

***

The United States government was not alone in the developed world where wastefulness, inefficiency, and corruption was involved. *Pravda,* the official Communist party newspaper, reported in 1988 that top officials of the Uzbekistan Republic stole at least $6.5 billion in a scandal involving bribery and falsifying production quota reports. They included the premier and deputy president as well as Brezhnev's son-in-law, who was the Soviet Union's first deputy interior minister.[30]

Italy was notorious for its corrupt political system. In 1974 rampant inflation of twenty-five percent was the result of bureaucratic excesses and spending created by a corrupt parliament. A typical comment by a businessman in Rome was, "I wouldn't claim that everybody in parliament is a crook, for there are some good people there. But there are so many crooks that it makes it difficult to tell the good from the bad. Most of them are dons, like in the Mafia, only looking after themselves, their relatives and their friends."

Little had changed in Italy by 1993 except, perhaps, to become worse. State spending on the public sector had ballooned from five percent in 1950 to twenty percent of Italy's output. The country's civil service was one of the primary causes. Government employees usually worked mornings only, received thirty-six days of vacation a year, and were guaranteed their jobs for life. Such security provided little incentive for hard work. Civil service positions were filled by politicians resulting in little regard for qualifications.

On a typical morning in an Italian post office, employees chatted idly while lines grew. It took as much as four hours to mail a package. Once a letter was mailed, it took as much as a week for a letter to arrive within the same city. A deputy-director of a post office branch in Milan said, "We have twenty employees, and we need only ten. On Saturdays we come in here and stare at each other because there's nothing to do. And, he said, "employees are normally paid despite absence from work. And believe me, you'll never get fired." [31]

Corruption in Italian politics finally reached the highest levels when magistrates notified Andreotti, a former prime minister, he was under investigation for corruption. He and other high-level political office holders were already being investigated for links with the Mafia.

Political corruption reached its extreme in Brazil. Robert Maksoud, a Brazilian hotelier, writing from Sao Paulo in 1989 said, "Among the various blocks of protected interests in Brazil, none is larger or more powerful than the bureaucratic aristocracy. The entire federal budget is used just to meet this elite clique's payroll, leaving not a penny available for maintenance or new investments in the country's undermined infrastructure ... (and an) inflation rate of thirty percent a month."

Brasilia, the capital, was built at a cost that nearly bankrupted Brazil. Here six-hundred thousand of Brazil's bureaucracy and politicians enjoyed beautiful subsidized housing and country-club privileges. They were the country's wealthiest and most self-centered, an enclave of privilege far removed from the nation's realities. Brasilia had little industry; nevertheless, the wealthiest of Brasilia's population earned seventy-five percent more than the nation's top ten percent elsewhere. These bureaucrats largely isolated themselves from the rest of Brazil's growing social problems where nearly a quarter of the citizens lived in abject poverty.

Government-run companies proliferated Brazil's economy. An example was Banco do Brazil, an enormous state-run bank that employed 125,000 government employees. Its payroll equaled one percent of the nation's gross national product. These and other government employees actually increased their real incomes while most other Brazilians lost purchasing power to runaway inflation created by these very same bureaucrats.

To meet these payrolls, to subsidize money-losing government-run companies, and to pay interest on the national debt, the government merely printed more money resulting in a higher inflation rate. The bureaucrats, under the banner of trade unions, constantly protested with mass demonstrations against the privatization of government-run industries. At the time, two-hundred and twenty-eight government-run companies had debts that exceeded their assets and were losing money. Repeatedly, Brazilian politicians failed to cut spending and reduce the deficit, an all too familiar problem everywhere in the world.

According to economist, Celso Martone, prices in Brazil multiplied a staggering twenty-two billion times since 1960. "Every economic team that comes to power makes the same diagnosis: The state is bankrupt, we have to do a tax reform, we have to privatize. But you can't convince the politicians of the gravity of the situation," said Francisco Gros, a former central-bank president.

Mr. Maksoud, the hotelier, summed up the desperate and frustrated feelings of the Brazilian voters, "People have become aware that big government is the sore spot of the Brazilian economy, and they are demanding a halt to job handouts and general corruption. It is these demands to which candidates from the left and the right are responding. Their proclamations to privatize government companies, dismiss millions of public servants and jail corrupt officials are non-idealogical, calculated responses to the reality of a system caving in on itself."[32]

In Spain, a similar situation unfolded; politicians bestowed favors on selected groups to the detriment of the entire nation. Freed of the shackles of General Franco in 1975, multinational companies rushed to invest in a great untapped market. Employment and wages shot up. In 1986 Spain joined the European Union, and development funds flowed in. But politicians, as usual, spent heavily on increasing government bureaucracy, social programs, and infrastructure, but didn't reduce its budget deficit. Free healthcare, heavily subsidized college education, and unemployment benefits far more generous than other European countries were granted. The government mandated that workers receive lifetime contracts from their employers.

Faced with large losses and unable to get workers to agree to layoffs or even salary cuts to preserve jobs, many big multinational companies closed up and pulled out of Spain by 1994. The nation lost over a half million jobs and the unemployment rate soared to twenty-five percent - one more example of government malfunctioning in the economy.

Just prior to the December 1995 elections in Turkey, the government went on a multi-billion dollar spending spree. Farm cooperative losses were forgiven, animal breeders assistance was increased tenfold, and Social Security payments were raised seventy percent. The result was a soaring budget deficit. Inflation then increased which caused the government debt to be financed by Treasury bills yielding 180 percent annually!

The classic example of detrimental government interference in the market- economy occurred in Venezuela. One of the richest oil producers in the world, Venezuela, was strangled by government economic controls. By printing excessive amounts of paper money, it had an annual inflation of seventy percent, savings rate plummeted, the deficit was out of control, and for three consecutive years the gross national product declined. Children suffered from malnutrition, social order broke down, and nothing seemed to work.

President Rafiel Caldera delayed cutbacks in subsidies, government-run companies, overregulation, and a huge government employee sector which employed fifteen percent of the work force. One of the subsidies allowed gasoline to sell for fifteen cents a gallon! The government imposed price and currency controls and unilaterally ordered business to pay workers a bonus causing layoffs and increased unemployment.

"It's not easy to take an economy that functioned without distortions and then implant hundreds of distortions, but this government managed to do it," said Robert Bottome, an economic consultant in Caracas.[33]

The examples of economic stupidity by politicians were endless. It seemed that their approach to government was always how can I benefit the voters so I will be reelected.

***

In the United States the problem with bureaucracies was not limited to the federal government. State and local bureaucracies employed over eleven million people in 1985, and employment grew even faster than in the federal government. Their compensation grew four times faster than for workers in private industry during the 1980s, and their average salaries exceeded private-sector wages. Two-thirds of state and local budgets were wages and benefits. Unions were the driving force of much of the explosion in costs of state and local governments requiring ever higher taxes. It was estimated in 1995, one-half of nearly everyone's income was taken in taxes of all types - federal and state income tax, sales tax, property tax, local tax and surcharge tax.

State and local government employees also averaged better benefits than employees in private industry. The American Legislative Exchange Council reported they had nearly four more paid holidays, twenty-five percent longer paid vacations after only one year, and pension and insurance benefits which averaged nearly a third more. In California, for instance, teachers' pensions indexed to inflation increased so much that anyone living beyond average longevity reaped thousands of dollars more than the current employed instructors.

Political favoritism in state and local governments was common. Typical was the appointment of eighty-year-old Tom Bane, who retired in 1992 after serving twenty-four years in the California Assembly. The California Assembly Speaker, Willie Brown, Jr., appointed him to the Unemployment Insurance Appeals Board at a salary of $92,460 a year.[34]

***

The problems of a democratic-form of government were quite obvious to many. The cause of these problems, in most cases, was the election of unqualified and inept government managers (politicians) and their desire to continue tenure indefinitely. This resulted in the sale of influence to special interests in return for reelection support to the detriment of the unorganized majority.

Specifically, this resulted in the growth of inefficient, wasteful, and corrupt bureaucracies. In turn, they created a government debt that became uncontrollable resulting in rising inflation. When the government-monster reached uncontrollable proportions, gridlock and indifference developed in its various institutions. Apathy and disgust then set in among the citizenry.

Herbert H. Jacobs succinctly described the problem in a letter to the editor of the *Wall Street Journal* in 1984, " ... there is a fundamental flaw in the Constitution. The national legislature does not work. ... it is not an efficient deliberate body committed to the furtherance of the national interest. (It) consists not of a body of wise, dedicated public servants, but simply a collection of over five-hundred ordinary job-holders motivated chiefly by an overriding need or desire for reelection ... replace them with a like number drawn at random from among all who aspire to public office and the result would undoubtedly be the same ... these people have a job to protect, a job that carries extraordinary personal power, and they are naturally led to place personal interest above that of their country."[35]

In most instances, the President and members of Congress were elected by a process mainly dependent upon fund-raising and self-advertisement on television screens. Although they were shrewd politicians, many were inexperienced for the position and had to learn on the job. Some were completely inept for the job for which they were elected. The electorate selected them primarily on name recognition, charisma, looks, and party affiliation. The tremendous ego-boost from the adulation of partisan crowds was another factor in stimulating incumbents to reelection. Cabinet members were selected principally on the basis of their support during the political campaign or to assuage various special-interest groups. Character, ability, education, and experience were secondary.

***

Voters, as well as legislators and government officials, chose legislation, appropriation, and taxes based purely on selfish interests rather than altruism and the public good. The result was a government that was captive to a coalition of interest groups whose support must be bought with special and discriminating benefits. In essence, the government collected citizens' tax money and redistributed the funds to a few powerful constituencies. Approximately one-half of the federal budget went directly for these transfer payments - the collection of money from taxpayers and transferred as income to select individuals and entities. Since this half of budget expense was not buying needed services or delivering goods for the benefit of all taxpayers, the majority receivied nothing in return for it. Yet, politicians urged ever higher taxes to pay for desperately needed services such as crime control and to pay off the national debt, and then used the money for transfer payments.

Throughout most of the world, politicians taxed labor, production, and savings while subsidizing non-producers, unneeded government workers, and the unemployed. The net effect was a diminishing group of producers and a rising group of non-producers. Governments also printed nearly valueless paper money in order to pay for much of the transfer payments resulting in runaway inflation. This resulted in the decline of the value of transfer payments which became nearly worthless in many third-world countries and the Soviet Union.

***

Even in ancient times the great Athenian philosopher, Socrates, perceived that democracy did not demand evidence of any special knowledge in its leaders, and societies suffered in the hands of men without true insight. By not demanding intellectual qualifications for office, democracy surrendered control of affairs to men with no expert knowledge. Furthermore, he observed that it treats any one citizen's opinion as of equal value with another's. At best, he thought the results would, therefore, lead to mediocrity, at worse to anarchy.

In 20th century democracies, many citizens didn't vote, and of those that did, a large portion were ignorant of the issues and motivated more by prejudice and emotion than reason. Often their votes resulted in doing them more harm than good.

A political knowledge poll was taken by Harvard University, the Kaiser Foundation, and the *Washington Post* in 1995-96 wherein 1,514 adults were randomly interviewed by phone. Three-fourths did not know the names of their own Senators and two-thirds could not name the person who served their congressional district in the House of Representatives. Forty percent could not even name the Vice President of the United States! Three-fourths did not know the term of office for a U.S. Senator, and half did not know the Supreme Court had final responsibility to decide a law's constitutionality. In answer to other questions, these uninformed citizens had deep misconceptions of how government functions.[36]

In other surveys, Michael Delli Capini of Barnard College found low-knowledge voters could not relate the political issues most important to them with the positions on those issues by candidates they voted for. This is a serious indictment of the democratic process to select the best government.

Futurists, Alvin and HeidiToffler, wrote, "Some day future historians may look back on voting and the search for majorities as an archaic ritual engaged in by communicational primitives." Commenting on American democracy, they said, " ... our Constitution or political structures are obsolete and in need of overhaul. Nowhere is obsolescence more advanced or more dangerous in our political life. And in no field today do we find less imagination, less experiment, less willingness to contemplate fundamental change."[37]

***

The politics of democracies became more of an arena for the promotion of conflicting interests rather than a process for solving problems and building purposes for the common good. Without common purposes, no basis for common priorities existed. Without priorities, there was no way to distinguish among individual interests and claims nor their effect on the whole of society.

In democracies, elected officials reacted to immediate crisis rather than making long-term plans to contain future crisis. They could not fully understand a problem before the next one arrived and overwhelmed them. Then the electorate demanded every problem be solved immediately. This resulted in hasty actions, sometimes detrimental, or with only short-term benefits.

Furthermore, even after the economic failure of socialism, an unwillingness remained in the world's capitalist countries to leave the free market system alone. Politicians continued to distort its mechanism with subsidies, tariffs, quotas, excessive regulations, special taxes, and price and wage controls.

Yet, after the collapse of socialism in the Soviet Union and the end of the Cold War, there were those who incorrectly said history had come to an end because it was the finality of mankind's ideological evolution. Francis Fukuyama, deputy director of the U.S. State Department's policy planning staff, said in 1989, "What we may be witnessing is ... the universalization of Western liberal democracy as the final form of human government." [38] Of course, it was not the final form of governance.

(The New Society)
The Committee on Governance, after studying the problems in former democracies, soon discovered that social need could not be met through the democratic political process. Although democracy had been the most successful form of government, the Committee was aware that it was fundamentally inept in handling society's problems in the future. Decision-making to meet the

peoples' needs, when left to politicians, had moved forward very little. Most important, decisions were based on the pressure from selfish minority interests or compromises with a consensus of dubious opinions of the unknowledgeable majority ignorant of the subject at hand, especially economics. The Committee felt democracy was merely the confession of an inability to arrive at a scientific answer to society's problems.

The Committee could see that as the legitimate functions of a democracy gradually broke down, the government was no longer responsive to the primary need of its people for protection from crime and other harmful forces. This was imperative even within primitive tribes. Consequently, the need for public order justified and usually resulted in absolute totalitarian authority.

The Committee felt there had to be another solution, another form of governance which was neither democracy nor dictatorship. They were aware that the greater the political power, the greater the eventual corruption. It was necessary to end all forms of political rule which were not only obsolete but barbaric, ending many times in coups, revolution, or war. After careful thought, they realized politics, once considered an essential part of democracy, was nothing more than a primitive method of selecting people to make laws and administer them for society.

Therefore, the Committee on Governance discussed a new governing structure. Instead of trying to improve existing methods of governance, it was suggested they be ignored as if they had never existed. A fresh outlook could only then develop. This could occur only after first deciding what should be the real purpose of government. Why did people form communities, and what did they expect the communities (government) to do for them?

After much research, analysis, and discussion the Committee arrived at the most logical purpose. It was not a complicated hodgepodge of special wishes and desires; it was very simple. It was decided the only need for societies to organize were two basic historical ones: (1) for mutual protection and (2) to create a community environment conducive for the creation of a better quality of life. This may have been the purpose of most individual nations at one time. All had strayed from it, and the methods had become unworkable.

With its purpose well established, the Committee was determined to proceed slowly in structuring the methods and to formulate them avoiding the old problems of a politicized democracy. They decided, as a primary function, the government should propose long-term goals and to broadly steer but loosely regulate means to attain them.

The government was to be a creator of broad social visions. The policies must not benefit individuals to the detriment of the rest of society. Additionally, government could only be effective if it confined itself to creating general conditions to which individuals and groups conformed under the law. It was ill-suited to make finer adjustments or to be an active participant. This was best left to the judgement and ability of the citizenry. The complexities of human life make it practically impossible for a government to intervene in detail effectively. It is beyond its grasp and power to adjust pragmatically. Therefore, the least number of decisions it has to make, the more competent it will be.

Thomas Jefferson correctly said, "That government is best which governs least." He and others of his time had a deep suspicion that government, if permitted by the voters, would waste the labors of citizens and ultimately reduce their freedoms, always under the pretense of taking care of the people.

Referring to overzealous politicians and regulatory bodies, Justice Louis Brandeis remarked, "Experience should teach us to be most on our guard to protect liberty when government's purposes are beneficient ... The greatest dangers to liberty lurk in insidious encroachment by men of zeal, well-meaning, but without understanding."

A sense that the electorate wanted their leaders and representatives to make long-term plans for various eventualities and to outline difficult things that must be done has usually prevailed. Most citizens had little time for such things because they were completely devoted to providing for their families on a daily basis. However, they did not want elected officials to merely respond to every move in the public-opinion polls to gain advantage over their political adversaries.

If this is what people expected, the Committee reasoned, why couldn't this be done in a scientific approach rather than a political one? Why couldn't society produce coherent long-term policies to provide the proper environment, to provide for an efficient economy and to preserve order in the world? Once the broad purposes and goals of government are determined, why was it necessary to obstruct their accomplishments with gridlock between political parties that were more prejudiced than logical in their thinking?

(Historical Background)

In 1932 an American movement called Technocracy arose that, among other things, believed the economy was too complicated to be understood and controlled by politicians. They believed control should be placed in the hands of scientists and engineers. Many complained that such a government would attempt to get too involved in the daily details of running the economy much like the central-controlled economies of socialist countries.

Some used the failures of the United Nations and the European Community as examples of failed technocracy, and it was true. Their problems were, however, due generally to the existence of prejudices, nationalism, and illiteracy in many portions of the world. In other words, decisions were still political.

(The New Society)

The Committee on Governance, reviewed the problems of centralized or politicized governments and decided the functions of government must be severely limited to the purposes that were earlier proposed: mutual protection and to create an environment conducive for the creation of a better life. All government functions must be clearly stated, with as many run by competitive private businesses as possible.

Governmental positions should be filled by qualified professionals with expertise in the fields of work encountered. The selection should be free of favoritism. Citizens should not be called upon to decide if these people are properly qualified in a massive politicized election. Nor should they be required to vote on matters so complex and foreign that a wrong vote could do them more harm than good.

On the other hand, citizens must have a method to appeal and correct any decision or grievance that may infringe upon their freedoms or rights which are not in conflict with society. They must have a method to propose deserving improvements or changes and to receive a prompt and satisfactory appraisal. All citizens, regardless of status, economic position, gender, or race, must be treated equally.

***

The Economic Advisory Committee already proposed a single world economy without borders which would not restrict the free movement of trade, workers, and ideas. It also included a single monetary system with one currency and a World Central Bank. It was obvious these measures had to be gradually adopted until new generations in the undeveloped world were on an educated par with more developed regions. Migration, in particular, had to be controlled so neither cultural shock nor primitive, uneducated masses would overrun the more developed peoples.

The seeds of animosity and conflict gradually receded after the founders of the new society banned cultural-nationalism and religious fanaticism; instigated the teaching of tolerance to children replacing ethnic and racial prejudice; adopted one language for the conduct of world-wide business, science, and government. The erradication of illiteracy through a standardized global education system was, undoubtedly, the greatest contribution to peace in the world.

***

A disarmament conference was called that abolished war. It was agreed that all weapons of war would be destroyed, all military forces would be disbanded, and the manufacture of lethal weapons would be banned. This was accomplished on a gradual and systematic basis. At first a world peace-keeping force took their place until all of the above was accomplished. Then it too was gradually demobilized until only regional security police maintained order. An enormous percentage of the world's wealth, began to be utilized to raise the living standards of all people through productive means rather than in destruction.

The abolition of war was only possible after an agreement was reached to eliminate cultural-nationalistic prejudice through the education of new generations and also in the elimination of political power under the new methods of governance. It became a serious criminal offense to attempt to manufacture arms or raise a military force.

If mankind was ever expected to be at peace with itself, a need for a single world government was apparent. This in itself would help eradicate isolation associated with regional prejudice. World government was also necessary to save the environment, for economic cooperation, and to banish illiteracy world-wide. Many thought the time had come for society to accept these responsibilities if it was ever to become truly civilized.

As world trade and communication technology grew, all regions evolved as part of the global community. The new world government was planned as a commonwealth of regions throughout the globe. Most were countries or nations of the past, but many nations were also divided into regions. Each had its own regional governance which conformed to world standards and laws in the Articles of Government of the United World Commonwealth.

Regional borders were defined within the worldwide community much like the individual states or provinces in earlier nations. Some ethnic areas existed within the borders of several countries. An example was the Kurds in Iraq, Iran, and Turkey. At first, the early planners endeavored to consolidate these cultural areas. This was not to encourage old prejudices but to assist in reducing conflicts before most prejudices could be erradicated in the schools. It was accomplished through a plebiscite that enabled inhabitants of those areas to vote for the particular regional control they would prefer to live under.

Once again, the borders have no significance except to define regional government control. Otherwise, they are not patrolled or defended and are open to trade and other world- communication much like individual states in the former United States. Each region is subject to world standards of behavior, education, environment, commerce, and government.

Today in the new society, all malevolent behavior adverse to the global society including the destruction of the world's resources and environment is prohibited. The world's citizens have finally come together for mutual protection. Together they are creating a better quality of life through universal education, cooperative scientific research, and a free global market-economy and monetary system.

To eliminate many complex functions which governments proved unable to perform efficiently and to reduce cost through competition, all functions possible have been contracted to competing businesses. They include such things as schools, postal services, mass transportation, administration and maintenance of parks, cultural and recreational areas, and many regulatory bodies.

(Historical Background)

The use of government employees, to perform functions private enterprise could do more efficiently, were commonplace before the United World Commonwealth was formed. Some examples of the general failure to function as efficiently as those motivated by the profit and loss incentive have already been described. Government-run services responded not to the pressures of the market system but to political pressures.

The U.S. General Accounting Office demonstrated that federal employees handling Medicare claims were paid more and produced less than their counterparts in private industry. Columbia University's Graduate School of Business found garbage collection cost the average municipal agency seventy percent more than it cost the average private firm. An audit by KPMG Peat Marwick projected a five year savings of $29 million from the privatization of Denver's Regional Transportation District.

Referring to the administration of government crop insurance to farmers, a major private insurer in Iowa was appalled and said, "The policy provisions they write actually deliver taxpayers dollars by the carload to farmers who don't deserve it. Their actuarial division in Kansas City has no idea what they're doing."

In 1983 Newark, New Jersey began to contract out about one-third of its services to private companies. Privatized street sweeping, alone, saved the city one million dollars annually while providing cleaner streets. Other cities, in financial trouble in the United States, were forced to lay off unneeded city employees, consolidate, eliminate unneeded services, and privatize many others through competitive bidding.

The Savings and Loan debacle was a classic example of government interference in the market mechanism gone awry. The purpose of deposit insurance was good, but the government should never have been in the insurance business. Instead, had it mandated deposits be insured by private insurance companies, who would have scrutinized bank loans carefully, no loss would have burdened taxpayers. Bank solvency, being an insurable risk, could have been priced properly on a risk-sensitive basis in private competitive markets. (i.e. If loans became risky, premiums would increase thus restricting the risk.)

The postal service in most countries was a monopoly run by the government. This was true in the United States until it became semi-independent. However, rate increases and other functions were still controlled by a government commission. Many anachronistic entrenched government methods were still used, so it continued to function like a government agency. It continued as a monopoly in most respects except in parcel delivery and express mail. Its expenses skyrocketed because competition didn't exist to force cost-control. Mail service continued to get slower, more expensive, and less reliable. A typical first-class letter in the United States took fifteen percent longer to arrive in 1989 than it did twenty years earlier.[39]

Because of competition from Federal Express and United Parcel Service, the postal service's portion dropped to about ten percent of express and three percent of parcel delivery sales. It could not compete for several reasons. Its costs were out of control, a carry-over from government service. Severe union contract restrictions created difficult work rules and banned layoffs. With an enormous work force of 756,000 employees (1990) averaging over $31,000 per annum there was a real problem in cutting unnecessary labor costs. Employees were paid nearly twice their counterparts in state governments and exceeded pay in comparable private-industry jobs.[40]

Automation was only used when absolutely necessary because the service had more employees than it needed. At twenty sites, mail was deliberately diverted from automated equipment to less efficient mechanical and manual processing to keep workers busy. To make matters worse, thirteen-hundred workers were fired or suspended in 1987 for mauling, destroying, or stealing mail. An audit found deliverable mail in trash bins at three-fourths of post offices. A similar problem occured on a large scale in Chicago in 1994. Yet, a Postal Inspection Service study revealed the few carrier routes contracted to private business, saved almost fifty percent in personnel costs.[41]

(The New Society)
The Committee on Governance felt there existed a need for government to prevent abuses and to regulate reasonable standards for commerce. The purpose would be to allow privately-run functions free access to competitive markets, to keep monopoly-functions efficient and responsive, and to protect the consumer from harmful products or services .

Nevertheless, the Committee believed the marketplace was ultimately the true regulatory agency. Through intensive competition, it regulates most economic activities with greater speed, effectiveness, and freedom than a multitude of government employees. Each business tries to outdo its competition by improving the quality of its product or service at less cost to the consumer. Government-operated enterprises, lacking competition, cannot do this. Yet, government must still be called upon to prevent abuses in the market place just as it does in other human relationships.

The Committee asked, "How could this be accomplished with responsible use of governmental power?" Many believed it should not slow technological advancement nor inhibit new ideas or products. Nor should it encourage excessive litigation that goes on for many years bankrupting small companies or passing these costs on to consumers in higher prices mainly for the financial benefit of attorneys. Nor should regulation encompass the prohibition of certain products, services, or activities that may be harmful to an individual such as addictive substances and gambling. The individual must bear the responsibility for their use providing he has been made aware of their harmful effects and is not harming others.

Regulatory boards look at many things before imposing new, more complicated regulations that may be inadvertently wasteful in the new society. These boards can't perpetuate themselves when they are no longer needed. They use such things as educating and instructing the consuming public as alternates to excessive regulation. They also ask, "Do methods exist to stimulate market solutions that are less expensive and burdensome than costly changes and excessive regulation." Former businessmen are also members of the boards so they look at forms and red-tape carefully to determine if they are overly time-consuming and impractical in the workplace. Because, in the end, the cost of excessive red-tape must be passed on to the consumer.

***

Despite the wisdom of keeping government to a minimum, the Committee realized some functions are probably best done under direct control of the world government. The various boards on long-term goals and policies, composed of professional experts in their various fields, is one example. Another is the protection of citizens through the judicial system and world and regional security forces. Criminal investigations, including that of lethal weapons, is the principal occupation of security people. The World Central Bank and monetary system is also operated by the government.

Finally, the control over the dispensation of natural resources and waste is the responsibility of government. Even here, the actual leasing of land and the harvesting and mining of natural resources and the processing of pollutants and waste is done by private competitive companies and monitored by the government.

Most functions of the government are regulatory and the monitoring of privately-run functions to insure broad guidelines and purposes of the world community are followed. These include such unique and diverse private operations as parental guidance instruction, education and boarding schools, narcotic dispensing clinics, gambling and prostitution, and rehabilitation for substance-abuse and compulsive gambling.

Other programs monitored include the global job-data system, testing for equal job-opportunities, the computerized global identification system, scientific research institutions for the development and improvement of social objectives including behavioral.

The World Funding Agency also funds enormously expensive projects which benefit all regions, such as space exploration and major one-time scientific and medical research projects. The financial requirements are so enormous, they can only be funded by the government. These are financed through the one-time consumption tax previously explained under A New Dynamic Economy.

The government also oversees the control of population, regulates the distribution of inheritance, and enforces the imposition of the individual's freedoms and rights. It supervises the personnel boards for testing and selection of government scientists, professionals, and other employees.

***

The need for government financing is greatly diminished as a result of the reduced functions of government, elimination of interest in the budget because there is no debt, adoption of more user fees, elimination of military expenditures, and abolishment of transfer funds. Finally, the enormous income from land leases more than pays for the unfunded operations.

Each regional government has a Regional Funding Agency composed of experts in the fields of accounting and finance whose job is to receive the region's income and apportion it to the various government functions in that region. Most of the income is fixed since it is derived primarily from land rentals. It is, therefore, easier to establish the annual income and calculate the budget. It is mandatory that the budget be balanced with the anticipated income so any difference is minimal at the end of the year. The Agency keeps a small surplus of working capital to cover any deficiency, and this has to be replenished the following year from the new budget. Therefore, a planned deficit or accumulating debt as in prior ages of government never occurs. Surpluses are allowed to accumulate and used only for an emergency such as a natural catastrophe.

A World Funding Agency receives a small percentage of each region's income and appropriates it for the operation of the various World Institutes and departments. Each region contributes the same percentage. With the assistance and advice of private professional accounting firms, representatives from all the world's Regional Funding Agencies meet once a year with representatives of the World Funding Agency to determine the appropriate percentage. The purpose of this is for regions to help control centralized spending to avoid the growth of centralized dominance.

The appropriations of the World Funding Agency, like those for regions, has to be budgeted and balanced. They fund the monitoring of the many regional boards and regulatory agencies. They also fund the World Central Bank, world security forces, and assorted World Institutes (World Education Institute, World Environmental Institute, and others).

Monies are no longer appropriated wastefully for special interests because long-range plans must be adhered to and lobbying is forbidden. Since there are no elected offices, there is no reason to exchange wasteful appropriations for votes. Should bribes be exchanged, it is considered criminal, and punishment is extremely severe because government officials and employees are considered trustees of the citizenry. Consequently, it is necessary to administer retribution much greater than for a comparable crime in private transactions unassociated with government functions. This is essential to prevent any spread of government corruption, the waste of citizens' monies, and the debasement of our social structure.

Private accounting firms are mandated to be contracted by both world and regional governments. They are required to annually audit all governmental functions, note any unusual expenses or procedures, and make recommendations for more efficient operations. Any waste or corruption must be immediately reported by them to the judicial authorities for investigation.

***

World institutes are essentially planning groups whose primary functions in a particular field are to establish long-term goals, conduct research, review suggestions for improvement of policies and regulations, assist regional boards, and handle citizens' grievances upon appeal from a regional board. They also create or change regulations, and on rare occasions amend a law. It is important to note that despite the successes of the world government, many of the regulations and policies require modification to improve especially as they are affected by human pragmaticism. The ability to change is an important function.

Any change can be challenged in the World Court which determines if a new law, regulation and even a policy change conform with long-term goals as defined in the Articles of Government of the United World Commonwealth.

Any important change in the Articles of World Government can also be challenged through referendum by the citizens. The pros and cons of a referendum are clearly outlined in a pamphlet that all voters are required to read. All adults are allowed to vote on a referendum providing they pass a literacy test on the subject matter involved.

***

Regional boards include every agency necessary to monitor and enforce laws, policies, and regulations in each particular field such as the regional Natural Resource Board, Population Control Board, Inheritance Administration, and the Education Board. These boards are also required to handle citizens' grievances and complaints that can't be settled in a court of law as well as proposals for improvements and changes in each board's respective field. Boards are required to take some reasonable action or be subject to investigation by judicial authorities. In addition to their main headquarters, Boards have local offices staffed by workers for the convenience and assistance of the local citizenry. Each board is comprised of a variety of professionals hired for their expertise in that particular field.

***

Both world and regional governmental services, are manned by hired professionals. For example, a board, for education may consist not only of educators and psychologists, but business-management experts to advise in the contracting of schools, and economists who can advise in the required educational needs to meet the demands of the workplace and a growing technological economy.

No longer are governmental positions filled by inept political appointees or by election wherein the will of the majority is the result of ignorance of many issues upon which the politician was elected. Moreover, political campaigns of long ago involved more than one issue. This made it necessary for voters to select a general balance of the politician's promises, plus party loyalty, habits, prejudices and other influences.

All government positions, incuding managerial, are now open through rigid competitive examinations including a psychological assessment and interview. Final acceptance is also based on previous experience in a particular field, aptitude, education, and especially analytical ability.

Thus, all standards, regulations, and decisions that effect the citizenry must be made unanimously by a group of competent professionals. They are not from only one restricted field, but from all fields affected by that decision. All decisions are based on the best interests of the public.

All offices and positions in the government are limited to specific terms consistent with efficient governance in that particular area. Upon the expiration of the term, the holder may apply for a transfer to another related government position that is open to competitive examination. The purpose is to prevent stagnated entrenchment, to encourage fresh ideas, and to eliminate the temptation to influence-peddle for favors.

Although there are only two layers of government, world and regional, it is necessary in larger regions to have more than one regional board for most categories. This is necessary to properly monitor various functions across a large area. The number of regional boards is usually determined by the population as well as the size of the area. Only two layers of government help overcome objections of some that creation of a world community would result in excessive layers of government.

***

Initially in overpopulated and less-developed regions, income from land rentals and other sources was far less than in more developed areas of the world. The operations of government, therefore, could not be fully funded so they functioned in a less sophisticated manner in the early decades of the new society. As an example, instruction in education closely followed that in the more-developed regions, but the facilities were much more rudimentary and crude. The use of boarding schools had to be delayed. Salaries and other expenses were very meagre; offices and equipment were more primitive.

As the population stabilized and gradually declined through population control, funds, available for governance per capita, began to increase. However, it took considerably more time to reach the ideal number of people in the overpopulated areas so living standards were considerably subpar for a much longer time. It took many decades to elevate all areas to the world standards prevalent in the United World Commonwealth today.

***

When the founders of the United World Commonwealth first met to write the Articles of Government, most nations were in favor of the purposes and long-term goals. As the specifics unfolded, and some methods appeared quite radical, there was hesitation and doubt in the minds of the representatives of some nations. Most developed countries with educated citizens were convinced of their need during the early days of the world crisis. However, a few nations, primarily in the Third World, refused to join. Their reasons were varied, but most hinged on deep seated religious or nationalistic beliefs.

As the new world economy grew, living standards benefited, and the behavior of its society improved, the non-members felt isolated and deprived. It was soon obvious to them, that unless they joined with the rest of the world to contribute to and receive mutual beneficial changes, many of their people would perish within a few generations. At best, they would be condemned to a primitive existence as compared to the vibrant United World Commonwealth. Today, even the most remote and primitive regions in the world are willing participants.

Chapter 13

A NEW WORLD ORDER
(Summary)

Much time has elapsed since the primitive days of the 20th century. A new world order has evolved to replace the old. Reflecting back, it is difficult to imagine that mankind in those early times could progress so far in the sciences and technology without a corresponding advance in behavior.

In those days the inhabited world gradually and inexorably disintegrated. It had to be fixed. Nevertheless, most people rebelled against new ideas and new ways to solve the problems. Some were outraged at the new radical social proposals. Old customs, prejudices, and methods handed down for decades and even centuries from each generation was difficult to eradicate. People, as a mass, would sometimes fight to the death to retain an established habit. The masses accepted ready-made beliefs and slogans and stuck to them despite absolute proof they were unsound. Most prejudice was political, cultural, nationalistic, and religious in origin. Mankind was endowed with fear and suspicion of change or anything or anyone that was different. So it was a monumental feat to educate the world's people to accept and adapt to these changes.

What made the new society successful? The first step to success was when most agreed the world about them was heading for disaster, and something had to be done.

Success is principally due to the employment of professionals and scientists, experts in each field of socio-economics; they replaced inept politicians and bureaucrats of yesteryear. These new architects of the future developed methods to improve society's behavior and to globally mandate competitive education for all. Standardized education has contributed to the reduction of economic disadvantage and the basis for a disciplined and civilized world. The new technocrats have ended wars, the population explosion, inflation, income tax, drug-trafficking, and most criminal activity.

They have provided basic economic security, equal employment opportunity, a progressive universal health-care system, improved commuting transportation, and a home in an idyllic environment for all workers. They have abolished governmental distortions in the free market encouraging a more productive economy and higher standard of living.

Most important, they have eradicated prejudice, illiteracy, and selfish greed for power.

A worldwide efficient market mechanism has been adopted without artificial borders to hinder the flow of free trade between the most efficient producers and their consumers. A free competitive market in industry and agriculture is now devoid of inefficient government-run businesses and malfunctioning interference, where unfettered supply and consumer choice estabish a natural equilibrium. This has resulted in an extremely efficient productive and distribution system throughout the world. The use of profit and loss measures this efficiency and also creates a necessary incentive for the individual.

Inheritance of vast wealth accumulation from one generation to another has been removed in order to create equal opportunity at birth for all.

The regional Land Use Boards control and lease all industrial, commercial, and agriculture land, and other natural resources in a sound and equitable manner. Coupled with population control, the environment has been restored and the quality of human life has improved worldwide. The environment and natural wealth are no longer ravaged by short-term, haphazard exploitation to meet the needs of an exploding population. Additionally, the elimination of wasteful and needless costs, including the abolition of military forces, and the income from land leases and user fees has eliminated the need for income taxes.

Savings and investment are no longer penalized by unfair taxes. Instead, increased savings foster growth of new and more productive industries and services that increase living standards for all. Systematic methods have been adopted to maintain a sound currency and eliminate inflation.

In turn, the success of all of the above has been due to the great bulwarks of our new society:

early behaviorial education
a liberal but disciplined order
freedom of individual choice but adoption of social responsibility.
population stabilization
scientific control of natural resources including land
a true market economy
exemption of labor and production from taxes
a non-political world government.

All of these changes have contributed to a significant improvement in the quality of life.

Yet, such success is only the beginning. The new society believes it cannot be satisfied with merely becoming civilized. A civilized mode of existence is only the basic foundation of human development. Society must move on to the more difficult challenges that lie ahead. It must have a profound purpose! We are now laying the groundwork for the future of mankind.

Chapter 14

FINAL CHALLENGES OF MANKIND

For man no rest and no ending. He must go on - conquest beyond conquest ... And when he has conquered all the deeps of space and all the mysteries of time - still he will be beginning. - H.G. Wells (from "Things to Come")

After the difficult times of socio-economic reconstruction, the scientific planners of the new society began to outline the far more difficult challenges facing mankind. Many decades of accomplishments in the new civilized world community were imperative but realistically were merely the means of survival. They asked, "Is survival and mere existence the goal of mankind, or are higher goals needed?" This and other questions were voiced as the architects of the United World Commonwealth pondered the future direction of the world. Most agreed mankind's inquisitive curiosity must never be curtailed. Instead, it must be encouraged to climb the explorative heights of scientific and physical achievement. The riddles of life and the universe must be uncovered. All excess resources must be allocated to this end.

The late Carl Sagan, professor of astronomy at Cornell University, said, " ... we're the kind of species that needs a frontier - for fundamental biological reasons. Every time humanity stretches itself and turns a new corner, it receives a jolt of productive vitality that can carry it for centuries."[1]

The architects of the new society posed many questions. What is the purpose of life? What should be the long-term purpose of society? Or does a purpose exist? How do we search for it?

Other innumerable and profound questions require answers. What is life? Where and how did it originate? Will it be possible to create it? What are the smallest life particles? Does life exist in other parts of the universe? If so, in what form?

Is survival the driving force of life? Is reproduction its primary weapon? What is the source or instigator of the reproductive process? What directs natural selection toward this goal? Why does life manifest itself in this manner, and what motivates it? Is it important to the universe?

What compiles the universe? Is it limitless? How did it originate and will it end? Are there other universes? Can the universe be perceived differently by other intelligence? What is the physical matter of the universe? Will we continue to indefinitely discover smaller particles of matter? Does what we perceive actually exist? Or does it exist only in relation to other perceptions? The questions are endless.

Does mankind have to know the answers to these and many other questions? Of course it does because they exist. It is one of the great purposes of life. In *A Brief History of Time*, Stephen Hawking, one of the great physicist-mathematicians of his time, said, "We still yearn to know why we are here and where we come from. And our goal is nothing less than a complete description of the universe we live in."[2] Alexis Carrel, the brilliant biochemist of the 1930s, said, "Men grow when inspired by a high purpose, when contemplating vast horizons."[3]

Sigmund Freud, however, postulated the behavior of humans revealed the purpose of human life was to seek happiness. This had a double goal: eliminating pain and discomfort and experiencing intense pleasures.[4] Such selfish goals cannot possibly replace man's noble destiny to seek the answer to all things.

The prospect of death, of non-existence, is frightening not because it terminates conciousness or happiness. It is because the civilized world and its inhabitants will go on without us, not missing or needing us if we have not contributed anything to that society. We will fade into history and nothingness. It is, therefore, important that individuals contribute to society in order to become an immortal part of it. True, reproduction is a necessary contribution, but the most noble is creative and analytical intelligence devoted to the solution of mankind's most perplexing questions and problems. Future generations can then build and extend their social structure on that understanding.

***

One of the greatest challenges to intelligent life will be to survive and perpetuate itself in the universe. This small fragile earth is the only inhabited planet in our solar system. It is merely a space-craft lost in a deep, hostile, and galactic void. Sooner or later life will suffer extinction either from collision with asteroids or comets, the decay of the sun, or some other unforeseen disaster such as the confluence of another star. Even the next Ice Age could seriously reduce life on earth. Therefore, it is imperative to eventually colonize other planets in other solar systems. This, by itself, is a necessary aspect of natural human evolution.

Robert Goddard, the American physicist who launched the first liquid-fuel rocket in 1926, said, "the navigation of interplanetary space must be effected to ensure the continuance of the race." Carl Sagan, remarked, "In the long-term, even if we were not motivated by exploratory passions, some of us would still have to leave the earth simply to ensure the survival of the rest of us. ... (our) eventual choice is spaceflight or extinction."

He also warned that collision with outer-space bodies was a serious problem.[5] Technology of the 1990s indicated one of the best ways to avoid this was to deflect an asteroid away from the earth by exploding nuclear weapons near it. However, Tom Gehrels, professor of planetary sciences at the University of Arizona, set up a Spacewatch Telescope on Kitt Peak in Arizona to scan the heavens for marrauding asteroids and envisioned the use of spacecraft implanted in an asteroid whose engines could guide it so it missed the earth. He said, "I would find it unforgiveable for human society to be eliminated because it failed to make this small effort ..."

Ray Bradbury, noted author of *The Martian Chronicles,* said "What grander priority is there than the life force, realizing its position in a strange and cold universe, struggling to survive not just here but on other worlds, forever and forever? ... the unborn speak to us from a million years ahead ... waiting to be secured ... save out a penny or a dime for tommorrow's rockets. When the sun dies, they will be our salvation."[6]

If mankind allows itself to be destined to oblivion, then what use is its regard for a civilized society? Surely, that is unacceptable. The evolution of life is not transitory but must continue to its ultimate destination.

Great challenges lie ahead for the new society: the discovery of an inexhaustable fuel or function that can propel at speeds approaching the speed of light, the unmanned exploration of other solar systems within the Milky Way galaxy, and finally the means to transport life to other habitable areas in the universe. Such dreams may seem incomprehensible today, but through eons the intelligence of the human organisim will prevail providing it continues to preserve and improve its fragile space-craft, the Earth.[7]

***

In the meantime it must not stagnate in leisure and comfort but must move on to develop more knowledge of the universe. Can it improve the human species with genetic engineering in order to accomplish the tasks ahead? Can micro-electronics create miniature armies, the size of fleas, to explore space? Will advanced computerization navigate humans to the stars? How can life-support systems and chemicals be used that are recyclable in space? How can moon stations near other planets be developed for further exploration in space? Does other intelligent life exist in the universe and is contact possible?

For pychological reasons it is difficult to accept that humans are alone in this vast universe. On the other hand, we must not be so egotistical as to believe we are the only intelligent life existing among the billions of planets orbiting billions of suns (stars) in billions of galaxies.

Radio-telescopes are faster, cheaper. and reach out farther than other methods of communication. However, after decades of listening for signals from other possible civilizations, none have been heard that can be verified. Yet, it just might be that as intelligent life in other parts of the universe develop to a highly advanced technical level, that level contributes to its own destruction. Is this why no contact has been made?

Survival of life in the universe is, of course, a priority purpose, but understanding the universe in which man lives may be the most important purpose of life.

***

Man is literally made from the dust of the earth. He is composed of chemicals found in the universe, and his body functions within the laws of physics. Still, animate matter is different than inanimate. Fundamental physico-chemical processes constitute living organisims. Why?

Indeed, intelligent life is so complex it boggles the mind. To take one example, the brain has a hundred billion neurons storing and retrieving information, with a trillion connections in each cubic centimeter, and firing ten million billion times each second in a fantastic network of unbelievable complexity. In nanoseconds the brain can retrieve any of one billion different facts. The mind, a product of evolution, is one of the most complicated mechanisms in the universe.

A.I. Oparin, the famous Russian biochemist of the 1930s and author of *The Origin of Life,* did not accept that "vital energies" existed in life organisims. He believed, "The complex combinations of manifestations and properties so characteristic of life must have arisen in the process of evolution of matter."[8]

He described how an atmoshere of superheated aqueous vapor came in contact with simple carbon compounds on the earth's surface. " Carbon is distinguished among all chemical elements by its exceptional ability to form atomic associations, and is found in all living things." The two types of matter, carbon and vapor, reacted chemically forming hydrocarbons and later, other complex organic compounds through oxidation from water. Simultaneously, hydrocarbons also reacted with ammonia, which during that period of time, was on the earth's surface. This reaction created other organic compounds containing nitrogen. As the earth cooled, the compounds of carbon, hydrogen, oxygen, and nitrogen, "endowed with tremendous chemical potentialities," reacted with each other and water in a vast primordial sea forming "complex, high-molecular organic compounds. Also by this process, the biologically most important compounds, the proteins, must have originated."[9]

These solutions of various compounds continued to mix forming "coazervates or semi-liquid colloidal gels. In this process organic substances become concentrated in definite spatial arrangements and separated from the solvent medium by a more or less distinct membrane. Inside ... the beginnings of some elementary structure appear ... This internal structure of the droplet determines its ability to absorb with greater or less speed and to incorporate into itself organic substances dissolved in the surrounding water. This resulted in an increase in size of the droplet, i.e. they acquired the power to grow." Competitive speed of growth, struggle for existence, and finally, natural selection determined such a form ... which is characteristic of living things of the present time."[10]

And what are the probabilities that life can be created in the laboratory? In 1966 research chemists, Clifford N. Matthews and Robert E. Moser, mixed methane and ammonia, then shot electricity through the gaseous mixture recreating lightning which abounded in primitive earth. The result was a poisonous hydrogen-cyanide gas which was allowed to stand and mix forming a black solid. When water was added, the result was a brown scum containing amino acids in large proteinlike chunks, the natural ingredient of all life-forming proteins.

Many problems arise in an effort to create life. The detailed knowledge of the internal structure of life is still unknown. But even in the 1930s Oparin believed synthesis of life was possible. He said, "The road ahead is hard and long but without doubt it leads to the ultimate knowledge of the nature of life. The artificial building or synthesis of living things is very remote, but not an unattainable goal along this road."[11]

***

If survival is the driving force of any life, then reproduction is the main biological purpose of life. All forms of life share a dominant drive: to extend the species and perpetuate themselves into future generations by any means available. But why is it meaningful?

Science knows how the reproductive process works in most higher forms of life. Even the division of one-celled organisms appears to be one of the commonest and most universal vital events, and it can be readily observed. The chromosone in the center of the most primitive one- celled animal duplicates itself with each half containing identical genetic information. The chromosone then separates and moves to each side of the cell. The cell then divides (binary fission). But, what motivates the separation and division remains unknown. It also appears to be the most primitive form of reproduction, but is it?

One group of bacteria, the mycoplasma, are the smallest cells that grow and reproduce. Still, they are not the smallest organisms; viruses are even smaller but are not cellular and cannot reproduce or grow outside of host cells. Some viruses can create genetic changes in the target host. This may be a crucial method for natural selection to effect evolution. Still, subviruses, such as prions, can be a hundred times smaller than viruses and appear to be little more than bits of live protein. What gives them life? Do even smaller bits of life exist?[12]

Some bacteria can live on glacier ice or in hot springs. A new form of life, archaea, was discovered in 1996 to have two-thirds of its genes foreign to any other living thing. A microbe, it lives in hot water spewed from ocean-floor vents two miles beneath the ocean at pressures two-hundred times surface atmosphere. It lives in complete darkness, lacks any oxygen, and thrives on hydrogen and carbon dioxide. Such organisms indicate parameters may exist that significantly increase the liklihood that life thrives in extremely hostile environments in other parts of the universe.

The source or motivation of reproductive cell-division may help answer the purpose of life. This and other complex events require seeking a scientific explanation. Navigation by migratory birds had been shown to be so extremely complex it boggled the mind. Nonetheless, it was eventually explained in scientific detail. Perhaps the fundamental reproductive force will be revealed in the same manner.

***

Some scientists were convinced the universe was formed to foster the complexity of life, permit highly complex life-objects to stay intact over long periods of time, and still allow for gradual change that leads to even greater complexity. Physicists B. J. Carr and M. J. Rees in 1979, after considerable mathematical examination, concluded, "Several aspects of our universe - some of which seem to be prerequisites for the evolution of any form of life - depend rather delicately on apparent coincidences among the physical constants." Paul Davies, a British cosmologist and author of *The Accidental Universe,* wrote, "Whether the laws of nature can force coincidences on the universe or not, the fact that these relations are necessary for our existence is surely one of the most fascinating discoveries of modern science."[13]

A universe deliberately created for habitation or directed by some unknown force seems unlikely. This seems to be the message of reductionists. They maintain the creative beliefs of consciousness is a product of brain chemistry, and life processes are governed by the DNA genetic program. And it, in turn, is directed by the laws of chemistry and physics of inanimate matter. Meanwhile many others, scientists included, believe an intelligence exists directing the universe and that life cannot be explained by the physical sciences alone. Living systems do show evidence of intelligent coping within their environments, but any conclusions are unproven todate.

It is interesting to note throughout history, if a natural event occurred that could not be readily explained, humans were quick to associate it with a godly being: the sun god, rain god, fire god, fertility and other gods. Steven Weinberg, the Nobel Prize-winning physicist, wrote in *Dreams of a Final Theory,* "The historian Hugh Trevor-Roper has said that it was the spread of the spirit of science in the 17th and 18th centuries that finally ended the burning of witches in Europe."

Mr. Weinberg continued, "We may need to rely again on the influence of science to preserve a sane world. ... the discovery of the final laws of nature will at least leave less room in the imagination for irrational beliefs. ... the only way that any sort of science can proceed is to assume that there is no divine intervention and to see how far one can get with this assumption."[14]

***

One theory, the chaos theory, holds that complex phenomena are inherently unpredictable. The supporters of this hypothesis believe secular, rational humanism is ill-suited to define the universe. In the 1920s the German scientist, Werner Heisenberg, theorized "the uncertainty principle" which holds it impossible to obtain an absolutely precise measurement of matter because the act of measuring disturbs the matter under scrutiny. A single particle of light, the photon, changes position whenever light rays are used to observe it. Therefore, it is impossible to predict with absolute certainty how it will behave in the future. Stephen Hawking noted that even if a " unified theory" of the universe is discovered, the uncertainty principle may inhibit man's ability to predict general events.

***

But what directs reproduction, natural selection, and the survival of life itself? Is life necessary to the universe? What is the complex relationship between mind and body? What explains the spontaneous tendency toward the formation of organs by their constitutive cells? The many manifestations of life and their sources will intrigue man until the answers are found. The process of making scientific discoveries to help answer these and many other questions will take considerable time. Therefore, much effort must be directed by the new society toward that end.

Is everything in the universe including mankind, preordained? Is it determined in advance? Do circumstances exist before a choice is made that makes that choice inevitable? (i.e. Is the body programmed in advance to arrive at the choice?) Can free will overcome a predetermined choice? The answer is probably yes to all of the above, but we are still seeking the answers.

Stephen Hawking believed a simple grand unified theory to explain the evolution of the universe was inevitable. It would, therefore, determine everything in the universe. Still, humans can never know what is preordained in everyday life because most events are too trivial and yet, too complex.[15]

***

The string theory was advanced by physicists in the 1990s as the framework for a unified theory which expresses all forces of nature as a single phenomenon. It assumes the basic constituents of matter are extended strings rather than particles, and that the universe possesses a strange structure, called super symmetry.

Steven Weinberg said, "Perhaps there is a final theory, a simple set of principles from which flow all arrows of explanation, but we shall never learn what it is. ...it may be that humans are simply not intelligent enough to discover or to understand the final theory. (Or it) may be centuries away and turn out to be totally different from anything we can now imagine."[16]

***

In the new society nearly all of the genes have been identified and located in the various chromosones of nuclei and many have been completely deciphered by molecular biologists. Nevertheless, the how and why of DNA remains unsolved. Scientists of the United World Commonwealth are also exploring artificial selection or induced genetic evolution, replacing natural selection, to propagate the strongest and most intelligent strain of Homo sapiens. This is thought to be a necessary prerequisite to successful space colonization and to solving the mysteries of the universe.

***

Much time has elapsed since the new society was founded, but tremendous gaps still exist in knowledge of the universe.

The universe as observed by man is composed of a vast empty space containing a small amount of physical matter. This matter appears to have formed into immense bubbles about 150 million light-years across. The interior of the bubbles seem to be empty of matter, but the walls consist of billions of galaxies. Each galaxy contains billions of stars like our sun; many probably have satellite planets and moons. Gallaxies appear to form from the gravitational collapse of matter consisting mostly of hydrogen gas. These massive clouds of dust and gases take billions of years to form stars.

Nevertheless, evidence indicates most of the universe's total mass cannot be observed. One can only speculate what the unseen mass is. Many prefer to describe some of this hidden mass as black holes, massive burned-out stars whose powerful gravitational force causes them to collapse. When its atoms are crushed, the matter is then squeezed into a small ball, so dense and so small that it would simply disappear. It is believed nothing can escape the tremendous gravitational pull, not even light. However, Stephen Hawking speculated that the uncertainty principle would allow particles and radiation to leak out thus escaping at a speed faster than that of light. If this is true, he believed the quantum principle would avoid a beginning of the universe. He further speculated that as the mass of a black hole becomes smaller, it becomes even hotter, explodes, and disappears. Where does the matter go?

As collapsing burned-out stars increase in the universe and eventually form black holes, will they eventually merge to form gigantic dark caverns - the huge undetected mass of the universe? What form of matter do these caverns take? It may be a form of subatomic particles yet undiscovered. The truth may be that the entire universe of universes is composed of many different types of subatomic particles that are constantly changing from one form to another. Evidence indicates, for example, that neutrinos produced by various nuclear reactions, are able to do this, and that some may possess a small amount of mass. Since the universe is packed with great numbers of neutrinos, they may be a major component of the undetected dark matter.

Are the unseen and undiscovered particles in the universe the stuff which creates the birth of new universes? Another Big Bang? But how?

***

Once it was perceived the basic element of physical matter was the atom. Later it was demonstrated another particle called the electron, one-thousandth the mass of the atom, existed as part of the atom. In 1932 it was shown electrons revolved around a positive-charged proton and a neutron without an electrical charge, comprising the nucleus of the atom. Much later it was discovered that a proton and neutron was composed of at least six smaller particles called quarks. Do even smaller particles exist? Probably, but only super colliders will divulge the answer. (The United States Congress failed to appropriate the financial resources to finish its construction in the 1990s.)

All particles are, in fact, waves according to quantum mechanics and comprise everything in the universe including light and gravity. In turn these particles are acted upon by four forces: the strong nuclear force, which binds quarks together in the atom's nucleus, the weak nuclear force, which triggers some forms of radioactive decay; electromagnetism, which builds atoms into matter; and gravity.

It is interesting that the heaviest elements can be reduced to the lightest such as hydrogen, and the electrons revolving about the lightest atomic nucleous are widely spaced as are the quarks in the nucleus. If quarks are composed of even smaller particles that are widely spaced, is matter primarily empty space? Infinite matter is not solidity but probably a system of inter-related events unknown, as yet, to human observers.

True, matter and its many forms appear physical while observed by humans, but is what they perceive different from what actually exists? What is observed evolves solely from the relationship of what has been previously observed. It is relative. All knowledge of the universe is comprised of events that occur in the conciousness of the mind. We cannot be certain, therefore, that it exists as it appears or only in relation to other human perceptions which may or may not be real. Whatever real means! Is it perceived differently by other intelligence in the universe?

When the fundamental event is finally discovered, will it be the building block of the universe? Is this event constantly in a state of fluctuation throughout the universe of universes, thus creating changing designs that are observable as predominately physical and fixed? These are questions that must be answered by future generations.

Sir James Jeans, the famous British mathematician and cosmologist, said, "Science, mainly under the guidance of Poincare, Einstein, and Heisenberg, came to recognize that its primary and possibly its only proper objects of study were the sensations that the objects of the external universe produced in our minds; before we could study objective nature, we must study the relation between nature and ourselves."

***

How did the universe originate? Einstein's general theory of relativity predicted that time must have had a beginning fifteen billion years ago with the Big Bang. The Big Bang was an explosion that most scientists believed created the present universe.

Another theory, the inflation theory, was proposed by Alan Guth, Massachusettes Institute of Technology physicist. He predicted, during a tiny fraction of a second after the Big Bang, the universe exploded at an increasing rate of speed faster than the speed of light from a size smaller than an atom to a size larger than can be seen today by the most powerful telescopes. Guth suggested the explosion was extremely hot, rather chaotic, and with very high energies. This, in turn, created a rapidly expanding universe in all directions that eventually slowed and the temperatures cooled much like an ordinary bomb explosion. Inflation theorists hypothesized billions of universes could be created in this manner.

The universe of universes apparently is composed of infinite space much of which is void of matter or events as we know it. This begs several crucial questions. If matter was created from the Big Bang or Big Bangs, in what form does it exist before the explosion? Stephen Hawking said, "The answer is that, in quantum theory, particles can be created out of energy in the form of particle-antiparticle pairs. But that just raises the question of where the energy came from. The answer is that the total energy of the universe is exactly zero ... negative gravitational energy exactly cancels the positive energy represented by matter." He put it another way: "The universe is neither created nor destroyed; it just is."[17] It may be possible, therefore, that physical matter is perceived only during certain periods in certain areas of the universe of universes. At other times its perception may be absent.

Also a beginning implies time existed before the Big Bang singularity. " ... the quantum theory of gravity has opened up a new possibility, in which there would be no boundary to space-time and so there would be no need to specify the behavior at the boundary. There would be no singularities at which laws of science broke down and no edge of space-time at which one would have to appeal to God or some new law to set the boundary conditions for space time." [18]

An infinite number of questions regarding these and other concepts of the universe proliferate. It would appear that some complex series of physical events occured that are, yet, not fully comprehensible using existing knowledge.

***

Theories must be substantiated through observation. Only intelligent life can create the means to make those observations. It may be one of the reasons life exists.

Other cosmologists proposed that universes have been perfectly designed for life in a manner that could not have happened by mere coincidence. Proponents of the weak anthropic principle suggested a universe simply passes through a phase in which conditions are right for life to exist; whereas, under the strong anthropic principle the basic laws of physics require life to evolve.

Many biologists believed the coincidences that occurred to produce intelligent life on earth were exceptionally unique and unlikely to be repeated on other planets anywhere in the universe. If this is true and humans are the only intelligence throughout the depths of space, the new society must begin colonizing our universe before some unforeseen tragedy ends this intelligence. It could be the final evolution of the universe, the manifest destiny of mankind.

***

As late as the 21st century, society was still not ready to seek its true destiny. It had not evolved intellectually or morally. It was too overwhelmed with the mundane problems of merely surviving on planet Earth.

Unlike the rulers and politicians of old, the planners and scientists of the new society were well aware of the real challenges of the future. To disregard them was unacceptable to the future evolution of mankind. The infinite questions about life, about intelligence, and their place in the universe must be answered. They stressed that knowledge builds on knowledge, and progress is the result.

The answers to questions of the universe, requiring incredibly complex answers, will eventually be forthcoming decades, centuries, and eons after the new society was created, providing mankind in the interim has not destroyed itself and its world. The challenge, the exploration, and the discovery should excite and fascinate our intelligence for centuries. They will elevate the purpose of human social effort to its greatest achievements and extend the evolution of man.

NOTES

Chapter 1

1 Todd Lewan, "Rio's Beaches and Tourist Havens Becoming Crime-Laden Battlefields," *Associated Press (Arizona Daily Star)*, May 13, 1990.
2 "World Trouble Spots," *Time*, 1990.
3 Stan Lehman, "South Americans Turn to Underground Economics for Survival," *Associated Press (Arizona Daily Star)*, October 1, 1989.
4 Thomas G. Donlan, "What Me Worry," *Barrons*, March 5,1990.
5 Roger Cohen, "Rio's Murder Wave," *Wall Street Journal*, May 9, 1989.
6 Carlos Ball, "Unmasking the Obscene Core of the Venezuelan Malady," *Wall Street Journal*, December 11, 1992.
7 Marcus W. Brauchli, "A Rising Middle Class Clamors for Changes in Troubled Pakistan," *Wall Street Journal*, December 14, 1995.
8 *The Environmental Fund*, Washington D.C.

Chapter 2

1 The expansion by the Soviet Union, prior to the German invasion, included the invasion of Finland, of Poland, and the occupation and annexation of the independent Baltic nations of Estonia, Latvia, and Lithuania.
2 Louis Snyder, *The War 1939-1945* (New York: Julian Messner, Inc., 1960)
3 Ivo Duchacek, "The February Coup in Czechoslovakia," *World Politics*, July 1950.
4 American Security Council's, *Washington Report*, July 1973.
5 Marx and other socialists advocated a classless society. Although he may not have referred directly to the redistribution of wealth, the abolition of class referred primarily to the elimination of class wealth which could only be accomplished through the redistribution of income and private property.
6 Dave Ricker, "From Leningrad to the Moon," *Green Valley News*, April 13, 1994.
7 Arnold Beichman, "Karl Marx Goes to College," *Wall Street Journal*, May 14, 1982.
8 *Chicago Tribune* and *Associated Press*, "Russian Exile's New Crusade Is Painful to West," *Seattle Times*, March 28, 1976.
9 In 1950 Klaus Fuchs confessed to being a spy for the U.S.S.R. wherein for 7 years he had funneled high-level secrets about nuclear weapons research including the hydrogen bomb to the Soviets. Evidence supplied in his confession led to the arrest of the Rosenbergs. Julius Rosenberg and his wife Ethel and Norton Sobell, all U.S. citizens, were found guilty in 1951 of conspiring to

commit war-time sabotage and were sentenced to death (except Sobell who received a 30 year prison term). The Soviet nuclear physicist, Sakharov, later admitted that their thermo-nuclear weapon model that they were working on in 1940's and early 1950's was the fruit of espionage.

Some disciples, in defense of the Rosenbergs, attempted to remake history many years later by accusing the government of abuse of power and suppression of the Constitution during the case. It is difficult to understand this defense considering the case had reached the Supreme Court in appeal no less than seven times and the verdict was guilty each time.

10 "Russia," *Time*, January 22, 1965.
11 "Russia," *Time*, February 12, 1965.
12 "Radio Free Europe," *Radio Liberty Newsletter*, December 1986.
13 Nikolay Shmelyov, *Novy Mir*, June 1987.
14 Ibid.
15 George Melloan, "Gorbachev Courts Capitalism, but Only Abroad," *Wall Street Journal*, December 8, 1987.
16 Robert G. Kaiser, "Like Its Leaders, Its Communism is Old, Tired, Sickly," *Washington Post*, October 1984.
17 Ibid.
18 Peter Gumbel, "Down on the Farm," *Wall Street Journal*, December 2, 1985.
19 Craig Forman, "East Bloc Lesson," *Wall Street Journal*, February 20, 1990.
20 Ibid.
21 Hedrick Smith, *The Russians* (New York: Quadrangle/New York Times Book, 1976)
22 Ibid.
23 Barry Newman, "Gorbachev's Test," *Wall Street Journal*, June 17, 1988.
24 Paul Johnson, "Has Capitalism a Future?", *Wall Street Journal*, September 29, 1978.
25 David Shipler, *Russia: Broken Idols, Solemn Dreams*, (New York: Time Books,1989)
26 Christopher Wren, "Whoever Steals Lives Better," *New York Times*, April 1976.
27 Lina Mathews, "Despite Exhortations at Top, Chinese Workers Still Loaf," *Los Angeles Times Service*, November 25, 1977.
28 Frederick Kempe, "Urge to Merge," *Wall Street Journal*, february 15, 1990.
29 Richard Lacayo, "Seizing the Moment," *Time*, October 16,1989.
30 Peter Gumbel, "Struggling Reforms," *Wall Street Journal*, November 20. 1989.
31 Elizabeth Rubinfien, "Soviets Slow to Embrace Market Economy," *Wall Street Journal*, September 5, 1990.
32 Ibid.
33 Ibid.
34 This chapter, "The Rise and Fall of Socialism," was first written in the early 1980s in which the author predicted the collapse of the Soviet Union. This prediction was based primarily on the inevitable decline of government-run industries and the government-controlled economy. Because the prediction became a

reality before the book was finished, it became necessary to modify the ending
35 Alvin and Heidi Toffler, *A New Civilization* (Atlanta-: Turner Publishing Co., 1995)

Chapter 3

1 Bruce Ramsey, "A Poor Work Ethic Breeds Poverty," *Seattle Post-Intelligencer,* 1982
2 Thomas Sowell, *Ethnic America* (New York: Basic Books, 1981)
3 Ibid.
4 Ibid.
5 Lee Lescaze and Steve Mufson, "Road to Russia," *Wall Street Journal,* July 15, 1985.
6 George Ayittey, "In Africa, Independence Is Far Cry From Freedom," *Wall Street Journal,* March 28,1990.
7 Ibid.
8 Lee A. Daniels, "L.A. High School Study Links Test Scores To Race, Income," *New York Times,* 1987
9 Susan Goldberg, "Why More Kids In Special Ed?", *Seattle Post Intelligencer,* August 8, 1982.
10 Mary Rothschild, "Black Students Shun Advanced Math," *Seattle Post Intelligencer,* February 19, 1984.
11 Charles Murray, "Here's the Bad News on the Underclass," *Wall Street Jounal,* March 8, 1990.
12 Guy Odom, *Mothers, Leadership and Success.* (Houston: Polybius Press, 1990)
13 Judy Belk, "Black Killers, Black Corpses: A Survivor's Story," *Wall Street Journal,* October 11, 1989.
14 Alex Kotlowitz, "Urban Trauma," *Wall Street Journal,* 1987.
15 Sylvestor Monroe, "Up From Obscurity," *Time,* August 13, 1990.
16 Thomas Sowell, *Ethnic America.* (New York; Basic Books, 1981)
17 Ibid.
18 Ibid.
19 Norman L. Munn, *Psychology: The Fundamentals of Human Adjustment.* (Boston: Houghton Mifflin Co., 1946)
20 Sandra Sear and Richard Weinberg, "IQ Test Performances of Black Children Adopted by White Families," *American Psychologist,* October 1975.
21 Many studies have shown that IQ tests are not culturally biased. It is only when they are applied to Hispanics and American Indians, they showed some evidence of bias because of language considerations.
Statistics generally showed that blacks had lower IQs than whites, and whites, in turn, had lower IQs than East Asians. In addition, statistically those in the lower socio-economic class had lower IQs. For example, chronic welfare recipients had a mean IQ of ninety-two; juveniles sentenced for crime had a mean IQ of ninety-three versus one-hundred and six for those who had never been in-

volved with the police; generally those without college degrees had lower IQs than those that did; those in higher skilled jobs (attorneys, physicians, engineers, business executives) tended to have IQs averaging one-hundred and twenty whereas those in lower-paying jobs had much less. As environment improved and became more uniform, IQ also improved.
22 Richard J. Herrnstein and Chares Murray, *The Bell Curve*. (New York: The Free Press, 1994)

Chapter 4

1 Richard J. Hernstein and James Q. Wilson, *Crime and Human Nature*. New York: Simon and Schuster, 1985.)
2 Clare Booth Luce, "The Significance of Squeaky Fromme," *Wall Street Journal*, September 24, 1975.
3 "Crowd Cheers as Girl Cuts Wrists, Aims Razor at Throat," *United Press International*, August 22, 1976.
4 Nancy Gibbs, "Wilding in the Night," *Time*, May 8, 1989.
5 Richard N. Ostling, "No Sympathy for the Devil," *Time*, March 19, 1990.
6 Richard Corliss, "X-Rated," *Time*, May 7, 1990.
7 Charles Krauthammer, "Crime and Responsibility," *Time*, May 8,1989.
8 Peter Fimrite, "Mob Scene at Slaying Horrifies Oakland," *San Diego Union Tribune*, August 22, 1993.
9 "Authorities Bemoan Latest Rash of Crimes," *Arizona Daily Star*, September 19, 1993.
10 Roger Cohen, "Rio's Murder Wave," *Wall Street Journal*, May 9, 1989.
11 Karl Zimmeister, "Illegitimacy in Black and White," *Wall Street Journal*, November 6, 1987.
12 "Children Having Children," *Time*, December 9, 1985.
13 Sharman Stein, "Poverty, Teen Pregnancies Constitute Vicious Cycle," *Chicago Tribune*, September 19, 1993.
14 J.C. Martin, "When Children Want Children Isn't Kid Stuff," *Arizona Daily Star*, February 12, 1989.
15 Harmeet K.D. Singh, "To Lower Infant Mortality Rate, Get Mothers Off Drugs," *Wall Street Journal*, May 1, 1990.
16 "Dropout Rate Has Broad Effects Educators Warn," *Associated Press*, 1986.
17 Gallup Poll, April 1976.
18 David E. Pitt, "Abuse of Elderly is Frequently a Family Affair," *New York Times*, 1987.
19 George McDowell, "Juvenile Crime Costing United States $4 Billion a Year," *Seattle Post-Intelligencer*.
20 "Spock Takes Blame," *Seattle Post Intelligencer*, 1979.
21 "Back to Basics in the Schoolhouse," *Newsweek*, October 21, 1974.
22 David K. Shipler, "Youth Problems in Russia," *New York Times*, March 5, 1978.
23 Robert C. McCormick, "Forum Members Hear About Children at Risk," *Green*

Valley News, August 20, 1993.
24 Fergus M. Bordewich, "The Country that Works Perfectly," *Reader's Digest,* February 1995.

Chapter 5

1 The dictionary informs us that intellect is the power or faculty of the mind by which one knows or understands, in distinction from that by which one feels or wills.
James Russell Lowell put it another way, "True scholarship consists in knowing not what things exist, but what they mean; it is not memory but judgement."
The term, intellectual, has many associated meanings, but perhaps the most common conception is as a social critic of the institutions and practices of his time.
2 "Prophets warn of potential danger to a civilization's well-being, and encourage change, but their prescriptions go unheeded. After all, changes beneficial to a society rarely suit the citizen's short-term self-interests," wrote Guy Odom in *Mothers, Leadership and Success.*
Even Albert Einstein once said the intelligence and character of the masses are incomparably lower than that of the few who will strive to take giant incomprehensible steps to improve the community. ("Letter to Posterity," by Albert Einstein, *Readers Digest,* 1938.)
3 Ants comprise ten to fifteen percent of the world's total animal weight or biomass. They are the most dominant social organism in the world and probably the most successful. (R. Z. Sheppard, "Splendor in the Grass," *Time,* September 3, 1990.)
4 Sigmund Freud, *Civilization and its Discontent.* ((London: Hogarth Press, 1939). The other two sources originated from the natural world about us and from our bodies. Since Freud's time, both of these have been largely overcome through the advancement of science in the new society.
5 Alexis Carrel, *Man the Unknown.* (New York and London: Harper and Brothers, 1935).
6 David Barash, *The Whisperings Within.* (New York: Harper and Row, 1979).

Chapter 6

1 David Barash, *The Whisperings Within.* (New York: Harper and Row, 1979)
2 Ibid
3 Ibid
4 Sonia L. Nazario, "Schoolteachers Say It's Wrongheaded to Teach Students What's Right," *Wall Street Journal,* April 6, 1990.
5 Ibid.
6 (none)
7 Julie Salamon, "Poverty Cycle," *Wall Street Journal,* August 10, 1982.
8 Childrens' Home Society of California, 5429 Mc Connell Ave., Los Angeles

900066.
9 Julie Salamon, "Poverty Cycle," *Wall Street Journal*, August 10, 1982.
10 Ibid.
11 B. Drummond Ayres Jr., "West Virginia Law Says No Driving for Dropouts," *New York Times*, 1989.
12 Michael McManus, "Report on Porn Turns Publishers Into Censors," *Wall Street Journal*.
13 *Journal of Personality and Social Psychology*, November 1989.
14 Dobson, "Bundy Interview," *Arizona Daily Star*, January 25, 1989.
15 Bob Greene, "Second-graders Love Mandingo," *Chicago Sun-Times*, June 15, 1975.
16 Richard Zoglin, "Home Is Where the Venom Is," *Time*, Aprol 16, 1990.
17 Neil Hickey, "How Much Violence," *T V Guide*, August 22, 1992.
18 Ibid.
19 Ibid.
20 Aurora Mackey, "Counselor Delves Into Family's Role in Individual Problems," *Los Angeles Daily News*, 1987.
21 Survey by Property Dynamics of Kirkland, Washington.
22 Stan Nast, "One Man's Tortured Life: A Case History," *Seattle Post Intelligencer*.
23 Bonnie Henry, "Psychologists Cite Dramatic Changes," *Arizona Daily Star*, March 12, 1995.
24 Eric Nalder, "Graduate Sues Schools Because He Can't Read," *Seattle Post Intelligencer*, September 22, 1977.
25 Lloyd Shearer, "Parents Make the Difference," *Parade Magazine*, September 16, 1984.
26 Gary Pulka, "Education Group Encourages Reforms for Urban Schools," *Wall Street Journal*, March 16, 1988.
27 R. Gustav Niebuhr, "Schools Resound With Four-Letter Words," *Wall Street Journal*, July 8, 1992.
28 Richard N. Ostling, "Shootouts in the Schools," *Time*, November 20, 1989.
29 B. Bruce-Briggs, "The Great Classroom Debacle," *Wall Street Journal*, July 20, 1976.
30 John Hood, "Education: Money Isn't Everything," *Wall Street Journal*, February 9, 1990.
31 B. Bruce-Briggs, "The Great Classroom Debacle," *Wall Street Journal*, July 20, 1976.
32 "Back to Basics in the Schoolhouse," *Newsweek*, October 21, 1974.
33 "Better Teaching Is Urged in High School Study," *Wall Street Journal*, May 1984.
34 Steve Stecklow, "Acclaimed Reforms of U. S. Education Are Popular But Unproven," *Wall Street Journal*, December 28, 1994.
35 Dr. E.D. Hirsch Jr., *Cultural Literacy*. (Boston: Houghton Mifflin Co., 1988)
36 Ibid.
37 Ibid.
38 Judge Warner Explains Juvenile System," *Green Valley News and Sun*, Sep-

tember 7,1994.
39 Richard Zoglin, "Is TV Ruining Our Children?" *Time*, October 15, 1990.
40 Douglas Kreutz, "High in School," *Arizona Daily Star,* May 14, 1989.
41 Dr. Maria Montessori, *Spontaneous Activity in Education.* (New York: Schocken Books, 1965)
42 James K. Wilson, *Public Interest*, Winter 1983 issue.
43 Dr. Alexis Carrel, *Man the Unknown*. (New York: Harper and Brothers, 1935.
44 Guy R. Odom, *Mothers, Leadership and Success*. (Houston: Polybius Press, 1990)
45 Joe Davidson, "Pre-School Program in El Paso Becomes a Model to Fight Dropout Problem at Early Age," *Wall Street Journal*, March 31, 1988.
46 Guy R. Odom, *Mothers, Leadership and Success*. (Houston: Polybius Press, 1990.
47 Ibid.
48 Kenneth H. Bacon, "Liberals Are Joining Conservatives in Urging Use of Free-Market Philosophy to Reform Schools," *Wall Street Journal*, June 5, 1990.
49 Ibid.
50 Dr. E. D. Hirsch, *Cultural Literacy.* (Boston: Houghton Mifflin Co., 1988)
51 Ellen Graham, "Values Lessons Return to the Classroom," *Wall Street Journal*, September 26, 1988.

Chapter 7

1 The National Institute of Justice, the principal research agency for the Justice Department.
2 Joseph A. Califano, Jr., "It's Drugs Stupid," *New York Times*, February 5, 1995.
3 "Restive Kids and the Path to Glory," *Associated Press.*
4 *Encyclopaedia Britannica.*
5 Joseph Pereira, "Baffling Plague," *Wall Street Journal*, August 1, 1989.
6 Jonathan Beaty, "Do Humans Need to Get High?" *Time,* August 21, 1989.
7 Dr. David F. Musto, "Lessons of the First Cocaine Epidemic," *Wall Street Journal*, June 11, 1986.
8 *Parade Magazine*, April 16, 1995.
9 "Kids Who Sell Crack," *Time*, May 9, 1988.
10 Ibid.
11 "Trafficker Forfeit Sets a Record," *New York Times*, December 10, 1995.
12 Jonathan Beaty and Richard Hornik, "A Torrent of Dirty Dollars," *Time*, December 18, 1989.
13 "The Drug Thugs," *Time*, March 7, 1988.
14 James Brooke, "Corrupt Police, Public Apathy Give Drug Lords an Edge," *New York Times*, August 14, 1994.
15 "U.S. Judge in New York Wants Drugs Legalized," *Associated Press*, December 13, 1989.
16 *Newsweek*, May 1, 1972.
17 Cox News Service, May 14, 1995.

18 Bob Ortega, *Wall Street Journal*, August 10, 1995.
19 "Thinking the Unthinkable," *Time*, May 30, 1988.
20 "Addicts Face Crackdown," *South China Post*, June 28, 1994.

Chapter 8

1 Richard J. Hernstein and James Q. Wilson, *Crime and Human Nature*.
2 In heavy crime areas such as New York City, people didn't report all crimes. Continual break-ins of automobiles was an example; and police discouraged the reporting because they were overwhelmed.
3 Warren T. Brookes, *Conservative Digest*, May 1985.
4 Justice Charles L. Weltner, "The Criminals Are Winning," *Atlanta Weekly*, May 2,1982.
5 Rita Kramer, "On the Case of Young Thugs," *Wall Street Journal*, June 3, 1986.
6 Ibid.
7 Richard J. Hernstein and James Q. Wilson, *Crime and Human Nature*.
8 David Rubinstein, professor of sociology at University of Illinoise, "Don't Blame Crime on Joblessness," *Wall Street Journal*.
9 Rita Kramer, "On the Case of Young Thugs," *Wall Street Journal*, June 3, 1986.
10 Eugene H. Methvin, "The Criminal Mind: A Startling New Look," *Readers Digest*.
11 Richard J Hernstein and James Q. Wilson, *Crime and Human Nature*.
12 James Webb, "What We Can Learn From Japan's Prisons," *Parade Magazine*, January 15, 1984.
13 Arthur S. Hayes, "Inner-City Jurrors Tend to Rebuff Prosecutors and to Back Plaintiffs," *Wall Street Journal*, March 24, 1992.
14 Jackson Toby, "Worst Things About U.S. Prisons Is The Prisonbers," *Wall Street Journal*.
15 "Con Job," *Readers Digest*, September 1994.
16 John Woolfolk, "Mind Boggling," *San Francisco Chronicle*, (compiled by Readers Digest), June 1994.
17 Ross Anderson, "Prisons: Nothing Works to Keep Lid on Powder Keg," *Seattle Post Intelligencer*, June 1975.
18 Guy R. Odom, *Mothers, Leadership and Success*.
19 "No Nonsense Inmate Wants Tougher Prisons," *Seattle Times*, March 27, 1977.

Chapter 9

1 *Wall Street Journal*, March 2, 1970.
2 "Pregnant Mother of 14 Lashes Back at D.C. Mayor," *Arizona Daily Star* (AP), April 1987. Kevin Noblet,

3 "Mothers' Day Is Nothing Special for Mom of 53 Children," *Arizona Daily Star* (AP), May 8, 1988.
4 Steve Mufson, "Little Is Being Done to Control Explosive Growth of Africa's Population," *Wall Street Journal*, July 3, 1985.
4 Adi Ignatius, "China's Birthrate Rises Again Despite a Policy of One-Child Families," *Wall Street Journal*, July 14, 1988.
6 Steve Mufson, "Little Is Being Done to Control Explosive Growth of Africa's Population." *Wall Street Journal*, July 3, 1985.
7 Ibid.
8 "Growing World Population Damages Basic Resources, U.N. Report Finds, " *Associated Press*, May 1988.
9 Eugene Linden, "How the U.S. Can Take the Lead in the Third World," *Time*, October 23, 1989.
10 Thomas Kamm, "The Global Population Streams Into Cities Raising Planners Fears," *Wall Street Journal*, August 30, 1994.
11 Ibid.
12 Steve Mufson, "Little Is Being Done to Control Explosive Growth of Africa's Population," *Wall Street Journal*, July 3, 1985.
13 Dr Louis Hellman, "The U.S. Role in Resolving the World Population Problem," submitted to the President upon request, January 1977.
14 *Congressional Record*, page S 3043, February 24, 1977.
15 John Vidal, *Manchster Guardian Service*, August 20, 1995.
16 Eugene Linden, "The Last Drops," *Time*, August 20, 1990.
17 Kunda Dixit, "Mass Extinction of Forest Species Feared in Asia," *Jakarta Post*, July 12, 1994.
18 Peter S. Greenberg, "Exotic Locales Forced to Put Limits on Tourism," *Arizona Daily Star*, July 16, 1989.
19 Dr. Carl Tiedcke, Letter to the Editor, *Santa Barbara News-Press*, 1978.
20 Steve Mufson, "Little Is Being Done to Control Explosive Growth of Africa's Population," *Wall Street Journal*, July 3, 1985.
21 Karl Lawrence, "Kenya Family Planning Fails to Check Population Spiral," *The Christian Science Monitor*, May 2, 1976.
22 "Common Sense About Population," *Wall Street Journal*, May 30, 1979.
23 President Theodore Roosevelt, Conference on the Conservation of Natural Resources, 1908.
24 Reuter, "A Quarter of Spain Is Said to Suffer From Erosion Woes," *Wall Street Journal*, May 1988.

Chapter 10

1 Paul Johnson, "Has Capitalism a Future?" *Wall Street Journal*, September 29, 1978.
2 A kibbutz is a commercial farm or workplace not unlike a collective farm.
3 Matt Moffett, "Barrio Brigades," *Wall Street Journal*, January 8, 1993.
4 Thomas Kamm, "Free Market Model," *Wall Street Journal, January* 23, 1993.

5 Norman Munn, *Psychology, the Fundamentals of Human Adjustment.* (Boston: Houghton Mifflin Co., 1946)
6 Milton and Rose Friedman, *Free to Choose.* (New York: Avon Books, 1980)
7 Ibid.
8 Ibid.
9 Kenneth H. Bacon, "The Savings Slump: No Easy Solution," *Wall Street Journal,* December 1988.
10 Robert Prinsky, "Britains Onerous Tax System," *Wall Street Journal,* March 28, 1977.
11 Marvin Olasky, *"Income Tax, the Monstrosity that Wouldn't Die,"*
12 Specifically in the United States, the Federal Reserve bought government bonds from the Treasury in exchange for newly printed currency or for entering a deposit on the Federal Reserve's ledgers to the credit of the Treasury. When the Treasury used this currency or credit to pay its bills for government programs, it eventually ended up in commercial banks where it increased the quantity of money.
13 At one time the the United States was on a gold standard. This produced trust in the future buying-power of the dollar because it provided a standard by which people could discipline monetary authorities. Generally, it appeared to keep the inflation rate low until it was abandoned in 1967.
14 Scott Kilman, "Market Maze," *Wall Street Journal,* May 20, 1991.

Chapter 11

1 Rousseau pointed out the "right to emigrate" is the ultimate safeguard of personal liberty.
2 *Health Management Quarterly.*
3 Joann Lublin, "British Health Service Is Ailing," *Wall Street Journal,* February 24, 1988.
4 Alan Otten, "Can't We Put My Mother to Sleep," *Wall Street Journal,* June 5, 1985.
5 Robert Bauman, "The VA's War on Health," *Wall Street Journal,* December 6, 1993.
6 Alan Otten, "Can't We Put My Mother to Sleep," *Wall Street Journal,* June 5, 1985.
7 David Marzolick, "Suffering Grandpa, Revived Unwillingly, Sues Hospital," *Arizona Daily Star,* March 18, 1990.
8 Peter F. Drucker, *The Unseen Revolution.*
10 Paul Harvey, "Two Million Americans Are Going to Waste," *Green Valley News,* June, 19, 1991.
11 Erle Norton, "Future Factories," *Wall Street Journal,* January 13, 1993.
12 Tom Peters, *A Passion for Excellence.* (New York: Random House, 1985.
13 Peter Drucker, *Management: Tasks, Responsibilities, Practices.* (New York: Harper and Row, 1974)
14 Ibid.

15 Ibid.
16 In 1971 when Intel invented the micro-processor, the Information Age evolved.
17 Peter Drucker, *The Unseen Revolution.*
18 In the 1990s a common incentive for management was stock options granted at current market prices. If management's performance resulted in the growth of profits, then the stock would reflect it and appreciate in value. The value of the stock options would, then, increase. If the performance resulted in a decline of profits or even losses, the stock would drop and the stock options would become worthless but no downside risk was assumed.

Chapter 12

1 Wieslaw Gornicki, "Horrors of the Holocaust in Cambodia," *Baltimore Sun*, April 22, 1979.
2 Ibid.
3 Ibid.
4 Ibid.
5 Beth Duff-Brown of *Associated Press*, "Chinese Scholars Rewriting History according to Mao," *Tucson Daily Star*, November 27, 1994.
6 Ibid.
7 John E. Yang, "Chaotic Congress," *Wall Street Journal*, 1989.
8 Ibid.
9 Doug Bandow, "Pigging Out at the Public Trough," *Wall Street Journal*, November 22, 1989.
10 Associated Press, "Congress Fueling Inflation," *Seattle Post Intelligencer*, June 1974.
11 Bob McHugh, "Fixed Sugar Prices Give Sweet Teeth a Sour Deal," *Tucson Daily Star* (A.P.), December 27, 1987.
12 Ann Hughey and Eileen Alt Powell, "Government Waste Panel Eyes $60 Billion in Cost Cutting," *Wall Street Journal*,
13 J. Peter Grace, "Little Things Mean a Lot, Grace Panel Found," *Wall Street Journal*, 1983.
14 Bruce Ingersoll, "Crop Insurance Fraud and Bungling Cost U.S. Taxpayers Billions," *Wall Street Journal*, May 19, 1989.
15 Karen Elliott House, "At Agriculture Agency, Bureaucracy is Huge, and the Living Is Easy," *Wall Street Journal*, April 12, 1977.
16 Ibid.
17 Ibid.
18 Ibid.
19 Anonymous, *Wall Street Journal*, April 7, 1995.
20 Karen Elliott House, "Civil Service Rule Book May Bury Carter's Bid to Achieve Efficiency," *Wall Street Journal*, September 1977.
21 Ibid.
22 Chares Peters, *How Washington Really Works,* (Redding, Mass.: Addison-Wesley, 1983).

23 Ibid.
24 James Bovard, "Welfare for Millionire Farms," *Wall Street Journal*, May 22, 1990.
25 Robert Schrum, "The Imperial Congress," *Seattle Times*, May 8, 1977.
26 Ibid.
27 John E. Yang, "Chaotic Congress," *Wall Street Journal*, 1989.
28 Robert Shrum, "The Imperial Congress," *Seattle Times*, May 8, 1977.
29 Ibid.
30 Mark J.Porubcansky, "Brezhnev's Kin Named in Corruption Scandel," (AP) *Arizona Daily Star*, January 24 1988.
31 Lisa Bannon, "Woe to Italy's Poor Civil Servants: Reformers Now Expect Them to Work," *Wall Street Journal*, December 31, 1992.
32 Roberto Maksiud, "Brazilian Politicians: Changing the Old Populist Line," *Wall Street Journal*, October 6, 1989.
33 Matt Moffett, "Populist Disaster," *Wall Street Journal*, August 16, 1995.
34 "Nice Work, If ...", (*California Journal*), *Readers Digest*, May 1994.
35 Herbert H. Jacobs, Letters to the Editor, *Wall Street Journal*, 1984.
36 Richard Morin, "Who's in Control? Many Don't Know or Care," *Washington Post*, January 29, 1996.
37 Alvin and Heidi Toffler, *A New Civilization*, (Atlanta: Turner Publishing Co., 1995.
38 John Elson, "Has History Come to an End?," *Time Magazine*, September 4, 1989.
39 Albert R. Karr, "Mail Monopoly Says Happy New Year," *Wall Street Journal*, March 7, 1990.
40 Ibid.
41 Ibid.

Chapter 14

1 Carl Sagan, *Pale Blue Dot*. (New York: Random House, 1994)
2 Stephen Hawking, *A Brief History of Time*. (Toronto: Bantam Books, 1988)
3 Alexis Carrel, *Man the Unknown*. (New York: Harper and Brothers, 1935)
4 Sigmund Freud, *Civilization and Its Discontents*. (London: Hogarth Press, 1939)
5 Carl Sagan, "A Warning for Us?" *Parade Magazine* June 5, 1994.
6 Ray Bradbury, "Can Man Refuse Eternity?" *Los Angeles Times*, August 1972.
7 Adrian Berry speculates in his book, "*The Next 500 Years*" that a ramjet spaceship could use diffused hydrogen gas in space as fuel for a nuclear fusion engine. Although this gas is exceedingly sparse in space, it becomes more concentrated if the spaceship is traveling at high speeds. The faster it goes, the more fuel it will suck into its engines so its speed will accelerate even faster. A spaceship could then reach the nearest star in about six years.
However, time moving on a vehicle this fast would slow down so that arrival time would drop from six to two and one-half years. This is because of the

advantage of Einstein's special theory of relativity.
For those seeking explanations of future scientific possibilities, Adrian Berry's *"The Next 500 Years"* (New York: W.H. Freeman and Co., 1996) is recommended.
8 A.I. Oparin, *The Origin of Life*. (New York: The Macmillan Co., 1938)
9 Ibid.
10 Ibid.
11 Ibid.
12 Steven D. Garber, *Biology, A Self-Teaching Guide*. New York: Wiley Publishing, 1989)
13 Eugene F. Moore, "Knocking on Heaven's Door," special to *Washington Post*, 1985.
14 Steven Weinberg, *Dreams of a Final Theory*, (New York: Pantheon Books, 1992)
15 Stephen Hawking, *Black Holes and Baby Universes and Other Essays*. (New York: Bantam Books , 1993)
16 Steven Weinberg, *Dream of a Final Theory* (New York: Pantheon Books, 1992)
17 Stephen Hawking, *A Brief History of Time*. (Toronto: Bantam Books, 1988)
18 Ibid

Index

A

Abalkin, Leonid Ivanovich 38
Absolutism 320
acid rain 210
addiction 82, 154, 155, 159, 165, 166, 170, 171
adolescence 145
adoption 217
Afanasyev, Yuri 30
Afghanistan 26
Afro-Americans 56, 59, 69 (see chapter 3)
Aganbegyan, Dr. Abel 39
Agency for International Development 336
Agriculture Department 46, 334
AIDS 5, 6, 7, 81, 158, 161, 192, 212, 215, 287, 290, 291, 339
aircraft 232
airports 309
Albania 22
Alcoholics Anonymous 171
alcoholism 83, 155, 156, 166, 183, 299
Allende, Salvador 26, 45, 233
American Civil Liberties Union 180
American Psychological Association 118
amino acids 376
Andreotti 344
Angola 25
Antarctica 210
aquaculture 223
archaea 377
Arctic Circle 201
Argentina 185, 267
arms race 32
asteroids 373

Athenian Republic 329
atom 382
Austria 21
Ayittey, George 57

B

baby-boom generation 87
Bacon, Sir Francis 28
bacteria 6, 7, 223, 383
Balkans 22
Ball, Carlos 13
Banco do Brazil 345
Bangladesh 211
bank loans 258
Barash, David 101, 104
Barbados 209
Barbarosa 19
base salary 283, 284, 293, 316
Basque 27
Batista 26
behavior 97, 98, 103, 105, 130, 132, 202
behavioral development 277
Behavioral Education 98, 106, 144, 146, 168, 188, 190, 197
Beijing 30, 209
Belarus 261
Belize 53
Bell, Terrel H. 136
Bellamy, Edward 28
Berlin 22, 223
Bermuda 210
Big Bang 383
bilingual teaching 127
Biopol 222
Birman, Igor 39
birth control 214
black holes 381
black market 34, 44
Black Panthers 59
Blanc, Louis 28
Blitzkrieg 20
Bloom, Allan 132
Blum, Richard H. 155
boarding schools 114, 146

Bogota 162
Bolivia 206
Bolshevik Revolution 36
Bonaparte, Napoleon 135
Booth, Clare Luce 73
border restrictions 111
borders 112, 356
Bottome, Robert 347
Bourne, Dr. Peter 155
Bovard, James 339
Bradbury, Ray 374
Bradshaw, John 121
brain 136, 171, 375
Brandeis, Justice Louis 353
Brasilia 345
Brazil 51, 55, 267, 344, 345
Brezhnev, Leonid 27
Britain 166, 267, 297
British Labor party 29
brothels 116, 185
Browder, Earl 24
Brown, Lee P. 166
Brown, Lester 205
Brown, Willie, Jr. 348
Bulgaria 46
bullet-trains 309
bureaucracy 243, 332, 333, 337, 338, 345-348
burglaries 84

C

caffeine 156
Cairo Conference 214
Caldera, President Rafael 347
Califano, Joseph A. 154, 326
Cambo 30
Cambodia 321
Canadians 285
Cape Verde 209
capital 256, 259
capitalism 232-234, 247, 253
carbon 375
Cardenas 26
Cardoso, President Fernando 51
carjackings 77

Carnegie, Andrew 253
Carpini, Michael Delli 350
Carr, B. J. 378
Carrel, Dr. Alexis 97, 103, 134, 372
Case, Anne 88
Castro, Fidel 26
catalytic antibodies 171
Catholics 214
censorship 118, 119
Center for the Study of Social Policy 88
Chaiken, Jan and Marcia 179
chaos theory 379
Chechnya 8
child abuse 81, 138, 156
child-support laws 198
Chile 26, 45, 233, 267, 301
China 7, 8, 23, 24, 40, 53, 58, 59, 180, 188, 204, 212, 216, 222, 224, 225, 244, 252, 334, 335
Chinese 55
choice 141
chromosones 377, 380
Chubb, John 141
circumcision 7
Civil Service Commission 337
civilized society 105
cocaine 155, 156, 157, 159
Cold War 21, 49
Coles, Robert 108
college 128
college diplomas 123
commodities 240, 273
Common Market 242
commonwealth of regions 356
Communism 24, 25, 27, 97
Communist Manifesto 28
competition 242, 246, 359
computers 124, 259, 279
conduct 98, 134, 138, 153, 187, 189 (see also-behavior)
Confederacy 113
Congress 323-329, 331, 340
constitution 89, 119, 276, 323, 328, 348, 350

consumption 266, 361
Continental Congress 266
contraceptives 215, 217
crime 76, 84, 89, 153, 158, 159, 160, 175, 180, 187, 190, 197, 201
Crimea 20
criminal justice system 177
Cuba 32
Cultural Revolution 322
culture 9, 104, 111, 112, 181, 268, 271
curricula 142, 143, 144, 145, 146, 150
Curtis, Thomas 343
Czechoslovakia 21, 25

D

Dash, Leon 80
data-banks 279
Davies, Paul 378
death 372
debt 348
Declaration of Independence 262
decriminalization of drugs 164, 165, 168, 172, 188
deforestation 208, 209
Delathre, Edwin 86
Delli Carpini, Michael 350
democracy 352
desalinization 224
Dewey, John 129
disarmament conference 189, 355
discipline 135, 155, 196
divorce 79, 121
DNA 378, 380
dowry deaths 7
drop-outs 83, 131, 140, 160
Drucker, Peter 301, 311
drug cartels 162
drug interdiction 162
drugs 82, 153 (see chapter 7)
Durant, Will and Ariel 252
Duster, Troy 77

E

East Berlin 22
East Germany 21, 46
East Prussia 21
Ebert, Roger 117
economic security 282
economy, the (chapter 10)
ecosystems 206, 210, 223
education 132, 137-140, 151, 188, 204, 207, 277, 281, 282, 368
Einstein, Albert 28, 383
El Salvador 26
electromagnetism 382
electron 382
Emerson, Ralph Waldo 135
employment 278, 311
energy 16, 208, 219
Engels, Friedrich 28
England 133, 261 (see also-Britain)
environment 104, 183
Environmental Fund 15
erosion 15, 205, 208, 212, 224
Ethiopia 25
European Community 272
Evans, Senator Daniel 328
evolution 103, 105
Executive branch 323
extinction, species 220

F

factories 306
family 120
Farmers Home Administration 12, 335
farming 206, 209, 273, 274, 339
Federal Crop Insurance 334
Federal Deposit Insurance Corporation 239
Federal grants 343
Federal Housing Administration 12
Federal Reserve Board 148, 268
Fenno, Richard 328
Finland 21
fire-arms 188, 189

fisheries 16, 208
fluoxetine 172
Foley, Thomas 335
forests 15, 205, 209, 210, 224
France 51, 231, 286
Franco, General 25
free market 234, 235, 237, 240, 249, 351
free trade 10, 111, 240-242
freedom to choose 277
Freeman, Richard 60
Freud, Sigmund 97, 104, 157, 311, 372
Friedman, Milton 123, 235, 250, 252
fringe benefits 280
fuel-cells 219
Fukuyama, Francis 351
future contracts 273

G

Galapagos Islands 210
galaxies 381
gambling 184, 186, 188
gangs 122, 154, 158, 161
gap in pay 124
garbage 211, 220, 221
Gehrels, Tom 373
Geiger, Keith 129
General Accounting Office 287, 333
General Agreement on Tariffs and Trade 242
genes 380
genetic engineering 374
Germany 21, 22, 266
Goddard, Robert 373
gold 271
Gorbachev, Premier 33, 40, 52, 286
Gordon, Sol 80
Gottfredson, Michuel 121
Grace Commission 333
Graham, Dr. Geoge 82
gravity 382
Great Depression 239, 241, 339
Great Leap Forward 322
Great Society 29

Greece 22
greenhouse effect 219
Grinspoon, Dr. Lester 156
Gromyko, Andrei 32
Gros, Francisco 345
Group Health Cooperative of Puget Sound 289
Guderian, General 20
Guth, Alan 383

H

Haiti 211-212
Hani, Chris 50
Hawaiian Islands 54
Hawking, Stephen 372, 379, 381, 383
Hayek, F.A. 48, 270
headquarter cities 304
health-care 284-289, 292
health-care costs 165
heavy-metal rock 75
Heisenberg, Werner 379
helicopter 309
Hellman, Dr. Louis 207
Hernstein, Richard J. 70
heroin 166
Hirsch, Dr. E.D 128, 143
Hirschi, Travis 121
hispanics 9, 204
Hitler 19, 20, 21
HMO 289
home-buyer 294
home-owners association 294
homeless 299
homes 293, 294, 295, 308, 309
House, Karen Elliott 334
House of Commons 325
House of Representatives 323, 325
Huba, Dr. Geoge 154
Hughes, John 155
hyperinflation 14, 18, 266

I

I.Q. 70, 137
Ice Age 373

illiteracy 113, 124, 126, 128, 148, 151, 368
immigration 9, 54, 207, 288
incentives 34, 35, 140, 246, 249, 314, 315, 316
income 280
income tax 261, 262, 263
incumbents 342, 343, 349
India 45, 78, 205, 209, 217
Indians 56, 57, 69
Indonesia 25, 209
Industrial Revolution 231, 320
inequality 250
infant mortality 81, 207
inflation 14, 50, 233, 260, 266, 267, 268, 269, 271, 343, 345, 346, 348, 349
inflation theory 383
Information Age 124, 259, 281, 282, 283, 313
inheritance 253, 254, 255, 368
Institutional Revolutionary Party 162
intelligent life 374, 375, 384
interdiction 162
interest rates 258, 260
interest 14, 260
Internal Revenue Service 12, 262
Internet 110
investment 256, 257, 258, 260, 261
Iquitos 237
Iran 224
Irish Republican Army 27
Israel 232
Italy 343, 344

J

Jacobs, Herbert H. 348
Jaguaribe, Helio 13
Japan 22, 223
Japanese 54, 55, 134, 191
Japanese Peace Treaty 23
Jeans, Sir James 383
Jefferson, Thomas 353

Jews 54, 56
John, Oldrich 25
Jung, Carl 104
juries 175, 192, 193

K

Kamin, Leon 137
Kant, Immanuel 104
Kaplan, Ira 71
Katz, Lawrence 88
Kennedy, Roger G 265
Keith, Hastings 338
Kenya 204
Keonjian, Edwaed 30
Kerensky 29
KGB 30
Khan, A.Z.M. Obaidullah 209
Khymer Rouge 321
Korea 23
Koreans 56
Kosygin 38
Kramer, Rita 177
Krauthammer, Charles 63
Kruse, Douglas L. 314
Krushchev 37, 38
Kuan, Lee Yew 55
Kuibyshev 20
Kuomintang 23
Kurdish Labor Party 27
Kurds 8, 356
Kurile Islands 22, 23

L

Labor Party 51
land 224, 225, 226, 227, 228, 229, 230 293, 368
language 112
Laos 26
Lasch, Christopher 87
laundering, money 161
law 119
Leary, Dr. Timothy 155
Lenin 29, 36
Leningrad 20
Liberman, Evsei 38

Libya 27
Lickoma, Thomas 107
Lincoln, Abraham 251
Lindbeck, Assar 296
litigation 359
living standards 12, 16, 237, 249, 256, 260, 314, 356 (see also standard of living)
Locke, John 104, 262
London, Herbert I. 144
long-term policies 354
longevity 3, 85, 144, 213, 303
love 184

M

Madagascar 208
Mafia 344
Magnitogorsk 43
Malaysia 25, 55, 194
malnutrition 212
management 312
Manson, Charles 74
Mao Tse-tung 322
Maoist 321
marijuana 172
Marraco, Santiago 224
marriage 184
Mars 374
Martone, Celso 345
Marx, Karl 28, 259
Marxism 25, 29, 132, 226, 244
Matthews, Clifford N 376
McDonnell, Sanford 133, 144
McNamara, Robert 215
media 117
Medicaid 292
Medicare 288
methodone 166
Mexico 45, 162, 206, 209, 233
micro-electronics 374
Milky way galaxy 374
Minigue, Kenneth 97
Moe, Terry 141
Mohammedanism 186, 214
money supply 269, 271

Mongol People's Republic 23
Montessori, Dr. Maria 132
Moore, Sir Thomas 28
morality 17, 107, 167, 326
Morris, William 28
Moscow 20
Moser, Robert E. 376
Mosher, Steven W 244
Moynihan, Senator Daniel 89
Mozambique 25
Mubarak, President 214
multi-national corporations 111, 281
Murphy, T.A. 235
Murray, Charles 60, 70
mycoplasma 377
Myers, Dr. Norman 209

N

Nahas, Dr. Gabriel 157
Narcotics Anonymous 171
National Academy of Sciences 127
National Commission on America's Urban Families 120
National Commission on Excellence in Education 124
national debt 258
National Health Service 292
National Institute of Mental Health 118
National Parks 265
National Rifle Association 180
nationalism 8, 10, 94, 98, 101, 108, 110, 111, 112, 114, 115, 323, 357, 358
Nationalists 23, 109
Natural Resource Reserve 283
natural selection 103
Nepal 209
nepotism 254, 103
Netherlands 166
neutrinos 381
neutron 382
New Deal 29
Nicaragua 26
nicotine 156

Niederhoffer, Victor 240
Nigeria 204, 214
Norplant 217
North Atlantic Treaty Organization 25
Northern Ireland 9, 27
nuclear fusion 219
nuclear waste 220
Nyerere, President 57

O

Odom, Guy 61, 135, 196, 204
Ojiombo, Dr. Lilia 215
Ollman, Bertell 31
Oparin, A.I. 375, 376
OPEC 238
opium 157
optical card 190
Oregon 310
Orwell, George 28
Outer Mongolia 23
Owen, Robert 28
ozone 16, 210

P

Pakistan 13
Palestinian Liberation Organization 27
parenting 120, 138, 168, 188
particle-antiparticle pairs 384
patents 316
Payne, James 181
Pension Benefit Guaranty Corporation 12
pension funds 301
people movers 305, 308
Peoples Republic of China 24
Peoples Republic of Guinea 46
Perelman, Lewis 142
Peres, Shimon 232
permissiveness 85, 86, 89, 155, 189
Persepolis 224
Peter Drucker 301
Peters, Tom 311
Philippines 26, 208

photon 379
Pinochet, General 233
planned economies 34, 37
Plato 28, 132
Pol Pot 321
Poland 21, 46
political cannibalism 323
politics 351, 352
pollution 210, 218, 219, 310
polygamy 184, 214
population 16, 205, 207, 211, 213, 215, 216, 218, 225, 368
Population Fund 205
population growth 206, 207, 212, 213, 216
postal service 336, 358
Potsdam Conference 21
poverty 66, 88, 181, 204, 215, 231, 267, 297
power structure 98
prejudice 99, 108, 109, 111, 112, 113, 128, 151, 367, 368
President 323
Price and wage controls 148
price controls 238
prions 377
prisons 158, 175, 180, 190, 194, 195, 196, 197, 199, 201
privatization 50
probation 179, 199
productivity 248, 256, 258, 259, 270, 314, 316
profanity 125
profit and loss 232, 243, 244, 245, 247
profit-sharing 314
prohibition 158, 163, 167, 171
prostitution 159, 184, 185, 188
protectionism 241, 270
proton 382
Puberty 145
punishment 194, 197, 201

Q

quality of life 96, 97, 99, 256, 293

quantum mechanics 381, 382, 383
quark 382

R

racism 181
radio-telescopes 375
Ramey, Craig 137
Rashcke, Carl 75
recession 268
recycling 219, 221, 222
Red Brigade 26
Red Guard 323
Redford, Robert 211
Reductionists 378
Rees, M. J. 378
Reformation 180, 185
rehabilitation 170, 183, 187, 195, 265
relativity, theory of 383
religions 150, 186, 214
religious fanaticism 98, 108, 109, 150
reproduction 377
responsibility 96, 166, 169
retribution 180
Revolution, Russian 30
Revolution, Youth 73
Rhodesia 25
Rio de Janeiro 4, 17, 78
risk-capital 259, 260
Rita Kramer 128
robberies 84
Roman Empire 231, 329
Romania 21
Ronstadt, Margaret 122
Roosevelt, Franklin 324
Roosevelt, Theodore 218
Rousseau 129
Rural Electrification Administration 335
Russia 267
Rwanda 108
Ryabov, Nikolai 50

S

Sagan, Carl 93, 371, 373
Sakhalin 22
salinization 209
Samenow, Stanton 182
Samoza 26
Sandinistas 26
Sao Paulo 11
satanism 75
satellite towns 305, 306, 310
Sato, Takashi 206
Saving and Loan Deposit Insurance 12
savings 260, 256, 257, 258, 369
savings and loan 239, 358
Schmidt, Pam 122
schools 122, 123, 125, 128, 129, 131, 138, 141, 142, 146, 149, 160
school's curriculum 136
Schwartz, Dr. Leny 287
Seibold, Eugen 112
Seidman, William 239
self-esteem 311, 316
selfishness 134
Senate 323
Sentencing 177
sex 113, 114
sexual aggression 115
Shalala, Donna 296
shelter 293
Shining Path 26
Shmelyov, Nikolay 38
shoplifting 83, 153, 197
Shrum, Robert 340
Siegel, Ronald K. 156
Singapore 55, 194, 197, 217
Singer, Max 149
Singh, Mrs. Harmeet 81
Sixteenth Amendment 262
Sizer, Theodore R. 127
slaves 67
Slemrod, Professor Joel 262
smart card 283
Smith, Adam 252

Smolensk 20
Smoot-Hawley Tariff 241
Snyder, Louis 21
Social Democratic party 29
Social Security 296, 300
Socialist Worker's Party 51
socialized medicine 285
Socialism (chapter 2), 234, 236
Socrates 350
solar energy 219
Solzhenitsyn, Alexander 17, 31
South Korea 23
Soviet Union (chapter 2)
Sowell, Thomas 53, 55, 65, 67, 204
space-time 384
Spain 25, 224, 346
Sparkman, Senator 207
special interest 328, 330, 331, 332, 341
Spencer, Herbert 251
Spock, Dr. Benjamin 86
standard of living 50, 207, 232, 235, 241, 281, 282
standards of conduct 85, 104, 106
Stans, Secretary of Commerce 203
Steele, Shelby 66
sterilization 216, 217
Stevenson, Dr. Harold W 125
string theory 380
strong anthropic principle 384
strong nuclear force 382
Stutman, Robert 159
subsidies 272, 273, 305, 308, 328, 331, 339, 340
subways 305, 308
Sugarman, Jule 337
super colliders 382
Supreme Court 261, 324, 343
Sweden 281, 296, 297
Sweet, Robert W 163

T

Taiwan 24
Tanzania 57
tariff 10, 240, 241, 270

Tax Foundation 263
taxes 229, 257, 347
Taylor, Jared 65
teachers 128
Technocracy 354
television 74, 118, 125, 130
Teutonic tribes 231
textbooks 133
Thailand 217
thievery 83
Thompson, William 28
Tiananmen Square 322
Tibet 24
Tiedcke, Dr. Carl 211
Tienamon Square 41
Tito 41
tobacco 166 (see also nicotine)
Tocqueville, Alex 252
Toffler, Alvin and Heidi 350
transfer payments 349
transportation 303, 305, 307, 308, 309
Trevor-Roper, Hugh 378
Trotsky 30
Truman Doctrine 22
Turkey 27, 346
twenty-second ammendment 324
Tytler, Alex Fraser 329

U

Ukraine 20, 30
ultimate fighting 74
uncertainty principle 379, 381
unemployment 262, 263, 279, 280, 281
unified theory 379, 380
United Nations 23, 205
universe 381, 382, 383, 384
user-fees 264, 265
utopias 28, 97
Uzbekistan Republic 343

V

Valle, Eduardo 162

Values Clarification 86, 107
Van Houten, Jan 31
vandalism 84
venereal disease 81, 82
Venezuela 13, 346
Vertix 222
Veteran's Health Administration 286
Vietnam 26, 41
Vietnamese 56
violence 118, 119, 189
virus 7, 11, 212, 377
Von Bock, General 20
voters 349, 350, 354, 363, 364

W

Wagenaar, Dr. Alexander 169
war 107, 355, 356
Warner, Judge Nanette 130
waste 16, 219, 220, 221, 222, 223
water 16, 209, 224
water table 212
weak anthropic principle 384
weak nuclear force 382
weapons 188
Weil, Dr. Andrew 156
Weinberg, Steven 378, 380
welfare 120, 159, 263, 264, 281, 296, 297, 298
Wells, H.G. 28, 371
West Berlin 22
West Germany 22, 281
West Indian 67
Wettmer, Justice Chales 175
Wilson, Professor James 87, 133
Wolfgang, Professor Marvin 179
women 233, 234
Wood, Joseph Krutch 97
World Bank 204
world church organizations 24
world government 101, 110, 111, 356
World Resource Camps 190, 197, 198, 199
Worldwatch Institute 205

Y

Yeltsin, Boris 40
Yew, Lee Kuan 55, 89
Yosemite National Park 210
Yugoslavia 8, 22, 37, 41

Z

Zambia 58
Zaychenko, Aleksando 47
Zemin, Jiang 50
Zheng Yi 322
Zorinsky, Edward 343

EPILOGUE

As this book is being printed, the world's economy is booming, no major war exists, and crime figures in the United States show a small decline.

Is this an aberration? Should we still be concerned with our future? Are dire predictions of declining behavior followed by major efforts to finally establish a truly civilized world still valid? The answer is yes to all of these questions.

The world economy is now booming because of three important developments. (1) The collapse of the socialist economic system in the former Soviet Union created the initiative for it and other socialist governments to develop dynamic free market-driven economies. (2) The computerized Information Age is creating a significant increase in productivity and thus, the ability for world consumers to buy more and thus raise their living standards. (3) Finally, the reduction of global trade barriers and the development of instant world-wide communications has enabled third world countries to benefit from foreign investment and multinational companies which have helped them establish state-of-the-art factories leading to thriving exports.

So, It is difficult to believe the virus of socialism is still alive in the school rooms of Cuba and North Korea and in government-run businesses of such diverse nations as China, India, Venezuela, Belarus, and even France. Che Guevara, the great exponent of revolutionary socialism, has recently been deemed a martyr by many throughout the world.

Recent polls in the United States indicate a majority favor more government benefits so the bureaucracy and controls that accompany them can only result in less responsibility and more restrictions on the individual. Fearful of losing their jobs in a competitive world, most in the polls favor more protectionism in world trade. Many third-world countries still harbor the fear of foreign investment. The cases of economic illiteracy are unending and continues to threaten our well-being. It will get worse when the current boom begins to cool.

Newly released crime statistics show a small decrease, but total crime figures continue to far exceed those of fifty years ago. History also indicates crime will increase again when the new baby-boom generation reaches adolescent age.

The use of abusive drugs by school children is on the rise again as the government's massive effort to stop the flow through prohibition only results in increased obscene profits with devastating effects on innocent non-users.

Education standards continue to hover far below those of the 1950s as well as below other nations. Dropouts and other illiterate applicants are unemployable in the current tight labor market. Illiteracy continues to overwhelm many third-world countries. Large pockets of poverty are the result.

As this is written, tremendous fires, set in Indonesia to clear tropical forests for farmland, are out of control and poisoning the atmosphere of vast areas in Southeast Asia. Exploding population demands more arable land. Yet we have no control to limit births.

Today, the American congress struggles to reform campaign financing hoping to alleviate the pressure of raising funds. But special interests proliferate as long as politicians' all encompassing efforts are aimed at reelection. Politicized democracy will remain seriously flawed until addressed.

Islamic fanatics are massacring entire villages in Algeria. Hutus slaughter Tutsis in refugee camps of Rwanda. Turks are bombing Kurdish camps. Ethnic, religious, and nationalistic prejudice continue to ignite terrorist acts and civil wars. It will not stop until prejudice and illiteracy are eliminated. Yet even in the United States today, people unknowingly encourage prejudice between cultural groups by subsidizing the teaching of ethnic beliefs, language, and politics—the seeds of future conflicts.

No major war exists today, but the build-up of sophisticated weaponry continues not only in the United States but in new developing world powers such as China. The spread of nuclear weapons exceeds that incurred in the cold war. Nuclear bombs that can be carried in a suitcase are now missing from the former Soviet's inventory, and no one knows how many or where they have gone!

Yes, we have a pause in our self-destruction. Let's not let it pass without making some effort to help insure the survival of future generations in the new millennium.

About the Author

Educated at Washington State College, University of Washington, Hayek School of Economics, MBA. Mensa candidate, aviator in Pacific Theatre WWII, Captain in United States Marine Corps. Entrepreneur, owner and manager of several successful businesses, member of board of directors of several corporations. Retired from active business at age 41 followed by becoming: Investor, financial analyst, world traveler and mountain climber.